ONAL
RELATIONS IN THE MODERN WORLD

'Incorporates a variety of political, social, cultural and economic factors and establishes solid links between ideas and action, ideology and political behavior.'

Lincoln Gordon, ... State *University*

'A wide-ra... ... from the French Revolution to t...

M.S. Anderson, Emeritus Professor, *University of London*

Cassels traces the part played by ideology in international relations over the past two centuries. Starting with the French Revolution's injection of ideology into interstate politics, he finishes by addressing present-day preoccupations with the legacy of nationalist discontent left by the collapse of communism and the resurgence of religious fundamentalism in world politics. Cassels includes discussion of Marxism–Leninism, Fascism and Nazism but, eschewing exclusive focus on totalitarian dogma, he also shows how the interplay of the less rigid belief systems of conservatism, liberalism and nationalism influence international affairs.

The focus and emphasis given to ideology in an historical survey of such broad scope make this book unusual, and even controversial. Social scientific and philosophical discussions of ideology make only glancing reference to foreign policy. Historians have generally touched on ideology only within the context of the case study, while the realist theorists of international relations play down its influence.

Alan Cassels is Emeritus Professor of History at McMaster University, Canada. He is also the author of *Fascist Italy* (1985) and *Italian Foreign Policy, 1918–45* (1991).

THE NEW INTERNATIONAL HISTORY
Edited by Gordon Martel, University of British Columbia, Canada

THE NEW INTERNATIONAL HISTORY SERIES
Edited by Gordon Martel
University of British Columbia, Canada

EXPLAINING AUSCHWITZ AND HIROSHIMA
History Writing and the Second World War, 1945–1990
R.J.B. Bosworth

Forthcoming:

WAR AND COLD WAR IN THE MIDDLE EAST
Edward Ingram

NORTH EAST ASIA
An International History
John Stephan

RUSSIA AND THE WORLD IN THE TWENTIETH CENTURY
Teddy Uldricks

IDEOLOGY AND INTERNATIONAL RELATIONS IN THE MODERN WORLD

Alan Cassels

London and New York

First published 1996
by Routledge
11 New Fetter Lane, London EC4P 4EE

Simultaneously published in the USA and Canada
by Routledge
29 West 35th Street, New York, NY 10001

© 1996 Alan Cassels

Typeset in Times by BC Typesetting, Bristol

Printed and bound in Great Britain by
Clays Ltd, St Ives PLC

British Library Cataloguing in Publication Data
A catalogue record for this book is available from the British Library

Library of Congress Cataloguing in Publication Data
Cassels, Alan, 1929–
    Ideology and international relations in the modern world/Alan
Cassels.
    Includes bibliographical references and index.
    1. International relations–Philosophy.   2. International
relations–History.   3. Ideology.   I. Title.   II. Series.
    JX1391.C327   1996
327.1′01–dc20   95-43631
                                                                  CIP

ISBN 0–415–11926–X (hbk)
ISBN 0–415–11927–8 (pbk)

Why do the nations so furiously rage together?
And why do the people imagine a vain thing?

Georg Frideric Handel, *Messiah*

CONTENTS

CONTENTS

SERIES EDITOR'S PREFACE

What we now refer to as 'international' history was the primary concern of those whose work is now recognized as the first attempt by Europeans to conduct a truly 'historical' investigation of the past, and it has remained a central preoccupation of historians ever since. Herodotus, who attempted to explain the Persian Wars, approached the subject quite differently from his successor, Thucydides. Herodotus believed that the answers to the questions that arose from the confrontation between the Persians and the Greeks would be found in the differences between the two cultures; accordingly, he examined the traditions, customs and beliefs of the two civilizations. Critics have long pointed out that he was haphazard in his selection and cavalier his use of evidence. The same has never been said of Thucydides, who, in attempting to explain the Peloponnesian Wars, went about his task more methodically, and who was meticulous in his use of evidence. Over the next two thousand years, men like Machiavelli, Ranke and Toynbee have added to the tradition, but the underlying dichotomy between the 'anthropological' and the 'archival' approach has remained. Diplomatic historians have been condemned as mere archive-grubbers; diplomatic history as consisting of what one file-clerk said to another. The 'world-historians', the synthesizers, have been attacked for creating structures and patterns that never existed, for offering explanations that can never be tested against the available evidence.

The aim of 'The New International History' is to combine the two traditions, to bring Herodotus and Thucydides together. While drawing upon the enormous wealth of archival research conducted by those historians who continue to work in the political tradition of formal relations between states, the authors in this series will also draw upon other avenues of investigation that have become increasingly fruitful since the Second World War. Ideology and culture, immigration and communications, myths and stereotypes, trade and finance have come to be regarded by contemporary scholars as elements essential to a good understanding of international history, and yet, while these approaches are to be found in detailed monographs and scholarly journals, many of their discoveries have not been presented in a readable and accessible form to students and the public. The New International History, by providing books organized along thematic, regional or historiographical lines, hopes to repair this omission.

Almost all historians who write on the subject of international history find themselves referring to 'ideology'. But it is a concept that is as elusive as it is pervasive, and perhaps for this reason there has been no attempt to treat it in a systematic, rigorous manner. While nodding in the direction of political philosophies, and the symbols and images, the myths and legends that are used to sustain them, historians of international relations have, more often than not, preferred to focus their attention on the realities of those relations. The 'realities' of who said what to whom, of who was making the decisions and how they made them, can be documented and detailed: and it is still documents in which most historians prefer to deal. Alan Cassels has dared to go beyond these limits, to attempt to bring some order out of the chaos and to apply some rigour to these concepts. Few historians would be bold enough to undertake such a task, and few of us have either the expertise or the range to accept such a challenge. Like its predecessor, *Explaining Auschwitz and Hiroshima*, this is a stimulating treatment of a provocative subject. I believe that historians and their students will be grateful to the author for taking on the task.

Gordon Martel

PREFACE

That ideology has played an important part in modern international relations is generally taken for granted. Yet the precise role played by ideology on the world stage has never been systematically analysed. Social scientific and philosophical works on ideology make only glancing and generic reference to foreign policy. On the other hand, historical studies which touch on the role of ideology do so only within the framework of case studies, and in addition tend to use the term ideology in a rather vague way.

The present book aims to identify the ideological component in the actual conduct of international affairs on a broad canvas. However, it should be understood from the start that this is not a matter of exploring specific ideologies, certainly not in any detail. In this book frequent reference is made to the great 'isms' of modern times – liberalism, conservatism, socialism, Bolshevism and communism, nationalism, Social Darwinism, imperialism, racism, Fascism, National Socialism or Nazism, among others. To say that the definition of most of these ideologies is contentious would be a massive understatement. It is not the function of this work to enter into hermeneutic debate, and therefore it is assumed that the reader has a rough understanding of what is meant by the well-known 'isms'. And, in truth, this study is not so much concerned with the content of ideologies as with the more generic phenomenon of ideological thinking, and with how the cast of mind recognizable as ideological has shaped foreign-policy making.

The starting point is the late eighteenth century because coinage of the word ideology in the French Revolution signalled also the onset of the use of ideas for political ends within a context of mass politics. We shall first consider the evolution of those general, relatively unstructured sets of beliefs and attitudes which informed international affairs in the nineteenth century. Then we shall examine their transformation into, or replacement by, the rigidly exclusive and all-embracing world views that have shaped – many would say poisoned – global politics in the twentieth century. Also observable along the way will be less coherent foreign policies of conviction, especially those bearing a nationalistic stamp, which none the less betray the ideological mentality. In other words, we shall be dealing with what have been called 'partial' ideologies or *mentalités* as well as 'total' ideologies.

Unfortunately, the concept of ideology and ideological thinking is a slippery one. Hence no one should write on the subject without first attempting some definition, if only to explain how one plans to use the terms. This I have sought to do in an introductory chapter which recounts the genesis of ideology, its appropriation by Karl Marx and his followers, and finally the connotation it has acquired in the twentieth century. After this preliminary excursus into the history of an idea, attention shifts to the political impact of ideology and the ideological mentality on the international scene. The rest of the book traces ideology in diplomatic history more or less chronologically over some two hundred years. Most of the subject matter concerns, if only for reasons of space, the major powers, and the concentration is on European issues for the simple reason that until the mid-twentieth century Europe remained the hub of world affairs. The final chapter, however, recognizes the new extra-European foci of international relations and ideologies since the end of Europe's second Thirty Years War, 1914–45. All of which necessarily involves a certain amount of historical narration (after all, this is intended as a work of history rather than international relations theory). However, the narrative is limited and directed as far as possible to illustrating those analytical themes regarding ideology in world politics which are then resumed in the conclusion.

J.H. Hexter in his book *On Historians* (1979) divides them into 'lumpers' and 'splitters'. Lumpers seek a grand synthesis; splitters refine the lumpers' broad theses by archival research. Given this present project's temporal and spatial scope, the end product plainly falls into the former category. The nature of the task constrains the lumper historian to pronounce on many historical matters without benefit of specialist knowledge. In consequence, I have frequently sought the help of generous friends and colleagues who gave of their time to render advice on topics where my own comprehension was superficial at best. Collectively, they have saved me from many grievous errors of fact and opinion and, needless to add, bear no responsibility for those that remain. In this connection my special thanks are due Robert H. Johnston and Kendrick A. Clements, both of whom read substantial portions of the text. I would also like to recognize here the scholarly assistance of Virginia Aksan, David P. Barrett, Robert L. Haan, Richard A. Rempel, James Stone, Wayne Thorpe, Thomas E. Willey, and also my wife, Nancy Gardner Cassels. And last but not least, I would be remiss if I did not point out that Gordon Martel, editor of the series in which this volume appears, has been a far from passive spectator. The idea of linking ideology and foreign policy originated with him, and his constructive participation throughout is gratefully recognized.

A.C.
September 1995

INTRODUCTION
Ideology – concept and use

Ideology is an enigmatic phenomenon. 'One of the most equivocal and elusive concepts . . . in the social sciences' is one expert opinion. Another writer has advanced its claim to 'a prize for the most contested concept'. And a third begins his study,

> Nobody has yet come up with a single adequate definition of ideology. This is not because workers in the field are remarkable for their low intelligence, but because the term 'ideology' has a whole range of useful meanings, not all of which are compatible with each other.[1]

Dictionary definitions are more impressionistic than exact, and faintly disapproving. A 'science of ideas' is an agreed lexicographical description, which suggests something more coherent and rigorous than any casual set of beliefs. But secondary definitions tend to undermine any notion of scientific rigour: typical phraseology includes 'visionary speculation', 'idle theorizing' and 'impractical theory'.[2] Such contradiction reflects at once the nebulousness of the concept of ideology and its shifting connotations over two centuries.

The word *idéologie* came into use in the French revolutionary era in order to characterize the beliefs of certain anti-metaphysical *philosophes* who followed Locke and Condillac in contending that all knowledge derives from sensation. The *idéologues* postulated a sure and encyclopedic form of knowledge upon which social engineering could be based. They endorsed the revolution as an opportunity to construct an ideal commonwealth founded on Enlightenment precepts of empiricism, human reason and natural law, although it was not until 1795 that their views won official approbation. They looked to the newly established Institut National to 'save the nation' by imposing from above proper rules of conduct. Indeed, one of its first acts was to launch a public competition on the topic 'What are the institutions for establishing morality in a people?' The principal voice of the *idéologues* and author of *Eléments d'idéologie* (1804), Destutt de Tracy, spoke frankly of 'regulating society'.[3] Thus, from the start, ideology had a sociopolitical purpose. To this day virtually

1

every commentator is agreed that ideology's natural habitat lies in the realm of social and political action.

The French Revolution was in part an attack on organized religion, and in the new revolutionary age ideology was to lay down moral guidelines previously supplied by the churches. It has often been suggested that the invention and rise of ideology was a collective psychic response to the waning of traditional religion in the West. In one scholar's shrewd words, ideologies 'did not arise until man decided that the "self" ceases to exist at death and that no supernatural explanation of the origin of the universe or man is necessary'.[4] And so ideological certitude replaced Christian dogma, and Europe's intellectuals became the new priests. Parallels between religious and ideological beliefs are easy to find – in the passion with which ideas that demand a 'leap of faith' are held or in the presumption to explain all phenomena by reference to a single theology. Yet, if 'all religion is ideology, . . . not all ideology is religion'. In fact, virtually all ideologists from the French Revolution onwards have been resolutely secular, their object the manipulation of power to create the perfect society in this world, not the next. In a well-worn phrase, modern ideologies are 'secularized religions'.[5]

The heyday of the French *idéologues* was brief, for Napoleon I denounced them as impractical visionaries out of touch with reality and their theorizing as 'shadowy metaphysics which subtly searches for first causes on which to base the legislation of peoples, rather than making use of laws known to the human heart and the lessons of history'.[6] In spite of the emperor's fall shortly thereafter, his blast was sufficient to put ideological theories out of fashion for some two generations. It was Karl Marx who brought the word back into intellectual circulation. No one can be sure why he decided to revive the concept of ideology, although the Napoleonic stricture of it as unscientific gives a clue, for under the rubric of ideology Marx and Engels developed the famous thesis of 'false consciousness'.

To Marx, reality consisted first and foremost in the material conditions of life, in the ownership and control of the current modes of production, and in the resultant class relationships. This provided the base of the social order, upon which rested a superstructure of morality, religion, law and, of course, the political system – all conditioned by and responsive to the basic material realities. To describe the whole complex of intellectual assumptions and behavioural attitudes associated with the superstructure Marx appropriated the word ideology. The first full statement of Marxism (1846) expounded the role of ideology by means of a famous metaphor. This compared it to that of a *camera obscura* which depicts the world by means of an upside-down image.[7] From the imagery used two things can be inferred. First, that ideology was formulated at least one remove from the material base, although whether it was part of or somehow distinct

2

from the superstructure has always been a subject of Marxist debate. Second, that ideology dealt in distortion and illusion, and thus deserved the title of 'false consciousness'. Ideology constituted a 'false consciousness' because reality began in 'the material process, not in the ideological reflex it left in the minds of the participants'.[8] It was Engels, not Marx, who actually invented the phrase 'false consciousness' and, in due course, established its place in the Marxist canon:

> We all laid, and *were bound* to lay, the main emphasis, in the first place, on the *derivation* of political, juridical, and other ideological notions, from basic economic facts . . . Ideology is a process accomplished by the so-called thinker consciously, it is true, but with a false consciousness. The real forces impelling him remain unknown to him; otherwise it would simply not be an ideological process.[9]

One question raised by this definition of ideology is whether the body of thought we call Marxism is not itself a false consciousness. One of the first to make such an allegation was the German revisionist socialist, Eduard Bernstein. Indeed, Lenin, writing in 1902 to refute Bernstein, used the phrase socialist ideology: 'the *only* choice is – either bourgeois or socialist ideology'.[10] By socialist ideology, of course, Lenin meant no false consciousness but the irresistible tide of materialist history. The orthodox Marxist line remained that ideological false consciousness as a reflection of the ruling mode of production would disappear with the overthrow of capitalism. Presumably, a true or proletarian consciousness would then prevail.

Until recently most theorists of ideology have been legatees of the concept of ideology as a false consciousness absorbed passively by all strata of society, even while they refined or challenged the full Marxian analysis. Typical was Karl Mannheim, founder of the 'sociology of knowledge' school. Within the framework of this academic subdiscipline he elaborated on the relativism of all ideologies, Marxism included, to the time and place of origin ('situational' and 'temporal determinations'). He distinguished between ideologies that mirrored the values of a dominant group or class and utopian ideas that expressed the beliefs of aspirant or rising groups and classes. Only a 'free intelligentsia', Mannheim argued, had any hope of breaking loose from this cultural relativism and of understanding reality without the blinkers of ideology and utopian dreams.[11] Another thinker to put faith in an intelligentsia was Antonio Gramsci, though his 'organic' intellectuals were to be activist workers for revolution by raising popular consciousness of the historical process. More important, Gramsci developed the construct of an 'ideological hegemony' to explicate how the ruling class wins consent of the governed, and in doing so he rescued Marxism from a sterile economic determinism.[12] Whereupon a cluster of sociologists set about investigating the role of ideas in the social control

3

exerted by elites. Out of this exercise emerged such theories as the process of 'legitimation' (Jürgen Habermas) and the 'ideological state apparatus' (Louis Althusser).[13]

All these writers portrayed ideology as a tainted form of knowledge. As one scholar of the sociology of knowledge puts it, 'Ideological thought is . . . something shady, something that should be overcome and banished from our mind.' 'A pernicious form of thinking' runs another's dismissive phrase.[14] These negative views find an echo in the current consensus. What started in the French Revolution as a scientific cult has found no more than a few defenders who equate ideology with rational thinking.[15] Rather, the twentieth-century version of ideology is of 'a myth written in the language of philosophy and science . . . [to] lend a partial credence to its assertions' which, apprehended irrationally, satisfy an 'emotional need'. In this scenario, ideology rests on 'some general law of all existence'. In the same vein, 'ideology is never content with a partial view; it intends to encompass all'; its aims are 'messianic'. Hence ideology is categorically and ruthlessly inclined 'to suspend ordinary ethical considerations, and to replace them by the prerogatives of the "historical mission"'.[16] Such typical opinions of ideology are, obviously, an accurate depiction of the single-cause, all-inclusive world views that Isaiah Berlin pilloried in his famous distinction between the hedgehog that knows one big thing and the fox that knows many little things.[17] This absolutist cast of mind is the hallmark of modern totalitarian systems. At which point, it may be germane to ask whether the greater part of modern scholarship, in tying its concept of ideology so closely to the totalitarian model, does not create an unduly restrictive and inadequate typology.

In daily speech, when the word ideology is used, most of us do not conjure up intimations of false consciousness or messianic visions. Plainly, something looser is intended, not so much 'propositional' beliefs as the expression of day-to-day attitudes. Terry Eagleton remarks that 'consulting the person-in-the-street has its uses' and holds that the view of ideologies 'as conscious well-articulated systems of belief is clearly inadequate'. It misses out 'the subject's lived, apparently spontaneous relations to a power-structure [that] comes to provide the invisible colour of daily life itself'. Other commentators make the same distinction between 'intellectual' and 'lived' ideology.[18] What is needed, therefore, is a less rigid formula than the received scholarly one.

In this connection the political philosopher John Plamenatz usefully observes that ideologies appear to operate on two levels, the sophisticated and the unsophisticated. On the former plane one encounters an 'explicit' world view (*Weltanschauung*) or 'total ideology'. Conceived by intellectuals, who are the real craftsmen of ideology, this enunciates an invariable law of history and points unerringly to a predetermined future. Conversely, 'partial' ideologies on the unsophisticated level denote the 'implicit' values of society at large and, by definition, lack some of the features of total ideologies, notably their structural rigour.[19] This is not to deny that a partial ideology is any more tolerant of other faiths or less demanding of absolute commitment by its adherents than its cousin. In a word, both types of ideology are prescriptive.

The temptation is to extend the definition of ideology indefinitely, and to open the door to 'the alarming cannibalism of the idea of ideology, its propensity to eat up *all* other ideas'.[20] Perhaps Plamenatz's unsophisticated partial ideologies are no more than 'belief systems'. These are less precise sets of principles than ideologies and are unearthed by means of behavioural psychology; they are 'lenses through which information concerning the physical and social environment is received [that] orients the individual to his environment, defining it for him and identifying for him its salient features'.[21] Alternately, we are dealing with what the French call *mentalités*, a collective unconscious (in a non-psychological sense) nurtured over a *longue durée*. It is worth noting that social scientists who write of belief systems and *mentalités* readily concede the 'blurring' and 'overlap' with ideology.[22] In a similar fashion, ideology may be said to encompass Georges Sorel's theory of 'social myths' which, though devoid of empirical evidence, still stimulate men to action, and Vilfredo Pareto's non-logical 'derivations' and 'residues' which mould communal attitudes.[23]

The admission of relatively unstructured conceptions into the category of ideology invites a further exegesis. Mainstream studies of ideology subscribe to the 'interest theory' – that is to say, ideology serves to gain or preserve the advantage of a particular group. Marxian false consciousness, of course, is a classic statement of this genre. But another school drawing inspiration from cultural anthropology has advanced an alternative 'strain theory', whereby ideological beliefs are considered a subconscious response to dislocations within the social structure.[24] One would expect ideologies originating from the latter source deep within society to take the form of inchoate, non-intellectual values widespread throughout a community. That is to say, the kind of thought patterns envisaged in the 'strain' model betrays a distinct resemblance to the unsophisticated or partial ideologies, belief systems and mentalities described above. Clearly, ideology has many mansions.

One conclusion to be drawn from the foregoing would seem to be that what we often mean by ideology is, in fact, no more than ideological thinking, a manner of thought and discourse rather than the dogma itself. Certainly, the word ideological as used in common parlance conveys a peculiarly intense way of holding an opinion as much as its substance. History is rife with cases of group action where doctrinal content has been secondary to fervency of belief, or where the basic ideas have changed, sometimes dramatically, but faith in the ideological cause has remained firm. Such episodes attest to the power of ideological thinking without reference to the substance of the message.

It follows that ideology in its historical context must be interpreted broadly. In the subsequent chapters of this book, therefore, it will be employed in both the total and partial sense, to embrace an intellectualized, comprehensive *Weltanschauung* as well as the amorphous values and assumptions held by the general public. In the latter category will be subsumed the generic phenomenon of ideological thinking. One specimen of this less determinate ideology or *mentalité* ought to be mentioned here in passing since it occupies so many of the following pages. That is the phenomenon of nationalism – the sort of ideology that, according to one authority on nationalism, 'can have a political impact only if presented in simplified forms and embodied in symbols and ceremonials'. In other words, nationalism lacks the intellectual structure of some other 'isms', and 'has never produced its own grand thinkers: no Hobbeses, Tocquevilles, Marxes, or Webers'.[25] Moreover, it is self-evident that no specific patriotic or nationalist sentiment can have the ecumenical appeal of the classic ideology. And yet, nationalist doctrines have historically evoked, and still evoke, convictions impervious to alternative opinion that are readily recognizable as ideological. Furthermore, as we shall see in a moment, nationalism was from the start instrumental in creating and spreading the modern vogue for ideology.

What, then, are the salient characteristics of ideology and the ideological mentality? All ideological belief comprises a set of closely related ideas held by a group; we may speak of an individual's ideology but such a figure is either representative of, or claims to represent, communal interests. Ideological beliefs supply a broad interpretation of the human condition, 'a cognitive and moral map of the universe'.[26] This requires a degree of historical consciousness, and the total ideologies advance a simplistic, monocausal explanation of all past and future history. In such accounts a key to understanding lies in natural law (or religion in a theocratic society). Secular true believers of an intellectual bent will adduce some empirical evidence and rational argument for their ideological convictions. Ideology is thus distinguished from myth pure and simple, although myths often accrue and add power to an ideology. But ratiocination contributes only marginally to ideological belief. At the end of the day, even total ideologies must be taken on trust and, in the realm of partial ideologies and unsophisticated ideological thinking, it is still more a question of emotional faith. An element of irrationality distances the ideological mentality from conventional philosophical speculation. Ideology, in one writer's phrase, 'is a doctrine whose special claim upon the attention of its believers rests much less upon its supposedly scientific or philosophical character than upon the fact that it is a revelation'. Or in another's simile, 'Ideology is to politics and religion what poetry is to music and literature . . . In the last analysis, its formulation and popularization may not be amenable to rational explanation'.[27]

Because of the emotional investment placed in ideological beliefs, they are prone to lapse into dogmatism and hostility towards unbelievers. Passively, a dominant ideology may provide the stability of shared values in a society, but more often ideological thinking demands active policies to safeguard or disseminate specific ideas. To encourage a rallying to the cause, the language of virtue and vice is customarily employed; the ideological formula is 'a tale that points a moral'.[28] For the same reason it usually postulates a golden age either in the past or in the future. In the former case, the task is to regain or preserve as much as possible of the ideal society; in the latter, it is to build an earthly paradise out of what Kant called 'the crooked timber of humanity'. In addition, most ideologues possess a certitude, not just that utopia can be built but that it is destined to be built. A fatalistic trust in the tide of history and the ideological frame of mind go together. However, history cannot be left alone to unfold; the 'passionate intensity' (W.B. Yeats) of ideological belief craves movement and deeds. It has been said that 'ideology is the transformation of ideas into social levers'. This activity is overwhelmingly political for 'the concept of ideology is linked closely with matters of power and political struggle.'[29] And with ideology's primary political function we arrive at the purport of this book: ideology in modern international relations.

The starting point must be the French Revolution of 1789. While one can certainly discern ideology and ideological thinking before that date, it was the revolution which supplied a galvanic impetus to secular religiosity in two particular ways: by spreading the habit of ideological thought and speech on a popular level, and by introducing it to the practice of international politics. Taking its cue partly from the American War of Independence and partly from the theory of the general will enunciated by Jean Jacques Rousseau, the French Revolution was promoted in the name of the inalienable rights of man.[30] Although the revolution in the short run served the interests of the French middle classes, the doctrine of equal rights took root, and not just in France. One might say that it spread to impose a Gramscian ideological hegemony first on Europe and then on the entire world. Furthermore, the cult of the rights of man opened the door to campaigns for popular sovereignty and democracy. The combination of the rights of man and popular sovereignty, by demanding that ordinary citizens concern themselves with public life, caused them to identify with the national group as never before. National identification served to assuage the alienation of modern society and to replace the old loyalties to church and village eroded by industrialization and urbanization. Technological developments in communication – in printing and radio, schooling and literacy – facilitated 'a greater degree of self-awareness on the part of all groups'.[31] The process whereby the inhabitants of the 'citizen state' were drawn into acknowledging an emotional stake in the group's status in the international arena has been called, in a famous case study of nineteenth-century Germany, the 'nationalization of the masses'. In this process 'the worship of the people thus became the worship of the nation, and the new politics sought to express this unity through the creation of a political style which became, in reality, a secularized religion.'[32]

In other words, ideology and the ideological pattern of thought supply a medium through which foreign policy issues can be transmitted to and perceived by a mass audience. Not surprisingly, Marxist theory, if not every Marxist, has traditionally regarded popular nationalism as typical false consciousness, an ideology geared to perpetuate the bourgeois state and sanctify international capitalist competition.[33] But it must be realized that, in an era of democracy and mass politics, nationalism or any other ideology can move both ways; the beliefs and actions of rulers may be shaped by values from below just as much as they may impose their own ideas on the citizenry.[34] But in the final analysis, the end of all ideological thinking is group consensus.

Mass politics evolved gradually, so too did concomitant ideologies. During the nineteenth century popular participation in political affairs made great strides but, on the other hand, did not achieve complete fulfilment. In the same way, nineteenth-century ideologies were in the main less than total; one scholar has termed them 'universalistic, humanistic'.[35] The twentieth century saw the maturation of mass politics, and the complementary ideologies have tended to fall into the category of exclusionary and aggressive world views. 'Ideologies – isms which to the satisfaction of their adherents can explain everything and every occurrence by deducing it from a single premise – are a very recent phenomenon', wrote Hannah Arendt. 'Not before Hitler and Stalin were the great political potentialities of the ideologies discovered.'[36] Twentieth-century systems of belief, even where a coherent intellectual structure has been lacking, have been held with a novel and fervent prescriptive conviction. In the field of international relations, it is no accident that the age of total ideological commitment has also been the age of total war and global confrontation.

1

RAISON D'ÉTAT MEETS THE ENLIGHTENMENT

Modern international relations began with the collapse of the medieval world. Out of the decline of feudalism and the breakdown of a united Christendom emerged the centralized sovereign nation state. Without any supranational authority competition among these units of international politics necessarily unfolded in a state of anarchy, mitigated only by the individual nations' sense of proportion and conscience.[1] The consequence was the appearance during the first centuries of the European state system of two categories of international conduct, conveniently termed the Italian and French methods of diplomacy.

The former derived from the 'wolf-like habits developed by the Italians of the Renaissance . . . a combination of cunning, recklessness and ruthlessness which they lauded as Virtù'.[2] The lack of scruple with which the Italian city states pursued their rivalry appeared to receive its imprimatur in Niccolò Machiavelli's *The Prince*, first published in 1532. Whatever the author's intent – and it has been endlessly debated – his name has resounded through the centuries as a term of political abuse. From its inception *The Prince* has exercised enormous influence in public life as an endorsement of force and fraud at the expense of morality and principle. *Raison d'état* justified all. By and large, international relations in the sixteenth and seventeenth centuries operated along Machiavellian lines. This was true not least during the series of religious wars that convulsed Europe. The Reformation had undermined the medieval Christian theory of a just war which had sanctioned war for the true faith; it was impossible to apply the just war theory to sectarian conflict.[3] The door was thus opened wider to Machiavellian amorality. While protesting loyalty to the Catholic or Protestant religion, states more often than not followed their own self-interest; Philip II of Spain was an almost lone exception and paid a steep price for his religious-political consistency. The Thirty Years War (1618–48), which opened as a climactic 'confessional' battle between Reformation and Counter-Reformation, ended as an unmistakable struggle for secular power.[4] And it was not at all inconsistent for his

9

most Christian majesty of France to side with the infidel Turk in order to curb Habsburg imperial power.

The sheer opportunism of this Italian system of diplomacy provoked in due course a predictable revulsion. Its most notable literary manifestation was *Of War and Peace* (1625) by Hugo Grotius, the first attempt to suggest on the basis of precedent and natural law, a code of international behaviour. It was reprinted or translated some fifty times between 1625 and 1758. The book played a part in the drive for a more honest diplomacy – the French system, so called not because the French were particularly virtuous but simply because it achieved prominence when the France of Louis XIV (1643–1715) was the dominant European power. In addition, its most able spokesman was a Frenchman, François de Callières, whose *De la manière de négocier avec les souverains* appeared in 1716. Essentially a manual of advice for diplomats, it stressed prudence, good faith and the will to compromise in negotiation. Diplomacy, to de Callières, was 'a civilized activity . . . equipped to cushion the forcefulness of power politics'.[5] An urbane approach to international affairs was furthered too by the dawning professionalization of diplomacy. The first training academy for diplomats was established in Paris in 1712; admittedly short-lived, it was nevertheless followed by similar schemes in other countries.[6] All of which reflected a desire to replace the lawless pursuit of self-interest with a degree of order and assurance in diplomatic practice.

International relations in the eighteenth century were conducted in a mix of the Italian and French styles. A perfect illustration was provided by Frederick the Great, king of Prussia (1740–86). Before reaching the throne he composed a tract critical of political expediency that, altered slightly by Voltaire, appeared under the title of *Antimachiavel* (1740). Yet, in the same year, his first action as Prussian monarch was the swift and violent seizure of the Austrian territory of Silesia – a coup straight out of the textbook of Italian diplomacy. '*Raison d'état*, with its appeal to the elemental impulses of power and grandeur in Man, triumphed in him . . . Frederick decided to follow in the reprehensible steps of Machiavelli.'[7]

The larger truth, however, is that, whether the Italian or French style of international relations prevailed, neither allowed any scope for ideology. The egotistical calculation of the Italian school precluded sacrifice for a larger cause. This was reinforced by the prevailing mercantilist theory of economics that lay behind the colonial wars of the age. In the context of *sauve qui peut*, old allegiances and enmities might be shelved at a stroke, as they were in the notorious diplomatic revolution of 1756. A few years later, an English diplomat complained that 'every court stands upon its own bottom, and lives from hand to mouth without any great principle of policy'.[8] On the other hand, the reasonableness of the French system ruled out strong emotional conviction. 'A man who is naturally violent and passionate', wrote Callières, 'is in no ways proper to manage rightly a negotiation of great importance'.[9] The entire political culture of the eighteenth century, in fact, was inimical to ideological thinking.

Even though some princes began to see themselves as servants of the state, politics remained overwhelmingly dynastic. International competition did not so much concern the Prussians against the Russians, or the French against the British, as the king of Prussia against the Russian emperor, and the king of France against the king of England (especially as the latter was also elector of Hanover). Foreign policy was primarily a matter for European courts and courtiers. Ambassadors had to pay many costs of a mission abroad out of their own pocket, which is why they came to expect a substantial parting gift from the court to which they were accredited. Notwithstanding the few halting steps to the professionalization of diplomacy, an ambassador was almost invariably a rich aristocrat. International relations rested in the hands of an elite who had much more in common with each other than with the populace of their own country. They all underwent the same classical education, perhaps topped off by the Grand Tour of European cultural centres; they spoke and wrote a *lingua franca*, increasingly French during the eighteenth century; monarchs and aristocrats intermarried freely across national frontiers.[10]

Such cosmopolitanism fostered a sense of community among states, what some theorists of international relations call 'solidarism'.[11] The sense of a 'family' of European nations also arose from the growing habit of calling international congresses, particularly at the end of a period of warfare. The agreements to emerge from such meetings – the Treaties of Westphalia (1648) and Utrecht (1713), for instance – attempted to bind together all participants in joint commitments. Writers in the seventeenth and eighteenth centuries regularly referred to Europe's nations as constituting a single commonwealth or republic.[12] The Hanoverian A.H.L. Heeren, writing in 1809, waxed nostalgic about the old regime's 'union of several contiguous states resembling each other in their manners, [Christian] religion and degree of social improvement, and cemented together by a reciprocity of interests'.[13] International rivalries were thus worked out in the ambience of a common European civilization based on shared values; the possibility of an ideological rupture was virtually nil.

'Diplomacy without armaments is like music without instruments', Frederick the Great is reported to have said.[14] But here again, international conflict was kept within bounds by certain features of eighteenth-century warfare. Although the brutalization of lower ranks everywhere sowed the seeds for acts of savagery in the clash of arms, berserk violence was episodic rather than characteristic of fighting in the century before 1789. In the main, this was because armies were composed of mercenaries, conscripts and volunteers whose enlistment was often less than an act of

11

free will. Mercenary troops were expensive to raise and deserted in droves if a commander exposed them too recklessly to slaughter. National recruits, many lured by penury to take the 'king's shilling' or coerced by press-gang, hardly constituted an effective fighting force. The day when millions would willingly lay down their lives for their country at little or no cost to the nation's treasury lay far in the future; Voltaire claimed that the inhabitants of France in his day did not know the meaning of the word patriotism.[15]

Furthermore, few advances in military technology and tactics were made in the century and more after 1648 – 'when time stood still', as one expert in warfare puts it.[16] Dependent on costly and unreliable troops and antiquated weaponry, military leaders in the eighteenth century preferred to concentrate on manoeuvring and set pieces like sieges, piling up 'minor successes until their aggregated weight and financial exhaustion compelled the adversary to make peace'.[17] Europe in the eighteenth century was much more often at war than at peace, but there was neither the inclination nor the wherewithal to indulge in crusading ventures to annihilate the enemy. Limited war was the other face of cosmopolitan diplomacy. Together, they ensured that 'Europe held itself at bay'.[18]

The framework within which this self-restraint was exercised was the balance of power, a phrase that came to enjoy wide currency after it was specifically mentioned in the Treaty of Utrecht. The functioning of the balance could not be described with any precision, however. Unquestionably, the very principle of a balance of power called for the formation of alliances to counteract the threat of a hegemonic state – hence the coalitions designed to thwart French continental ambitions between 1689 and 1713, and British naval and commercial pretensions during the American War of Independence. But apart from these *ad hoc* arrangements, the balance was volatile. It might, as at the opening of the eighteenth century, comprise a rough counterpoise between the traditional royal houses of Habsburg and Bourbon, or with the mid-century rise of Prussia and Russia a multiple equilibrium involving several great and secondary powers. The balance could be invoked to protect the rights of small states; conversely, it could be used to justify the dismemberment of Poland (1772–95) as a means of preserving the peace among Russia, Prussia and Austria. To some, the balance of power was a self-regulating mechanism, a kind of Newtonian law of international affairs. Others saw it more as an ideal to be aspired to, a moral imperative. However interpreted, the idea of a balance of power entered fully into eighteenth-century assumptions about international relations; it was 'an orthodoxy whose acceptance was . . . formal and explicit'.[19] Above all, the eighteenth-century balance demanded of national foreign policies a flexibility that, in turn, ruled out ideological alliances and enemies.[20]

The international system made up of cosmopolitan diplomacy, limited war and balance of power was a peculiarly eighteenth-century phenomenon. Bitter memories were held of the religious wars of the previous century, whose horrors were often embellished in the telling. Especially appalling in retrospect was the religious fanaticism of the Thirty Years War – or more accurately, the religious guise given to dynastic rapacity. The Catholic–Protestant contest having been settled according to the formula of *cuius regio, eius religio* (a nation's religion would be decided by its ruler), religion in the eighteenth century ceased to be a basic cause of conflict between states. If this did nothing to reduce international competition and war, it did lower the temperature of international politics; for example, it permitted the moderate diplomacy of the French style to emerge.

Moreover, the fact that humankind had introduced a degree of order into the anarchic state system was consonant with the philosophy of the eighteenth-century Enlightenment. In its optimistic fashion, this set great hopes by humanity's ability to understand and control the world it lived in. In human reason lay the expectation, perhaps the certitude, of progress. The advance from the ferocious wars of religion to the comparatively restrained international relations of the eighteenth century seemed a step in the right direction. Even the Machiavellian pursuit of self-interest in the age of Frederick the Great implied the exercise of rationality in calculating the probable profit and loss of any move on the world stage. In this sense, the secular diplomacy and restricted warfare of the eighteenth century was a function of the Age of Reason.

But eighteenth-century international relations appealed to the contemporary spirit of rationalism only up to a point. Inasmuch as the essence of the system remained power politics with war the final arbiter, it failed the absolute test of reason. It was not difficult to argue that interstate hostility was wasteful of a nation's treasure and its citizens' lives, and detrimental to human happiness at large. This utilitarian argument, sometimes married to a moral condemnation of war, gave rise to blanket critiques of an international order based on sovereign nation states. Schemes for a perpetual peace resting on a federation of nations flowed from the diverse pens of William Penn (1693), the Abbé de Saint-Pierre (1712), Jean Jacques Rousseau (1761) and Immanuel Kant (1795). Their plans were frankly utopian and made no impact on world politics in their own day. But it is worth noting that they were the forerunners of the twentieth-century creed of universalism. Advocates of the League of Nations and the United Nations frequently harked back to the writings of the eighteenth-century peace enthusiasts.[21]

A more pragmatic criticism of the existing international system came from the ranks of the *philosophes*.[22] The school of thought known as the physiocrats was concerned to promote economic efficiency on the home

13

front, and it also subscribed to the notion of a natural harmony of economic interests among the nations. The physiocrats deplored the pursuit of dynastic and political objectives in the international arena partly because of the burdens imposed on the domestic economy, partly because of the obstacles raised to the free flow of goods throughout the world. France's parlous financial situation on the eve of the revolution of 1789 – after a century of intermittent hostilities with Britain culminating in expensive involvement in the American War of Independence – was adduced in support of physiocrat arguments. But at least the physiocrats more or less accepted governmental structures as they were; their aim was to see their own economic prescriptions taken up by the more enlightened rulers of the day. The physiocrats did, in truth, attract not a few admirers among European royalty.

Other *philosophes* adopted a more radical tack. Rousseau, the most influential if not the archetypal *philosophe*, planned but never completed a study of international politics to complement his famous *Social Contract*. Nevertheless, from this and other writings his scorn for the diplomacy of the *ancien régime* was evident. For Rousseau, man's situation in the state of nature was benign; his fall was brought about by society – a notion summarized in the celebrated aphorism that 'man is born free, but is everywhere in chains'. A wholesale reconstitution of society into small national units, in which the general will might be readily determined, would resolve every difficulty of both a civil and international order. Indeed, virtually all radical *philosophes* proposed this 'second-image solution' to the problem of peace and war: 'establish ideal states all over the world and peace will follow'.[23] Humans being regarded as inherently good and peace-loving, Machiavellian power politics, the balance of power and war were dismissed as the work of wicked governments, or in Diderot's words, 'the blind passion of princes'. What was needed was to get rid of rulers with dynastic ambition and the privileged elite who ran eighteenth-century international relations. Theorists of the rights of man, such as Condorcet, called for the submission of foreign policy issues to a popular assembly. Arguably the most forceful advocate of popular sovereignty as the path to peace, however, was not a French *philosophe* but the radical Englishman Tom Paine. Paine relished the day when 'all the governments of Europe shall be established on the representative system', for then 'nations will become acquainted, and the animosities and prejudices fomented by the intrigues and artifice of courts will cease'.[24]

As the primary concern of the radical *philosophes* was not foreign policy but the drastic reformation of their own societies and government, their influence was to be felt first in the realm of internal politics. Their swingeing critique of the *ancien régime* became the ideology of the revolution of 1789 in France. But the doctrine of the rights of man, like any other ideology, could not be constricted within national frontiers. As we shall see in the next chapter, the revolutionary ideology reverberated throughout Europe, enlisting followers and provoking counter-ideologies, while reshaping international politics utterly.

In one notable instance the international ramifications of Enlightenment thought were demonstrated well before 1789. Behind the revolt of the thirteen American colonies in 1776 lay political theories regarding a ruler's obligations under a social contract and the iniquity of absolute monarchy or despotism. Stemming from John Locke's apologia for Britain's own revolution of 1688, they became fashionable in French intellectual circles through the works of Montesquieu and Rousseau, whence they returned to the English-speaking world across the Atlantic. The intellectual debt that the American rebels owed the French *philosophes* was symbolized in the famous embrace in a Paris theatre exchanged between Voltaire and Benjamin Franklin soon after the latter's arrival as diplomatic agent in the French capital. Needless to say, King Louis XVI's aid to the Thirteen Colonies sprang not from admiration of revolution, but from *raison d'état* alone. It was a rare occasion on which the French monarchy and its Enlightenment critics stood on the same side of the fence.

For their part, the Americans were determined to base the foreign policy of their embryonic republic on correct principles. When it was a matter of arranging cooperation with France in the war against England, two ideals came into apparent conflict. On the one hand, many colonists had turned their back on Europe in the hope of creating a better society elsewhere. As Tom Paine wrote in the bible of the American revolution, *Common Sense* (1776), 'with a blank sheet to write upon' Americans had it in their 'power to begin the world over again'.[25] Would association with an old corrupt Europe tarnish this dream? If so, the answer was strict isolation. On the other hand, if the New World's social experiment were truly unique and superior, was there not a duty to impart the secret of success to others? Such a course required relations with other countries and hinted at interference in their domestic affairs. This was the dilemma of American exceptionalism. In practice, the American Continental Congress formulated a compromise. No political commitments were to be made to any other state, not even those at war with England during the revolutionary struggle. Yet formal diplomatic relations would be necessary in order to negotiate commercial treaties and, in a challenge to current mercantilism, the offer of free trade was to be extended to all states equally. Thus, the early foreign policy of the United States 'was idealistic and internationalist no less than isolationist'.[26]

The tension between the desire to preserve the New World from contamination and the compulsion to promote law and reason in international affairs by active participation can be found in the classic commentary on the new republic's international position – President Washington's Farewell Address of 1796. Hence, both American isolationists and

15

internationalists have cited the address in support of their position.[27] The document, in fact, suggested a means of reconciling the two visions: 'It will be worthy of a free, enlightened, and at no distant period a great nation to give to mankind the magnanimous and too novel example of a people always guided by an exalted justice and benevolence.' The words recalled John Winthrop's biblical metaphor of America as 'a Citty upon a Hill, the eies of all people are upon us'.[28] To instruct by setting a shining example would allow the USA to wield influence without entanglement in the politics of the Old World. The pose of aloof paragon of virtue was sustainable until imperialism and two world wars sucked the USA into total involvement in international affairs. But already in the last quarter of the eighteenth century one may perceive the outline of the two ideologies which have characterized American foreign policy in the twentieth century. The isolationist impulse would be juxtaposed with postwar crusades to bring American values, derived incidentally from the eighteenth-century Enlightenment, to the rest of the world community.[29]

If the *philosophes* played a part in bringing the Thirteen Colonies to rebellion, the American victory sent back the 'intellectual contagion' of revolution to Europe. It was not that representatives of the new US government deliberately fostered revolution, though some made no secret of their distaste for the *ancien régime* by ostentatiously shunning both the dress and ceremony of European courts. Their message was reinforced by word-of-mouth testimony of those Europeans who had fought on the American side; the largest contingent was French and the most vocal in support of liberty was the Marquis de Lafayette. Of course, French radicals required little prompting to draw conclusions from events across the Atlantic. Condorcet in an anonymous pamphlet exulted, 'America has given us this example . . . The spectacle of a great people where the rights of man are respected is useful to all others, despite differences of climate, of customs, and of constitutions.'[30] Seizing on the example, one Parisian reformist group took the name of 'les américains'. An eager disciple of the American revolution was Jacques Pierre Brissot, a pamphleteer whose Gallo-American Society was short-lived and an object of ridicule. But his passion for 'a crusade of all peoples against all kings' would surface to greater effect in a few years' time.[31] In more general terms, it was only in the wake of the American War of Independence that the word 'democracy' entered European political parlance to denote 'a new feeling for a kind of equality, or at least discomfort with older forms of social stratification and formal rank . . . [and] against the possession of government, or any public power, by any established, privileged, closed, or self-recruiting groups of men'.[32] In this push for equality lay a clear challenge to dynastic control of international relations.

The threat of the democratization of diplomacy carried with it the portent of ideology in world politics. Most *philosophes* 'were concerned

with Man in the abstract . . . What was required for good government, it
was assumed, was a firm grasp of correct principles, not detailed study of
particular problems and conditions.' This habit of generalization had its
counterpart in prescriptions and programmes couched in absolutist terms.
When the rights of man were achieved,

> men would at last be free; but this would not lead to the emergence of
> differing opinions and parties among them. On the contrary, unfettered
> reason would produce complete harmony and unanimity. Such a society
> would also be one of perfectly virtuous men . . . Side by side, therefore,
> with the mocking, critical, worldly, sometimes cynical spirit . . . there
> lurked within the Enlightenment another which was utopian, messianic
> and potentially totalitarian.[33]

On the surface, the eighteenth-century cult of reason appeared to rule out
ideological fanaticism. But in the disaffection of the *philosophes* the seeds
of ideology were germinating.

The formalized international relations of the *ancien régime* constituted
an interim between the frenzied wars of religion and the wars of nationalist and ideological passion to come. Yet, in one respect, the monarchs of
the eighteenth century unwittingly prepared the way for the future confla-
grations. The enlightened despots, with their rationalist zeal for efficiency,
brought a new degree of centralization to their respective states; this was
as true of diplomatic and military service as of internal administration.
The nation state left behind by Prussia's King Frederick, Catherine the
Great of Russia, and even Joseph II and Leopold II of Austria, was a
more streamlined and therefore more formidable instrument operative in
the balance of power than they had inherited.[34] It was this newly powerful
nation state that, increasingly after 1789, was to be put at the service of
the sovereign people. Whereupon the centralized, populist nation state
would become the engine of ideological foreign policy.

2

THE BIRTH OF IDEOLOGY
The French Revolution

THE FIRST MODERN WAR OF DOCTRINE

Debate swirls about the French Revolution of 1789 as a historical watershed, a clean break with the past and the beginning of modern times.[1] In the realms of intellectual and economic history, continuities pre- and post-1789 are readily traceable. But in matters of war and peace there is no doubt that the French revolutionary era ushered in novelty. Moreover, of the two famous solvents of the *ancien régime*, the French and industrial revolutions, it was the former that had the more immediate impact. Industrialization and urbanization, probably more than anything else, would in the long run bring the masses a role in political decision-making (see Chapter 5). Yet it was the French Revolution's promotion of the rights of man which first injected a populist and ideological note into the conduct of international relations.

Alexis de Tocqueville compared the French Revolution's scope to that of Christianity – 'catholic in the exact sense'.[2] From the start, there were portents that the upheaval in France would not be confined to one country. The Declaration of the Rights of Man and Citizens by the revolutionary National Assembly in August 1789 was addressed to 'all mankind', although this conventional Enlightenment phraseology no more implied a decision to export revolution than it did in the mouth of the American revolutionaries. On the other hand, just such an interpretation was self-servingly placed on the declaration by thousands of enemies of the *ancien régime* and refugees from all over Europe who congregated in Paris. Conversely, aristocratic emigrés who fled France cited it as proof positive of the danger of revolutionary subversion everywhere; it was the fount of their campaign to invoke foreign intervention in France to reverse 1789.

In addition, more specific issues of international politics were raised immediately by the revolution in France. The Treaty of Westphalia, which in 1648 had ceded Alsace to France, also guaranteed seigneurial rights there, including those of the small German princes who in 1789 were still members of the Holy Roman Empire; they were understandably

18

incensed by the National Assembly's abolition of feudalism. Another anomaly was the papal enclave of Avignon which, on the petition of its inhabitants, was occupied by French forces in 1790 and the following year formally annexed to the French state. Both cases clearly pitted the old order of monarchical, clerical and aristocratic prescription against the democratic, egalitarian challenge. Not surprisingly, the two parties used Alsace and Avignon unsparingly in their ensuing propaganda war, though neither the German princelings nor the pope were able to command much sympathy, and in the long haul the questions proved to be mainly of symbolic importance.

Indeed, for some two years the main forces of revolution and counter-revolution showed distinct reluctance to join issue with each other. The French revolutionaries were too involved in their constitution-building to look beyond France's frontiers, and said as much. More important, the European powers initially found various reasons for leaving the French alone to wrestle with their problems. Most likely to be involved was Austria, whose alliance with France in 1756 had been sealed by the marriage of the Habsburg princess, Marie Antoinette, to the future King Louis XVI. But the familial tie was not particularly affectionate, and Marie Antoinette's brother, Leopold, who succeeded to the imperial throne in 1790, expressed approval in principle of the overthrow of France's absolute monarchy. *Raison d'état* likewise dictated caution. The 1756 alliance notwithstanding, the prospect of a France too weakened by internal strife to act vigorously on the international stage was pleasing to Vienna. In particular, it would inhibit France from pursuing its traditional ambitions in the Austrian Netherlands (Belgium), where the attempt to impose uniform administration on all the Habsburg dominions had provoked a ferment. Similarly, revolutionary France's 'disjointed and inefficient government' appeared a boon to the British, as anxious as the Austrians to keep France out of the Low Countries.[3]

At the other end of Europe also local problems took priority over what was happening in Paris. King Gustav III of Sweden railed fiercely against the revolutionaries and spoke of leading a counter-revolutionary crusade, but in 1789 his nation was occupied by war with Russia. Empress Catherine of Russia claimed to be physically sickened by news from the French capital, but her country was engaged in warfare not just with Sweden but the Ottoman empire too. The Prussians were prepared to move on an enfeebled France, though for territorial gain rather than any ideological cause; but contrariwise, they were equally ready for an alliance with the French revolutionaries against Austria. Above all, the three East European powers feared to overcommit themselves in the west lest the Polish question should suddenly explode. Further partitions of Poland were always on the cards after the first one in 1772, and Russia, Austria and Prussia watched each other warily to prevent a neighbour stealing a march. Preoccupation with their own backyard was summed up in Catherine the Great's remark that she would combat the revolution on the Vistula where Polish patriots were promoting an independent constitutional monarchy. In consequence, the entreaties of Marie Antoinette and the emigrés at first fell on deaf ears, and Austria even expelled the emigrés from Belgium.

The Austrian attitude changed, however, after 21 June 1791, when Louis XVI's attempt to flee was thwarted at Varennes, and the French royal family returned to Paris as virtual prisoners. Claiming her own and her family's lives to be in imminent danger, Marie Antoinette's appeals to her brother grew more frantic. Leopold II at last responded, somewhat impetuously: 'Everything I have is yours: money, troops, in fact everything!' The imperial mood was perhaps revealed in Leopold's sour reception of Mozart's opera, *La Clemenza di Tito*, composed for his coronation on the untimely theme of royal mercy to rebellious subjects. Recent unrest throughout his empire suggested that Austria might be susceptible to 'this pernicious French epidemic'.[4] Moreover, the summer of 1791 was a diplomatically propitious time for Austria to give attention to France. Fitful hostilities with Turkey were drawing to a close and, more crucially, a *rapprochement* with Prussia seemed to promise security in the Polish question as well as cooperation in Western Europe. The latter prospect brought together the Austrian emperor and Prussian king at Pillnitz. Their joint statement issued on 27 August 1791 introduced a fresh asperity into the ideological confrontation between the old order and the new. It declared the situation in France to be 'an object of concern to all the sovereigns of Europe' and called on monarchs everywhere to 'employ the most effective means to place the king of France in a position to affirm, in the most perfect freedom, the basis of a monarchist government'. Meanwhile, Austrian and Prussian troops were put in a state of readiness to march. Yet this threat of intervention was hedged with a serious reservation, namely, that it was to be implemented only on the basis of an international action.[5] In other words, Austria and Prussia would not move without the help of at least one other power, and in 1791 it was hardly conceivable that either Britain or Russia would join an attack on France.

The Declaration of Pillnitz, then, was no clarion call to arms against the French Revolution. Its intent, in Vienna at any rate, was to exert sufficient pressure without fighting to check the radical tide in France. When, in September, Louis XVI accepted a limited monarchical constitution, it did indeed appear that the revolution had been contained. The new *modus vivendi* between the French monarchy and the revolution convinced the Austrians that their minatory stratagem had succeeded.[6] None the less, Austria and Prussia went out of their way to emphasize the growing ideological divide. Not only did they announce that their declaration at Pillnitz was issued at the behest of the reactionary French emigrés, but they also allowed the emigrés to attach to it a provocative letter urging Louis to reject any new constitution. Even so, the Declaration of Pillnitz might have created little stir – it first received hardly any notice in French journals – but for the fact that there were in Paris politicians with diverse motives for publicizing its ideological challenge and for replying to it in kind.

All along, the French revolutionaries had indulged in the rhetoric of universal revolution. For instance, the National Assembly permitted the Prussian self-styled 'orator of the human race', Anacharsis Cloots, to bring before its bar a delegation of 'the oppressed nations of the universe', so that he might declaim that, 'encouraged by the glorious example of France, all the peoples of the universe sighing equally for liberty would soon break the yoke of the tyrants who oppress them'.[7] But the temptation to adopt a positive policy of internationalizing the revolution was resisted until the election of a legislative assembly under the 1791 constitution. Members of the National Assembly having quixotically agreed not to stand for the Legislative Assembly, the latter was a new body in every sense and free to strike out on new and radical paths. It did so by declaring war on the *ancien régime* throughout Europe.

War afforded the possibility of shaping the future direction of the revolution in France. The moderate faction in the Legislative Assembly (the Feuillants) believed war would entail a halt to radical experimentation and bring the sansculottes or mob to heel. To others, notably Lafayette, war offered the opportunity of gaining martial glory and personal advancement, and then of arbitrating between the king and the assembly. In court circles, of course, war was a welcome prospect because, it was hoped, it would not just curb the revolution but destroy it entirely. At the other extreme, the republicans (chiefly the Girondins) saw war as the chance to push the revolution further and topple the monarchy. Among the Girondins the most influential warmongers were the followers of J.P. Brissot, a journalist with a chequered career before 1789 – prisoner in the Bastille, exile and police spy. In addition to their domestic republican agenda, the Brissotins endorsed war for the ideological purpose of liberating Europe from monarchical rule.

The campaign for war gathered momentum in October 1791 with a notorious speech by Brissot to the Legislative Assembly which relied heavily on rhetorical questions and has been described as 'a farrago of truths, half-truths and misinformation'.[8] War was presented as the solution to all French ills, including growing economic difficulties. Austria was the source of every problem: the Austrian alliance had marked the beginning of the end of France's greatness; French foreign policy was being made by the 'Austrian committee' at court; the king was in treasonable correspondence with the Austrian emperor and the emigrés; the

Declaration of Pillnitz was proof of an international conspiracy against the French Revolution. Much of this was the stock-in-trade of current radical demagoguery; what was daring was the call for a crusade to carry the rights of man beyond France's frontiers.

In the coming months this note was struck continually. Henri-Maximin Isnard dwelled on the revolutionaries' duty to carry their message abroad: 'The French have become the foremost people of the universe . . . As slaves they were bold and great; are they to be feeble and timid now they are free?' In any event, Isnard argued, it would be a simple process: 'At the moment that the enemy armies begin to fight with ours, the day-light of philosophy will open their eyes and the peoples will embrace each other in the face of their dethroned tyrants and approving heaven and earth.' Or as Brissot himself explained to the Jacobin club:

> It will be a crusade for universal liberty . . . Each soldier will say to his enemy: 'Brother, I am not going to cut your throat, I am going to free you from the yoke you labour under; I am going to show you the road to happiness. Like you, I was once a slave; I took up arms and the tyrant vanished; look at me now that I am free; you can be so too; here is my arm in support.'[9]

The war debate was conducted with 'operatic intensity'. The Legislative Assembly met in a former riding school with ample room for the public to attend. This they did daily and in numbers; debates were regularly punctuated by interruptions from the gallery. Brissot, by common consent, was a consummate publicist and thrived on the public's presence. In this frenzied atmosphere every issue was polarized and personalized; one was either totally for or against the revolution; one was for war or else a traitor. Those who harboured qualms about war, as initially many did, were marginalized; extremism carried the day. In short, Brissotin oratory 'converted the deputies of the legislative from politicians to crusaders'. As 1791 drew to a close, the assembly's president looked ahead exultantly: 'If the Revolution has already marked 1789 as the first year of French liberty, the date of the first of January 1792 will mark . . . the first year of universal liberty.'[10]

The outbreak of war itself was attended by much miscalculation on both sides. In the belief that the Declaration of Pillnitz had temporarily cowed the revolutionaries, the Austrians, alarmed at mounting Brissotin bombast and the Legislative Assembly's bullying of King Louis, had further recourse to intimidation during the winter of 1791. The Rhineland princes, protectors of the emigrés, were given assurances of military help if attacked by France; demands for a return to the *status quo ante* 1789 in Alsace and Avignon were accompanied by a warning of 'inevitable consequences, not only from the head and members of the Holy Roman Empire, but also from the other sovereigns who have united in a concert,

22

for the maintenance of public order and for the security and honour of monarchs'. Such provocation was predicated on the assumption that France, crippled by domestic turmoil, was incapable of effective military resistance. 'The highest degree of anarchy reigns in all departments', concluded one intelligence report.[11]

In Paris an utterly contrary opinion prevailed. In the Legislative Assembly it was an article of faith that Europe's *ancien régime* was on its last legs, the populace on the edge of revolt everywhere, and the monarchs too selfish to hold together long in an anti-revolutionary alliance. The new spirit engendered by the French Revolution would carry all before it. 'Louis XVI, with his 400,000 slaves, knew how to defy all the powers of Europe; can we, with our millions of men fear them?', was a typical sentiment. Brissot adduced Genghis Khan and Tamerlane as tyrants unable to overcome 'free soldiers'.[12] To cap all this, the minister of war presented an unreservedly optimistic report on France's military preparations. 'It is not the actual distribution or balance of power which is vital,' a keen observer of modern wars has written, 'it is rather the way in which national leaders *think* that power is distributed.'[13] Misperceptions at the opening of the French revolutionary wars sprang directly from the ideological divide that had come to separate France from the rest of Europe. In the first place, it made intelligence gathering unduly hazardous and haphazard. Second and more important, both parties were so certain that history was on their side that they blundered cavalierly into war. One author terms this gullibility the 'Coppelia effect' after the magic spectacles that, when worn by the hero in *The Tales of Hoffmann*, turned a doll into a beautiful woman.[14]

The propensity to war being so great, it mattered little who declared hostilities first. In the event, it was France on 20 April 1792. The motion for war put before the Legislative Assembly was debated scarcely at all; there was much cheering and only seven hardy souls voted nay. Interestingly, one sceptic outside the assembly was Robespierre who, apropos the welcome due to be accorded the French liberators, warned that 'no one loves armed missionaries'.[15] At first, in truth, it proved to be less a matter of propagating the revolution abroad than of preserving it at home as the Austro-Prussian forces swept from Belgium deep into France and a manifesto published in the name of the Duke of Brunswick threatened to raze Paris if the French royal family was harmed. But the allied army was checked, or, more accurately, failed to advance further, at Valmy in September. Then suddenly the tide turned. On 6 November General Dumouriez, former Brissotin foreign and war minister, won a stunning victory at Jemappes, which opened all of Belgium to French forces. By the end of 1792 France's armies had penetrated into the Germanies as far as Frankfurt, and in the south had taken possession of Savoy and Nice. The 'crusade' to spread liberty could now take off.

France's dramatic metamorphosis from monarchy into republic in September 1792 automatically broadened the doctrinal gulf between Paris and the monarchist capitals. Therefore, when news of Jemappes arrived, the National Convention, the new French assembly elected to draft a republican constitution, seized the chance to drive home the point. On 19 November the Convention promulgated a fraternity decree that offered assistance to 'all those [peoples] wishing to recover their liberty'. 'War on the castles, peace to the cottages' was the pithy expression popular in the Convention.[16] To appeal to disaffected elements in the enemy country was nothing new; it had been a regular feature of the earlier wars of religion. But to make subversion of a whole social order an explicit war aim was startlingly novel.[17] As a symbol of the new ideological factor in international affairs, the fraternity decree left a deep impression; its cancellation as impractical policy some months later went all but unremarked.

In the meantime, the Convention on 27 November issued another and equally significant decree, in reality a set of instructions for administering the territories occupied by French arms. While ordering the suppression of all feudal privileges in accord with revolutionary philosophy, it also made plain in no uncertain terms that populations would have to pay for their own 'liberation'. Financial levies, often mere substitutes for the abolished feudal dues, and requisitions in kind were to meet the cost of French armies of occupation in Belgium and elsewhere. The distinction between liberation and French conquest was immediately blurred. Furthermore, by the end of 1792 Brissot and Dumouriez among others were to be heard calling for the acquisition of France's 'natural' frontiers – the Rhine, Alps and Pyrenees. Here were early signs that the ideological crusade might easily turn into French imperialism.

The French occupation of Belgium widened the war by involving Britain, for the Low Countries were, in Edmund Burke's words, 'as necessary a part of this country as Kent'. In London a quarrel with France was no more than a continuation of the second Hundred Years War which, since 1689, had been fought for material gain. A century later, the British government's eyes were still fixed on colonies, the commercial regime in the Scheldt and the balance of power in northwestern Europe. Ideological motivation was suspect in London, and the Pillnitz declaration derided as 'ill-conceived and undignified'.[18]

Yet, although British foreign policy was driven overwhelmingly by economic and geopolitical considerations, decisions were taken in 1792 against a background of ideological turmoil on the home front. Britain produced the two greatest tracts on the French Revolution of the age. Burke's *Reflections on the Revolution in France* prophesied in 1790 the anarchy and bloodshed soon to engulf France, and incidentally laid down the tenets of counter-revolutionary conservatism. Paine's *Rights of Man* (1791–2) was an express rebuttal of Burke and defence of the revolution's

Rousseauite theory; his reward was honorary French citizenship and a seat in the Convention. The French Revolution also had immediate effect on the campaign for British parliamentary reform. This movement, born of the American revolutionary experience, had been largely restricted to the upper classes. But after 1789 it took on a new life and drew in thousands of new adherents from all social strata. Links with the French Revolution were flaunted; the London Corresponding Society, the largest reform group, exchanged pledges of loyalty with both the Legislative Assembly and the Convention, and promised to resist any British attempt to join an anti-French coalition. The zenith of agitation for parliamentary reform, coupled with food riots, coincided with the drift to a Franco-British war. All of which enabled the Tory government of William Pitt the Younger to brand the reformers subversive, and to extend by simple government fiat the definition of sedition so as to drastically curtail civil liberties.

In actual fact, despite the fervour of the broadsheets and the street riots, the country as a whole stood behind the government and supported war against revolutionary France. The British conservative *mentalité* complemented a John Bullish Francophobia.[19] Even the opposition Whigs, from whom radicals in both Britain and France expected sympathy, were split. Their leader, Charles James Fox continued to proffer the revolution an olive branch, but he was sabotaged by conservative Whigs who assured Pitt of their backing in the event of war.[20]

Events leading up to Franco-British hostilities followed the pattern of those before the Austro-Prussian war with France. France's ambition to carry the revolution and its armies from Belgium into Holland was well known in London and, in November 1792, Britain signed a treaty with Holland guaranteeing Dutch integrity, very similar to the earlier Austrian pledges of aid to the Rhenish princes. In Paris the French foreign minister, Charles François Lebrun, issued a public demand that Britain desist from intervention in the Netherlands; predictably it was rejected. Compromise was hard to achieve because the same ideological blinkers that had distorted Austrian and French estimates of each other's strength were still being worn in London and Paris. In December the French were forced to evacuate Frankfurt, so Britain clung to the belief – the continued French hold on Belgium notwithstanding – that the revolution had fatally weakened France's military capability. On the other side, French agents in Britain informed their home government that 'England offers precisely the same prospect as France did in 1789'. Lebrun assured his colleagues that 'the situation throughout the British Isles was so combustible that only a spark was needed to ignite England, Scotland and Ireland simultaneously'.[21] On 1 February 1793 a revolutionary government in Paris once more anticipated an assault and declared war first; the vote for war this time was unanimous.

Thus started the War of the First Coalition. Britain's motives and war aims might be explicable by *raison d'état*, but the monarchies of Europe were also drawing closer together in common fear of revolution on the march. Pitt began the process of providing money to construct anti-French coalitions, the first of which soon included, besides the three major powers, Spain, Portugal, Sardinia, Naples and a number of German states. For their part, the French advertised the ideological quarrel with their foes. An appeal, composed with the help of Paine in exile and in the spirit of the fraternity decree, was made to the British people to rise up against their rulers. Then, on the eve of the Franco-British war, came news of the execution of Louis XVI. Regicide could not fail to sharpen ideological passions as Danton, now influential in shaping French foreign policy, recognized: 'They threaten you with kings! You have thrown down your gauntlet to them, and this gauntlet is a king's head, the signal of their coming death!'[22]

The crusade for universal liberty was launched by the Girondins but inherited by an extremist group that took over the Jacobin club and emerged victorious from the factional infighting in Paris. Many of these Jacobins, not just Robespierre, were lukewarm towards universal revolutionary war. Even Danton, for all his fiery public utterances, worked surreptitiously if unsuccessfully to extricate France from its crusading entanglement.[23] A token of the Jacobins' attitude was provided by the case of Thaddeus Kosciusko, whose Polish resistance movement against the Russian predators ostentatiously adopted many of the trappings of revolutionary France. In 1792 the Girondins had granted Kosciusko French citizenship; a year later a Jacobin ministry met Kosciusko's pleas with stony silence. On the other hand, when it was a matter of French national security, the Jacobins were all thoroughly belligerent. And in 1793 the cry of *la patrie en danger* was growing insistent. French armies were on the retreat again, even in Belgium; Lafayette who had deserted to Austria earlier was followed by Dumouriez in April; the economic situation was desperate, provoking bread riots by the sansculottes. The Jacobin answer was centralized control of the war effort, the like of which was not to be seen again until the twentieth century. To some extent, this was enforced through terror, but the greater part was accomplished by voluntary action won by manipulating the passions of the French populace. The dominant sentiment roused was a fervent national pride.

One of the immediate causes of the French Revolution had been the failure of a patriotic reform movement under the *ancien régime*. Nationalist sentiment had then turned to revolutionary means for fulfilment. The result was that 'nationalism . . . became the spearhead of an attack on feudalism', and from the start of the revolution the appellation *patriote* was practically synonymous with revolutionary. Once all Frenchmen were in theory equal citizens, they were expected to rally to the defence of what was now their own national community, and as early as December 1789 the phrase 'every citizen a soldier, every soldier a citizen' was heard in the National Assembly.[24] The epigram was not without substance. When the Declaration of Pillnitz hinted at the formation of an international anti-revolutionary combination, some 100,000 volunteers, many of them from the revolutionary National Guard and wearing the tricolour, flocked to the colours 'as an earnest of their devotion and friendship for their fellow citizens'.[25] In leading France into war, Brissotin oratory had regularly mixed calls for a revolutionary crusade with appeals to national honour, Austrophobia and, on occasion, xenophobia, including ugly boasts of French innate superiority over other peoples.

Given the Jacobins' reservations about supranational crusades, their capture of power in 1793 guaranteed a still greater emphasis on patriotism as the guiding force behind the war effort. However, to leave things to popular spontaneity was not enough. The peasantry, the bulk of the French population, had contributed relatively few recruits to the volunteers of 1791; the volunteers of 1792 proved less numerous and of poorer quality than their predecessors; a levy to raise 300,000 troops authorized in February 1793 proved disappointing and fanned smouldering counter-revolution in the Vendée into conflagration. The situation was remedied by the famous directive of 23 August 1793 for a *levée en masse*. This aimed not just at raising a mass conscript army, but also at energizing the entire French people:

> Young men will go to the front; married men will forge arms and transport foodstuffs; women will make tents, clothes, and will serve in the hospitals; children will tear rags into lint; old men will get themselves carried to public places, there to stir up the courage of the warriors, hatred of kings and unity in the republic.[26]

In an attempt to inflame public opinion the Legislative Assembly had printed and circulated nationally the minutes of its hyperbolic session before the outbreak of war. But nothing hitherto matched the galvanic impact of the *levée en masse*. In the first place, it mobilized more than a million men, of whom over three-quarters were on active service at any one time. All males between eighteen and twenty-five were liable for military service, although marriage and paternity conferred exemption. Marriage and birth rates shot up, of course, and other forms of evasion from flight to bribery of officials were not uncommon. Nevertheless, helped by a high rate of unemployment, the numbers enrolled were formidable. Equally remarkable were achievements on the home front. Given extensive powers of requisition by the Committee of Public Safety, a sort of war cabinet, commissioners for armaments and food transformed private concerns into virtual state enterprises. By 1794, it has been estimated, 3,000 workers were producing 700 guns a day, the smelting of church bells supplying much raw material; 6,000 workshops were manufacturing gunpowder, much of it with saltpetre scraped off damp cellar walls; in Paris alone 258 open-air forges were in operation in such areas as the Invalides, Tuileries and Luxembourg gardens; the grounds of the Tuileries were planted with potatoes. Most of this improvisation was financed by *assignats*, a paper currency secured against confiscated church property. They were now printed in massive quantities, and in 1793–4 exchanged at between 20 and 30 per cent of face value. To curtail the subsequent inflation, the command economy was for a short time stretched so far as to include wage and price controls.[27]

These feats were made possible by the wave of nationalist emotion that swept France. The printing presses and theatres of Paris indulged in an orgy of patriotic sentiment and sentimentality, while the brush of the painter David, himself an active revolutionary, provided images of noble heroism. In the provinces local zealots and government representatives *en mission* vied with each other in whipping up patriotic ardour. The gist of their propaganda was that the revolution was threatened not just by external foes but also by enemies within. The consequence was national paranoia, best exemplified by the infamous Law of Suspects which gave watch committees throughout France frightening powers. In turn, the paranoia was fed by the increasing numbers dispatched by M. Guillotin's humane execution machine; the discovery of so many 'enemies of the people' in all walks of life appeared to testify to an internal danger. In this frenzied atmosphere ideological thinking flourished. Amid the bloodletting of 1793–4 it is admittedly hard to discern the ideals of liberty, equality and fraternity. Yet the behaviour of the Committee of Public Safety betrayed an unmistakably ideological cast of mind.

This body claimed authority on the basis of a Rousseauite general will. Against this notion of an absolute good, diversity of opinion is irrelevant, in fact intolerable. Put bluntly, 'freedom consists in doing what is right'. In the 'flaming, unreasonable desire of coming to grips with the promise of an abstract felicity', all means, no matter how savage, are justifiable. The men who ran the Terror sought the perfect society, a heaven on earth.[28] This involved not just outward change, for example in the form of constitution or adoption of a revolutionary calendar beginning in 1792. It required a transformation of beliefs – hence the zealots' dechristianization programme symbolized by festivals of reason held in many churches, including Notre Dame cathedral. The outcome was to be the moral regeneration of the French citizenry. Once opposition to progress was removed by the guillotine, the new citizen would emerge, imbued with revolutionary *vertu* which was declared to consist of 'courage, patriotism, probity'.[29] The vision was apocalyptic, the long-term intention social engineering on a grand scale.

Meanwhile, in the short run, the organization of the war effort under the Terror was so successful that the unity of the First Coalition was seriously breached and the danger of foreign invasion of France banished for twenty years. How much this military success was due to the ideological fervour stirred up by Robespierre and his colleagues is a moot point, though it was certainly a factor in revolutionary Year II (1794).[30] At all events, it is beyond question that the French Revolution dramatically improved France's military capacity. The relationship between the army and the revolution was a close one. The disappearance of many emigré officers, who owed their rank to social position rather than ability, opened up a military career to talent. The newly promoted young officers were indeed of superior quality to the displaced aristocrats and had a personal reason for gratitude to the revolution for hastening their advancement. As for the rank and file, most lived close to the civilian population, in quarters not barracks, and therefore participated in the general revolutionary enthusiasm. Volunteers for military service tended to bring the revolutionary spirit with them. In 1793 an amalgam of professionals and volunteers, to which were soon added the conscripts raised by the *levée en masse*, produced the 'final and definitive form of the nation in arms'.[31] Not surprisingly, the egalitarianism of 1789 that drew officers and men closer together gave rise to a sense of camaraderie but also to problems of discipline. The latter were dealt with by the Committee of Public Safety whose emissaries to the armies meted out political indoctrination in *vertu* and capital punishment to looters and unsuccessful generals alike.

This mix of exhortation and coercion worked. From 1794 French armies, reorganized by Lazare Carnot, became the scourge of Europe. French troops learned to accept unusual hardships, lived a Spartan existence off the land and moved swiftly; they skirmished rather than fought pitched battles. 'Raggedly charging as fast as musket-and-bayonet-carrying men could go, to the accompaniment of revolutionary drums, songs, slogans and yells', their tactics disconcerted the *ancien régime* armies.[32] Their casualties were large by eighteenth-century standards. But these were acceptable to the commanders because of the huge pool of manpower created by the *levée en masse*, and to soldiers in the ranks so long as a spirit of self-sacrifice for *la patrie* and its revolutionary ideals held sway.

The international conflict sparked by the French Revolution has been called the first modern 'war of doctrine'.[33] As far as the years 1792–4 are concerned, the term is apt. An ideological frame of reference was established early by the Declaration of Pillnitz and the Girondin crusade for universal liberty. If the Jacobins later stressed patriotism at the expense of international revolution, the war effort under the Terror was no less fired by revolutionary ideology: 'In the course of this radical phase of the Revolution, the principle "national sovereignty" was finally equated with "popular sovereignty".'[34] It was perhaps inevitable, once the ideology of the French Revolution spread from the political classes to the populace at large, that the notion of personal liberty should succumb to the collective idea of the nation. The populist aspect of French nationalism in 1793–4 endowed it with a peculiar intensity, 'a religious character and . . . a veritable ethic'. It is no accident that the word chauvinism derives from the name of a superpatriotic French folk hero of this era.[35] Here, one discerns the beginnings of a shift from patriotism, meaning an innocent love of country, to the sort of exclusive nationalism that connotes hostility to the foreigner. In other words, France pioneered a development that would engulf the rest of Europe in the nineteenth century and in due course the rest of the world – the creation of an ideology out of nationalism itself.[36]

In light of nationalism's impact, the subject has naturally spawned a vast literature. It is worth distinguishing between two generic interpretations of the origins of nationalism, one historical, the other sociological.[37] Into the former category fall those scholars who regard nationalism as essentially an outgrowth of modern, that is to say post-1789, society. As such, it has allegedly been inculcated from above by intellectuals and more pragmatic publicists 'teaching the right determination of the will', or else disseminated in the form of a literate 'high culture' responsive to technological progress.[38] At the other extreme is to be found the 'antiquity of nations' argument, which suggests that nationalism is more mysterious, self-generative and rooted in ethnicity.[39] This divergence of views reflects the fact that in some instances the nation state preceded the growth of strong and widespread national feeling, while in others pre-existent nationalism was a mainspring of state formation. In Britain and France, and even the United States, nationalism's evolution occurred almost as an act of will within the framework of a nation state already in place. By contrast, a nationalist spirit was apparent for all to see in Central and Eastern Europe in the nineteenth century, and later in the Third World, long before political self-determination was achieved. The truth is that no single paradigm has yet been devised to encompass all nationalist experiences. Nationalism both wells up more or less spontaneously within a community and may be taught from the top down by an intelligentsia or predominant power structure.[40] Usually the two processes intersect, which is precisely what happened in France under the Jacobins. It is scarcely credible that a few years of revolutionary and nationalist exhortation were sufficient to produce the extraordinary outburst of nationalist sentiment of 1793–4. The Jacobins tapped, channelled and augmented an already extant patriotism that, to an indeterminate degree, antedated the revolution and the Terror.[41]

Walter Bagehot's comment on nationhood still holds true: 'We know what it is when you do not ask us, but we cannot very quickly explain or define it.' The problem of definition is compounded by the very dynamic of nationalism that causes it to be diffused as a consciousness throughout a particular group. Whatever its genesis from above or below, its purpose is to end up as a popular emotion, a reality acknowledged in Ernest Renan's celebrated description of a nation as 'a daily plebiscite'.[42] Ideas seeking a mass audience thrive best on imprecision and lack of clear definition. Nationalism is no exception, and it is arguably the least intellectual of ideologies. One cultural historian indeed intimates that national self-consciousness may belong in the realm of the mythic. In this interpretation nations are 'imagined political communities' where 'a deep, horizontal comradeship' (fraternity in French revolutionary parlance) requires that 'fiction seep quietly and continuously into reality'.[43]

The surmise has already been made in the Introduction that, as an example of ideological thinking, nationalism falls properly into the category of belief system or *mentalité* that roots itself deeply and impenetrably in the mass mind. Or it is an unsophisticated ideology in the sense propounded by Plamenatz. Nothing of which detracts from nationalism's potency. On the contrary, it has shown itself repeatedly capable of expressing a community's most ardent longings and inspiring the most fervid political action. More than any other single force, nationalism has been responsible for the injection into international affairs of that 'passionate intensity' that is the quintessence of ideology.

Ideological fanaticism, though, is difficult to sustain, as the French discovered in 1794. Battlefield victories removed the sense of imminent peril, and French troops began to make their way homeward. The severity of the Terror no longer appeared vital to national survival, and in July it came to an end with Robespierre's execution. The ideological quotient in French foreign and military policy declined commensurately. In 1790 the National Assembly had approved a motion that 'the French nation will undertake no war for conquest and will never use its forces against the liberty of any people'. Four years later, the Convention was told 'the Republic must dictate laws to Europe'.[44] In these two statements is revealed the sea change that overtook French policy towards 'liberated' territories. France now sought to impose its will on others; old-fashioned power politics were set to return.

Annexations to achieve France's 'natural' frontiers started under the Convention; Belgium, much of the Rhineland and part of Savoy were unambiguously incorporated into France. The Directory, which succeeded to power after the Terror, put into practice a policy first advocated by the Girondins, of establishing a chain of 'sister republics' which were given classical names. These ultimately stretched from Batavia (Holland) in the north to the Parthenopean Republic (Naples) in the south. Under both dispensations the French pretended to respond to the will of the people. In the case of the annexations, euphemistically called *réunions*, the French received petitions from the local Jacobin clubs asking to join France. In the dependent republics French arms installed in all positions of authority Francophile Jacobins, who obediently signed treaties permitting French troops to remain on their soil. But these non-French Jacobins were without exception everywhere a minority, although a noisy and articulate one.

The rejoicing with which the fall of the Bastille had been greeted, especially by Europe's intellectuals, was considerably muted after the events of 1793–4. Moreover, the policy of making the indigenous populations pay for French occupation was extended by way of levies and requisitions into contributing to the price of the ongoing War of the First Coalition. It has been calculated that a quarter of Directory revenues came from the conquered lands.[45] Wordsworth's encomium of 1789, 'Bliss was it in that dawn to be alive', gave way to

> And now, become Oppressor in their turn
> Frenchmen had changed a war of self-defence
> For one of conquest, losing sight of all
> Which they had struggled for.[46]

Popular resentment against France grew with the passage of time, and many middle-class radicals who had welcomed the French now invoked the principles of the French Revolution against the occupiers. In their case, to the cry of freedom from tyranny was added the corollary of freedom from foreign oppression. Nationalism, a product of the revolution within France, was turned against the French. Italy in particular witnessed the first stirrings of national sentiment in opposition to French policy. Sometimes anti-French feeling arose from a different ideological source, as deeply religious peasants resented the anticlericalism that accompanied the invaders. In brief, France did not rule by virtue of revolutionary ideology but by force of arms.[47] This was proved in 1798 when the elite of the French army departed Europe for an Egyptian expedition; the satellite republics without adequate French military support collapsed, albeit temporarily.

If by the turn of the century French policy revealed the triumph of national self-interest over ideology, the same can be said of the counter-revolutionary coalition. Prussia was an exemplar. At the first check administered to the allied advance in 1792, Prussian forces were transferred to the east to ensure Prussia's participation with Russia in the second partition of Poland. This pattern was seen again after the even more emphatic French victories of 1794–5. Prussia once more found compensation in the final division of Polish territory among the three East European powers, and for good measure withdrew from the war against France altogether. Russian policy was cut from the same cloth. While breaking diplomatic relations with republican France, St Petersburg refrained from military action until French penetration of the eastern Mediterranean in 1799 violated a Russian sphere of interest. Two years earlier, an exhausted Austria had come to terms with France in the Treaty of Campo Formio. By this and subsequent diplomatic arrangements Austria deserted the Rhineland princes, subjects of the Holy Roman Emperor and the most zealous ideological opponents of revolution; they were either expelled from their domains or else became French clients. In return, Austria was permitted to take Venetia. Like the three partitions of Poland, this was a typical old-regime transaction dictated by *raison d'état*.[48] Clearly, the powers were as yet reluctant to accept that the French Revolution necessitated any serious change in their international behaviour.

On the other hand, the rhetoric of revolutionary ideology had entered international discourse to stay. Much allied spleen was vented at the machinations of French agents and the intrigues of an international Jacobin conspiracy. French agents abroad there certainly were; Edmond Genet in Washington, for example, was active in founding democratic clubs. But an international network of revolutionaries was fantasy, fed to a great extent by Augustin Barruel's *Memoirs, Illustrating the History of Jacobinism*, published simultaneously in English and French in 1797. This work, which argued that the French Revolution was a Masonic plot because the words liberty and equality were part of the Freemasons' creed, may have wielded more influence in its day than Burke's *Reflections on the Revolution in France*.[49] Fear of a 'democratic international' also owed something to the reappearance of several Brissotins, the original crusaders for universal freedom, in a ministerial capacity under the Directory. Possibly, Count Talleyrand, the foreign minister, had them in mind when he commended an Egyptian campaign to the Directory with the argument that the subjects of the Turkish empire 'will greet us with rapture; for they have long wished that we would come to deliver them from their oppressors'.[50] In addition, Napoleon Bonaparte, who was to lead the eastern expedition, harboured the dream of reaching India where, he imagined, the Sultan of Mysore might be enlisted in a war of liberation from the British. A call for popular revolt similar to the fraternity decree of 1792 accompanied the launch of the Egyptian venture in 1798, but the peoples of the Ottoman empire, lacking the middle-class radicals who had made the ideological ploy credible in Western Europe, remained generally unmoved. The French were perhaps looking the wrong way; uprisings within the British Isles offered greater possibilities. Although some Irish rebels chanted the Marseillaise, it is questionable how far they were inspired by French revolutionary principles. But the chance to foment revolution of any stripe was let slip; the French authorities were dazzled by the eastern mirage and their expeditions to Ireland were badly mismanaged.

It was the Directory's policy of national expansion and empire, rather than Europe's ideological rift, that gave rise to a second anti-French coalition in 1799. This was, however, short-lived. Napoleon's return to Europe was quickly followed by more military victories against the Austrians, wrecking the coalition and stabilizing the rickety republican ring around France's borders. Within France these successes more than compensated for the disappointments of the Egyptian campaign. Napoleon rode them to political dominance, initially as the first of three consuls in 1799 and then as emperor in 1804. Thereafter for the next decade the nature of international affairs was shaped very much by one man.

THE SPREAD OF IDEOLOGY IN THE NAPOLEONIC ERA

The equivocal character of the French emperor has always posed a major problem. His collaborators confessed to being rarely aware of what was in his mind. His correspondence was geared to telling others what to do, not to revealing himself, and he worked conscientiously at creating an artificial self-portrait to leave to posterity.

Predictably, historical opinions of Napoleon have diverged wildly.[51] Broadly speaking, schools of thought fall into two categories. On the one hand are those for whom Napoleon remained the true heir of the French Revolution, whose goal, the brutal means notwithstanding, was the selfless one of spreading the ideology of 1789 throughout Europe. Significantly, the crusading spirit survived longest in the ranks of Napoleon's *grande armée*. On the other hand, it is possible to see the Napoleonic empire as no more than the realization of a self-centred vision. Napoleon's own coronation by the pope in Notre Dame, his later marriage into the Habsburg family, the replacement of France's 'sister republics' by satellite kingdoms whose crowns were worn by his sundry relations – all betoken an imperial megalomania. In which case the emperor's genuflections to the revolution may be dismissed as mere opportunistic show. Napoleon himself did nothing to clarify things by talking alternately the language of liberation and of conquest. The most simple explication may be the best, namely, that success went to his head and transformed him from heir of the revolution into egotistical conqueror.[52]

As we have seen, Napoleon had scant regard for the *idéologues* of the French Revolution. In reality, political as much as philosophical differences lay behind his dislike, for he accused them of intrigues against his rule. Moreover, although his own pragmatism was indeed at odds with ideological blueprints, Napoleon sprang from the same intellectual environment as the *idéologues*; 'his precocious mind had ripened in a doctrinaire age and he never wholly freed himself from that early conditioning.'[53] Above all, he absorbed from the Enlightenment a trust in the power of human reason to build a more perfect world. Napoleon came to the fore militarily in the service of the Jacobins as they were engaged in trying to force a rationalist utopia on France, and he shared their dream. Like the Jacobins he admired order and discipline. Therefore he welcomed the totally unintended but momentous consequence of a decade of revolution – a quantum leap in the centralization of France's national administration.

It was this rationalizing aspect of the revolution that Napoleon carried forward. In Napoleonic France uniformity was imposed from the centre on civilian as well as military affairs – on local government, the law, education at all levels. Napoleon's outstanding talent was that of a modernizing bureaucrat. 'What a head for organization he has got!', exclaimed Prussia's Frederick William III after meeting him.[54] Napoleon's martial feats owed at least as much to farsighted logistical planning as to battlefield manoeuvres. In turn, his military successes allowed him to attempt on a European scale what he achieved in France, namely 'the imposition of a new and uniform model of administrative modernization'. 'The profound belief in the possibility of creating a Europe in the image of France underlay Napoleon's reconstruction of Europe,' and the implementation depended on the creation of 'new ruling elites of service, which would cut across former national loyalties'.[55] He wanted to play Charlemagne to a new united Europe.

Napoleon, then, evinced a typical eighteenth-century faith in rational progress, but he reinterpreted the original ideals of the French Revolution and jettisoned the shibboleths of 1789. Liberty was suppressed by the secret police and censorship, equality yielded to a new nobility of the *légion d'honneur*, and the fraternity to be fulfilled by an integrated Europe was, in fact, French political, economic and cultural imperialism.[56] Napoleon's drive for rationalized and administrative order has been called the 'Indian summer of enlightened despotism'.[57] But crucially he sought to extend eighteenth-century reform from the single nation to a universal domain. In this way, prosaic bureaucratic modernization became something of a transcendental vision, even an ideology in a rough sense.

To the other European powers, however, Napoleon was simply French expansionism personified, bent on hegemony in Europe and even beyond.[58] But their resistance continued to be fatally uncoordinated. The Third Coalition brought Britain, Austria and Russia together in 1805, but was effectively broken when Napoleon defeated the Austrians at Austerlitz. Prussia belatedly joined the fray only to be overwhelmed at Jena, after which the Russians were dealt with at Eylau and Friedland. Napoleonic domination of the European continent was recognized in the famous meeting of the French and Russian emperors at Tilsit on 25 June 1807. Two years later, Austria took on Napoleon again and suffered another catastrophic defeat at Wagram. This string of glittering triumphs enabled Napoleon to tighten and enforce more widely the so-called Continental System, his one weapon against the sole undefeated enemy,

Britain. Protected by its sea power as it was, that nation might still, he thought, be brought to heel by stifling its trade with the Continent.

In the meantime, the continental powers' collective humiliation was at last forcing them to accept the lesson that, in order to defeat France, it was necessary to imitate what the revolution and Napoleon had wrought in France itself. The message registered most forcibly in Prussia where reformers had been pushing in vain for change from the top down while the country stayed out of war between 1795 and 1806. Now, in the post-Jena despair and led by the royal ministers, Baron Stein and Prince Hardenberg, their moment had come. In September 1807 Hardenberg wrote to his king:

> The French Revolution, of which the current wars are an extension, has brought the French people to a new vigour, despite all their turmoil and bloodshed . . . It is an illusion to think we can resist the Revolution effectively by clinging more closely to the old order, by proscribing the new principles without pity. This has been precisely the course which has favoured the Revolution and facilitated its development. The force of these principles is such, their attraction and diffusion is so universal, that the State which refuses to acknowledge them will be condemned to submit or perish . . . Democratic rules of conduct in a monarchical administration, such is the formula, it appears to me, which will conform most perfectly to the spirit of the age.[59]

This suggestion took practical form in a royal edict of 9 October 1807, for which Stein as Prussian chief minister was mainly responsible, 'on the facilitation of property ownership, the free use of land, and the personal condition of peasants'. It attacked the rigid division of Prussian society into estates (*Stände*) and promised an end, in just over three years, to feudal obligations tying the peasantry to the land, after which 'there will be only free people'.[60]

Stein, whom the conservatives dubbed the 'Prussian Jacobin', would have liked to go further by bringing all estates together in a national assembly. For his efforts he incurred the wrath of Napoleon, who correctly saw Prussian recovery as a challenge to France. Napoleonic pressure compelled King Frederick William to dismiss Stein, who decamped to St Petersburg where he joined a coterie of expatriate reformers from all over Europe committed to using the French model of national renewal to liberate their own countries. Meanwhile in Prussia a military reform commission undertook an overhaul of the army parallel to the civilian reform. Following French precedent, the officer corps was made less exclusive and more professional, and the principal military reformer, General Scharnhorst, urged a 'more intimate union' with the nation.[61] The linkage between overall national policy and waging war was not lost on the reform-minded Prussian officer, Carl von Clausewitz, who remarked on 'the colossal weight of the whole French people, unhinged by political fanaticism, [which] came crashing down on us'. Or in the words of his well-known aphorism, 'war is simply a continuation of political inter-course, with the addition of other means'.[62]

The Prussian reform programme edged towards a nation in arms roused by popular resentment of the French tyrant. What was awaited was the trumpet call for all Germans to rally against the traditional Gallic foe. National feeling in the Germanies and elsewhere in the French empire, first stimulated by the occupation policies of the Convention and the Directory, was bound to grow when subject to Napoleon's high-handedness, his constant levies and looting of art treasures. Nationalism, save in France itself, was of course antithetical to his dream of an integrated Europe ruled from Paris. If his redrafting of the European map encouraged national consciousness in Italy, Germany and Poland, it was accidental; the Kingdom of Italy, the Confederation of the Rhine and the Grand Duchy of Warsaw sprang purely from power-political considerations.[63] His true sentiments were disclosed in the execution of local patriots who opposed French rule – Johann Palm in Nuremberg, Andreas Hofer in the Tyrol.

The first serious uprising against the French since 1799 occurred in an unlikely quarter. When in 1808 Napoleon invaded Spain and deposed the reigning monarch, a coalition of clerical conservatives and patriots began a sanguinary guerilla war which, together with a British army in Portugal, locked up a sizeable French force in the Iberian peninsula for the duration of the empire. In Central and Eastern Europe, though, the powers hesi-tated to issue the summons for grass-roots resistance. Courts and notables, remembering the Parisian sansculottes, feared an uncontrollable populace. In fact, they were still inclined to regard the French emperor himself as a shield against revolutionary anarchy. In any case, Napoleonic France remained too strong to confront militarily – until, that is, the breakdown of the Treaty of Tilsit over the Continental System led to Napoleon's fateful invasion of Russia in 1812.

The re-emergence of the bedraggled rump of France's *grande armée* from the snows of Russia in 1813 occasioned the Fourth Coalition. It also emboldened the princes finally to gamble on a peoples' war of liberation. Five years earlier, Austria had tried to raise a citizen army but with-out much success; now Prussia took the lead. By a series of measures in February and March King Frederick William decreed universal military service and activated a proposal, bruited since 1806, for a *Landwehr* (militia) of all men between seventeen and forty not on active service. This duplicate *levée en masse* raised over a quarter of a million men. Public pronouncements struck the twin notes of egalitarianism and Germanic identity: 'Germans, we are opening up to you the ranks of the Prussian army, where you will find labourers' sons fighting side by side with princes' sons – any difference in class is obliterated by the words "King, Honour and Country".' A new military decoration, the Iron Cross, was struck and explicitly opened to both officers and men. Frederick William addressed an appeal 'To my people', in German 'An mein Volk', an emotive word that the king made clear included all Germans. Stein's promise of an uprising of the *Volk* encouraged Tsar Alexander I to continue his pursuit of the Napoleonic forces beyond Russia's frontiers. The impressionable Russian emperor, professing his allegiance to 'the hereditary and imprescriptible rights of free nations', was in fact more eager than the Prussian monarch to exploit popular and patriotic resentment against Napoleon. Thus a proclamation to the German people and princes was published jointly in the names of Alexander and Frederick William.[64]

German writers were swept up in a ferment of nationalist ideology. Since the Enlightenment a species of German cultural nationalism, based on the study of language, had thrived. But it took the events of 1806–13 to fuse cultural and political sentiment. Ernst Moritz Arndt advocated a rational, democratic and united Germany; Father Jahn in more baleful fashion postulated a *Volk* purified of all alien elements. Johann Gottlieb Fichte, however, best typified the intellectual politicized by the struggle against Napoleon. His *Reden an die deutsche Nation* (1808) became a sacred text of Germanic nationalism. In February 1813 he dramatically suspended his lectures at the new University of Berlin and urged his young listeners to enrol in the campaign for liberation. The artistic community did not lag behind. Carl Maria von Weber, to cite only one example, set about to liberate German music from foreign influences. At a more popular level, the Germanies in 1813–14 were subjected to a barrage of nationalistic symbolism – meetings and ceremonies bedecked with Teutonic insignia, the participants often clothed in folk costume, and the publication and recitation of stories, poems and songs about German greatness.

All this had little to do with the actual downfall of Napoleon, whose crushing defeat near Leipzig in October 1813 was inflicted by superior numbers and regular troops. Even after Leipzig there was no mass German uprising, except in the Tyrol, and no guerilla warfare as in Spain. None the less, such few clashes as did occur between the French army and German popular forces were turned into mighty exploits by the intelligentsia and popular artists. The poet Theodor Körner, for instance, was killed serving in a free corps of non-Prussian German patriots under the command of a young officer, Baron Lützow; Körner's poetic rhapsodies spread the fame of Lützow's Black Rifles throughout the literate public of the Germanies. Out of the euphoria of the time grew a legend: the war of liberation had been won by the German people inspired to heroic deeds by a noble patriotism. 'Those glorious days', as Arndt fondly recalled them, constituted a myth that German nationalists would find most useful in the future.[65]

The French revolutionary and Napoleonic wars bequeathed an unquenchable ideological legacy to the world. In the first place, the political phrases 'right' and 'left' derived from the French National Assembly of 1789, where those supporting the royal prerogative adopted the habit of standing on the right of the hall, those favouring revolutionary change on the left. For at least a century afterwards the terminology of left and right specifically connoted a position pro or con the French Revolution and all it entailed. The rights-of-man ideology, which had propelled France into war in 1792, stood for a measure of representative government, equality before the law and the classic civil liberties – freedom of thought and speech, of assembly and movement, and freedom from arbitrary arrest. By the end of the Napoleonic age this cluster of left-wing tenets took the form and name of liberalism. Liberalism, a term culled from Spanish politics of the time, was to be the universal nineteenth-century doctrine for the advancement of the rights of man.

A second and in the long run more potent ideology to emerge from the revolutionary era was the new cult of nationalism, which had operated both for and against French interests. But it would be wrong to make an exact equation between the nationalism that had animated the French war effort and that of the war of liberation in 1813–14. The enthusiasm with which the French greeted Napoleon on his return from exile in Elba suggested that, over twenty years, military glory had grown addictive and that nationalism had taken root in a broad swathe of French society. In contrast, the peoples' war east of the Rhine was a brief flowering, and the imitative radical nationalism was conjured up, not by revolutionaries, but by monarchs and their ministers who were still cut off from the mass of their subjects; state and nation remained separate. Whether rulers in Central and Eastern Europe after Napoleon's overthrow would countenance the popular nationalism they had summoned to their assistance, or honour the liberal promises made in the heat of war, had to be doubted.

Before 1789 there had existed no such thing as a conservative ideology. The *ancien régime*, being under no threat, had no need of self-justification. Consequently, the emigrés and others who began the struggle against the French Revolution were reactionaries in a literal sense; they reacted to events as they arose. But the assertive spread of the rights of man and their concomitant, popular nationalism, craved a riposte. The conservatism that was formulated in the generation after 1789 did not reject change out of hand, but rather required that it occur within traditional bounds. It took its cue from Burke's critique of the revolution's wanton disregard of experience and wholesale destruction of long-established institutions and, more positively, from his advocacy of the organic society. Burke set greater store by ancient communal liberties than the abstract individual liberty of the rights of man. This argument was echoed by Joseph de Maistre and Louis de Bonald, although with the addition of a divine origin of prescriptive rights. In the German-speaking world the conservative philosophy was assiduously propagated by Friedrich von Gentz whose career embraced both the study and the diplomatic conference chamber. Gentz, whose ideas sprang mainly from Kant and Burke, translated the latter's works into German.[66] By 1815, then, a third ideology was in place alongside the other two. For the next fifty years and more international relations would respond to the triangular interplay among liberalism, conservatism and nationalism.

3

CONSERVATIVES, LIBERALS AND NATIONALIST IDEOLOGY

THE METTERNICH 'SYSTEM'

As its name implies, the restoration of 1815 was an attempt to go back to the *status quo ante* 1789 – or at least to an image of pre-revolutionary society idealized in retrospect. In particular, a return to dynastic rule and aristocratic cosmopolitan diplomacy was intended to exorcise the ideological passions that had lately invaded international relations. Yet, in spite of their aversion to ideological constructs, the victorious allies could not entirely escape the spirit of the new age born of the French Revolution. In the words of a contemporary French aristocratic diplomat:

> Transactions are nowadays delayed by hindrances of which previously we were free. Yesterday it was only a question of material interests, of an increase in territory or commerce; now one deals with moral interests; the principles of social order figure in dispatches.[1]

Accordingly, it was deemed necessary to enunciate the principles of authority that were to buttress the restored order. To answer in kind, as it were, the ideology of Jacobinism that was the all-purpose bogey word of the day, denoting the mix of populist revolution and nationalism that had plunged Europe into more than two decades of war. In consequence, the architects of the restoration announced their attachment to the twin concepts of legitimacy and a concert of Europe. Anti-Jacobins as well as Jacobins were now playing the game of ideological self-justification.[2]

The doctrine of legitimacy was not a coherent body of thought. At its simplest, it held that the only valid governments were those based on tradition, proven over time and, for some Catholic writers, sanctified by the Church.[3] In its reverence for the past it followed Burkean conservative theory; in practice it implied a return of the princes toppled by revolutionary upheaval. But legitimacy was not merely a recipe for internal state formation; it also had consequences for relations between states. Legitimacy won for a government acceptance, not just by its own people, but by other rulers. The triumph of legitimacy thus implied a restored European

41

homogeneity which, in turn, 'meant a recognition of the necessity of norms and law in international affairs'. Without legitimacy in the broadest sense, there was no possibility of restoring the familiar order of eighteenth-century international affairs. Legitimacy, in other words, was the precondition of building anew what Burke had called the Commonwealth of Europe.[4]

Like monarchical legitimacy, the eighteenth-century Concert of Europe was taken for granted, neither codified nor given concrete shape. It was Napoleon's gross violation of the tacit norms of international behaviour that created a groundswell for the formalization of the hitherto vague sense of European communality. As early as 1804 Tsar Alexander I, in negotiations with Britain, spoke of prescribing proper rules of international conduct within a European confederation, an idea Pitt professed to endorse.[5] The same ideas informed the Holy Alliance to which Alexander in 1815 invited all Christian sovereigns to subscribe. The signatories were to bind themselves together in an 'indissoluble fraternity' wherein 'the precepts of Justice, Christian Charity, and Peace . . . must have an immediate influence on the councils of Princes, and guide all their steps, as being the only means of consolidating human institutions and remedying their imperfections'.[6] Although most European states eventually joined the alliance, they did so as a token gesture to gratify the tsar whom most hard-headed statesmen of the day regarded as an impractical visionary; not for nothing had Napoleon included him amongst the despised *idéologues*. Yet Alexander's rather mystical notions were not at variance with more pragmatic proposals advanced by Britain, specifically by Viscount Castlereagh, foreign secretary at the end of the Napoleonic wars.[7]

Castlereagh's proudest achievement was first to arrange a political understanding among Britain, Austria, Prussia and Russia before the military offensive against Napoleon in 1814 (the Treaty of Chaumont), and then to prolong the coalition beyond victory and expand its function. The outcome was the Quadruple Alliance of 20 November 1815, article VI of which read:

> To consolidate the connections which at the present moment so closely unite the Four Sovereigns for the happiness of the World, the High Contracting Parties have agreed to renew their meetings at fixed periods, either under the immediate auspices of the Sovereigns themselves, or by their respective ministers, for the purpose of consulting upon their common interests, and for the consideration of the measures which at each of these periods shall be considered the most salutary for the repose and prosperity of Nations, and for the maintenance of the peace of Europe.[8]

All this was a marked advance on the inchoate eighteenth-century family of nations.[9] 'In either form, Quadruple or Holy Alliance, the principle was asserted of the common responsibility of the rulers of Europe, or at least all but one major member, for the orderly future functioning of the whole.'[10] France, of course, was left outside the Quadruple Alliance, whose initial purpose was to restrain France. But even before the alliance's signing, the Congress of Vienna, which met from October 1814 to June 1815 to draw up a post-Napoleonic settlement, had accepted France's full participation. The inference was that in due course the embryonic concert would embrace all five major European powers.

The choice of the Austrian capital for the postwar congress was symbolic. Since the Declaration of Pillnitz in 1791 Austria had been the standard-bearer of the old order, and had taken up arms against revolutionary and Napoleonic France more often than any other continental power. In their staging of the peace congress the Viennese authorities went out of their way to recreate the ambience of the lost world of pre-1789. Diplomatic negotiations and intrigue were interspersed with a constant round of glittering aristocratic entertainment and sometimes conducted to the strains of music wafted from a nearby ballroom; 'the congress dances' was one summation.[11] The Viennese locale also guaranteed the highest profile and maximum influence of Prince Metternich, Austrian foreign minister and later chancellor, and his associate, Gentz, who served as secretary to the congress.

Not surprisingly, these archetypal representatives of post-revolutionary conservatism seized on the episode of Napoleon's Hundred Days to drive home their message. The escape from imposed exile of the 'great usurper', as Metternich called Napoleon, and the welcome given him by many, if not all, Frenchmen were represented as Jacobinism on the march once more. The allies scurried to complete the Final Act of the Vienna Congress, which they did on 8 June 1815, before returning to the battlefield to inflict on Napoleon his final defeat at Waterloo.

In its Final Act the Congress of Vienna resurrected the eighteenth-century notion of a balance of power, or what one historian prefers to call 'political equilibrium'.[12] But, by whatever title, power was distributed according to two precepts. First, it was necessary to build a security ring around the recent aggressor, France, and second, to provide the customary cartographical compensation for all the allied partners. Thus, Belgium, the former Austrian Netherlands, was attached to Holland to create a buffer to the north of France. Austria's compensation took the form of Lombardy and Venetia. Piedmont gobbled up the Republic of Genoa and was expected to help Austria in resisting French penetration of northern Italy. On the Rhine France was confronted by an enlarged Prussia, now given possession of most of the left bank. Elsewhere Prussia secured some of Saxony, although less than coveted and not enough to upset Austria's pre-eminence in the German world. But the big gainer in Eastern Europe was Russia; in a rearrangement of Polish lands St Petersburg was awarded the lion's share, out of which was carved a nominally independent kingdom of Poland under the tsar.

It will be observed that, in all this shuffling of territories and peoples, the principle of legitimacy often took second place to *raison d'état* and an international equilibrium. Napoleon's extinction of the Holy Roman Empire stood, and the invention of a Germanic confederation of thirty-nine states under Austrian presidency in its stead ignored the rights of over three hundred Teutonic princelings expelled by Napoleon. In truth, legitimacy was invoked at Vienna primarily to aid the restored Bourbons in France. On ascending the French throne in 1814, King Louis XVIII emphasized his legitimacy by insisting that 1814 was the nineteenth year of his reign. It was to enhance his stature that France was admitted to the councils of the Vienna congress. And it was no coincidence that Talleyrand, French foreign minister again in 1815, should be the statesmen at Vienna to argue most forcefully for legitimacy as the basis of the European concert.[13]

Legitimacy became a dogma after, rather than during, the Congress of Vienna. It was applied to the entire settlement of 1815 which, as the legitimate order, was to be defended at all costs. Such was the conviction of Metternich who, for the next thirty-three years, imposed his stamp on Europe. In his only 'profession of political faith', composed in 1820, he inveighed against the 'presumption' of middle-class intellectuals who believed they could construct a commonwealth in an instant, as the French had tried to do. Against this had to be set 'the fruit of human experience in every age'; this amounted to 'historic right', which Metternich preferred to the word legitimacy. Those princes who had been restored in 1815 therefore deserved protection, for 'monarchy is the only government that suits my way of thinking'. The diplomatic settlement of 1815 was similarly inviolable because international engagements must be honoured 'so long as they are not abolished or modified by common agreement between the contracting parties'. If popular nationalist feelings, aroused in the French revolutionary era, had been ignored at the Congress of Vienna, that was of no account; they engaged Metternich's attention only as a facet of democracy, 'a principle of dissolution, of decomposition'.[14] Nor should it be overlooked that nationalism was a deadly virus for the state in whose service Metternich, a Rhinelander, had risen to prominence; the Habsburg empire was a mélange of differing national groups.

When German *Burschenschaften* (student groups) agitated in 1819 against the betrayal of the liberal and nationalist hopes of the war of liberation, Metternich persuaded the diet of the Germanic Confederation to accept the Carlsbad Decrees which imposed political tutelage and censorship on German universities. The next question was whether the *Burschenschaften* were a local phenomenon or part of a wider discontent. The latter view gained ground in 1820 with the assassination of the king's nephew in Paris, anti-government conspiracy in London and open revolts in Italy and the Iberian peninsula. 'We have come to one of those fatal epochs', wrote Gentz, 'when one cannot count on anything.'[15] Legitimacy required upholding on the international stage.

The essence of Castlereagh's 1815 proposal for a European concert was periodic meetings of the great powers, and in the next seven years four international congresses were held. The first, at Aix-la-Chapelle in 1818, dealt with the problems of containing France and reintegrating it into the family of nations, which was, in Castlereagh's view, the proper and principal object of the concert. But the next three meetings, all held on Austrian territory, revealed Metternich's appropriation of the British foreign secretary's project for the ideological purpose of suppressing revolution throughout Europe.

The congresses at Troppau and Laibach in 1820–1 addressed themselves primarily to the disturbances in Italy, which had begun in Naples and spread to the Papal States and Piedmont. These uprisings aimed at curbing absolute monarchical or papal power by a representative assembly, a demand typical of liberalism after the French Revolution. In addition, however, the revolts evinced resentment of Austria, and the crowds waved banners in what were to become the Italian national colours of red, white and green. All of which threatened Austria's predominance in Italy, 'one of the pillars of Metternich's policy'.[16] The combination of liberalism and nationalism, not just in Italy, was the nightmare that would haunt Metternichian conservatives until 1848. In 1820, though, Austria won international sanction to send its own troops to crush the Italian constitutional movements. More important, at Metternich's behest the Congress of Troppau issued a blanket approval of the principle of intervention to quell revolution at large. The Troppau protocol of 19 November 1820 announced:

> States which have undergone a change of government, due to revolution, the results of which threaten other states, *ipso facto* cease to be members of the European Alliance . . . If, owing to such alterations, immediate danger threatens other states, the powers bind themselves, by peaceful means, or if need be by arms, to bring back the guilty state into the bosom of the Great Alliance.[17]

This was an even more notable success for Metternich in that it signalled the conversion of Tsar Alexander I to conservatism. For many years the idealistic tsar had flirted with the revolutionary ideologies of liberalism and national self-determination. His original text of the Holy Alliance had referred to a universal brotherhood among subjects as well

as sovereigns, and it had required Metternich's intervention to remove the hint of democracy from the final document. After 1815 Russian agents were suspected of liaisons with liberal groups throughout Europe, and the tsar was known to be unsympathetic to the Carlsbad Decrees. Alexander's friends included notorious nationalists. The Polish patriot, Adam Czartoryski, was instrumental in persuading the tsar to tolerate a shadowy Polish independence. Alexander's chief advisor at Troppau was Count Capodistrias, proponent of Greek liberation from the Turks as well as of liberal constitutionalism. In fact, the congress witnessed something of a struggle for the soul of Tsar Alexander between Metternich and Capodistrias. Metternich's anti-revolutionary hand was strengthened by news of a Russian army mutiny which reached Alexander in mid-congress. The impressionable tsar swung violently around to the Austrian's way of thinking, and the obedient Capodistrias drafted the actual Protocol of Troppau.[18]

Yet, if at Troppau Metternich succeeded in binding Russia to the conservative cause, as he had bound Prussia and the German states at Carlsbad, he also opened up a breach with Britain. While Castlereagh had no objection to the military intervention of Austria alone in Italy, its own sphere of influence, he balked at the use of the concert as a European policeman. In a famous state paper dated 5 May 1820 he insisted that it 'never was, however, intended as an Union for the Government of the World, or for the Superintendence of the internal Affairs of Other States'.[19] Britain refused to endorse the Troppau protocol, and worse was to follow. After an adjournment of the Troppau congress, the powers reassembled at Laibach to complete their Italian business and arranged to meet again at Verona. Prominent on the agenda of the Congress of Verona, which met in October 1822, was Spain, where the revolutionary movement had assumed a radical aspect reminiscent of France in 1793–4. It was over Spanish issues that the gulf between the Metternichian concert and Britain became unbridgeable.

Before the Verona congress an overworked Castlereagh committed suicide and was replaced by George Canning. Unlike his predecessor, Canning was not a member of the 'Vienna club' of 1815 and was inclined to a more insular 'English' than 'European' policy. Moreover, although a rigid Tory at home, Canning was considerably to the left of Metternich and could be counted on to implement forcefully the message of Castlereagh's state paper.[20] It was no surprise, therefore, when Britain objected to intervention to restore Spanish reactionaries. The French took it upon themselves to carry out the task, even before receiving the authorization of the Verona congress where a British protest was registered in vain. Canning thereupon bent his efforts to safeguarding British interests in Portugal through bilateral negotiations with France and, more momentously, in Latin America by seeking cooperation with the United States.

The inspiration provided by 1789 to reformers and would-be revolutionaries extended beyond Europe. In Spain's Latin American colonies, with the United States' revolutionary example close at hand, liberals under the leadership of Simon Bolívar had seized the opportunity presented by Napoleon's invasion of the mother country to declare independence. This frank affront to legitimacy now came under the scrutiny of the Congress of Verona. If legitimate rule was restored in Spain itself, reasoned the now conservative Tsar Alexander, why not in Latin America too? It would have been a parlous enterprise in the best of circumstances; against the opposition of the British fleet, which Canning threatened, it was unthinkable. Undoubtedly, the British foreign secretary was motivated by a genuine ideological distaste for Metternichian conservatism, but the additional fact that London merchants, hampered by Napoleon's continental system, had established a flourishing trade with the new Latin American republics was an incalculable but weighty factor. Not for the first nor the last time in international affairs, the coincidence of moral imperative and self-interest clouds the issue of motivation. In the case of British nineteenth-century policy, George Bernard Shaw puts the matter in a nutshell when, in his play *Man of Destiny*, he has Napoleon express his sardonic opinion of 'every Englishman' whose 'watchword is always Duty: and he never forgets that the nation which lets its duty get on the opposite side of its interest is lost'.[21]

In the Latin American question Canning hoped to confront the European conservatives with a joint Anglo-American stand. In this he was only partially successful. On the advice of Secretary of State Adams, President Monroe acted unilaterally when, on 2 December 1823, he informed the US Congress that from that time forward no parts of the American continent, north or south, were 'to be considered as subjects for future colonization by any European power'.[22] In reality, the efficacy of Monroe's doctrine depended for the next century on the shield provided by the Royal Navy, so at least a tacit complicity between London and Washington was born. Canning later turned the situation to his advantage by boasting that it was he who 'called the New World into existence to redress the balance of the Old'.[23] The phrase had both ideological and geopolitical meaning.

Anglo-American relations were cordial enough a bare decade after the War of 1812 ended. In that conflict, it is worth noting, the United States had taken the moral high ground in defence of neutral rights in wartime. In the same vein, the presidential statement of 2 December was presented as a ringing declaration of principle. Inevitably, there were in 1823, as there had been in 1812, material considerations at work. Much of Monroe's speech warned against Russian penetration of the Pacific Northwest, and equally pertinent was pressure brought by US merchants in competition with their British counterparts for Latin American markets.

None the less, whatever its proximate cause, Monroe's message refurbished the notion of the New World as a society apart possessing its own lofty values. It has already been remarked that this self-image pointed American foreign policy in two different directions: intervention abroad to bring the blessings of the American way to humanity at large, and detachment to preserve purity at home. In wrestling with this dilemma, both Washington and Jefferson had inclined to the latter, and Monroe's words too appeared to endorse a policy of non-entanglement.

From a different perspective, however, the US step in 1823 amounted to a claim to speak for the Latin American states and implicitly to bring the entire American hemisphere within its province. Secretary of State Adams put it bluntly shortly before Monroe's statement: 'American affairs, whether of the Northern or Southern Continent, cannot henceforth be excluded from the interference of the United States.'[24] The Monroe Doctrine, as future generations came to call it, might reaffirm isolation from European affairs as a fixed maxim of US foreign policy, but most Americans saw no contradiction between the principle of isolationism and hemispheric hegemony.

The idea of a common destiny for all the Americas enjoyed something of a vogue in the 1820s, and Bolívar instigated the first Pan-American Congress which was held in 1826 in Panama. The congress rather compromised its pan-American identity by inviting Britain and Holland, and there was talk of a universal league of liberal states to set against the Metternichian concert. Moreover, the Latin Americans pondered awhile before sending an invitation to the United States.[25] The Panama meeting was less than a total success; the two US delegates did not arrive in time and Bolívar could not attend. Most important, it remained to be seen whether, for Washington, pan-Americanism would imply cooperation with its southern neighbours or a cloak for their domination.

The related questions of Spain and Latin America did not kill the Concert of Europe. It convened frequently during the remainder of the nineteenth century in both conference and congress form, but it did so on an *ad hoc* basis, 'free from its earlier determination to govern the world'.[26] Between 1815 and 1822 Castlereagh's vision of regular periodic meetings had given rise to the now outmoded label of the 'congress system'.[27] But the four post-Vienna congresses were too unpremeditated to be termed systematic; they were called as issues arose. On the other hand, the mere idea of regular consultation had enhanced the concert and sense of international community enormously. The post-1815 principles of international cooperation were undoubtedly set back when Canning, after Verona, refused all invitations to further congresses. Specifically, the British defection brought to an end the utilization of the concert to impose a particular ideology on the world. This is not to say that Metternich did not strive with some success to maintain his conservative grip on much of Europe, simply that he could never again rely on a muster of all the great powers for assistance. A century would pass before the next experiments in international policing. The twentieth-century essays in collective security, however, would be aligned not with conservative but with liberal and democratic ideologies.

The change in the nature of the concert after 1822 soon became apparent in the question of Greek independence. Although the French appeal to the subject peoples of the Ottoman empire to rise up in support of the Egyptian expedition had gone largely unheeded, the nationalism stirred up by Napoleon did not leave Southeastern Europe unaffected. And revolutionary exiles from Italy and Spain encouraged the educated Greeks scattered around the Mediterranean and on the Aegean islands to enlist in a regional 'liberal international'.[28] But whatever the liberal sentiments of Greece's middle-class dissidents, political calculation pointed in the opposite direction. It made sense to turn for help to Russia, always eager to undermine and supplant Turkey's decaying empire. In the Corfu-born Capodistrias there existed an excellent channel of communication to Tsar Alexander.

Inopportunely, though, the Greek rising of 1821 coincided with Alexander's conversion to legitimacy and capitulation to Metternich's influence. Faced with a choice between Greek Christians fighting Muslim Turks and support of established authority, the Austrian chancellor's political ideology overcame any religious sentiment. Thus, the Greeks were left to fend for themselves until 1825 when a new tsar, Nicholas I, ascended the throne. Unlike his predecessor, Nicholas was an uncomplicated reactionary autocrat but, crucially, he would not let his concurrence in principle with Metternichian conservatism stand in the way of the pursuit of traditional Russian goals in the Near East.[29] Russia's backing of the Greek revolt was in the short term a more serious blow to the Metternichian concert than the British desertion.

Meanwhile, Britain too, together with France, had grown exercised about the Greek issue. Interests and emotions jostled together in the policy of the Western powers. Strategic concerns militated against infringement of Turkish integrity lest Russia prove a dangerous beneficiary. Commercially it was necessary to balance long-standing ties with the Ottoman empire against such trading preferences as a grateful new Greek state might offer its liberators. In Britain's case, having endorsed the cause of national determination in Latin America, it was difficult not to follow the same route in the Mediterranean, above all in view of the wave of philhellinism sweeping the country.[30] The study of ancient Greece and Rome formed the core of the education of the governing and professional classes, and the fallacy was widespread that, in supporting the Greek rebels, one was defending the culture of Socrates and Aristotle. Classical sensibilities were upset by reports of Turkish massacres of Greek populations, though both sides were guilty of horrendous atrocities. A London Greek committee floated a loan for the Greek government-in-waiting which netted £472,000; one of the committee's most illustrious members was Lord Byron, who duly returned to the war to meet his romanticized death at Missolonghi. Philhellinism also had a stronghold in French governing circles. Even King Charles X, soon to lose his throne because of his ultra-royalist policy, sympathized with revolution in the Hellenes. In any event, France's centuries-old involvement in the Levant dictated that Paris demand a say in resolving the Greek–Turkish quarrel.

Given the West's diverse motives in the Near East, British and French diplomacy was directed to brokering an agreement between Greeks and Turks, which meant working with Russia while at the same time limiting Russian aggrandizement. In 1827 these ends were largely achieved in the tripartite Treaty of London, by which the three powers agreed to impose mediation on the warring parties. The sultan's reluctance was overcome by judicious military-naval pressure. In a series of protocols signed in London in February 1830 Greek independence was recognized and guaranteed by Britain, France and Russia. The powers insisted that the new Greece accept a monarch drawn from German royalty, a sop to conservatism that disappointed a number of Greek liberal republicans. In retrospect, the Greek crisis can be seen to have held portents for the future. It disclosed the difficulty that the restored old order faced in trying to contain the force of nationalism. But still more, it was an object lesson in how the Eastern Question could divide Russia from the other conservative states; this was a tale to be repeated many times up to 1914.

No sooner had an eastern problem been surmounted in 1830 than another, and potentially much graver, revolutionary storm blew up in the West. In July the returned Bourbons proved they had forgotten nothing and learned nothing, as the saying went, by promulgating five ordinances which curtailed the press and parliamentary activity guaranteed on their restoration. Revolutionary barricades were immediately erected in the streets of Paris. Ominously, there were shouts of 'Vive Napoléon! Vive l'empereur!', invoking the spectre of revolution and French imperialism marching in tandem again.[31]

The threatened recurrence of the 1790s proved a false alarm, however. The radicals and the Bonapartists were held in check. The veteran republican Lafayette embraced the Duke of Orleans of the cadet branch of the Bourbon family as his king, and in return Louis Philippe honoured the revolutionary tradition by accepting the title King of the French (not of France) and the tricolour as the national flag. To prevent a regrouping of the anti-French alliance of 1815, the new regime in Paris hastened to offer reassurance abroad. French emissaries to Vienna and St Petersburg were instructed to describe the July revolution as a 'catastrophe' and depict King Louis Philippe as the sole bulwark of order. As proof of respect for the restoration of 1815, France scrupulously avoided giving aid and comfort to uprisings in Italy, the Germanies and Poland which had been encouraged if not set off by the events in Paris.[32] To some extent placated, and also distracted by these insurrections on their own doorstep, the conservative powers gave their diplomatic recognition to the new July monarchy, although Tsar Nicholas refused to address the new French king by the customary title of 'Monsieur, mon frère'.[33]

France did, in fact, send an expedition to the Papal States in 1832 to reassert its status as a Catholic power, but otherwise did nothing to hamper Austria's suppression of revolts in Italy. In Poland, Russia was left free to suppress a nationalist uprising that had counted heavily on French support, and St Petersburg followed this by cancelling the autonomous constitution granted in 1815. The one nationalist rising to involve the international community occurred in Belgium. Here, a coalition of Catholics and liberals, again energized by the July revolution in France, declared their country's independence from Holland. Immediately, Prussia, fearful of two revolutionary states bordering its Rhineland provinces, wanted to send in troops, and the tsar was ready to do the same. France countered by threatening its own intervention. In the event, the situation was defused when the new French regime established an understanding with Britain.

Like France, Britain favoured Belgian independence. But it would be quite wrong to assume that, having sided with liberal nationalists in Latin America and Greece, Britain was ideologically consistent in backing liberal nationalism everywhere. This was one of the fallacies of the Whig interpretation of British history.[34] Neither the Tory government nor the Whig ministry that replaced it in November 1830 evinced much sympathy for Italian, German or Polish rebels. In the Belgian question Britain was primarily concerned at the twin prospects of the removal of the buffer built on France's northern frontier in 1815 and French domination and possible absorption of Belgium itself. The Belgians' willingness to accept a French prince as their king was well known. British opposition to French designs in the Low Countries repeated the stand taken in 1793.

At the same time, it was generally recognized in London that the artificial union of Belgium and Holland could not survive; the British objective, then, was 'an independent Belgium, free from French and Dutch alike'.[35] In his eagerness to win international acceptance Louis Philippe sent the evergreen Talleyrand as ambassador to London with urgent orders to find common ground. In less than two weeks, Britain and France announced agreement on non-intervention in Belgium and submission of the question to the international conference already sitting in London to handle Greek independence. On 20 December 1830 the London Conference issued a protocol that acknowledged the need to break the Dutch–Belgian tie. Mainly because of Dutch recalcitrance it was a further nine years before the powers signed a final international guarantee of Belgian independence. Nevertheless, the largely painless solution of the Belgian problem indicated that the European concert could still work effectively on occasion, its internal divisions notwithstanding.

In another sense, however, the concert's success in Belgium was deceptive, for the 1830s saw the great powers acutely divided on ideological grounds. The French regime after 1830 was constitutionally not drastically changed from its predecessor, but its spirit was entirely different. Politically, economically and socially, the *haute bourgeoisie* came into its own, giving rise to the apt title of the bourgeois monarchy. The ideology of the thrusting upper middle class was liberalism; freedom from old feudal and absolutist royal restraint was a prerequisite for business enterprise and profit. The French monarchy of 1830–48 was a classically bourgeois liberal regime, its ministers responsive to a chamber of deputies elected on a narrow propertied franchise, and the rights of all its citizens protected by law if not always honoured in the breach. As the wits of the day put it, the system was 'a throne surrounded by republican institutions'.[36]

In the meantime, across the Channel a Whig government pledged to parliamentary reform succeeded in placing the great reform bill of 1832 on the statute book. This undermined the sway that landed interests had exercised in Parliament; the beneficiaries were the new manufacturing and commercial centres. Although the new property qualification to vote almost doubled the electorate, the composition of the House of Commons remained in the short run unchanged. What happened was that the rising middle class was co-opted into the traditional aristocratic power structure – the renowned Victorian compromise. The French July monarchy was based on the same synthesis: a section of the French nobility of Orleanist persuasion colluded with the *haute bourgeoisie* to ward off radical revolution. The congruence of the French revolution of 1830 and the British reform bill was not lost on Metternich; both were the heritage of 1789. 'There exists in Europe only one issue of any moment,' he wrote in 1832, 'that issue is Revolution.'[37]

Pushing the middle classes and their liberal doctrines into prominence was the first industrial revolution, which was well under way by the 1830s throughout northwestern Europe. The smaller countries of Holland and Belgium followed the liberal pattern of Britain and France. Thus, there came into being a solid bloc of Western European states, all of them limited or parliamentary monarchies, with a growing urban middle class and the rights of man enshrined in law. The contrast with mostly agrarian, still quasi-feudal Eastern Europe was inescapable. Out of alarm at the 1830 revolutions and the consequent western liberal phalanx the three eastern conservative nations moved closer together. By a 'chiffon' of Carlsbad, Austria, Russia and Prussia agreed in August 1830 on non-intervention in French affairs but on stern action if France should try to export its revolution. An Austro-Russian convention signed at München-grätz three years later was, in Metternich's eyes, more substantive because it addressed concrete issues. The two powers undertook to uphold the *status quo* in the Ottoman empire and their Polish provinces. Soon after, in October 1833, Prussia subscribed to the Münchengrätz accord in a Berlin convention that also bound all three parties to cooperate in suppressing revolution everywhere – a restatement of the Troppau Protocol of 1820, in fact.

The ideological divide between liberal Western and conservative Eastern Europe was perceived clearly at the time. Britain's Whig foreign secretary, Lord Palmerston, referred to 'the new confederacy of the west' in counterbalance to the 'triple league of despotic powers'. To Metternich, Palmerston was the embodiment of dangerous liberalism: 'He thinks he is pushing an English line of policy, but really it is a revolutionary one . . . Lord Palmerston is wrong about everything.' As for the Concert of Europe and conference diplomacy, the Austrian chancellor conceded ruefully that 'from the time Liberalism gained the upper hand in France and England, these meetings have degenerated . . . The temper of the Left clashes with the temper of the Right, and the two are mutually destructive.'[38] Even allowing for the propensity of both Palmerston and Metternich to indulge in ideological propaganda, it is clear that a doctrinal gulf had opened up between the western and eastern powers.

It is worth noting here, too, that this division between a liberal west and conservative east remained a constant feature of European international politics for the next sixty years. (Even the aberrant second Napoleonic empire, to be discussed later, was an enemy of the forces of the 1815 restoration and, in its closing years, tried to imitate Louis Philippe's compact with liberalism.) Moreover, it is over the long haul that the influence of ideology in the nineteenth century is probably best appreciated, as a persistent, sometimes insensible ambience moulding attitudes before a precise question was taken up. Still, on innumerable occasions, ideological predisposition was overridden by calculations of self-interest. The so-called Anglo-French 'liberal alliance' between 1830 and 1848 illustrated perfectly both the pull of ideology and its limits.

In the wake of their collaboration in the Belgian question Britain and France advertised their liberal credentials by affording refuge to Europe's failed revolutionaries. The congregation of Poles in Paris, most famously Chopin, confirmed the tsar's view that France was still the fount of subversion. In the ongoing dynastic strife in Spain and Portugal, London and Paris supported the liberal cause and together tried to cut the supply of arms sent by the eastern states to Iberian conservatives. Yet, in 1840 Britain and France almost went to war over colonial competition in the Mediterranean.[39] The Eastern Question, which had split the conservative powers in the 1820s, now disrupted the western liberal partnership.

For years Mehemet Ali, Egypt's pasha, had been quarrelling with his nominal overlord, the sultan, and renewal of warfare between the two in 1839–40 brought the Ottoman empire to the verge of collapse. France, once more trading on the Napoleonic link with Egypt, seconded Mehemet Ali's claim to Syria, only to be opposed by both Britain and Russia. An influential segment of French opinion pushed the ministry headed by Adolphe Thiers to adopt a bellicose stance that saw France isolated, as in 1815, against a concert of European powers. (One side-issue was a flare-up of popular Franco-German animosity ominous for the future.) A volatile situation was defused only when an apprehensive King Louis Philippe forced Thiers' resignation and allowed Anglo-Russian forces to bring Mehemet Ali to heel. After which an international conference in London devised a new order in the Near East. Anglo-French relations never recovered from the setback, although the attempt was made to patch up the liberal association. But after 1840 the best that could be achieved was an expression of general cordiality which both London and Paris summed up in the phrase *entente cordiale*.[40]

Even the vague *entente cordiale* did not survive long. François Guizot, the French architect of the entente, trusted in 'la politique générale' to surmount 'les questions spéciales', only to disprove the theory himself. In Spain, Britain and France might uphold liberal constitutionalism but they also jockeyed for pre-eminence. When Guizot engineered the marriage of two Spanish princesses to Francophile husbands in 1846, Palmerston declared the entente at an end. For the next two years Britain and France engaged in an angry war of words. The Anglo-French ideological tie was always a fragile one. overly dependent on the personal relationship between individual statesmen and monarchs. The two nations' diplomats remained hostile to each other, and public opinion was variable. The crisis of 1840 showed how easily French popular hostility to the old English enemy could be aroused. In Britain the liberal entente was supported most wholeheartedly by those Whigs loyal to the Foxite tradition of sympathy for French revolutionary ideals. But this was a fading memory, and much public opinion remained indifferent to foreign affairs.[41] The Anglo-French disarray of 1846–8 allowed Metternich more control of Europe's international affairs than he had enjoyed for some time – ironically on the very eve of his fall.

ROMANTIC MESSIANISM

Of the first half of the nineteenth century it has been written that 'no period before or after has experienced so luxurious a flowering of Utopian schemes'. Instrumental in stimulating this 'political messianism' was the cultural vogue of romanticism, fundamentally a reaction against that 'prime enchantress' of the Enlightenment, reason.[42] In its stead the romantics exalted nature and feeling. The frank appeal to and reliance on the emotions was singularly conducive to 'passionate' or ideological thinking. Furthermore, romanticism served to promote specific ideologies. One of the features of the romantic revolt against the eighteenth century was an uncritical nostalgia for the distant past, especially the Middle Ages, whose organic corporate order was contrasted favourably with the selfishness of the bourgeois age. By inference, this depiction conferred a lustre on the institutions of the *ancien régime* – the alliance of crown and altar, the ascendancy of a landed nobility – and in this way romanticism at first fortified the restoration of 1815. In brief, the romanticization of the past lent credibility to legitimacy.

However, from about 1820 romanticism became increasingly an ally of the forces of change. This was arguably a natural position, since romantic poetry, painting and music all deliberately flouted classical convention. Even more significant was the romantic artist's concentration on self; where the Enlightenment had concerned itself with the condition of humanity at large, romanticism fixed attention on the plight of the individual. In cultural terms this was the counterpart of the political campaign for the rights of man or liberalism. 'Romanticism', declared Victor Hugo, 'is liberalism in literature.'[43] The fusion of romantic art and liberal politics has been most famously captured in Delacroix's painting *Liberty Leading the People*, a bare-breasted Marianne waving the tricolour on the Parisian barricades of July 1830 (now the iconography of France's hundred-franc note). It seemed but a small step from preaching the freedom of the individual artist and citizen to advocating the liberation of subjugated national groups. By making this leap, romanticism helped greatly to link the ideologies of liberalism and nationalism between 1815 and 1848.[44]

In this period two strains of nationalism may be discerned. One was that pioneered in the French Revolution and derived from the sovereignty of the people, that is, 'the conscious and voluntary consent of the various elements of the population'. The other, less legalistic and more organic, flourished particularly east of the Rhine and 'was based on an unconscious community of race, language or customs'.[45] The distinction still exists linguistically: in English and French the word 'nation' can mean either a state or people, while in German *Staat* and *Nation* convey two forms of nationality, one legal, the other cultural.

Romanticism was particularly influential in promoting the latter, more mystical sort of nationalism. It did so through its fascination with the past and rediscovery of folk tales and songs of an ancient community. Historical novels, enormously fashionable at the time, likewise reminded people of their national roots. The 'springtime of the nations' before 1848 consisted largely of the romantic revival of the cultures of the suppressed peoples of Europe – German, Italian, Magyar, Slavic in their many ethnic forms. Frequently this cultural nationalism served to construct a single national language out of a throng of regional tongues; for example, Alessandro Manzoni rewrote his popular historical novel, *I promessi sposi* (1827), in a conscious attempt to establish an Italian linguistic benchmark. It is telling that the *risorgimento*, connoting a rebirth of Italian culture, is still regarded as the *sine qua non* of that country's political unification.[46]

It follows that the nationalism of 1815–48 was almost exclusively confined to those who were literate and familiar with the arts. By definition, these were people of substance and property, and in assessing their motives, one encounters the inevitable mixture of idealism and ambition. Very likely, many, perhaps most, of the professional and commercial classes, who comprised the bulk of European liberal nationalists, believed themselves sincere when they protested their attachment to liberty. On the other hand, it is undeniable that their careers flourished best, indeed only, within the framework of a constitutional nation state. The German bourgeoisie in 1834 therefore greeted with acclaim the *Zollverein*, a Prussian customs union with a number of German states, small and halting step though it was towards national unity. What was really required was 'all the highly organized administrative machinery of a large national state, all its innumerable political openings, all the opportunities it could provide for the exercise of the talents of lawyer, journalist, scholar, public official and industrialist'.[47]

In other words, nationalism in the 1830s and 1840s was no artificial construct of the intellectuals. It sprang from the moral and material aspirations of a thrusting and rising segment of society receptive to fashionable romantic writers and painters who, by definition, were anti-intellectual. Intellectuals, of course, put their gloss on nationalist sentiment and thereby helped to spread the nationalist gospel. But liberal nationalism was not primarily an intellectual movement; nationalism, it bears repeating, was and is *mentalité* rather than firm doctrine.

By 1848 maybe not all liberals were nationalists; but most were, and most nationalists were likewise liberal. They were forced together by a common enemy, the Metternichian system. But they were drawn together as well by the romantic confusion of individual freedom with national self-determination. In reality, liberalism and nationalism, if not downright incompatible, pulled in contrary directions, which of course is why their alliance lasted no more than one generation. Liberalism encouraged its audience to act as free-thinking individuals; nationalism invited them to find their identity by submersion within a national group, to waive their rights for the good of the commonweal, especially in time of war. In so far as the liberal nationalists confronted this problem, they did so by envisaging consensual rule. When government rested on consent of the governed, any curtailment of liberty by the state was *ipso facto* sanctioned by the citizenry; freedom thus remained inviolate. Some took the argument further and suggested that, with the triumph of popular sovereignty, humanity would attain so high a level of civilization as to resolve the conflict between individual rights and national group dictates altogether.[48]

The archetypal ideologue of this persuasion was the Italian Giuseppe Mazzini. He repudiated the title of nationalist because it connoted competition with others and preferred to call himself a patriot. Nevertheless, he was the authentic voice of romantic and liberal nationalism in his day.[49] Exiled from Italy after the 1830 uprisings, Mazzini founded in the following year Young Italy, which was intended to be the cornerstone of a youthful revolutionary international. In 1834 Young Europe came into existence calling itself a 'holy alliance of the peoples'. Mazzini's influence, however, lay not in his conspiratorial activities, which were characterized by zeal rather than organization, but in his widely read writings. Although a liberal in his veneration of liberty, Mazzini was no bourgeois liberal; he was more a republican democrat in the Jacobin tradition. As a patriot, he believed that God had chosen Italy to preach the gospel of democratic nationalism to the world; this was the mission of a 'third Rome'. But the achievement of national longings everywhere was not an end in itself; it was rather a milestone on the road to what Mazzini called Humanity. According to a divine design,

> the map of Europe will be remade. The Countries of the People will rise, defined by the voice of the free, upon the ruins of the Countries of Kings and privileged castes. Between these Countries there will be harmony and brotherhood. And then the work of Humanity for the general amelioration, for the discovery and application of the real law of life . . . will be accomplished by peaceful and progressive development.

Mazzini's followers were instructed that their first duty was to Humanity, for 'you are *men* before you are either *citizens* or *fathers*'.[50]

Mazzini was not the only liberal nationalist 'to find justification of national particularity in the service of a universal ideal'.[51] The Polish poet Adam Mickiewicz, a close friend of Mazzini, believed in world regeneration through national fulfilment, and so too did the French historian Jules Michelet. Almost all of these romantic nationalists shared the ideological conceit that utopia was not only attainable but near at hand. The outbreak of revolution all over Europe in 1848 appeared to bear out this sanguine expectation.

By and large, the revolutionary upsurge was guided by the liberal and nationalist visions with which artists and some intellectuals had won the affections of a considerable section of Europe's bourgeoisie. But to call 1848 a 'revolution of the intellectuals' is strictly speaking a misnomer, for the real movers and shakers were the professional classes and the romantics. None the less, the familiar appellation does convey something of the clash of ideas and the ideological excitement that came to a head in this year of revolutions.[52]

1848: ZENITH OF LIBERAL NATIONALISM

Serious revolution, as usual, occurred first in Paris, this time triggered by economic distress and too narrow a franchise. But unlike the July revolution of 1830, the storm that broke in February 1848 gathered momentum. A republic was instantly proclaimed, and the post of foreign minister in a provisional government went to the poet Alphonse de Lamartine – a token of romanticism's influence. On 4 March Lamartine issued a manifesto of contrived ambiguity. It announced that 'the treaties of 1815 no longer exist in the eyes of the French Republic', but accepted that they were 'facts only to be modified by common accord'. In addition, France promised to protect 'legitimate movements for the growth of peoples' nationalities'.[53] As events were to prove, this threat to internationalize revolution was a verbal effusion to placate the radicals and foreign refugees in Paris. The conservative powers predictably took fright, but were soon occupied with revolts in their own territories which, of course, had been encouraged by the Lamartine manifesto. But Palmerston, while by no means complacent, recognized the hollowness of Lamartine's words, and the Anglo-French entente was partially repaired.[54] Through British good offices France was able to reach a tacit *modus vivendi* with the other European states based on mutual non-interference in each others' affairs. As in earlier French revolutions, pursuit of a revolutionary and ideological foreign policy depended on the relative strength of the right- and left-wing factions in Paris. Therefore, the bloody suppression of the radicals in the June Days confirmed that the cautious line already adopted in practice by Lamartine would be continued.

But the impact on international relations of the French revolution of 1848 had yet to be felt. On 10 December 1848 an election, using universal male suffrage for the first time in France since 1792, was held to choose the president of the second French republic. Louis Napoleon, nephew of Napoleon I, garnered three-quarters of the vote. The Bonapartist success stemmed from the unpopularity of the other three candidates, all tarred with the brush of factionalism and bloodletting earlier in the year, and from fear of socialism on the part of both the bourgeoisie and peasantry, who looked to Louis Napoleon to restore order and protect property. However, it also reflected the power of myth and the French popular thirst for *la gloire* associated with the name of Bonaparte. This Napoleonic legend was a classic instance of what French historians have styled *un lieu de mémoire* (a focal point of historical memory), and Louis Napoleon was the beneficiary.[55]

The Napoleonic legend originated in the great emperor's memoirs dictated in exile after 1815, which depicted him as a defender of the French Revolution and the principle of nationality, trumpeted his military victories while ignoring the cost and attendant dictatorship, and ascribed his fall to British machinations.[56] Romanticism's cult of the individual easily translated into worship of the heroic figure, from which Napoleon's reputation profited immensely in the years before 1848. Moreover, the July monarchy foolishly attempted to trade on the growing Napoleonic legend. In 1840 the French persuaded the British to return Napoleon's body, whereupon it was entombed with great pomp in Les Invalides. Unfortunately, the ceremony coincided with France's surrender in the Near Eastern crisis of that year and, in comparison with the memory of Napoleonic glory, the pacific policy of the July monarchy was made to look thoroughly ignoble.

On the death of Napoleon I's only son in 1832, Louis Napoleon had succeeded to the Bonapartist inheritance. For a time he had consorted with the *carbonari* (charcoal burners), as the secret societies of Italian nationalists called themselves. He was an unlikely French nationalist hero, by no means charismatic, and spoke French with a German accent. In a pamphlet, *Idées napoléoniennes* (1839), he recast the Napoleonic legend as 'not an idea of war, but a social, industrial, commercial, humanitarian idea'.[57] Twice, in 1836 and 1840, he tried to invade France with a few companions; on the latter occasion, hoping to exploit the July monarchy's retreat in the Near East, he carried a tame eagle in a cage as an imperial symbol. But there was no mass rallying to his cause; the government deported him after the first abortive coup and imprisoned him for four years after the second. It was easy to dismiss Louis Napoleon as a serious threat. By 1848, in contrast, France was 'bored' (Lamartine's word), and was ready for another bout of Bonapartist excitement.[58] The Napoleonic legend was pervasive if muddled; a number of peasants believed they were voting for the first Napoleon in the presidential election.

At home and abroad Louis Napoleon was an unknown quantity. His presidency was marked by only one initiative – the dispatch of a French army to restore the pope ejected by Roman republicans. This was not a peculiarly Bonapartist move; it repeated the July monarchy's foray into the Papal States in 1832, and the chief intention in 1849 was to allay Catholic opinion within France. But Napoleonic precedents were directly recalled on 2 December 1851 when the president seized absolute power and, exactly a year later, transformed himself into Emperor Napoleon III. Significantly, these coups were accompanied by plebiscites which gave over 90 per cent approval to the constitutional changes. The new emperor had risen to power by popular opinion and his plebiscites acknowledged the fact. That is to say, he was not just the beneficiary but also the prisoner of the very Napoleonic legend he had sold to the French people. Thus, if not the war-lover his uncle had been, Napoleon III was nevertheless driven to pursue an activist foreign policy and court prestige on the international stage.

Unexpectedly, the European powers welcomed the emergence of a second Napoleonic empire. By stifling the memories of 1815 and discounting Napoleon III's capacity for international mischief, they greeted the demise of the second French republic as the final act in the demolition of the European revolutionary movement set in motion by France's own upheaval of February 1848. None of the uprisings outside France succeeded in either their liberal or national objectives. On the other hand, their very failure changed the ideological climate in which international relations would be conducted for the remainder of the nineteenth century and, it might be argued, created the conditions for the first of the next century's world wars (see Chapter 5).

As in France, the 1848 revolutions elsewhere carried all before them at first. Student riots in the streets of Vienna forced Metternich's resignation on 13 March, and the doyen of European conservatism fled ignominiously by means of a common cab and passports in false names. Simultaneously, the Magyars coerced the beleaguered Austrian emperor into acceding to a series of March laws that provided Hungary with a liberal constitution and wide-ranging autonomy. By June a pan-Slav congress assembled in Prague to demand equal national rights for Austro-Slavs. With Austria's Italian provinces also in revolt, rampant nationalism threatened the heterogeneous Habsburg empire with dismemberment.

Meanwhile, in Berlin King Frederick William IV, faced with street demonstrations, made liberal concessions and promised Prussian leadership of the movement for German unity. But the more serious drive for German unification unfolded at Frankfurt where an unofficial assembly sat from May 1848. It was the brainchild of liberal parliamentarians from the diets of various German states who supervised hasty elections ostensibly on a universal male franchise. The self-styled parliament of the German peoples spent many months debating the shape of a putative Germany. To what extent this dilatoriness may be ascribed to *Sprechsucht*, literally a passion for speaking or the congenital verbosity and hairsplitting of liberal intellectuals is a moot point.[59] In any event, delay was costly, for, by the time consensus was found at Frankfurt, armed reaction was in full spate in central Europe. Frederick William spurned Frankfurt's offer of the crown of a united Germany, and the deputies from Austria, Prussia and some smaller states obeyed a royal command to quit the assembly. A year after its first sitting, the Frankfurt parliament disintegrated.

The shortcomings of German liberalism in 1848 have been endlessly analysed. What is most relevant here is the school of thought that holds that the Frankfurt Assembly was fatally flawed by the attitudes it took in the nationality questions of the day.[60] In spite of the lip service paid to the national rights of others, wherever German and non-German claims collided the majority of the assembly tended to adopt an unbending nationalist stance. In the mixed German-Danish duchies of Schleswig-Holstein, the assembly encouraged use of the Prussian army to enforce German rights and even declared war on Denmark. Hostilities between two groups of liberal nationalists, German and Scandinavian, loomed until Anglo-Russian diplomatic pressure imposed a compromise. When Prussia moved to crush a Polish uprising in its province of Posen, it won endorsement in Frankfurt by a vote of 342 to 31. In the same vein, many deputies expressed satisfaction when Austrian forces subdued the rebellious Slavs in Prague. In short, the Frankfurt liberals shared the general Teutonic disdain for Slavic pretensions.

Inevitably, the nationality issue came to the fore in considering the complex matter of Austria's relationship to the putative united German state. Should all of Austria's imperial domain be included, or merely the German-speaking lands? How to distinguish German from non-German territory in such mixed areas as Bohemia and the Tyrol? Or should the Habsburg empire be excluded altogether? After much agonizing the Frankfurt Assembly proposed a compromise to incorporate into the new Germany those parts of the Habsburg empire belonging to the Germanic Confederation of 1815, leaving the remainder to be joined to Vienna by dynastic ties alone. However, in March 1849 the Austrian government of Prince Schwarzenberg made clear its intention to preserve the empire as a single unit. This effectively scuttled the plan for a *Grossdeutschland* (large Germany), and the Frankfurt Assembly *faute de mieux* fell back on a *kleindeutsch* (little German) scheme, which left Austria out of a unified Germany. This paper programme, too, of course evaporated with the demise of the Frankfurt Assembly itself.

What the questions of Schleswig-Holstein, Posen and the Habsburg ethnic minorities brought into the open was most Germans' axiomatic assumption of the superiority of their own culture. As one Frankfurt deputy put it, 'It was from ancient times the historic task of the Germans to draw to themselves the alien nationalities, to permeate them, to mature them for modern times.' The German mission, above all, was to dominate and civilize the backward Slavs, 'to be the bearer and mediator of culture, science, and freedom toward the east'. All of which could be used to justify the yearning for a pan-German *Mitteleuropa*, 'a gigantic Reich of seventy, eighty, a hundred millions; to stand armed against east and west, against Slav and Latin peoples'.[61] Lest it be thought that such sentiments were confined to the firebrand 'frontiersmen', German nobles living on the borders of the Teutonic world, it is worth quoting Heinrich von

Gagern, no xenophobe but a reflective middle-class liberal from Hesse and president of the Frankfurt Assembly, who mused:

> I wonder if in the national interest we can . . . in future leave the non-German provinces of Austria to themselves and to chance. I believe that it is the role of the German people to be great, to be one of those who rule . . . What kind of unity must we strive for? A kind that will enable us to fulfil our destiny in the East; a unity that will enable us to make those peoples along the Danube that have neither the vocation nor the right to independence satellites of our planetary system.[62]

German nationalism continued to be bedevilled by reveries of a *Drang nach Osten* (drive to the east), with its overtones of racial superiority, for the next century to come.

Given the international role that Germany was destined to play, the defeat of the Frankfurt liberals would have worldwide and lasting repercussions. But the frustration of liberal nationalism was not an exclusively German episode. Nowhere did the liberals succeed in fulfilling nationalist expectations. Italy provided a case second only to that of Germany. Broadly speaking, three ways to Italian unification presented themselves in 1848, all generically liberal. First, there was the Mazzinian prescription of a democratic republican Italy. Second, that of a confederacy under the papacy, an alternative given currency in Vincenzo Gioberti's *Del primato morale e civile degli italiani* (1843). His neo-Guelph scheme received a great impetus with the election in 1846 of Pope Pius IX. Pio Nono was a liberal pope by comparison with his predecessors, and at first he did nothing to refute the popular impression that he favoured Italian unification along liberal lines. The third approach to national unity was under the leadership of the House of Savoy which ruled Piedmont-Sardinia. Its king, Charles Albert, was persuaded, even before the outbreak of France's February revolution, to grant a liberal constitution. Like Frederick William of Prussia, the Piedmontese monarch was tempted to join the liberal nationalists; unlike his Prussian counterpart, Charles Albert did not resist the temptation.[63]

News of Metternich's downfall in March 1848 precipitated an uprising in Milan that drove the Austrians out of Lombardy. Charles Albert promptly invaded the province, although his motive was as much dynastic ambition as nationalism. Mazzini persuaded the Milanese revolutionaries to accept Piedmontese military command for practical reasons, and even a papal contingent of troops arrived to fight for Italian unity, only to be soon withdrawn following protests by Catholic Austria. In any event, the Austrian army, once regrouped and under the command of General Radetzky, proved too strong. In little more than twelve months it defeated the Piedmontese army twice, reconquered Lombardy, put an end to a revolutionary Venetian republic, and restored legitimate rule as far south as the Papal States. Radetzky was promoted to field marshal, and Johann Strauss the elder saluted the hero by composing what has become almost a second Austrian national anthem (the Radetzky March). Meanwhile, in Rome radical unrest culminated in the murder of the pope's chief minister, the flight of Pio Nono and, in February 1849, the establishment of a Roman republic which summoned Mazzini to its aid. For a few months Mazzini was able to live in microcosm his dream of a democratic, anti-clerical Italian state. The Roman republic survived until July when, Catholic sentiment triumphing over common republican ideology, it was overthrown by the forces of the second French republic.

Pope Pius returned to Rome threatening his subjects with excommunication, and duly became a bitter enemy of Italian nationalism. Mazzinianism too, having shown itself too weak to resist the armed strength of conservative Europe, was no longer a viable road to Italian unification. But Piedmont lived to fight another day. King Charles Albert abdicated, although Piedmont itself was saved from Austrian wrath lest punitive measures bring a French army across the Alps. In addition, Radetzky conceived an admiration for the new king, Victor Emmanuel II, who, without much effort on his part, now became the focus of Italian nationalist hopes. Conveniently, the letters of the surname of Giuseppe Verdi, known for his nationalist sentiments, matched those of the slogan 'Vittorio Emanuele, re d'Italia' (king of Italy); thus the cheers of opera-goers could be, and were, construed as a political statement.

The clearest sign of the rout of the liberal nationalists by mid-1849 was the revival of Habsburg power and prestige, both within the Austrian empire and in central Europe at large. Metternich was gone, but under Prince Schwarzenberg his autocratic methods returned. Vienna reasserted control over its multifarious subjects partly by the time-honoured method of playing off one group against another, and partly by brute military force. Austria's military task was eased immeasurably by help from Russia in Hungary where, in March, the Magyars, swayed by the inspirational Louis Kossuth, declared total independence. Ever fearful of the nationalist contamination of his Polish provinces, Tsar Nicholas I committed 140,000 troops to assist the Habsburg emperor against revolution, 'Our common enemy'.[64] Overwhelmed by the combined weight of the Austro-Russian armies, Budapest surrendered and Hungarian independence was nullified. The Austro-Russian conservative alliance, which had served Metternich since the Troppau congress in 1820, seemed still in good working order. Moreover, it assisted Austria in restoring its influence in the Germanies. When Prussia floated the idea of a new league of German princes under its own leadership, Vienna, sure of Russia's friendship, objected so forcefully that the scheme was dropped. The loose Germanic Confederation of 1815, which Metternich had manipulated with such skill and liberal German nationalists perceived as a major obstacle to unification, re-emerged with few changes.[65]

Everywhere in 1849 liberalism went down to defeat. But national sentiment, once roused, could not be rescinded. When, as in Germany, liberalism and nationalism came into competition, the latter eclipsed the former. Here was an accurate pointer to the intrinsic strengths of liberalism and nationalism as ideologies. In its heyday between 1815 and 1848 classical liberalism was a tolerant creed; its vision of freedom for all presupposed a pluralistic world in which a variety of philosophies would compete in a free market. In this respect, liberalism fell short of those absolute ideologies that countenance no truth but their own. Liberalism's quandary was, and still is, that its own beliefs allow freedom to those who would destroy libertarian pluralism itself. But nationalism, for its part, has not customarily called on its followers to suffer their enemies. Already by the mid-nineteenth century nationalism showed signs of assuming a self-righteous and bigoted mien, which made it a much tougher if less attractive ideology.

The inability of the liberals to satisfy national aspirations simply gave an opportunity for other and more conservative groups to appropriate nationalism for their own ends. In fact, 1848 signalled the beginning of the transition of nationalism from a revolutionary to a right-wing ideology. Furthermore, the events of 1848–9 discountenanced the romantic nationalists. After the failure of political messianism, national goals would be pursued in a more pragmatic fashion. This constituted a 'revolution of the spirit' that was the most significant consequence of the 1848 revolutions.[66] The standard word to characterize the new atmosphere is realism, 'which involved the repudiation of the whole system of sentiments and myths with which international society had in the immediate past been inspired'. This realism was visible in all walks of life. As another text puts it, 'The realistic attitude can be seen in politics, in the conduct of international relations, in class relationships, in a new emphasis on science and technology, as well as in literature.'[67] In the dawning age of realism, there was no place for utopian dreaming. Ideological thinking would fall somewhat out of fashion, although not out of existence.

4

IDEOLOGY AND *REALPOLITIK*

WHIG IDEOLOGY AND LITTLE ENGLANDISM

In the history of ideas and ideologies 1848 marked a watershed. But in international relations a much more meaningful turning point was the Crimean War of 1854–6. The war originated in a comparatively trivial dispute between France and Russia over each nation's entitlement to protect Christianity's holy places in the Ottoman empire. This quarrel was exacerbated by the mutual antipathy between the two emperors. Tsar Nicholas I refused to recognize Napoleon III's imperial title lest it confer legitimacy on the Bonapartist line; in the French emperor's eyes, the tsar's unflagging support for the 1815 settlement cast him as the automatic foe of the second Napoleonic empire. But the crisis did not escalate seriously until Britain became involved.

In the wake of the Anglo-Russian cooperation that had settled the Near Eastern crisis of 1840, Tsar Nicholas visited Britain and left convinced he had a tacit agreement that the two powers in concert would partition the Ottoman lands when the moment was ripe. In 1853 Nicholas, challenged by France, suggested the time had come, and moved his troops into the Danubian principalities of Moldavia and Wallachia on the specious legal pretext of protecting the Christian communities there. But the tsar had miscalculated; London never had any intention of killing off the Turkish empire. The response of Britain's public and press was fierce. Not only was Russian aggression denounced as a threat to British interests and the balance of power, but British opinion succumbed to what Lord Macaulay called 'one of its periodical fits of morality'. In this case liberal righteousness about the evils of Russian despotism led to the Crimean War.

By the middle of the century Russophobia had become a fixture on the British scene, its intensity fuelled by Russia's repressive actions in the revolutions of 1830 and 1848. First Polish exiles, and later the Hungarians, were extremely successful in peddling their anti-Russian sentiments. Kossuth, for example, addressed crowds of 200,000 and was fêted by city fathers. The position of susceptible British radicals was expressed in a

Chartist leader's simplistic formula: 'Policy, alliance with the oppressed nations; object, the annihilation of Russian supremacy.'[1] A left–right division over war with Russia was perceptible in the coalition cabinet of Lord Aberdeen, where the Whigs were generally 'hawks', and the Peelite Tories 'doves'.[2] One authority ascribes huge influence to 'Whig ideology . . . the vital idealistic counterpoint to the concern for British honor and prestige that was most responsible for getting her into the war and keeping her there'. Its political expression was 'the British desire to promote European progress and ordered liberty against both reactionary despotism and radical revolution, and to replace the old oppressive international order with a new constitutional liberal one built around England'.[3] Such an evolution would, no doubt, have delighted British public opinion, though one should beware of ascribing too schematic an aim to government policy. On the other hand, it cannot be denied that on occasion, and particularly in 1853–4, British foreign policy did march to the beat of Whig ideology.

Russia's reply to diplomatic protests at its incursion into the principalities was uncommonly mild and even promised their evacuation. But London was in no mood to believe these fair words. The Turks, thus emboldened, declared war on Russia. Despite the tsar's promise to refrain from acts of war while negotiations among the European powers were in progress, an engagement at Sinope saw the Russians destroy the Turkish Black Sea fleet. Most of the British press, Whig and Tory, reached for pejorative terminology; massacre was the favourite description. In this rabid atmosphere Britain and France declared war on 28 March 1854. Napoleon III was not averse to fighting Russia so long as he had an ally, but public opinion in France was much less Russophobe than in Britain, and the emperor had made several efforts to effect a peaceful Near Eastern compromise. In effect, Britain led and France followed on the road to war.

In August the Russians withdrew from the principalities, which were promptly occupied by Austrian and Turkish forces. Objectively, there was no reason for the war to continue, but reason did not prevail.[4] In Britain war fever still raged and the Aberdeen government was its prisoner. Lord Aberdeen himself was a known opponent of the war, and he stayed in office only on Queen Victoria's tearful plea to save her from the war faction. Accusations of lack of patriotism and worse were hurled at the 'Kremlin school', and at one point a crowd gathered outside the Tower of London on the rumour that both the prime minister and prince consort were to be committed there for treason.[5]

The government, under attack over its leader's alleged pacifism, ran into further difficulties for its maladministration of the war effort. The Crimea was selected as the theatre of war because it seemed the area of Russia most vulnerable to Anglo-French naval power, but the choice also posed enormous logistical problems. Moreover, the Crimean War was journalistically perhaps the most 'open' war ever fought, in that modern technology allowed it to be instantly reported back home with graphic pictures by a British press as yet neither censored nor manipulated by officialdom.[6] The superpatriots and parliamentary opposition were quickly supplied with ample evidence of military and civilian bungling – most notoriously the charge of the Light Brigade and the squalid field hospitals against which Florence Nightingale raged. A parliamentary motion for an inquiry into the conduct of the war, moved predictably by a radical member, was tantamount to a vote of confidence. It was carried by 305 to 148. The beneficiary was the cabinet's most prominent hawk, Palmerston, who took over the prime ministership in January 1855.

But Palmerston was no radical; he had entered politics as a Pittite Tory and his support of liberal causes was selective. At home, his refusal to espouse the swelling liberal demand for further parliamentary reform blocked it for the next decade. In foreign affairs, though, he was in tune with progressive opinion 'out of doors', that is to say, outside parliament. As 'an incarnation of John Bull . . . he would keep Britain in her rightful place as the leading world power. It was, of course, a benevolent power which would uphold "free" governments and check tyrannies.'[7] Abroad, then, Palmerston embodied the Whig ideology. But his fiery words often outstripped his actions, and so it was in the Crimean War. As a fervent Russophobe, his war aims were to roll back Russia's frontiers everywhere, not just in the Near East but in central Asia and Poland as well. But none of his inordinate ambitions were realized at the Congress of Paris that closed the Crimean War in 1856. The peace settlement, in fact, closely followed plans developed by Europe's diplomatic community before Palmerston became prime minister – with one significant addendum. The neutralization of the Black Sea deprived Russia of any naval defence on a vital southern frontier.

In the British public mind, however, the war had been fought not for strategic gain, but for the nobler if vaguer purpose of liberation from tsarist tyranny. As demonstrably nothing of the kind had been accomplished, the Peace of Paris was greeted in Britain with resignation rather than enthusiasm.[8] In the postwar disillusionment anti-war voices were able gradually to win back an audience. Foremost among them were those of the radical members of parliament Richard Cobden and John Bright – testimony that not all on the left looked kindly on overseas crusades. Cobden and Bright represented a quite contrary liberal strain. Derived from the eighteenth-century *philosophes* and transmitted to Victorian England by Jeremy Bentham, this held that leaving the peoples of the world to themselves to communicate via culture and commerce was the best surety of peace and prosperity. Wars were caused by governments that interfered with this natural process. Liberalism should and could be encouraged around the world by Britain's example, not its foreign intervention. This was the same rationale as that used by American isolationists. In Britain the policy of non-entanglement went by the name of Little Englandism; it was encapsulated in Cobden's favourite toast, 'No foreign politics'. Under this rubric he advocated 'as little intercourse as possible between Governments', but rather, with international trade in mind, 'as much connexion as possible between the nations of the world'. Bright, while the memory of the Crimean War was still fresh, dismissed 'this regard for "the liberties of Europe"', and in a memorable phrase, condemned foreign involvements as 'a gigantic system of outdoor relief for the aristocracy of Great Britain'.[9]

Cobden and Bright both lost their parliamentary seats in an election fought on patriotic grounds in 1857. Nevertheless, they were soon back in the House of Commons, and their ideas began to gain ascendancy. This was due in no small measure to the fact that they were preceptors in the Manchester School of free trade. As the leading manufacturing and commercial nation of the mid-nineteenth century, Britain stood to profit from a reduction in tariffs on exports of finished goods and imports of grain. An end to tariff wars was expected to promote international harmony, and cheap bread harmony among the classes at home. The Cobdenite stress on trade at the expense of politics and ideology in foreign relations thus had both an abstract and material appeal. The conclusion in 1860 of a wide-ranging Anglo-French commercial treaty, negotiated by Cobden himself, marked the heyday of free trade and Little Englandism. Four years later Cobden noted a 'remarkable change in the temper of the House [of Commons] since the Crimean War . . . as a consequence of extended commercial operations'. To hail Cobden as 'the real Foreign Secretary of the early eighteen-sixties' is an exaggeration but not a great one.[10]

An interesting test of Little Englandism arose in 1861 with the outbreak of the American Civil War, not least because both parties to the conflict proclaimed principles that appealed to the liberal conscience. On the one hand, the Southern Confederacy claimed the same right of self-determination as German, Italian and other liberals had advanced in 1848. On the other hand, the South's adherence to the 'peculiar institution' of slavery was a blatant contradiction of the liberal tenet of individual freedom. William Ewart Gladstone personified this liberal dilemma. Early in the war he was decidedly sympathetic to Southern self-determination, but by the close in 1865 he had been converted by Bright to regard slavery as the key moral issue at stake and to switch his allegiance to the Union cause. Bright was one of the radicals consistently supportive of the North, credited with persuading the Lancashire cotton operatives to stay loyal to the Union side despite the curtailment of supplies of Southern raw cotton by the Northern blockade. In actual fact, British working-class opinion throughout the land was as divided as in the rest of the population; on the American Civil War there was no clear-cut divide between right and left.[11]

It is true, however, that most of the British establishment at the war's outset favoured the South, primarily out of dislike of the North's democratic reputation. Prime Minster Palmerston, for example, was not averse to intervention, or at least a benevolent neutrality, to aid the Confederacy. But he could not carry the cabinet with him and, as always, was attuned to feeling in the country, which on the whole was against bellicosity.[12] Consequently, London pursued an even-handed policy and steered clear of involvement. Palmerston's self-restraint in the American Civil War stands in sharp contrast to his gusto for confrontation with Russia a decade earlier; it was a tribute to the current Little England atmosphere.

The innate isolationism of the Cobden and Bright brand of liberalism also helped to relegate Britain to the periphery of the momentous European events that the Crimean War set in train. The Black Sea clauses of the Treaty of Paris were naturally resented in Russia and, almost overnight, transformed that country from the staunchest upholder of the international *status quo* into a revisionist power. Austria's postwar situation too was drastically altered. Vienna had upset the western states by refusing to enter the war against Russia. More important, the Austrian threat in December 1855 to do just that was instrumental in forcing Russia to accept allied peace terms. Habsburg ingratitude for the tsar's help in suppressing the Hungarian rebellion in 1849 rankled in St Petersburg as much as the new regime in the Black Sea. Both Russia and Austria, then, emerged from the Crimean War isolated. And with Britain in a Little England mood, the Concert of Europe in effect disintegrated. Especially subversive was the split between the conservative regimes in Vienna and St Petersburg whose alliance had been for forty years the most secure bulwark of the 1815 restoration. This settlement was now vulnerable, and its sworn enemy stood ready to act. Napoleon III, liberated from the restrictions of the defunct European concert, could dream of a Bonapartist retaliation against 1815, his weapon the nationalist sentiment revealed but left unassuaged in 1848.

THE NAPOLEONIC LEGEND AND ITALY

As we have seen, the nationalist revolts of 1848 were fired by a passionate and romantic belief in freedom. The Crimean War, in its guise as a crusade against Russian absolutism, was perhaps the final flowering of this sentimental liberalism. But in the harsh new climate of realism nationalist aims would be pursued by illiberal means and by politicos whose attachment to nationalist ideology was opportunistic. Napoleon III proved their willing dupe, to be exploited without scruple. In brief, we now enter the era of *Realpolitik*.

Realpolitik is one of those words that it is easier to apply as an adjective than to define as a noun. Fundamentally, it denotes an emphasis on ruthlessness, force and fraud. The term was coined by Ludwig von Rochau whose *Grundsätze der Realpolitik, angewendet auf die staatlichen Zustände Deutschlands* (1853) argued that it was unreasonable to expect power to be subject to law or principles. Almost simultaneously Auguste Comte published *Cours de politique positive* (1854) wherein he contended force to be the basis of all political relationships. Indeed, *Realpolitik* may be seen as a counterpart to Comte's mid-century scientific positivism, cold-blooded and materialistic.[13] In its chief characteristics *Realpolitik* reflected the sharp break made with the past after 1848; its worship of strength and acceptance of violence was a rebuke to liberals, such as those in the Frankfurt Assembly, who believed goodwill and rational argument could carry the day. The concomitant pursuit of untrammelled self-interest became possible with the Crimean War's disruption of the Concert of Europe.

Realpolitik had much in common with the practice of *raison d'état* in the eighteenth century. The approach of both to international relations was completely amoral and, more germane to this study, both concentrated on geopolitical and strategic gain to the apparent exclusion of ideological considerations. Yet, there is a crucial difference: whereas *raison d'état* constitutes the end purpose of a foreign policy, *Realpolitik* implies no more than a methodology to achieve any sort of goal, ideological or non-ideological. Certainly, in the 1850s ideology took a temporary back seat, principally because conservative–liberal discord, which had exploded in 1848, abated thereafter. The propertied classes had been surprised and shocked by the lower-order radicalism that burst forth in 1848, especially during the June Days in Paris. Common alarm brought conservatives and bourgeois liberals to a reconciliation, or at least a truce, and not just in Western Europe; a rough equivalent of Britain's Victorian compromise began to emerge in the heart of the Continent. The right expedited this synthesis by taking up the salient ideology left over from 1848 – the formerly liberal cause of nationalism. In like vein, the conservatives' attitude to war underwent a significant change. Since 1792 war had gone hand in hand with revolution; now the right in *Realpolitik* fashion were prepared to risk war. For this reason *Realpolitik* has been described as 'the mark of conservative desperation'. And by employing war for nationalist purposes, the conservatives guaranteed that '*Realpolitik* did not mark an end to ideology, but . . . represented the most realistic and ruthless pursuit of it'.[14]

A prime illustration of the foregoing was Count Camillo di Cavour's Machiavellian diplomacy in the course of Italian unification. But first one confusion must be removed, namely, that Cavour was known as a liberal. Indeed, he had been in the van of those who founded a Piedmontese parliamentary system in 1847–8, and his polity as premier from 1852 was impeccably liberal, anticlerical and economically modernist. However, his support came from a *connubio* (marriage) of conservatives and liberals, and his following is best described as 'the party of order'.[15] As his conduct at the height of the struggle for Italian unity would demonstrate, he was no friend of radicalism and democracy, and it goes without saying that his *Realpolitik* distanced him from Italy's idealistic liberals of 1848. Labels apart, Cavour was as much a man of the right as of the left.

Cavour's reputation as Italian nationalist has more substance. After all, it was his newspaper, *Il Risorgimento*, that in 1847 baptized Italy's nationalist movement; and he worked closely with the Società Nazionale Italiana, from its founding in 1856 the principal mouthpiece of Italian nationalist ideology.[16] Even so, some qualification is in order. His first objective was to supplant Austria in northern Italy and replace Austrian influence throughout the Italian peninsula with Piedmontese. This was not the same thing as unification. On the other hand, the House of Savoy was the only authentic ruling Italian family, and its aggrandizement therefore was consonant with Italian self-determination. Cavour's nationalism was simply hard-headed and restricted to what appeared possible, exemplified perfectly in his rejection of the old romantic notion that 'L'Italia farà da sè' (Italy will do it alone).

Piedmont joined the military action against Russia in the Crimea solely to cultivate western goodwill, without any assurance of a *quid pro quo*. In reality, Cavour gained an immediate reward. Both he and the British foreign secretary, the Earl of Clarendon, were permitted to lecture the Congress of Paris on the iniquities of Neapolitan and papal rule and of Austria's stranglehold on northern Italy. But gratifying though this was, the situation on the ground stayed the same. Moreover, welcome as the moral support of British liberals might be, it was France which over the centuries had tilted against Austria in Italy. To effect real change in Italy the Second Empire had to come into play.

To his contemporaries Napoleon III was scarcely less enigmatic than his uncle. The British ambassador in Paris confessed that 'to fathom the thoughts or divine the intentions of that one individual would sorely try the powers of the most clear-sighted'.[17] 'The sphinx of the Tuileries' was a well-deserved epithet. It is difficult, therefore, to estimate how committed he was to his oft-expressed mission to redraw the map of Europe according to a *politique des nationalités*. Without doubt, his convictions were shaped by his Bonapartist inheritance. He attributed his uncle's fall to the force of nationalism, while the mandate of the Napoleonic legend demanded an assault on that 1815 settlement which had ignored the principle of national determination. In addition, Napoleon III was very much a product of the age of romanticism, and shared the belief of the messianic nationalists until 1848 that the satisfaction of nationalities would lead to European harmony through the creation of larger federations and, after

1856, a resurrection of the shattered concert. He was assuredly no *Realpolitiker*. Contrariwise, it would be hyperbole to call Napoleon III an ideologue; none the less, his foreign policy disclosed certain fixed ideas to which he clung doggedly.[18]

After 1856 the configuration of international politics was propitious for the realization of Bonapartist and nationalist goals. Thus, at the end of the Crimean War the French emperor traded on the prevailing Russophobia to push for Romanian self-determination in the Danubian principalities. More important, however, was Italy, where the great Napoleon had first made his name and his nephew had begun his rackety political career as a *carbonaro*. The overthrow of the 1815 settlement in Italy, it was hoped, might cause the entire international edifice constructed out of the Bonapartist defeat a half-century earlier to crumble away peaceably.[19] Napoleon III gave an earnest of his intentions by encouraging the anti-Austrian outbursts of Cavour and Clarendon at the Congress of Paris. A French *coup de main* to drive the Austrians out of Italy carried a risk, though it seemed an acceptable one. Post-Crimean Austria was diplomatically isolated, and England and Prussia were mainly concerned lest Napoleon's revision of the Vienna settlement be directed at Belgium or the Rhineland, not Italy.

Such political calculation fused with the vaunted principle of nationality to produce the secret pact struck between Napoleon and Cavour at Plombières on 20 July 1858. The Second Empire undertook to declare war if Austria attacked or threatened Piedmont. The outcome of the war would see Piedmont acquire Lombardy, Venetia and some other north-central Italian states; France was to be rewarded with the Piedmontese territories of Savoy and Nice. The rest of Italy would consist of a central kingdom ruled by Napoleon III's cousin (shades of the first Napoleon's nepotism), the truncated Papal States and the Kingdom of Naples. These four segments of the Italian peninsula were to be joined together in a federation under the pope. Plombières demonstrated the cautious approach to nationalism of both negotiators. For Napoleon, a loose Italian confederation contained enough disparate elements to please all shades of French opinion while forestalling the emergence of a powerful neighbour state. Cavour, for his part, was content to follow the Piedmontese road to Italian unity by an 'artichoke policy' of 'peeling off' provinces one at a time.[20]

Piedmontese recruitment of fugitives from Austria's Italian provinces was a designed provocation and a triumph of unscrupulous *Realpolitik*. Unwisely, Vienna delivered an ultimatum that justified activating the Plombières agreement. The Franco-Austrian war of 1859 saw the Second Empire emerge victorious from two military engagements but fail to overwhelm Austria, whereupon Napoleon III shocked his Piedmontese ally by signing an armistice at Villafranca. By its terms Austria ceded most of

Lombardy to the French emperor, who then transferred the territory to the House of Savoy, but the rest of the Plombières programme was left uncompleted. Napoleon's action arose in some measure from his physical nausea at the carnage of the battlefield, but mainly from a threatening mobilization of Prussian troops on the Rhine frontier.

Prussia's gesture was one of several made since 1848 to take over the German nationalist movement, in this case by saving the embattled Viennese government from the traditional Gallic foe. Of course, there was an Austrian price to pay – acceptance of Prussian hegemony in the Germanies. Had Austria been willing to make concessions to Prussia in central Europe and to Russia in the Near East, it is not impossible that the old conservative front of eastern powers might have come back to life. In that event, Napoleon would have been totally isolated; he had the sympathy of Palmerston's Whig-Liberal government in the Italian question but no prospect of concrete British help. But Vienna refused to save its position in Italy by yielding elsewhere; it would be another dozen years before the triad of conservative states would be reassembled. In 1859–60 no concerted international action proved possible, although there were numerous congress proposals. In the meantime, with the Villafranca armistice imposing a stalemate on France and Austria, the initiative passed to the Italian nationalists. Cavour, who had resigned in despair after Villafranca, returned in January 1860 to orchestrate the nationalist ideology – up to a point.

Nationalist uprisings, engineered in part by Piedmontese agents, were already under way in the central Italian duchies. To secure their annexation Cavour intervened further by sponsoring plebiscites under the watchful gaze of Piedmontese forces. His use of the plebiscite card was aimed squarely at Napoleon III, who could hardly deny the basis of his own authority or, in the words of his own foreign minister, 'principles which he might need to apply and invoke himself later'.[21] But Napoleon still balked at Piedmont's acquisition of Tuscany, and to make doubly sure that France would continue to ward off Austrian interference, Cavour secretly promised to grant the deferred Plombières recompense – Savoy and Nice. A great deal of duplicity was involved. The plebiscites in the duchies, which duly delivered healthy majorities in favour of annexation to Piedmont, were shamelessly rigged, as were later votes held under French auspices in Savoy and Nice. The credibility of Napoleon III as champion of the nationalities was seriously impaired by France's absorption of foreign terrain, while predictably Cavour came under heavy fire for trading away Italian lands, in particular Nice (Nizza) which was unmistakably Italian.

Cavour, in fact, almost overreached himself. Nice was the birthplace of Giuseppe Garibaldi, who in May 1860 emerged centre stage and threatened to undo all Cavour's careful arrangements. In the whole story of Italian unification Garibaldi was the one leader whose appeal transcended class and region. An anticlerical and democratic patriot, his reputation rested on his military exploits in 1848–9, especially in defence of the short-lived Roman republic. Like many other republicans of 1848, though, Garibaldi was willing to accept King Victor Emmanuel for the sake of a united Italy. But disgusted with Cavour's devious *Realpolitik* and caution, Garibaldi, ever the man of action, gathered a thousand volunteers and set sail from Genoa for Sicily with the intention of overthrowing the Bourbon monarchy in Naples and then advancing north to expel the pope from Rome – all in the name of *italianità*. Cavour was trapped. Such was Garibaldi's popularity with ordinary Italians, and even with Victor Emmanuel, that Cavour dared not openly oppose the Sicilian adventure. Yet Garibaldi's redshirted paramilitary force suggested social radicalism and popular nationalism, excesses that appalled the bourgeois Cavour. Just as important, an attack on Rome, where French troops had been protecting the pope since 1849, would invite foreign intervention and possibly the reversal of all Cavour's achievements to date.

The Sicilian expedition met with success beyond wildest expectation. The British fleet posed no obstacle in the Mediterranean. Garibaldi had once been a lion of British drawing rooms, and the Liberal government maintained its watching but friendly brief over the course of Italian unification. Gathering recruits along the way, Garibaldi overran Sicily, crossed the Straits of Messina and captured Naples within a matter of weeks. By September he was ready to march on Rome, at which desperate juncture Cavour gambled. With Napoleon III's grudging permission, he sent a Piedmontese army into the Papal States to confront Garibaldi. The redshirts, however, offered no resistance, and on 26 October 1860 Garibaldi met Victor Emmanuel and handed over his conquests to the new king of Italy. Ritual plebiscites in Sicily and on the mainland afforded the pretence of popular legitimation of the south's attachment to 'Italy one and indivisible'.[22] The phrase conveniently ignored the fact that neither Venetia nor Rome were yet part of united Italy. Just as the events of 1859–60 had been precipitated by French action, so the incorporation of Venetia and Rome into the Italian state would later be the work of an external agency.

Dependence on foreign help was not the only respect in which Italian unification fell short of the nationalist ideal. The truth was that only a small minority of Italians participated in the process. By and large, Cavourians and the Società Nazionale Italiana came from the same narrow upper middle-class stratum of society that had nurtured Italian nationalism before 1848. Garibaldi's fame notwithstanding, the cause for which he fought left the great mass of Italian peasantry untouched, physically and mentally. Many historians have lamented the exclusion of most Italians from the birth of their own national community as an opportunity lost, 'una rivoluzione mancata' (a revolution that failed).[23]

From the start, then, the new Italy had to face the problem of popular alienation, which was compounded by the betrayal of Cavour's earlier promises of regional autonomy. To the question of how the new state was to be administered, the victors answered by extending arbitrarily Piedmontese laws and practices throughout the peninsula, a policy that was set in motion well before Cavour's untimely death in June 1861. Resentment was predictable, and particularly acute in the south where rule by northerners was *ipso facto* alien rule. The sense of a Neapolitan world tuned upside down by Italian unification is nowhere better caught than in an authentic masterpiece of twentieth-century literature, *Il gatto-pardo* (The Leopard, 1958) by Giuseppe di Lampedusa, himself a direct descendant of one of those Sicilian nobles dislocated by the convulsion of 1860. The south's response was frequently violent. In united Italy's first years more Italian lives were lost in the suppression of 'brigandage', a term of convenience to cover insurrection by disaffected Bourbon royalists, aristocrats and clericals, Mafia outrages and desperate peasant *jacqueries*, than in all the wars of unification put together.[24]

Italy might be made in 1860 but Italians had yet to be created, as the oft-quoted contemporary remark put it.[25] The unification of Italy, unlike the French Revolution, did not spawn a widespread nationalist ideology. The failure of the expanded Piedmontese liberal parliamentary system to produce a cohesive nation state resulted ultimately in the resort to fascism. Much of Mussolini's career was to be consumed in trying to rouse a spirit of *italianità* among the populace.

PRUSSIA AND UNITARY NATIONALISM

German unification, which followed hard on the heels of the Italian, bore some obvious similarities. The centralizing role of Prussia matched that of Piedmont, and Otto von Bismarck equalled Cavour in *Realpolitik* diplomacy. A united Germany, like Italy, faced the problem of regionalism. But there was one important difference. No matter how inefficient and corrupt the new Italian state, it operated within a liberal framework – a constitutional monarchy, statutory individual rights and *laisser-faire* economics. Thus, the principles of the Mazzinians and other idealistic liberals of 1848, who for pragmatic reasons had rallied to the House of Savoy, were compromised but not utterly blighted in 1860. In contrast, German unification was accomplished by conservative forces for conservative reasons; the break with 1848 was sharp, and liberalism was completely swallowed up by the nationalist movement. Out of this experience would grow a German nationalism of a fervent and ideological kind, an unintended but undeniable legacy of Bismarckian *Realpolitik*.

Bismarck's appointment as Prussian first minister in September 1862 was an explicitly anti-liberal manoeuvre. The refusal of the liberals in Prussia's *Landtag* (parliament) to vote for taxes for the reorganization of the army had pushed the king to the verge of abdication and Bismarck was brought in to outface the liberals. His exploitation of the so-called 'gap' in the Prussian constitution to collect taxes without parliamentary approval at first exacerbated the crisis, which was resolved only by Bismarck's accomplishment of German unification.

Yet Bismarck was emphatically not a German nationalist. Just as Cavour worked first and foremost for Piedmont, Bismarck's prime objective was to strengthen the Prussian state. This meant maintaining monarchical authority and the ascendancy of Bismarck's own class of *Junker* landowners, the traditional backbone of Prussia's civil and military administration.[26] German nationalism in 1862, however, connoted revolution, or at least liberal constitutionalism, which, in Bismarck's eyes, was only a slightly lesser evil. Its voice was the Nationalverein, founded in 1859 in imitation of the Società Nazionale Italiana and located in Coburg, the capital of German liberalism. In its bourgeois membership and liberal nationalist programme, the Nationalverein was the Frankfurt Assembly reincarnate and, as such, anathema to all Bismarck's convictions.

On the other hand, Bismarck was no doctrinaire and, ever alert to what he called the *imponderabilia* in a situation, was capable of great mental flexibility. Convinced of a divine purpose in the universe over which humans had little control, he aspired to travel with the 'stream of time'. 'By plunging my hand into it', he once wrote, 'I am merely doing my duty. I do not expect thereby to change its course.' On another occasion he warned against imagining 'that we can hasten the march of time'.[27] Specifically, he recognized that German unity was an idea whose time had come. The trick was to make it conform to Prussian conservatism.

Bismarck was soon able to begin the process. In 1863 a nationalist revolt erupted in Russia's Polish provinces. A Bismarckian emissary, General Alvensleben, was dispatched to St Petersburg where he signed a convention for Russo-Prussian cooperation on their common border in order to capture and disarm the rebels. This provoked a storm of protest among western liberals, especially in 'polonophile' France. Napoleon III, anxious to refresh his tarnished image as a paladin of oppressed nationalities, called for a free Poland, and Empress Eugénie, an increasingly important political figure in the Second Empire, astonished the Austrian ambassador by unveiling a European map with a wholesale realignment of frontiers to accommodate an independent Poland. But elsewhere in Western Europe there was less enthusiasm. London's liberal sympathies for suppressed nationalities proved not to extend from Italy to Poland, certainly not to backing another liberationist campaign of the volatile

Napoleon. Left to plough a lonely furrow, France could offer no material assistance to the Poles who were left to their own devices and defeat.[28] In the meantime, Bismarck had scored three clear points. The Alvensleben convention reaffirmed Prussia's official stand against revolutionary nationalism; it helped to safeguard Prussia's own Polish provinces; and it gave Prussia a claim on Russian goodwill in whatever diplomatic incident might arise in the near future.

Almost at once, in fact, Prussia was drawn into a diplomatic imbroglio. Denmark again tried to alter the status of the mixed-nationality duchies of Schleswig and Holstein and, in particular, to absorb the former. In such a north German problem it was incumbent on Prussia to come forward to protect Teutonic rights, as it had in 1848. Fifteen years later Bismarck too was constrained to take up the nationalist cause lest either the Nationalverein or the Germanic Confederation step in first. In fact, the confederation authorized Prussia and Austria to take joint action, but Bismarck refused to recognize the mandate, and it was on orders from Berlin and Vienna that Prussian and Austrian troops invaded Schleswig-Holstein. By mid-1864 Denmark was forced to surrender the duchies, which remained under Austro-Prussian occupation pending their final disposition. Bismarck was determined all along that they should be annexed to Prussia, although he bombarded the Austrians with a variety of solutions, none of which proved acceptable in Vienna. But the fate of Schleswig-Holstein was not the real issue; the duchies were merely the cover for a larger Austro-Prussian struggle for supremacy in the Germanies.

Between 1864 and 1866 this diplomatic war was fought in two arenas. Since 1815 the Germanic Confederation had usually responded to Austrian wishes, and in the 1860s the small federal states, fearful of Prussia's growing power, were still inclined to seek shelter under the Austrian umbrella. Consequently, Vienna advanced more than one scheme to overhaul the confederation, while stopping short of advocating real German unity. They were all blocked by Prussia, and one Bismarckian tactic was to outbid Austria by proposing that elections to the federal diet be based on universal male suffrage. As Bismarck had calculated, Vienna recoiled in horror at such a radical suggestion. But it was significant that Bismarck was willing to invoke democracy to further his own ends.[29]

While the Germanic Confederation was locked in stalemate, Prussia gained a distinct advantage on the wider European stage. Before the Austro-Prussian quarrel escalated into war, Bismarck needed to ensure that Vienna would fight without allies. After the Alvensleben convention he could count on Russian benevolent neutrality, and also on Britain's Little England isolation. The key player in the game was the Second French Empire. In the short term, Napoleon III was obsessed with Venetia and the memory of his chequered role in Italian unification. For this reason he offered both Prussia and Austria his benevolent neutrality in their prospective conflict in return for the transfer of Venetia to France and thence to the supposedly grateful Italians. The operative understanding was reached in October 1865 when Napoleon met Bismarck at Biarritz, an encounter sometimes called the German Plombières. Indeed, both pacts envisaged war against Austria, but whereas at Plombières the French emperor undertook to fight against Austria, at Biarritz he promised merely to stay neutral. Anticipating a lengthy struggle at the end of which he would mediate and state his price, Napoleon was content to exchange vague promises about securing Prussian dominance in north Germany against French compensation in the Rhineland, Luxemburg or Belgium. Bismarck readily agreed and, some months later, made a military alliance with Italy to open a second front against Austria, with Venetia as the prize.[30]

Although Napoleon continued to deal secretly with Austria about Venetia up to the outbreak of war, in effect three revisionist states – Prussia, France and Italy – were now ranged against an isolated Austria. Vienna might have learned a lesson from the Danes whose machinations in Schleswig-Holstein had been made in expectation of help from other powers that never arrived. But at the time the common consensus was that in head-to-head combat with Prussia (or even with Prussia and Italy combined) Austria would prove victorious. It was therefore a confident Austria that responded to Prussian goading in June 1866 by mobilizing the forces of the Germanic Confederation. For the same reason surprise was the dominant European reaction to the Prussian victory at Sadowa, achieved by superior staff preparation, in the ensuing Seven Weeks War.[31]

The decisive battlefield victory allowed Bismarck, via the pretence of Napoleonic mediation, to reach a quick peace settlement that excluded Austria from German affairs. Prussia annexed Schleswig-Holstein and other German states in order to render its territory a compact block. The old Germanic Confederation was dissolved and replaced by a Prussian-dominated confederation of all states north of the River Main. Out of deference to France rather than Austria, four south German states were permitted to retain their independence, for the time being.

Almost overnight Bismarck became the nationalist hero who had engineered a revolution from above. But, in reality, the triumph was not Bismarck's alone. Certainly, there was little input from the German masses, but Bismarck built on a foundation of middle-class nationalist consciousness raised by those liberals who were his ideological enemies. It was more, in one historian's phrase, 'a revolution from two sides, Bismarck's and the nationalist movement's'.[32] Nevertheless, 1866 was a decisive turning point in German political ideology. Bismarck's international success marked the final appropriation of the nationalist cause by Prussian conservatism. By and large, the liberal guardians of the nationalist flame acquiesced. Their euphoria at the recent nationalist triumphs was manifested in the Prussian *Landtag*, which approved by 310 to 75 a bill indemnifying Bismarck for his illegal collection of taxes since 1862. The year following the Seven Weeks War saw the founding of the National Liberal Party, whose constitution proclaimed that 'the Unification of Germany under one and the same Constitution is for us the highest task at the present time'. The document continued, 'We do not entertain the hope of being able to meet our many needs all at once . . . Our pressing experience has taught us that one cannot fight with the same weapons at all times for the same tasks.'[33] In other words, nationalist ends took priority over liberal means.

Meanwhile, Napoleon III stepped forward to claim his reward for neutrality in the Austro-Prussian war. Faced with the shock of Sadowa, Empress Eugénie among others had urged a French mobilization on the Rhine in belated retaliation for Prussian mobilization against France in the Italian crisis of 1859. But her husband chose to regard the construction of a north German confederation as vindication of his own nationality principle, and to await the reward supposedly promised at Biarritz. Venetia, although without some Alpine territory, passed from Austria to Italy as arranged, but Bismarck had given no other hard and fast undertaking. He now informed Napoleon that cession of any of the Rhineland would affront German patriotic feeling heightened by the recent war, while international sanction was necessary for French compensation in Luxemburg and Belgium.[34] The French emperor was not only rebuffed but his importunity played directly into Bismarck's hands. It so alarmed the south German states that they accepted the military pact that the Prussian premier offered them as well as membership in the Prussian *Zollverein*. From 1866 full German unity of the *kleindeutsch* variety was always on the horizon.

Napoleon III's failure to extract a French *quid pro quo* to offset Prussia's aggrandizement was only one in a catalogue of foreign policy frustrations in the 1860s. The Second Empire's Italian policy had won few kudos, least of all among the Italian nationalist constituency, which continued to be deprived of its natural capital, Rome, by France's military protection of the pope's temporal power. French vociferous advocacy of Polish independence foundered on the unyielding hold that the eastern powers retained over the Poles. But perhaps the most ignominious blot on the Bonapartist record was a foray into Mexico, where the first Napoleon had once nursed the dream of a French empire. What began in 1861 as a joint Anglo-French-Spanish intervention to compel a new republican government to honour Mexico's foreign debt soon turned into an exclusively French expedition to restore the Catholic religion. Napoleon III persuaded the Habsburg Archduke Maximilian to accept a Mexican crown. But with the end of the American Civil War, Washington was free to reassert the Monroe Doctrine and to demand the withdrawal of French troops from the New World. By 1867 Napoleon complied, leaving Maximilian to his fate. Shortly after, Maximilian was captured and executed by the Mexican republicans. In France official pressure prevented exhibition of Manet's famous paintings of the execution. But a Paris journal summed up French opinion in a literary analogy: 'Who would have believed that in our age invisible witches could still sweep an honest Macbeth into the abyss by telling him: you will be king?'[35]

Under the first Napoleonic empire despotism at home had been redeemed by *la gloire* abroad; under the second, despotism was accompanied by an accumulation of international setbacks, inevitably undermining the regime's internal support. To counter a growing opposition, Napoleon III invoked one of the more fictitious elements in the Napoleonic legend, namely, that the great Napoleon was on the verge of liberalizing his regime when cut down in 1815. Such was the theoretical justification for the transmutation of the 'authoritarian empire' of the 1850s into the 'liberal empire' of the 1860s.[36]

Progressively throughout the latter decade the trappings of a liberal parliamentary system were introduced. Elections to a *corps législatif* were geared to appeasing the liberal bourgeoisie whose economic power had grown during the boom years of the 1850s. Workers too found themselves with new rights embodied in trade union legislation, a token of Napoleon's vague St Simonian socialism. The amalgam of social paternalism and nationalism has invited comparisons with the fascist dictators of the twentieth century.[37] But in the final analysis, the liberalism of the 1860s was largely a façade; the ultimate arbiter was always Napoleon. It is a matter of debate how far international failures compelled him to liberalize his government. But there is no questioning the impact that liberalization had on foreign policy-making, especially from 1867 when a round of constitutional reforms coincided with Napoleon's post-Sadowa humiliation. In the 1790s the leftward drift of the French Revolution had been marked by a concomitant rise in nationalist sentiment which demanded an aggressive foreign policy. In the same way, a wider participation in the political process of the Second Empire, circumscribed though it was, forced Napoleon III to adopt a belligerent posture towards Prussia. The mood of the French political classes, if not perhaps the public at large, was caught by the liberal Thiers who complained that the emperor acted in the interests of Italians, Germans and Poles, but never the interests of France.[38]

Between 1867 and 1870 foreign policy on both sides of the Rhine was conducted in an atmosphere of inflamed nationalism, which accounts for the risk-taking practised in the affair of the Hohenzollern candidature for the vacant Spanish throne. To be hemmed in by German monarchs to both the south and east was understandably intolerable to France, and the Prussian king admitted as much when he withdrew his relative's candidacy. But Paris clearly played to the nationalist gallery in demanding a guarantee that the candidacy would never be revived. Bismarck's riposte was to manipulate the telegraphic report of the encounter at Bad Ems between the king and Count Benedetti, the French ambassador, so as to make it appear, quite falsely, that the king, in refusing the French request, had gratuitously insulted the ambassador. The Ems telegram ploy was a blatant *Realpolitik* provocation, and France fell into the trap. It exploded in nationalistic indignation. Without waiting for Benedetti's full report, the *corps législatif* voted overwhelmingly for war which, the emperor's liberal chief minister announced, 'we enter with a light heart'. Even allowing for the limited range of public opinion at the time, the Franco-Prussian war that opened in July 1870 was a genuine 'peoples' war' on both sides.[39]

France fought alone, as had Austria in 1866. Vienna refused Napoleon III's overtures to join him and seek revenge for Sadowa. The Austrians judged it wiser to concentrate their attention on the Balkans, as Bismarck advised. In addition, ideological factors held Austria and France apart. The rift between the traditionalist house of Habsburg and the upstart Bonapartes was never overcome, and Emperor Francis Josef, who declared himself still 'a German prince', worried lest a French victory bring Napoleon into southern Germany.[40] As for the other powers, Russia still judged Prussia and France by their attitude to Polish revolutionary nationalism; conservative Bismarck fought against it, Napoleon III encouraged it. For Britain the criterion was Belgium, and in another Machiavellian coup Bismarck assured British goodwill in 1870 by revealing correspondence in which Napoleon, after the Biarritz meeting, had rashly committed to paper his designs on Belgium. The Italians continued to show no gratitude for Napoleon's contribution to their unification, and looked forward to a Prussian victory in order to expel the French from Rome.

Italy and the rest of the European states which favoured Prussia got their wish. The French military machine proved as unexpectedly fallible as the Austrians' four years earlier. Under Napoleon's liberal empire the *corps législatif* had been allowed to curtail military expenditure, and no French Bismarck had appeared on the scene to defy the constitution and the liberals. Lack of preparation, indifferent strategic planning and poor leadership resulted in France's emphatic defeat at Sedan in September 1870 and Napoleon III's abdication.[41] Since France had launched the war, Bismarck's military alliance with the south German states came into effect. Fighting together against an ancient common enemy supplied the platform for Bismarck to arrange the incorporation of south Germany into a new political union. Well before the signing of a formal peace treaty with France, the German empire was proclaimed. The ceremony took place on 18 January 1871 at one of France's most historic sites – the Hall of Mirrors in Louis XIV's palace at Versailles. This was a piece of German nationalistic self-indulgence, but not untypical of the insensitivity and excess that *Realpolitik* had injected into international relations.

With hindsight we can see that the creation of a united Germany, even minus the German-speaking Habsburg lands, betokened a threat to the European balance. Some apprehension on this score was voiced in 1870, although in muted fashion. By and large, Bismarck's accomplishments were greeted with either equanimity or resignation which must be attributed, at least in part, to the advance made by nationalist ideology over the previous half-century. By 1870 self-determination was becoming the accepted norm of European international relations, and so German unification was regarded as a natural political evolution. Most Britons (with Benjamin Disraeli a notable exception) took this attitude. True, Britain would have preferred a liberal Germany, but took comfort in the circumstance that the heir apparent to the new imperial throne followed the prompting of his wife, a strong-willed liberal daughter of Queen Victoria. In any event, a powerful Germany of any ideological hue was welcome as a counter to Russia. Conversely, Russia would have liked a weaker German union than Bismarck had forged, but was happy with its conservative nature. Both accepted the new Germany's entrance into the European states system without protest.[42]

The generally equable reception accorded German, and Italian, unification also owed something to the fact that these were nationalist triumphs in a restricted sense. They had been orchestrated from the top by ministers of the crown; the nationalist societies were overwhelmingly middle-class; mass involvement was marginal and spasmodic. Put another way, the spectre of popular and revolutionary nationalism, which had so terrified the Metternichian conservatives of 1815, was kept at arm's length. Both Cavour and Bismarck, in short, were cabinet politicians.

On the other hand, they were *Realpolitiker* for whom the end justified sometimes repugnant means. The narrative of Italian and German unification exposed their willingness to traffic with popular nationalism when opportune. Cavour held his plebiscites. Bismarck, more daring, resorted to universal male suffrage; he suggested its introduction into the Germanic Confederation, and employed it in elections for the *Reichstag* (the lower parliamentary house) in both the North German Confederation and the new empire. Neither plebiscites nor universal suffrage offered any assurance of government responsive to the popular will, and the democratic gestures of Cavour and Bismarck were as fraudulent as Napoleon III's plebiscites and sham liberal empire. But all three leaders discerned that mass opinion, suitably handled, might be enlisted in support of the existing social order. Nationalism supplied the bridge between democracy and conservatism; a successful foreign policy was counted on to allay domestic tensions. Napoleon III tried but failed disastrously to put this proposition into practice, Cavour was more successful, and Bismarck most successful of all. Collectively, though, Louis Napoleon, Cavour and Bismarck proved that nationalism did not have to be Jacobin. Here, they pointed the way to the post-1870 future when all states, authoritarian and parliamentary alike, found in nationalist and imperial ideologies a means of coping with the rise of the masses.

Still one further development had occurred since 1848 to give impetus to ideological tendencies. For a generation a battle had been raging to determine the shape and nature of the nation state. On the one side were the proponents of a 'federative polity' whereby state formation would be loose and tolerant of regional and other particularist rights. On the other stood the advocates of a 'unitary' or centralized state framework. Everywhere victory went to the latter.[43] In Italy Napoleon III's scheme for a confederation under the pope came to nought; instead, Italy was united on rigid Piedmontese lines. Similarly, the forces of federalism in central Europe – Austria, the small German states and the 1815 confederation – were swept aside, and the emergent German empire was Prussia writ large. The movement towards a tighter sort of national unity was global. The American Civil War was an explicit contest between the unitary principle and states' rights, and by 1865 the northern Unionists prevailed over the Confederate South. In Japan, where for centuries two authorities had coexisted – the emperor and the feudal clan chief known as the Shogun – another struggle ended in the same way. By the Meiji restoration of 1868 the Shogun and the clans renounced their powers, and henceforth the emperor became the focal point of Japan's transformation into a modern nation state. Even where federative polity survived, as in the Habsburg empire, it did so by admitting a degree of centralization. The revamped constitution or *Ausgleich* of 1867 granted the Magyars the devolution for which they had fought in 1848–9. But although the *Ausgleich* created a dual monarchy, by concentrating power in Austro-Hungarian hands it turned away from a truly federative solution to the Habsburgs' multinational problem, which would have entailed a triple (or trial) division of powers with the Slavs.

The drive to national centralization in the mid-nineteenth century was not novel; it was a continuance of the work of the enlightened despots of the previous century. It was rather that the process was dramatically speeded up between 1848 and 1870. The result was a closer relationship than ever before between the state and its citizens. The scope for the dispersion of the values and ideology of the government and power structure throughout society was increased accordingly. So too was the opportunity in an age of democracy for subterranean belief systems and *mentalités* to flow upwards and influence official decision-making. Given the part that nationalism and imperialism would be expected to play in harmonizing the interests of the ruling classes and a mass electorate, international relations stood little chance of escaping an upsurge in ideological currents of thought after 1870.

5

IDEOLOGY AND MASS DEMOCRACY

BISMARCK AND MONARCHICAL SOLIDARITY

For some years after 1870 the ideological lineaments of international relations reverted to their pre-Crimean War shape. Specifically, on 6 June 1873 the three conservative powers, Austria-Hungary, Russia and the new Germany, joined together in a *Dreikaiserbund* or league of three emperors. This harked back to Münchengrätz in 1833, and indeed the *Dreikaiserbund* was formed for the same reasons and in the same way as the Münchengrätz convention. Recent events had served to concentrate minds in Vienna and St Petersburg on the Near East. Austria-Hungary, having been excluded from Italy and Germany, was looking to recover prestige in the Balkans; Russia had used the cover of the Franco-Prussian War and Bismarck's goodwill to repudiate the post-Crimean demilitarization of the Black Sea. Fear of working at cross purposes in the crumbling Ottoman empire first brought Vienna and St Petersburg together in 1872, as it had at Münchengrätz. Also, as in 1833, Prussia (or in 1873 Prussianized Germany) joined later, and the agreement was cemented by the three powers' reiterated attachment to 'monarchical solidarity'. The *Dreikaiserbund*, however, was a vague instrument. It involved no firm commitments, merely mutual consultation, and it depended on fallible Austro-Russian cooperation. In this sense, it was 'a fair-weather system' at best.[1]

The *Dreikaiserbund*, as an extension of the Austro-Russian *rapprochement*, was Bismarck's work. Now chancellor of the new *Reich*, he was to put his stamp on an era of international relations, just as Metternich had done half a century earlier. And like Metternich, he sought to contain the forces of revolution symbolized in a recently Bonapartist France. In reality, the Third French Republic which succeeded the Second Empire was anything but revolutionary; it quickly developed into what has been aptly termed a 'stalemate society'.[2] However, the republican regime had only established itself by stifling the radical Paris Commune of 1871, and the memory of the Commune haunted Europe's propertied classes to the end of the century. It suited Bismarck to emphasize the French

85

revolutionary tradition in order to isolate the Third Republic diplomatically. In his own words, he wanted to be 'one of three, so long as the world is governed by the unstable equilibrium of five great powers'.[3] (He discounted the new Italy in this equation.) With Britain still holding aloof from continental affairs and the conservative *Dreikaiserbund* ideologically estranged from the Third Republic, France was left friendless.

Bismarck's concern lest France become *bündnisfähig* (a credible ally) arose from the dire legacy of the Franco-Prussian War. Whereas the Austro-Prussian conflict had bequeathed surprisingly little rancour, Prussia's victory of 1870 stoked a bitter French resentment. Consanguinity preserved a bond between Austrians and Prussians while by the *Ausgleich* the Magyars had actually profited from the Habsburg defeat; but in France the spirit of revenge feasted on the postwar Treaty of Frankfurt by which the Germans annexed Alsace-Lorraine ostensibly for reasons of military security. The issue of the 'lost provinces', which had been part of France since 1648, ruled out any *détente* between Paris and Berlin for the next fifty years. France's postwar economic recovery and swift payment of the indemnity imposed by the Frankfurt treaty redoubled Bismarck's alarm at the country's nationalist temper. Moreover, the Third Republic by 1873 fell into the hands of the monarchists whom Bismarck accused of masterminding a clerical international to thwart his *Kulturkampf* which aimed to extend state power over the Catholic Church in Prussia. In the fight against ultramontanism Bismarck sought allies among secular liberals at home and abroad, demonstrating his readiness to manipulate ideological passions without becoming a slave to them. Accordingly, he had recourse to any ideological stick to beat the French, who were thus denounced simultaneously as revolutionary republicans and clerical reactionaries.[4]

All this culminated in the war scare of 1875, an apparent German threat to reopen the war of 1870 conveyed through inspired press revelations under the heading of 'Is war in sight'?[5] Almost certainly, Bismarck was bluffing, but as a diplomatic gambit the war scare failed. Russia joined Britain in protesting Germany's brinkmanship, which infuriated Bismarck. If nothing else, the Russian attitude revealed the fragility of the *Dreikaiserbund* and its ideological foundations.

But the real danger to the unity of the monarchical states lay not in the west but in the east. In the 1820s and the 1850s the Eastern Question had nullified the ideological affinity between the courts of Vienna and St Petersburg; in 1878 it did so again. Over the previous three years the Slavic peoples of the Balkans had one after another risen in armed revolt against their Turkish suzerain. The agitation began in Bosnia and Herzegovina, although Bulgaria was destined to be the flashpoint of the crisis. The nationalist rebels turned to Russia for help, as had the Greeks half a century earlier. But there was now a new ingredient in the situation;

racial pan-Slavism for the first time was a prominent factor in the Eastern Question. The sense of a common identity and interests among all Slavs was promoted by the presence of a pan-Slav Russian ambassador in Constantinople and the appointment of a pan-Slav Russian general to command the Serbian army. And if a scene in Tolstoy's *Anna Karenina* is to be believed, Russian volunteers were sped on their way with the toast, 'To serve the Faith, humanity and our brothers!'[6]

The threat to Austria-Hungary was twofold. Not only did Russian encroachment in the Balkans challenge the Habsburgs in their only remaining sphere of influence, but pan-Slavism was a siren call to the disaffected Slavs within the empire's frontiers. Yet, for almost three years, the bond formed by the *Dreikaiserbund* kept Vienna and St Petersburg from open conflict. Russian policy was, in fact, driven less by pan-Slav fantasies than the Austro-Hungarians feared, and twice in 1876–7 the two powers exchanged formal recognition of each other's legitimate interests in the Balkans. Bismarck, who had encouraged Russia in the Near East up to a point, was now willing to promote an Austro-Russian understanding in order to control both states. On the other hand, the German chancellor tried to steer clear of direct involvement in a Balkan tangle that, he maintained, was 'not worth the bones of a Pomeranian musketeer'.[7]

Predictably, an eastern crisis brought Britain out of its shell. As in the Crimean War, Britain's reaction was highly emotional. But whereas liberal sentiment in 1854 had fulminated against tsarist despotism, it was inflamed this time by lurid press reports of Turkish atrocities in Bulgaria. Britain's liberal conscience was articulated in Gladstone's pamphlet, *Bulgarian Horrors* (1876), which sold 40,000 copies in a few months. Therein Gladstone, who had supported the Crimean War, dropped his Russophobia and urged an Anglo-Russian partnership to save the Bulgars. However, Gladstone was out of office, and Disraeli's Tory administration viewed the Eastern Question without sentiment. In 1875 Britain purchased a controlling share in the Suez Canal Company from the impecunious Egyptian khedive, and the following year Disraeli contrived the title of empress of India for Queen Victoria. Hence, any Russian threat to Ottoman integrity, including the Straits and Constantinople, appeared a danger to the Suez lifeline to India and had to be resisted for imperial reasons. Victoria herself went in the reverse direction to Gladstone: an opponent of the Crimean War, she now encouraged her cabinet to oppose Russian expansion. At a lower social level, too, the Russian bogey excited artless passion. Audiences joined lustily in the music-hall chorus that added jingoism as a term for bellicose patriotism to the English language.[8] The split in British opinion was to a large extent a function of party politics and of the personal duel between Gladstone and Disraeli. But it was also a clash of political philosophies. Gladstone was striving to revive the sort of idealistic liberalism that had peaked on the Continent in 1848. Disraeli, on the contrary, trafficked in a populist nationalism and the 'new imperialism' which was about to revolutionize international affairs. In any event, the furore caused by the Eastern Question in 1875–8 marked the demise of strict Cobdenite isolationism.

The Balkan crisis came to a head when Russia, trusting to its agreements with Austria-Hungary to preserve that country's neutrality, declared war on Turkey in April 1877. By the beginning of the following year Russian troops had occupied Sofia and were moving on Constantinople. Did this augur, at last, the demise of the Turkish 'sick man of Europe'? In March 1878 the Turks were compelled to sign the Treaty of San Stefano, the main feature of which was the creation of a large, independent Bulgaria expected to be a compliant Russian satellite. This was too much for both London and Vienna; the former sent a fleet to anchor off the Ottoman capital, and between them they forced St Petersburg into a secret disavowal of San Stefano. Russia's retreat was to be disguised as the outcome of an international congress, the Concert of Europe *redivivus*. In spite of Bismarck's reluctance to be sucked into Balkan affairs, Berlin was the natural site for the congress – testimony in fact to the German empire's diplomatic stature. Furthermore, it was paradoxical that Bismarck should preside over the restitution of the concert since he had done more than anyone to wreck it in the 1860s. With Germany now a 'sated' power, though, he was somewhat less hostile to a community of nations that could be invoked to maintain the *status quo* or at least limit change. In other words, the European concert was for Bismarck an agency to be used only if and when expedient.[9]

None the less, Bismarck utterly dominated the Congress of Berlin held in the summer of 1878; he allegedly appropriated Louis XIV's epigram in order to boast, 'Le congrès, c'est moi'. Of course, it meant all praise, or blame, for the outcome of the congress fell to the German chancellor. Most participants went away satisfied. Disraeli's unease about German unification was quieted, and he returned home claiming peace with honour and Cyprus. Bismarck persuaded the French to divert their gaze from the blue line of the Vosges to the colonial territory of Tunisia. In the Balkans administration of Bosnia and Herzegovina passed to Austria-Hungary, and the independent Bulgaria envisaged by the Russians in the San Stefano treaty was much reduced in size by the detachment of eastern Roumelia. Russia was thus the sole power to leave Berlin aggrieved. Bismarck had, truth to tell, conducted his brokerage honestly, but the Russians, remembering his earlier sympathy for their Near Eastern ambitions, accused him of duplicity. The Congress of Berlin, said Tsar Alexander II, was 'a European coalition against Russia under the leadership of Prince Bismarck', and the pan-Slavs were even more vehement.[10] The international ramifications were serious. With the *Dreikaiserbund* shattered, Bismarck was forced to redesign the relationship among the trio of conservative powers.

The immediate cause of the fateful Austro-German alliance of 1879 may have been Russian umbrage at both countries, but other and deeper motives were also at work. As early as 1872 Bismarck had assured Count Andrássy, foreign minister in Vienna, that he was unalterably opposed to a disintegration of the Habsburg empire under the impact of Russian-sponsored pan-Slavism; such an eventuality threatened his Prussianized *Kleindeutschland* with an influx of ten million Austrians. His preferred solution to the problem of Austria-Hungary's German population, expressed more than once, was 'a lasting organic connection' consisting of 'uniform arrangements in the areas of jurisprudence, legislation, and administration – as well as in economic and social-political matters – a cooperation that could undoubtedly be most beneficial for two common-wealths that are so well suited to complement each other'.[11] However, when Bismarck submitted this sort of proposal in 1879, Andrássy rejected it in favour of a plain military pact; a Hungarian who had fought for inde-pendence in 1848, Andrássy wanted German protection against Russia but no absorption into the larger Teutonic world. As a result, the Austro-German treaty signed on 17 October provided for German aid if Russia attacked Austria-Hungary, though the latter's commitment to help Germany was conditional on an attack by France supported by another power. On paper the alliance was couched in conventional political terms, but in spirit it was much more. Bismarck's abortive proposal for an organic association hinted at the ethnic and cultural links between Berlin and Vienna. Bismarck himself emphatically repudiated pan-Germanism; it smacked of the windy romanticism of 1848. Yet, he was wont to refer to Austria-Hungary as part of Germany and described Trieste as 'Germany's only port on the southern seas'.[12] The Austro-German alliance, then, could hardly escape the semblance of a pan-German riposte to the pan-Slavism witnessed in the eastern crisis of 1875–8.

The question was whether the new nationalist and racial ideologies would supersede the older 'isms' – conservatism and liberalism – in shaping international alignments. Bismarck was determined and confident that this would not happen. He insisted that the Dual Alliance of 1879 did not automatically entail Russian estrangement. Indeed, one purpose in tying Austria-Hungary to Germany was to prevent Vienna from drifting into any future 'Crimean coalition' against Russia. Above all, the Dual Alliance was not meant to give Austria-Hungary licence to follow a provocative policy in Southeastern Europe. Just the reverse in fact; Bismarck intended to use it to restrain Vienna from Balkan adventures.[13] In the short term, Bismarck's prognostication was borne out as a chastened Russia returned to the conservative fold. On 18 June 1881 a three emperors' alliance was concluded for a three-year term, and was duly renewed for a further three years in 1884. It was an advance on the *Dreikaiserbund* in that it was a military agreement for benevolent neutrality if any party found itself under attack. But the Three Emperors' Alliance was merely a supplement to, not a replacement of, the 1879 Austro-German pact. What made it possible at all was a straight power-political deal: recognition of an Austro-Hungarian zone of influence in the western Balkans (especially Bosnia and Herzegovina) and a Russian sphere in the east (Bulgaria). The conservative ideological tie was less in evidence in 1881 than in 1873. Nevertheless, anxiety at the rise of socialism ran high, and Bismarck invoked the need for a 'triangular rampart' to preserve both peace and conservative principles.[14] In domestic politics he had just transferred his support from the National Liberals to right-wing groups; the switch paralleled his strategy in the Three Emperors' Alliance of bolstering conservative pro-Germans in St Petersburg against the revolutionary pan-Slavs.

While ideology might do something to sustain the Bismarckian system in the east, it stood in the way of its extension to the west. It remains unclear how far the German chancellor nourished a genuine desire to bring Britain into his diplomatic net. In the wake of the Congress of Berlin, where he had enjoyed a fruitful collaboration with Disraeli, he sent out feelers for an Anglo-German understanding for the containment of Russia. But the moment passed, and the British general election of 1880 ensured it would not return. One of the few British elections to hinge on foreign policy, it was marked by Gladstone's celebrated campaign in the Midlothian electoral district of Scotland – 'a battle', he wrote in his diary, 'of justice, humanity, freedom, law, all in their first elements from the very root, and all on a gigantic scale'. Resuming his Bulgarian 'atrocity agitation' of some years ago, he savaged the Disraeli government for its neglect of the 'right principles' of British foreign policy. These he particularized as the cultivation of the Concert of European Christian states to 'neutralise and fetter the selfish aims of each', the acknowledgement of 'the rights of all nations' and a foreign policy 'inspired by love of freedom'.[15] The thunderous oratory and vitality of Gladstone's Midlothian campaign, remarkable in a man of seventy, swept the Liberal party into office.

Nothing could have been more antithetical to Bismarck's conservative *Realpolitik* than the Gladstonian cult of liberal and Christian morality in world politics. After 1878 Bismarck had little use for the Concert of Europe, and Gladstone's endorsement of self-determination was a fillip to pan-Slavism. The German made no secret of his hostility. From 1880 to 1885 he waged a propagandistic 'ideological war against Gladstonism', which suggested *inter alia* that British liberalism was a disguised and creeping republicanism. As ever with Bismarck, though, there was method in the ranting. Gladstone was built up as a bogeyman in the campaign to discredit liberalism within the *Reich*, while his 'unacceptably antimonarchical, revolutionary, unpeaceful' conduct was fed to Vienna and St Petersburg to frighten the monarchs into remaining loyal to the coalition of the three emperors.[16]

The conservative–liberal divide between Bismarck and Gladstone was reminiscent of the polemic between Metternich and Palmerston exactly fifty years earlier. But the international ambience of the 1880s made it increasingly difficult to pursue either a traditional conservative or liberal polity. Pressures quite unknown to their predecessors inhibited both Gladstone and Bismarck. In the former's case, imperialism was the bane. As prime minister, Gladstone found his liberal critique of Disraeli's pre-occupation with empire in 1878 a distinct encumbrance as his ministry was sucked in one colonial quagmire after another – in the Transvaal, Egypt (conquered in 1882 for the sake of the Suez Canal), the Sudan, Afghanistan, and even in Ireland, which could be regarded as a colonial problem where coercion violated Gladstonian ideals. For Bismarck, it was the familiar obstacle of the clash of national wills in the Balkans that again tested his ability to hold the bloc of conservative powers together. As in the great eastern crisis of 1875–8, Bulgaria was the source of trouble. Nationalists in that country were understandably distressed at the abridgement of their territory by the Congress of Berlin. Their king, Prince Alexander of Battenberg, shared these sentiments and, in 1885, unilaterally announced the incorporation of eastern Roumelia into Bulgaria. Neither Britain nor Austria-Hungary, architects of a truncated Bulgaria at Berlin, approved. The Three Emperors' Alliance came under immediate strain, although its terms allowed the sort of frontier change Sofia now envisaged. Serbia, at that time an Austrian client state, attacked Bulgaria but was swiftly repulsed, after which the powers agreed to recognize an enlarged Bulgaria. The Three Emperors' Alliance was shaken and, in fact, its days were numbered.

One reason why Austria-Hungary was reconciled to Bulgaria's success was that the expected Russian protegé of 1878 had turned out to be a great disappointment to the pan-Slavs. Prince Alexander, in particular, proved so dismissive of St Petersburg's tutelage that in 1886 the Russians kidnapped him in the hope of the accession of a more amenable personage to the Bulgarian throne. However, the Bulgarians elected as king Ferdinand of Saxe-Coburg, an Austro-Hungarian favourite and another anti-Russian candidate. The Austro-Russian stand-off allowed Ferdinand to survive and Bismarck to preserve the peace; his policy of using the Dual Alliance of 1879 to deter Russia while restraining Austria-Hungary appeared to be working.[17] European public opinion found it difficult to take seriously these Balkan episodes which supplied plots for Ruritanian romances. The Serb–Bulgarian war was the setting for G.B. Shaw's *Arms and the Man* (1894), a burlesque of the ideology of romantic patriotism; Prince Alexander's kidnapping was the inspiration behind Anthony Hope's adventure story, *The Prisoner of Zenda* (1894) and also Winston

Churchill's single excursion into fiction, *Savrola* (1897). The trivialization of Balkan crises contributed to the complacency with which Europe first greeted that of July 1914 (see Chapter 6). More immediately, the second Bulgarian crisis provoked an international upheaval. It created so much bad blood between St Petersburg and Vienna that the Three Emperors' Alliance expired without renewal in 1887. The destruction of the conservative nucleus of his system plunged Bismarck into a frenzy of diplomatic activity to repair the damage, with the consequence that 'a more complicated chapter of diplomacy than that dealing with the year 1887 could hardly be found in the history of European international relations'.[18]

The German chancellor's problems were exacerbated by the appearance on the French political scene of the charismatic General Boulanger, a Napoleonic 'man on horseback' whose message was that France should turn its gaze away from its overseas empire and back towards Alsace-Lorraine. A popular Boulangist song, besides 'vowing death to the Prussians', also made significant reference to the tsar as a French ally.[19] Despite their contrary political ideologies, Russia and France were edging closer together. Both states found common cause in opposition to Britain in the colonial field, yet as Boulangism demonstrated, a Franco-Russian collaboration against Germany in Europe could no longer be discounted. Boulangism proved a passing phenomenon, but in the meantime Bismarck hastened to repair the wire between Berlin and St Petersburg. The upshot was the Reinsurance Treaty of 18 June 1887 by which both parties promised neutrality if the other was involved in war, save in the case of an attack by Germany on France or by Russia on the Habsburg empire. This last proviso technically squared the Reinsurance Treaty with the Austro-German pact of 1879, and to prove it, Bismarck showed the exact terms of the latter to the Russians. But whether Bismarck's alliances with Austria-Hungary and Russia were morally compatible must be a matter of dispute.[20]

The intricacy of Bismarck's new arrangements did not stop with the Reinsurance Treaty. Five years earlier Italy, piqued at France's seizure of Tunisia from under its nose, applied to join the Austro-German alliance. Bismarck agreed because it freed his Austro-Hungarian ally from the danger of a two-front war. This was no imaginary threat for Rome's primary foreign policy goal was the recovery of 'unredeemed Italy' (*Italia irredenta*), the South Tyrol and Trentino still under Habsburg rule. In other words, the Triple Alliance of 1882 linked Italy uneasily with its 'natural' enemy, and at each renewal of the alliance the Italian price for continued loyalty increased. The first occasion fell in the midst of all Bismarck's other concerns in 1887, when Italy demanded, and obtained, the promise of consultation and compensation in the event of any change of the *status quo* in the Eastern Question.

Given the volatility of the Eastern Question, it behoved Bismarck to make a further bid to maintain stability in the area. During 1887 he instigated two Mediterranean agreements involving Austria-Hungary, Italy and, now that the conservative Marquis of Salisbury had replaced the liberal Gladstone, Great Britain. By these agreements the signatories pledged support of the *status quo* first in the Mediterranean, then in the Near East. They were aimed in turn at curbing France and Russia, although the latter was the principal target.[21] On the other hand, the Reinsurance Treaty committed Bismarck to back Russia in Bulgaria and at the Straits. Thus, the Reinsurance Treaty was at odds with both the Austro-German alliance and the Mediterranean agreements. The German chancellor's system had by 1887 become 'a network of fundamentally contradictory policies. It has nevertheless been regarded as Bismarck's crowning achievement.' Historians have bestowed on his balancing act praise and condemnation in equal measure.[22]

The complex manoeuvres to which Bismarck was driven presaged the end of his dominion over the European states system. His grip faltered precisely because those populist forces against which he had fought for twenty years had now grown almost irresistible. It has been observed that on occasion Bismarck exploited 'public diplomacy' in the course of German unification and in Franco-German war scares. But these were spasmodic and tactical incidents, for Bismarck had no sympathy with the principle of democracy or mass democratic forces. His social values were those of the Prussian *Junker* aristocracy. In domestic politics, despite elections by universal male suffrage to the *Reichstag*, he worked steadfastly and successfully to thwart ministerial responsibility to that same *Reichstag* and thence to the popular will. In like vein, his preference in foreign policy was for cabinet diplomacy, the confinement of international politics to princes, aristocratic statesmen and upper-class career diplomats in the eighteenth-century style. To open the door to democratic opinion was to admit dangerous passion and prejudice. But after 1870 mass politics, first augured in the French Revolution, finally came into its own. Conservatism and liberalism had now to adjust to the new democratic environment, and the relatively novel doctrine of socialism hoped to flourish within it. International relations could not be quarantined. To be specific, the ideology of nationalism was spreading to all ranks of society, sometimes assuming the extremist forms of imperialism and racism. In resisting this populist trend as long as it did, the Bismarckian system was the last hurrah of the *ancien régime*.

POPULIST IDEOLOGIES

Modern democracy, it has been remarked earlier, sprang from two sources: the French Revolution and industrialization. Only after 1870 was the combined effect of the two forces fully realized.

Throughout the nineteenth century the notions of popular sovereignty and the rights of man bequeathed by the revolution spread with gathering momentum. The pace was proportional to the ability of their advocates, the liberals, to establish an ideological hegemony. Liberalism, in spite of its surrender to illiberal nationalism after 1848 carried the day in many other walks of life. The 1870s saw 'the fruition of liberalism' in the shape of *laisser-faire* economics, anticlericalism and the success of liberal parties in burgeoning parliamentary systems.[23] Even old-fashioned conservatives like Bismarck colluded with liberals in these areas. As for the vote, classical liberals held that its exercise called for social responsibility, equated in practice with ownership of property. It would take time and progress to elevate the labouring masses to an appropriate degree of property-holding and trustworthiness that the liberals saw as a prerequisite to full democratic rights. But as the Metternichian conservatives had warned, faith in progress was naïve and events might not wait on progress. Indeed, the fruition of middle-class liberalism signalled the onset of the next stage of political evolution – the rise of the masses. The catalyst was the vast socio-economic change overtaking Europe.

At the opening of the nineteenth century twenty-two European cities had a population of 100,000; by 1895 the number was 120. By 1850 more than half the British population lived in urban areas; by the century's close over four-fifths of the British and half of the German populations lived in cities.[24] This urbanization, the inevitable consequence of the industrial revolution, supplied the physical impetus for modern democracy. The uprooting of millions from their traditional agrarian pursuits and habitat destroyed old loyalties both regional and spiritual, for the churches were administratively geared to serve rural, not urban, communities. Once congregated in factory towns, workers derived comfort and strength from their numbers and closeness. Ease of communication among themselves created a collective awareness and sense of class. Working-class consciousness found many outlets – most notably the trade union movement but also cooperative ventures, workers' educational organizations and a host of self-help schemes. It was but a short step to political organization, often in socialist and labour parties. Democratic agitators and publicists always had before them the example and hortative methods by which the bourgeois liberals of previous generations had won representation and influence. But fundamentally it was the sheer weight of the newly formed urban masses that, in the last quarter of the nineteenth century, gained them a voice in national policy-making.

The involvement of the masses took two main forms. The first was enfranchisement. Political equality of the one-man, one-vote sort was pioneered in the United States where, by the 1830s, it was the norm. In Europe it was heralded in 1867 by the second British parliamentary reform bill, which, though stopping short of universal male suffrage, made its accomplishment only a matter of time. In the period up to 1914, France, Germany, Austria, Italy, Spain, Belgium, Holland, Switzerland, Sweden, Norway, Serbia, Bulgaria, Greece and Turkey – all accepted the principle of a universal male franchise. This did not in many cases guarantee government by the popular will. Nevertheless, at regular intervals millions of ordinary citizens now participated in the ritual, whether meaningful or token, of government-making and breaking. And in prospect was a further increase in the electorate by means of female suffrage, already in place in some American states.

Second, many workers were brought under the protection of compulsory state-sponsored insurance plans. Bismarck was a leader in this 'state socialism', by which he aimed to stave off socialism of the Marxist variety. During the 1880s the *Reichstag* approved insurance against industrial accident, sickness, invalidity and old age. These precedents were widely followed throughout the industrialized world. Such schemes were initially intended to be funded by employer and employee contributions, but the trend ran to increasing use of general revenues for social insurance; the British budget of 1909 and National Insurance Act of 1911 constituted a giant step in this direction. These measures, together with a growing mass of factory inspection laws and labour codes, meant that the national government had a direct impact on the everyday life of ordinary workers in ways unimaginable in their grandparents' day.

Through the vote and the embryonic welfare state, then, the average male worker for the first time in history had a stake in his national community. But in return for his new rights or privileges, he assumed commensurate obligations. He was expected to abide by the law and eschew revolution and, more relevant here, to give unqualified allegiance to his nation state in the international arena, to the point of making the supreme sacrifice, as many did in two world wars. At the very moment democracy promised greater freedom to the citizen, nationalism took it away again.

The historian Heinrich von Treitschke, liberal German nationalist in 1848 and later votary of Bismarckian authoritarianism, put the situation starkly in his celebrated lectures at Berlin University:

Social selfishness and party hatreds must be dumb before the call of the State when its existence is at stake. Forgetting himself, the individual must only remember that he is a part of the whole, and realize the unimportance of his own life compared with the common weal.

The grandeur of war lies in the utter annihilation of puny man in the great conception of the State, for it brings out the full magnificence of the sacrifice of fellow-countrymen for one another. In war the chaff is winnowed from the wheat.[25]

Treitschke's words constitute a classic statement of 'integral nationalism', a variant that 'casts off all ethical ballast, obligating and totally subordinating the individual to one value alone, the nation'. As a concept, integral nationalism has been applied above all to those states that achieved unification late, saw themselves as 'disadvantaged competitors' and, out of a 'collective inferiority complex', developed a peculiarly aggressive nationalism. 'One nation as the Absolute' pointed the way to the totalitarianism, practised or attempted, between the two world wars, in the 'belated nations' of Germany, Italy and perhaps even Japan.[26] Ironically, it was a Frenchman, Charles Maurras, who supposedly coined the phrase integral nationalism.

To seal the compact between democratic rights and national duty three agencies proved particularly useful: schools, the press and the military. 'Universal teaching must precede universal enfranchisement,' wrote that archetypal liberal, John Stuart Mill.[27] In reality, the sequence was reversed. It was political change – the need for the newly enfranchised to be able to read a ballot paper and be conversant with public issues – that sparked the explosion in basic education beginning around 1870. As one parliamentary opponent of the British reform bill said: 'It will be absolutely necessary that you should prevail on our future masters to learn their letters.'[28] Given this civic purpose of mass education, the state demanded control of the process. The 1870s witnessed, besides the establishment of publicly funded school systems, an international drive to curtail the role of private, mostly clerical, foundations; the Prussian *Kulturkampf* was only the most notorious case in point. Church schools survived, even rebounded, but in the main national governments directed what the children of the new electorate should be taught. The French ministry of education went to the extreme of boasting that, at any given moment, the same lesson was being taught everywhere in the country.

Education for citizenship easily translated into instruction in patriotism and exclusive nationalism. Teaching pupils the national anthem was an obvious illustration, the words of the *Marseillaise* being an egregious example of patriotic gore. History and geography were subjects especially susceptible to a nationalist slant. As countless autobiographies have testified, the swathes of red that marked imperial possessions on the world map hanging on classroom walls throughout the British Empire left their stamp on impressionable young minds. An international inquiry into the prejudicial influence of school texts carried out after the First World War highlighted the biased accounts of the origins of the Franco-Prussian

War of 1870 to which pupils in both countries were exposed. The new German nation state was uncommonly anxious to teach nationalism. Emperor William II told a schools conference in 1890: 'It is our duty to educate young men to become Germans, not young Greeks or Romans,' and he urged teachers to develop 'the "National" in questions of history, geography, and heroic tradition'.[29] Probably the most overt instance of patriotic education, however, was to be found in the United States, which were then faced with a swift influx of millions of non-English-speaking immigrants. Great pressure was put on US schools to 'Americanize' the newcomers' offspring; this they did through the use of the English language and the daily pledge of allegiance to the flag. 'The strange and dissimilar races which come to us are, in one generation, assimilated and made Americans,' claimed one US enthusiast. 'The school for the Nation! All education for the nation! Everything for the Nation!' exulted another.[30]

Furthermore, it is important to recognize the limits of mass education in the late nineteenth century. Almost everywhere school attendance was required for no more than a few years and seldom beyond the age of twelve or fourteen. Instruction generally consisted of the three Rs and a smattering of geographical and historical 'facts'. The short and shallow curriculum produced awareness of issues but hardly understanding, not to mention rational enquiry; it was a recipe for 'an increase in gullibility'. 'Schools taught everyone to read and pay attention to what the teacher said. If one read something with one's own eye, one was inclined to believe it; if a licensed teacher vouched for it, it must be true.'[31] In this way, a modicum of education programmed the mass mind to receive nationalist and other ideological messages.[32]

By the end of the nineteenth century the level of literacy in the industrialized world had made a remarkable advance. In round figures, between 80 and 95 per cent of adult Britons, west Europeans, Germans, Scandinavians and white Americans born in the USA could read and write; the comparable figure for the peoples of the Russian empire was 20 per cent. Where the literacy boom occurred, it was a godsend to the newspaper trade; in Europe alone the number of journals doubled in twenty years.[33] But more significant than numerical increase was the change in the style of the popular press in the 1890s. It was no coincidence that this decade, which saw the coming of age of the first mass literate generation, also hatched the so-called 'yellow press', a phrase that, although derived from a comic strip, has stuck because it manages to suggest the tawdriness that was the new journalism's hallmark.

For some years several newspapers had tried to extend their readership beyond the middle classes by reducing their selling price, relying on advertising to balance costs. The yellow-press revolution carried this trend forward but, more momentously, sought a wider circulation by pitching the presentation of news to the lowest common denominator of the literate masses' understanding. Brevity here was the rule; reports and paragraphs were kept short and subservient to headlines in large type. Inevitably issues were simplified and sensationalized. To a certain extent, the content of news changed; crime and gossip received more space. But international relations remained a staple, though trivialized as a matter of course.

In fact, international news proved ideally suited to yellow journalism because it could be combined with another novel topic in the press. Professional sport stemmed from the changing lifestyle of the late nineteenth-century factory worker. While leisure time was increasing, the introduction of assembly-line mechanization suppressed any sense of personal worth and gratification on the shopfloor. Commercialized football and baseball arose and flourished in urban centres to fill the empty weekend with excitement and colour lacking in the workplace and drab townscape. The spectators were invited to lose themselves in partisanship for their team; fanatic supporters became fans. In parallel fashion, the yellow press now encouraged them to cheer for their team in the greater game of international competition, especially in the contest for empire. Bismarck's reference to colonial skirmishes as little 'sporting' wars was not out of place.[34]

Yellow journalism was most spectacularly successful in the English-speaking world. In 1895 William Randolph Hearst bought the *New York World* and immediately set out to challenge Joseph Pulitzer's *New York Journal*, already known for its sensationalism. The *World* and the *Journal* vied with each other in scurrility and bellicose American nationalism. Their inflammatory reportage of Cuban unrest and the sinking of the US battleship *Maine* in Havana harbour shaped US popular opinion, which in turn propelled Washington into the Spanish–American War (1898) and the subsequent annexation of the Philippines. Britain had its counterparts, notably the *Daily Mail*, launched by Kennedy Jones and Alfred Harmsworth in 1896 to be 'the Voice of Empire in London journalism'. Not to be outdone, the rival *Daily Express* announced in its first issue in 1900: 'Our policy is patriotic; our faith is the British Empire.'[35] Needless to say, Britain's yellow press enthusiastically backed war against the Boers (1899–1902) and can be held accountable for much of the populist jingoism expressed at the time. London's dominance of British journalism gave the *Daily Mail* and *Daily Express* circulation figures and a notoriety that no continental paper could match, which is not to say, though, that sensationalist and xenophobic journalism was absent in the more fragmented markets of the European nations. One historian has listed 'the poisoning of public opinion by the newspaper press' among the major causes of the First World War.[36]

Lastly, young adult males on the Continent were liable to an additional dose of indoctrination. Prussia's victories in 1866 and 1870 appeared to teach the lesson that a mass army of civilians in uniform could henceforth overwhelm a small professional force. This short-sighted conclusion (the *Landwehr* was far from being the sole reason for Sadowa and Sedan) led the European states, large and small, to enact or extend their own systems of compulsory military service. Even modernizing Japan joined the stampede in 1873; of the major powers only Britain and the US eschewed conscription. By the dawn of the twentieth century exemption from conscription was reduced or abolished altogether as all the European states embraced the French ideal of 1793, the 'nation in arms'. The consequence was militarism in the sense of 'the excessive permeation of civil society with the military outlook and behaviour values', a transnational phenomenon, though 'strikingly evident' in Prussianized Germany.[37]

A term of two or more years with the colours, followed by several more in the reserves, amounted by definition to a further tuition in nationalistic culture. Indeed, in France the proselytizing influence of professional military officers on raw conscripts grew into a *cause célèbre*. The controversy arose not over any nationalist message, but rather the monarchist and clerical views disseminated by the highly conservative officer corps. When, in the Dreyfus affair (1894–9), the latter came into open conflict with the Third Republic and lost, retribution followed. A witch hunt of allegedly anti-republican officers hurt France militarily, but the minister of war gloried at one and the same time in the army's new political correctness and its educative function: 'The regiment is more than a family. It is a school. The officer is the extension of the teacher, the nation's instructor.'[38]

The late nineteenth century, therefore, brought about a conjunction of those two socio-economic factors that the theorists of nationalism have identified as its twin generators. On the one hand, the so-called second industrial revolution created a social climate in which collective thinking and action flourished more or less spontaneously. On the other, the national power structures, through elementary education, the press and conscription, subjected the masses to a barrage of patriotic propaganda. As a result of this potent combination, the old dichotomy between state and people began to fade away; hence integral nationalism. Even in France, where popular nationalism was nothing new, the process of nationalizing the masses was carried further as peasants were transformed into Frenchmen.[39]

All this was Metternich's nightmare of 1815 brought to life, for the popular nationalism whipped up by the Jacobins had known no bounds. The romantic Mazzinian nationalism of 1815–48 had been tempered by deference to humanity and universalism; the *Realpolitik* manipulation of nationalism between 1848 and 1870 had kept plebian excitability under control. But the genie was now out of the bottle. Democratic nationalism, like that of 1793–4 in France, would be excessive, frenzied and intolerant. 'My country, right or wrong' moved nationalism another step away from simple patriotism and further in the direction of a mass fanatical ideology. It was not by mere chance that crowd or mob psychology entered the realm of social scientific study in the late nineteenth century.[40]

The ideological temper of the new nationalism was soon disclosed by its deviation into the byways of racism and imperialism. The attraction of these collateral 'isms' owed much to the cult of Darwinism spawned by the publication of Charles Darwin's *Origin of Species* (1859). Within the next fifteen years a stream of books appeared by such natural scientists as T.H. Huxley, Ernst Haeckel and Darwin himself 'underscoring the essential oneness of the human race with other animals and with plants'.[41] The explicit application of the biological 'laws' of natural selection – struggle for existence, survival of the fittest and evolution – to human transactions was the work of Social Darwinists; for example, Herbert Spencer, 'Darwin's bulldog' in Britain, Ludwig Gumplowicz on the Continent, and William Graham Sumner in the USA. But perhaps just as important in the dawning age of democracy as the Darwinian vogue among the intelligentsia was its 'trickle-down' effect. A vulgarized Darwinism percolated throughout all levels of public opinion. In part, this can be attributed to the reduction of the cosmic mysteries to a simple formula composed of a few easily understood natural laws. In addition, the popularity of Darwinism also appeared to derive from its easy justification of the drift of western society in the 1860s towards competitiveness; the law of the jungle rationalized *laisser-faire* economic practices and *Realpolitik* international rivalries. When the yellow press later in the century embraced undiluted Social Darwinism, it was to an extent preaching to the converted.

Disputatious international relations offered an activity ripe for Social Darwinian analysis, with the nation state taking the part of Darwin's species. But there seemed a more exact and biological equivalent – the ethnic or racial group. Moreover, Darwin himself, however unwittingly, encouraged this parallelism, because the subtitle of his seminal work 'made a convenient motto for racists': *The Preservation of Favoured Races in the Struggle for Life.*[42] Significantly, Darwin's own notoriety caused the Comte de Gobineau's hitherto obscure four tomes *Sur l'inégalité des races humaines* (1853–5) to vault into prominence.

One of the first fruits of the racism fostered by Darwin and his theory, then, was the flowering of the pan movements – parties and factions based on ethnic identification. In some ways, these were throwbacks to the romantic, cultural nationalisms of the earlier nineteenth century, and they betrayed the same messianic tendencies. None more so than pan-Slavism, which made its advance in Russia against the backdrop of a campaign to modernize the country in the wake of the Crimean defeat. In some ways pan-Slavism was a reaction against the liberalizing measures of Tsar Alexander II, for it took much of its inspiration from traditional Slavophile culture, which was exalted by writers such as Dostoevsky and by the group of five nationalist composers improbably christened 'the mighty handful' (*moguchaya kuchka*). Political pan-Slavism, though, found its high priest in a scientist, Nikolai Danilevsky, whose *Russia and Europe* (1871) soon became the authoritative statement of the old Slavophile argument for the superiority of Russian over Western civilization. Danilevsky went beyond 'a historical cultural concept' to imagine a veritable pan-Slav union whose hypothetical boundaries coincided roughly with the future Stalinist empire of 1945. Furthermore, he happily contemplated a war with the West as 'the only way to heal our Russian cultural disease and to develop Pan-Slav sympathies'.[43] The Slavophiles had always tended to be purblind in their beliefs; Darwinian natural law confirmed them in their ideological certitudes.

Pan-Slavism and pan-Germanism were symbiotically linked in mutual antipathy. Danilevsky's pan-Slavic bible was intended as a response to German unification. In turn, many Germans eagerly espoused the Aryan myth propounded in Houston Stewart Chamberlain's *Foundations of the Nineteenth Century* (1899). On the political plane, Habsburg alarm at pan-Slavic rumblings in the eastern crisis of 1875–8 fractured the *Dreikaiserbund* and, as we have seen, pushed Bismarck towards the Austrian alliance with its whisper of pan-Germanism. So long as Bismarck was in control, though, pan-Germanism would play no role in German foreign policy. It was not until 1891, after the iron chancellor's fall, that a pan-German league was formally inaugurated, and even then its initial aim was colonial expansion as much as an *omnium gatherum* of all Teutons in Europe.[44] On the other hand, as the Dual Alliance dragged Germany deeper into the Balkan morass in the years leading up to the First World War, Berlin and Vienna presented what looked very like a pan-German front against Slavdom. In St Petersburg pan-Slav leverage on Russian foreign policy waxed and waned over the years, but on the eve of the First World War it was not to be discounted. It would be too fanciful to interpret the outbreak of war in 1914 as a straightforward collision of two major ethnic movements, but they contributed to the confrontational mood of the day (see Chapter 6).

A variety of other tribal doctrines, some on the bizarre side, indicate the prevalence of racial thinking at the opening of the twentieth century. Pan-Mongolianism was supposed to express the aspirations of the yellow races, pan-Turanianism those of a historical racial community of Finns, Magyars and Turks. Pan-Islam was first heard from. A vague Anglo-Saxonism was mooted in 1898 to construct an ideological platform for a British–American–German diplomatic alignment that never materialized. More successful was the United States' use of pan-Americanism to regulate the economies and politics of its Latin neighbours on the grounds of Social Darwinian fitness.

Social Darwinism and race came together again in the 'new imperialism', the European powers' scramble to appropriate the remaining uncolonized areas of the globe in Africa and Asia. As official policy, extra-European imperialism had fallen out of favour in the early nineteenth century following the collapse of empire in the American hemisphere. Not that the colonial drive ceased altogether; the British empire flourished and grew, albeit in an 'informal' and mostly non-political manner.[45] What was new about end-of-the-century imperialism was the unprecedented enthusiasm of both peoples and governments in more nations than had ever before indulged in overseas empire. Moreover, whereas earlier empires had been built on white settlement, the new colonies were located in zones often unsuitable for European habitation. The principal material motive remaining was economic exploitation. The new imperialism, in fact, coincided with serious economic difficulties in the industrialized world, although whether that made it merely an economic episode is far from proven.

The great depression of 1873 and further economic downturns in the next two decades spelled the demise of mid-nineteenth-century *laisser faire*. European businessmen, especially in newly industrializing countries without ready access to traditional world markets, and farmers hurt by the import of cheap grain and refrigerated meat from the Americas and the Antipodes looked to national governments for help. This arrived in the shape of protective tariffs and government contracts. The more each nation's economy became exclusionary, the more the Social Darwinian notion of incessant struggle among nation states was reinforced. This economic nationalism revivified the seventeenth- and eighteenth-century mercantilist view of colonies as mere adjuncts to the national economy, a means of serving the mother country's prosperity. Similarly, the neo-mercantilism of the late nineteenth century depicted overseas possessions as an opportunity to escape economic depression at home. The new imperialism was to open up new markets, raw material supplies and, above all, outlets for surplus capital investment.

Marxists have interpreted the new imperialism as a crisis of capitalism brought on by overproduction and marked by a shift from entrepreneurship to finance and monopoly capitalism. Building on J.A. Hobson's *Imperialism* (1902) and Rudolf Hilferding's *Das Finanzkapital* (1910), V.I. Lenin gave this view definitive form in his *Imperialism, The Highest Stage of Capitalism* (1916). Responding to the wartime environment, Lenin argued that, when the 'colonial policy of monopolistic possession' had produced a 'world which has been completely divided up', the internal contradictions of capitalism and its national rivalries would return to Europe. Thus, 1914 marked the outbreak of an imperialist, capitalist war. This monocausal exposition of events has not fared well under non-partisan scrutiny, which has found its basic premise flawed. The statistics show that the business community profited only marginally from the new colonies and by and large was reluctant to invest in them. Admittedly, this might simply mean that the bankers and industrialists, who lobbied for empire, discovered their expectations to be misplaced. More to the point, close examination of the specific steps by which each of the major powers expanded its formal empire reveals much more non-economic than economic motivation at work.[46]

In truth, the same demons that were whipping up popular nationalism also stimulated the imperialist 'fever'. As early as 1919, Josef Schumpeter took direct aim at the economic interpretation of the new imperialism. Capitalism, being a rational exercise, could not be responsible for 'object-less tendencies toward forcible expansion, without definite utilitarian limits – that is, non-rational and irrational, purely instinctual inclinations toward war and conquest'. The blame was laid at the door of 'atavistic' and 'instinctual tendencies' which, he optimistically forecast, were disappearing with the advance of civilization.[47] Schumpeter's atavistic tendency sounds very like the unthinking pursuit of national glory for its own sake which captivated the late nineteenth-century masses. As movements engaging the enthusiasm of whole national communities, non-rational or ideological modes of thought were necessary to make both popular nationalism and the new imperialism tick.

Imperialism, however, was in some ways a more potent ideology than nationalism. As the ethnic movements demonstrated, the Darwinian hierarchical doctrine was more conveniently applied to race than to nations. Consequently, it vindicated the imposition of white, Western culture on the brown and yellow races. Indeed, it could be taken further to mandate the process for the betterment of all humankind, out of which doctrine grew the genus of 'ethical imperialism'. A paternalistic attitude to the indigenous inhabitants of the colonies corresponded to the upper-class paternalism at home that brought about the first worker insurance programmes. At the core of the new imperialism, then, there existed a sense of mission, 'a group of ideologies . . . within the framework of traditional civilization, systems of thought with a humanitarian, idealist or Christian cast'.[48] This missionary urge, in both the religious and secular sense, gave imperialism a moral dimension and appeal. At the worst, it allowed nationalists to cloak selfish interests in the mantle of the service of humanity. Ideology is ever the more effective for being supranational.

A brief glance at three of the nation states involved in the colonial race reveals that the new imperialism was a compound of all the above factors – economic exigency, national pride and sense of mission. Intermixed, they exercised a powerful attraction on the least likely nation state. Bismarckian Germany, a continental power *par excellence*, adopted an official colonial policy in 1884. Bismarck did so, not to create a global empire, but to safeguard specific German economic interests in East Africa and to cause trouble for his British *bête noire*, Gladstone. But he quickly came to regret his embrace of colonialism because it merely whetted the appetite of the colonial lobby and the sort of cosmic ambition voiced by Treitschke: 'We want and ought to claim our share in the domination of the earth by the white race.' 'My map of Africa lies in Europe,' was the German chancellor's response. 'Here lies Russia and here lies France, and we are in the middle. That is my map of Africa.'[49] None the less, world politics or *Weltpolitik*, not Bismarckian concentration on Europe, was to be the wave of the future in Germany.

The case of the United States, another newcomer to the colonial game, again illustrates the multifaceted nature of the new imperialism. In a rapidly industrializing country big business pressure for overseas outlets was visible in Washington's espousal of the principle of the commercial open door, especially in China.[50] However, political and ideological factors were equally evident. Alfred T. Mahan's *Influence of Sea Power on History* (1890) played an incalculable role in persuading the US to join the imperialist parade. Furthermore, the creed of manifest destiny, previously evident in the mid-nineteenth-century annexation of Texas and the post-Civil War threat to Canada, was now applied beyond the American hemisphere. The deliberate export of American values was at open variance with the pristine and isolationist intent to serve as freedom's beacon to inspire the rest of the world. As such, manifest destiny has been castigated as a perversion of the United States' true mission: 'Manifest Destiny and imperialism were traps into which the nation was led in 1846 and 1899.' For all that, the urge to carry the American message abroad rooted itself deep in the national psyche during the age of the new imperialism. A 'dominant vision equating the cause of liberty with the active pursuit of national greatness' proved a heady brew.[51] It would become the ideological rationale for the US role in twentieth-century world affairs.

The familiar interplay of material and idealist motives manifested itself as well in the most venerable of imperialist nations. In Britain the Tory party entered the 1906 election on a platform of partial 'tariff reform', by which was intended an imperial and preferential trading bloc.[52] The Tory defeat could hardly disguise the leverage exerted by economic protectionist interests in an age of imperialism in the very homeland of *laisser faire*. At the same time, the note of ethical imperialism was struck more insistently in late Victorian and Edwardian Britain than anywhere else. Kipling regarded the British empire as the trustee of a divine purpose:

> God of our fathers, known of old,
> Lord of our far-flung battle-line,
> Beneath whose awful Hand we hold
> Dominion over palm and pine.

The British public school was a prime vehicle for instilling the lesson of imperial duty into the ruling classes. 'The boys of today are the statesmen and administrators of tomorrow,' said the headmaster of Harrow. 'In their hands is the future of the British Empire. May they prove themselves not unworthy of the solemn charge!' As for those lower down the social scale, the British class system and habit of deference ensured that 'Britain's unique imperial mission . . . was apparent to all'.[53]

The struggle to carve out and retain overseas empire could not fail to have an impact on great power alignments. Not for nothing have international relations of the 1890s been called 'the diplomacy of imperialism'.[54] It has already been noticed how a colonial quarrel with France over Tunisia caused Italy to throw in its lot with Germany and Austria-Hungary, thus setting up the Triple Alliance in 1882. As we shall see later, extra-European issues contributed even more to the building of the countervailing organism, the Triple Entente. Imperialism thus rebounded on Europe to create the bipolar balance that made the Continent such a dangerous place before 1914.

The whole complex of popular nationalism and imperialism, Social Darwinism and racism posed a challenge to the traditional nineteenth-century forces of right and left. Conservatism and liberalism catered for the interests and beliefs of the propertied classes, not mass opinion. Yet, in necessarily adjusting to the new democratic environment, the conservatives had certain intrinsic advantages. In the first place, conservative political philosophy before and since Burke regarded society as an organic unit, holding the individual's worth to be best preserved within a communal framework. Conservatives therefore had little compunction about implementing the collectivist ideologies of the late nineteenth century. It was generally men of the right, the Bismarcks and Disraelis, who promoted labour legislation and social insurance schemes. The conservatives, in fact, were trading on their lineal descent from the old agrarian aristocracy by updating ancient nostrums to suit the age of democracy. The early welfare state was old-fashioned *noblesse oblige*, with the state instead of the aristocracy dispensing charity. In the patriotic and imperialist field also the conservatives were able to exploit their patrician affiliation. Under the *ancien régime* the profession of arms was a conventional upper-class career, and as empire and nationalist expansion predicated war, conservatives appeared the natural champions of these causes.

Liberalism, by contrast, was hamstrung by its mid-century legacy. *Laisser faire* had a declining clientele. Some business interests, seduced by economic nationalism, deserted liberal groups and parties, while those who remained liberals and cited Darwin to justify freedom of contract between employer and employee antagonized the working class. Likewise, in international affairs, the internationalist visions of the 1848 liberals, of Cobden and Gladstone, were totally out of tune with the emotional mood of popular xenophobia. The dilemma of liberalism, squeezed between a new socialist left and a resurgent right, was reflected in the violation of classical liberal tenets by self-styled liberal statesmen in pursuit of mass support. David Lloyd George in Britain and Giovanni Giolitti in Italy accepted the principle of state intervention in the economy. Still more liberals submitted to the prevailing nationalism and imperialism. The German National Liberals had made their surrender in 1866. Twenty years later, those British liberals who could not swallow Gladstone's home rule for Ireland were proud to call themselves Liberal Imperialists and went on to join the Conservative Unionists. Giolitti took Italy into a colonial war for Libya in 1911. Lloyd George, vociferous critic of the Boer War, and Georges Clemenceau, liberal advocate of individual rights in the Dreyfus affair, both turned into nationalistic war leaders, in which capacity they showed scant regard for personal liberties.

Conservative success in cornering the nationalist-imperialist market and in co-opting prominent liberals, and even socialists, has given rise to the quasi-conspiratorial diagnosis of 'social imperialism'. Trotsky was the first to use the phrase sarcastically to describe social democratic support of the war efforts of 1914. But more recent interpretations concentrate on the rallying of elements in the national power structures faced with the consequences of democratization, and on their manipulation of imperialism so as to avert genuine change at home. In this scenario parliamentarianism was ineffectual and conservative social legislation a mere paternalistic placebo in lieu of real egalitarian measures. Imperialism allegedly operated as a diversion from class differences by sustaining domestic prosperity despite uneven economic growth and by persuading the masses to take satisfaction in national prestige.

The concept of social imperialism has transnational relevance but has been applied most cogently to two imperialist nations – Britain and Germany. In Britain the combination of cross- and above-party groups, although decidedly right-wing, was less overtly preoccupied with the maintenance of the social structure than with the development of 'national efficiency'. The fruition of this social imperialism was Lloyd George's wartime coalition of 1916.[55] More attention has been focused on the phenomenon in the second German *Reich*. There, it has been argued, 'manipulated social imperialism' grew out of Bismarck's revolution from above, and out of the conservative reconciliation he effected in 1879 between big business and large-scale agriculture. This alliance of 'steel and rye' provided the nucleus of the cartel of elites that exploited imperialism as a 'taming' policy to preserve their own status. Social imperialism constituted 'an ideology of integration which could be deliberately applied from above to combat the antagonisms of German class society'.[56] Whether Bismarck should bear responsibility for German social imperialism is debatable, for

106

its heyday came in the 1890s when Berlin embarked on thoroughgoing *Weltpolitik*.[57]

Any *tour d'horizon* of late nineteenth-century nationalism and imperialism must make mention of a concurrent revolution in the realm of higher thought. In the 1890s a cluster of social scientists and philosophers, though working independently of each other, arrived at a concerted critique of the narrow positivist methodology of enquiry and the pseudo-scientific certitudes it bred; hence one target was fatalistic Social Darwinism. At the forefront of this intellectual revolution was the 'recovery of the unconscious' as a mainspring of human action. Yet, with the notable exception of the revolutionary syndicalist Georges Sorel, none of the intellectual giants had at the time any intent to preach a philosophy of social or political action.[58] Nevertheless, as happened with Darwin, certain followers of Nietzsche, Freud, Bergson *et al.* were eager to translate their ideas into praxis.

Seizing on recent investigations into the non-rational, some became 'frank irrationalists'. For the most part, this 'generation of 1905' was made up not so much of scholars as of writers and artists – Maurras, Barrès and Péguy in France, the Futurists in Italy. They constituted a neoromantic movement, and like the earlier romantics, they extolled nationalism and glorified war and empire as theatre for the display of the noblest human sentiments.[59] This was essentially the same attitude as that of countless upper-middle-class young men who acclaimed the outbreak of the war in 1914 as a release from the bourgeois materialism of the second industrial revolution. The poetic voice of this soon-to-be-lost generation, Rupert Brooke, rhapsodized that now 'the central purpose of my life, the thing God wants of me, is to get good at beating Germans . . . I'm the happiest person in the world'.[60]

It must be granted that the influence of the 1890s' intellectual revolution was strictly limited; Social Darwinism was in the air everywhere, social Freudianism awaited the mid-twentieth century. Perhaps the Freudian revolution should be seen not as a contribution to the spirit of the age but its mirror. Were the anti-positivists and neoromantics creatures of their own environment, whose writings were simply reverberations of the irrational and emotional political fashions of the day? If so, they were no different from the statesmen and diplomats who, on the surface, ran international affairs in 1914. Overwhelmingly, these were drawn from the same aristocracy, or at least *haute bourgeoisie*, as their predecessors a hundred years earlier.[61] They subscribed to the international values nurtured in the eighteenth century – the Concert of Europe, balance of power, cabinet diplomacy, limited war. But they were no longer their own masters. In an age of democracy the professional diplomats were buffeted by mass nationalist passions, whether they realized it or not. Social imperialist elites inculcated such feelings from above, whereupon, in the style of

Frankenstein's monster, they in turn propelled the decision-makers along the road to Armageddon. In contrast, parliamentary regimes were naturally susceptible to popular nationalist pressures from below, often exerted by well-organized pressure groups. The independence of a foreign minister was curtailed by his party's need to win the next election and that of his ambassadors by the invention of the telegraph. The international atmosphere *in toto*, the entire weight of Social Darwinian popular consciousness, all the 'unspoken assumptions' before 1914, now militated against the practice of old-fashioned cosmopolitan diplomacy.[62]

COUNTER-NATIONALIST IDEOLOGIES

The dangers that democratic nationalism and imperialism implanted in international relations are more apparent with hindsight than they were at the time. What soothed most contemporary qualms was a naïve faith in the idea of automatic progress. This was a direct inheritance of the Enlightenment's exaggeration of the power of human intelligence, reinforced by the stupendous technological achievements of nineteenth-century science, and confirmed by Darwinian evolutionary theory, which implied moral as well as material advance.[63] The idea of progress, 'despite its vagueness, . . . became part of the general mental outlook and for many years provided the basis for a working faith of great vitality'.[64] Against this collective self-confidence, voices raised in warning and dissent waged an uphill struggle.

Such was the fate of the peace movement that emerged at the close of the nineteenth century. On this topic scholars have found it useful to make a distinction between pacifism and pacificism. Pacifism, strictly speaking, has always been the preserve of individuals who, on grounds of religion or conscience, cannot sanction the taking of life in any circumstances. Since they are absolutists, their position might be called ideological. Their main achievement has been to make conscientious objection to military service respectable and legitimate in certain parts of the world, but otherwise their influence on international relations has been imperceptible. Pacificism, for its part, is more concerned with peace advocacy in a sociopolitical context. It preaches institutional reform to prevent or abolish war, and 'it can thus be derived from any "reforming" philosophy – from, for example, liberalism, radicalism, socialism'. Although often urged with ideological fervour, pacificism also implies a partial acceptance of the realities of international competitiveness. In practice, it countenances war for just or defensive purposes, and has therefore sometimes been called 'patriotic' or 'political pacifism'.[65] This was the tradition set by the *philosophe* critics of eighteenth-century Machiavellianism and carried forward in the next century by the liberal internationalists who followed Mazzini, Cobden and Gladstone. Pacificism or internationalism,

108

a virtually synonymous term, was the driving force behind the pre-1914 peace movement.

It was not only the rise of popular nationalism that gave the pacificistic internationalists cause for alarm. In the age of neomercantilism governments found it expedient to stimulate burgeoning national industries by armaments contracts. The resultant arms race suggested that the next war would be far more destructive than the recent limited conflicts. An impressive six-volume work by Ivan Bloch, first published in Russia and entitled *The Future of War* (1898), argued that war had become 'impossible except at the price of suicide' and, for good measure, threw in the prospect of a 'convulsion in the social order'.[66] Bloch, an East European entrepreneur, gained the ear of Tsar Nicholas II and his foreign minister, not least because Russia was under severe economic strain to keep up in the arms race. Out of a mix of principle and political calculation, St Petersburg launched an initiative for an international conference to consider some arms limitation and the arbitration of international disputes. Twenty-six nations convened at The Hague from May to July 1899, but none of the great powers had any sympathy for Russia's modest proposals. All endorsed the pious resolution that 'the restriction of military budgets is highly desirable for the moral and material benefit of humanity', but the steps to accomplish this were deferred to 'further study'.[67] A scheme for an international arbitral tribunal to sit at The Hague was agreed, but only with the proviso that the tribunal should have no power to compel arbitration. A further Hague Conference in 1907, attended by forty-four states, was similarly devoid of concrete achievement. Rather than promoting internationalism, the Hague Conferences exposed the debility of the international concert in the face of forceful self-centred nationalism.

The new literacy and the regard paid to public opinion in the age of democracy meant that the peace movement had little difficulty in putting out its message; it was simply that it went largely unheeded. The case of the pseudonymous Norman Angell is instructive. In 1909 this British journalist published a pamphlet, *Europe's Optical Illusion*, which appeared the following year in expanded form as *The Great Illusion*. The illusion of the title was that modern war could bring profit to any party, victor or vanquished – essentially the same homily as preached by Bloch. Angell built his case on the interdependence of all national economies; war would bring down the universal economic structure on everyone's head. Due to Angell's racy style and prowess in self-advertisement, *The Great Illusion* became an instant bestseller – two million copies sold by 1913 in several languages – and in due course helped to win its author the Nobel Peace Prize. The peace movement rallied behind the book. Yet, there is reason to believe that its impact was the exact opposite of what was intended. If none benefited from war, nobody in a rational world would

109

start one. And a world populated by rational creatures making enlightened decisions was the very premise on which the pervasive idea of progress rested. To stress war's irrationality in this sanguine climate of opinion was to teach not so much that war would be catastrophic but that its outbreak was impossible; reasonable capitalists would not permit it. In this sense, Angell 'psychologically disarmed' both the peace movement and a wider public.[68] Complacency was not a negligible factor in bringing on war in 1914.

However ineffectual in its day, the peace movement at the turn of the century pointed ahead to the later popularity of anti-war and internationalist ideologies – after the Great War had proved Bloch and Angell correct. Pointers to the future were strongest where a tradition of liberal internationalism was most firmly entrenched, namely in Britain. There, from the opening of the twentieth century, a group of radicals and disaffected liberals mounted a captious examination of British policy. They directed their fire at ever-rising naval expenditures and colonial policy. Moreover, they revived the critique, first voiced by Paine and Bentham, of the secrecy in which diplomatic decisions were shrouded. Their strictures reached a high pitch around 1912 as rumours of clandestine Anglo-French military and naval pledges abounded. Here was the genesis of the campaign for democratic or open diplomacy that found its niche in US President Wilson's programme for the reform of international politics in the aftermath of the First World War.[69]

The pacificistic opposition to popular nationalism and armaments was both moral and pragmatic; the socialist censure was more firmly grounded in ideology. All the major socialist movements, with the exception of the British and the American, culled their doctrines from the writings of Karl Marx. But on nationalism, war and peace, the master was somewhat ambiguous. At least two paradigms can be traced.[70] Up to 1848 Marx appeared to believe that nationalism was alien to the working class and would vanish with the success of proletarian revolution. Such was the inference to be drawn from the famous remark in the *Communist Manifesto* (1848) that 'the workers have no country to defend, you cannot take from them what they have not got'. But in the remaining thirty-five years of his life Marx could not avoid the evidence of popular national feeling, and he took to arguing that it constituted part of the superstructure of bourgeois society and a phase through which it was necessary to pass. Nationalism in an advanced country was a sign that history was unfolding as it should, bringing revolution nearer; but the same sentiment in 'peasant nations' was dismissed as irrelevant. The prototype of the former was German unification, which Marx applauded, although as a Rhinelander he resented the role played by Prussian militarism. Conversely, he was scathing about most Slavic nationalisms and, significantly, he endorsed the efforts of the united Germany, deemed a bourgeois state, to hold feudal Russia in check. The two Marxian paradigms are not irreconcilable. Both sprang from an economic determinism, and both anticipated the day when the 'vertical division' into nations would yield to the 'horizontal division' of classes.[71]

All the above facets of Marxism found their way into the experiments in international socialist cooperation. The First Socialist International (1864–76) was bedevilled by arguments between Marx and the anarchists who, like the romantics, had a touching faith in the innate goodness of man to solve the problems of national rivalries – a view totally at variance with Marxian scientific socialism. Even so, the First International was united in condemning current global politics. Much more important was the Second International. Not only was it larger, encompassing all manner of socialists, but its founding in 1889 coincided almost exactly with the rise of popular nationalism and imperialism. From the outset, the Second International concerned itself with the danger of the masses being swept up in what Marx on more than one occasion had referred to as 'foreign policies in pursuit of criminal designs, playing upon national prejudices and squandering the people's blood and treasure'.[72] Therefore, the International regularly approved resolutions condemning military expenditures and standing armies, which were adjudged instruments of domestic tyranny and aggression abroad. For national defence socialists advocated a people's militia along the lines pioneered by the American revolutionaries and taken up by the French in 1793 and the Germans in 1813; in socialist lore a popular force could not by definition commit aggression.

It was the rise of a revisionist or reformist Marxism, however, that made the deepest impression on late nineteenth-century socialism's attitude to war and peace. The reformists' readiness to support governments that promised worker legislation, even to the point of entering a bourgeois cabinet, meant that the nation state had begun to absorb not only the proletariat but some of its self-styled leaders as well. In 1904, at the Amsterdam Congress of the Second International, the issue of reformism was thrashed out and the orthodox Marxist repudiation of reformism won a majority. Similarly, at Stuttgart in 1907, when the question of socialist backing for a bourgeois state in an international quarrel came to a head, the hardliners were able to reassert the principle of non-cooperation:

> Should war break out . . . it is their [socialists'] duty to intercede for its speedy end, and to strive with all their power to make use of the violent economic and political crisis brought about by the war to rouse the people, and thereby to hasten the abolition of capitalist class rule.[73]

Here was a hint that war might serve as the catalyst for proletarian revolution, a doctrine to be developed later by both the syndicalists and the Bolshevik Lenin.

111

But the Amsterdam and Stuttgart resolutions were paper triumphs for the orthodox Marxists. In practice, most socialist parties continued to pursue an evolutionary road to socialism by constitutional means, and in foreign affairs they often championed the national interest. It was indicative that the Second International, in spite of the bravado at Stuttgart and other congresses, never formally approved the use of the general strike in the event of war. This was partly out of fear of inciting a repressive state apparatus, but it also indicated that many socialists envisaged a case in which they might want to enlist in the national cause.

In all this the members of the International took their cue from the strongest and outwardly most successful socialist party – the *Sozialistische Partei Deutschlands* (SPD). By 1912 the SPD polled over four million votes to emerge with 110 seats as the biggest party in the *Reichstag*. Although German conservatives equated socialism with revolution, the impressive electoral figures suggest how completely the SPD was being integrated into the political structure and society of the second *Reich*. One clear token of this was the party's adoption of traditional German nationalist values. Like their liberal forbears of 1848, the German socialists combined arrogance towards the Slavs with a fearful hatred of tsarist autocracy. Marx had bequeathed his own legacy of anti-Slavism, which, after his death, Engels reiterated forcefully to both the SPD and the early Second International. In 1893 August Bebel, the orthodox Marxist leader of the SPD, castigated Russia as 'the champion of cruelty and barbarity, the enemy of all human culture', and opined that in the event of a Russian attack, 'we are as much and more interested than those who stand at the head of Germany, and we should resist Russia, for a Russian victory means the defeat of social democracy.' And a few years later, 'If it came to a war with Russia . . . I would be ready, old boy that I am, to shoulder a gun against her.' Many emigrés from tsarist oppression made their way into the SPD, especially after the failed Russian revolution of 1905, and embroidered the image of Russia as socialism's principal enemy.[74]

German socialists revealed their nationalist proclivities in other directions too. In conversations with their French counterparts the most they would concede on Alsace-Lorraine was autonomy, not return of the lost provinces. French socialists responded in kind. Thus Jean Jaurès, ardent anti-militarist that he was, observed that 'those Frenchmen, if there are any left, who say that it is all the same to them whether they live under French troopers or German troopers . . . commit a sophism which by its very absurdity makes its refutation difficult.'[75] Nevertheless, the nationalist trendsetter in international socialism continued to be the SPD which seemed to grow more bellicose with time. In 1913 the party voted for the annual military expenditure bill, albeit on the excuse that the money was to be raised by progressive taxation. Finally, when the moment of truth arrived in 1914 and the Russian bogey was invoked, opinion within the

SPD was overwhelmingly in favour of voting for war credits. The French socialists, deprived of the leadership of Jaurès, who had been assassinated by a nationalist fanatic, followed suit, and so did the majority of socialists throughout Europe. 'Social imperialists', 'social patriots', 'social chauvinists' were some of the taunts hurled by the stubborn but outnumbered left-wingers who resisted the call to arms.

In the struggle for the hearts and minds of the masses nationalism won a resounding victory over the international brotherhood of the working classes almost everywhere in 1914. In the process the Second International was cast into oblivion. The socialist failure stemmed at least in part from the evident gulf between precept and practice, for to the end the official doctrine of the International made no concession to either revisionism or nationalism. The refusal to countenance such realities was the acme of ideological thinking. In terms of ideological theory, socialism showed itself less malleable than other nineteenth-century creeds. Conservatism and even liberalism came to terms more easily with the new democracy, the one by promoting variants of social imperialism, the other out of deference to representative institutions and opinion. But mainstream, that is Marxian, socialism could not and would not grant the possibility of genuine democracy within a capitalist system. Equally, it found it hard to take cognizance of workers' new-found partisanship for their respective nation states. Moreover, the catastrophe of 1914 did not shake Marxist socialism out of its dialectical rigidity. After the First World War it assumed the form of the 'total' ideology of Marxism–Leninism.

Although the anti-war agitation before 1914 by both socialists and pacificists was ineffectual, the two movements none the less set the stage for the postwar clash of international ideologies. While orthodox Marxists rallied to Lenin, liberal critics of power politics put their hopes in Woodrow Wilson. Leninism and Wilsonianism would offer a war-torn world two starkly different prescriptions for a new international order.

6

IDEOLOGY AND THE GREAT WAR

IDEOLOGY AND A BIPOLAR BALANCE

Most histories of the twentieth century begin in 1914. However, there are plenty of reasons to regard 1890 as a more realistic point of departure for the new century, and certainly so in the field of international politics. It was in 1890 that Europe started on the road to the First World War.[1]

Bismarck's forced resignation in that year followed hard on the accession of William II to the German throne. Such was the 'dread or reverence' in which the iron chancellor was held that every European chancellery registered the shock. Moreover, the new emperor promised a 'new course' in German policy, although the phrase was mainly a rhetorical flourish and William had no very firm objective in mind other than closer ties with Britain.[2] William II's advent and Bismarck's exit also marked the start of a period that saw Germany achieve the status of economic superpower.[3] Within a generation the second *Reich* had become an industrialized giant which by most economic standards outstripped all continental rivals, while crucially the nation's social patterns remained stuck in a pre-modern age. Behind the dislocation wrought by rapid economic growth lurked the continuing *Gründerkrise*, the founding crisis of 1870 that left Germany in a schizoid state in which constitutionalism clashed with authoritarianism, and the national with the dynastic principle. Both socially and politically the question of national identity remained wide open. Such is the gist of the much-debated *Sonderweg* thesis, which holds that Germany's peculiar socio-economic unfolding took the country on a 'special path' distinct from that of the other modernizing European states.[4]

Out of Germany's identity crisis, it has been alleged, grew a national fretfulness to explore new horizons that was perfectly mirrored in the volatile imperial personality.[5] Under William II, and in no small degree because of the emperor, German foreign policy reached new heights of stridency and assertiveness. A turning point arrived in 1897 when the emperor appointed Admiral Tirpitz as state secretary for the navy with a mandate to build a high-seas fleet. The decision by the hegemonic continental power to pursue a *Flottenpolitik* was an unmistakable signal that Germany now also nursed global pretensions to be pursued by *Weltpolitik*.[6]

To the German historian Fritz Fischer must go most of the credit for reasserting the primacy of internal politics (*Primat der Innenpolitik*) by arguing that Germany's shift to wholehearted imperialism was a response to domestic problems. According to the Fischerites (and many of Fischer's disciples are more emphatic than Fischer himself), *Weltpolitik* was intended to be a solution to the strains produced by rapid modernization not just in the economic sphere, but in social relationships too. It is worth remembering that this phase in German policy accompanied the further rise of socialism. Unquestionably, a *Sammlungspolitik* or rallying of right-wing agrarians and industrialists banked in some degree on *Weltpolitik* both to sustain prosperity and to neutralize the left by allaying discontent at home. In other words, a strong element of social imperialism was at work. Its roots in the domestic scene gave *Weltpolitik* a particular urgency and, needless to add, it looms large on the charge sheet of German war guilt in 1914.[7]

A harbinger of things to come and the most immediate consequence of Bismarck's departure was Berlin's decision not to renew the 1887 Reinsurance Treaty with Russia, which lapsed in June 1890. In point of fact, Russo-German relations had been going downhill well before Bismarck's resignation, not least as a result of the chancellor's own economic measures. His compact with the *Junkers* for domestic political reasons in the 1880s compelled him to raise the tariff on imported Russian grain, and in 1887 he put a stop to the sale of Russian bonds on the Berlin money market. But it was only after Bismarck's departure that the German foreign ministry persuaded the emperor that the political tie with Russia was incompatible with obligations to Austria-Hungary; without Bismarck himself his complex diplomatic system was deemed inoperable.[8]

With the end of the Reinsurance Treaty Russia was bereft of an ally among the great powers, the same position in which France had languished since 1870. What was more natural than that the two isolated states should come together? Even before 1890 portents of this were apparent. The Paris *bourse* was delighted to replace Berlin in floating loans for Russian industrialization, and in a different milieu Russian music enjoyed a Parisian vogue.[9] A political relationship had been held at bay by a mix of Bismarckian adroitness and the ideological antipathy between Russian autocracy and the French revolutionary tradition. But the disappearance of both Bismarck and his Reinsurance Treaty was sufficient to overcome ideological inhibitions. Between 1891 and 1894 France and Russia progressed from a generic entente for consultation in the event of an international disturbance to a full-blown military alliance. The burial of traditional ideological enmities was symbolized when a French naval squadron visited Kronstadt in 1891 and the tsar stood bareheaded during the playing of the revolutionary *Marseillaise*.[10]

The Franco-Russian alliance put to an end the right–left divide in international politics dating from 1791. Above all, it sealed the fate of the Austro-Russo-Prussian consortium that had served as a bastion of conservatism since 1815. Long threatened by the conflict between Vienna and St Petersburg in the Eastern Question, it foundered ironically at a moment when the Eastern Question was relatively quiescent. None the less, the shift in Russian policy represented a clear triumph of national self-interest over ideology, even if Berlin was slow to recognize it. William II, in particular, continued to count on the ideology of royalism. Writing in English in 1895 to his cousin, the newly-crowned Tsar Nicholas II, he expatiated on the perils of the French connection:

> It is not a *fact* of the *Rapport* or friendship between Russia and France that makes one uneasy . . . but the danger which is brought to our principle of Monarchism . . . The blood of their majesties is still on that country! Look at it, has it since then ever been happy or quiet again? Has it not staggered from bloodshed to bloodshed? And in its great moments did it not go from war to war? Till it soused all Europe and Russia in streams of blood? Till at last it had the Commune over again? Nicky, take my word on it, the curse of God has stricken that people for ever![11]

This sort of commentary, frequently encountered in the 'Willy–Nicky' correspondence, was not without its impact. In 1905 the two emperors met at sea off Björkö and signed a treaty that would have undercut Russia's commitment to France, not to mention Germany's to Austria-Hungary. Not surprisingly, each ruler on his return home was assailed with protests by ministers and officials, and the Björkö treaty was cancelled by mutual agreement. In the end, the episode was a further illustration of the eclipse of old ideologies.[12]

The 1894 treaty between France and Russia was explicitly directed against the Triple Alliance, and was to remain valid so long as the Triple Alliance lasted. Five years later, this time limitation was removed lest the Habsburg empire should collapse, leading to the demise of the Triple Alliance and the unwelcome creation of a Teutonic *Mitteleuropa* stretching to the Mediterranean.[13] At all events, the Franco-Russian alliance created a bipolar balance with its attendant threat that any and every international crisis might draw in most of the powers, as indeed happened in the July crisis of 1914. On the other hand, in the 1890s, the escalatory danger of a bipolar balance was mitigated by one of the novel ideologies. During this decade of the new imperialism day-to-day issues pitted France and Russia not against the Triple Alliance powers, but against Great Britain. China and India were the theatres of Anglo-Russian, and Africa the scene of Anglo-French confrontation. But of course the sting could only be drawn from bipolarity in this way so long as Britain itself remained extraneous to the two power blocs.

British foreign policy prided itself on its pragmatism: no permanent friends or enemies, simply permanent interests, as the dictum attributed to Palmerston had it. Yet one point of principle evolved during the nine-teenth century, specifically a resolution to keep aloof from continental entanglements. Thus, Castlereagh and Canning withdrew Britain from the Metternichian concert, and after disillusion with the Crimean War a Cobdenite emphasis on trade rather than political ties reigned for a time. By the mid-1890s the catch-phrase 'splendid isolation' came into common usage. In Britain isolationism never achieved the status of a diplomatic ideology that it did in the United States. Nevertheless, every foreign secretary had to pay lip service to isolationist precepts, as did Sir Edward Grey in 1906 shortly after assuming office: 'Alliances, especially continental alliances, are not in accordance with our traditions.'[14] Whether Grey went on to practise what he preached is another matter.

Britain's involvement in Europe was unexpected and unpremeditated. The tidal wave of animosity that engulfed the premier imperial power in the Boer War, climaxing a decade of colonial troubles, persuaded London to embark on a series of agreements to resolve extra-European problems. First was the Hay–Pauncefote treaty of 1901, which gave the US *carte blanche* to build a canal across the isthmus of Panama, only five years after President Cleveland had invoked the Monroe Doctrine in a dispute over the Venezuela–British Guiana boundary. Next, in 1902, to check Russia in the Far East, Britain signed an alliance with Japan, the first such formal accord with another power since the Crimean War. In the same vein, Britain welcomed overtures from the French foreign minister, Théophile Delcassé, to avoid a repetition of the Fashoda affair in Africa, where in 1898 the two countries had almost gone to war. The result in 1904 was a comprehensive colonial settlement, at the core of which was an exchange of French support for Britain in Egypt in return for British backing of France in Morocco.

All these arrangements served a strategic purpose as well. They enabled the British Admiralty to withdraw some of its over-extended resources from distant parts of the globe so as to concentrate them in 'home waters' against the prospective German battle fleet. But there was no conscious intent to lessen Britain's detachment from Europe. Quite the contrary; it can be argued that these strictly regional accords were designed to prevent colonial rivalries from inveigling Britain into quarrels with European powers. In truth, the Anglo-Japanese pact was a substitute for an Anglo-German colonial understanding which could not be achieved because Berlin's unacceptable price was a British pledge to defend the *status quo* in Europe. In this sense, 'the alliance was not the end of isolation; rather it confirmed it.'[15]

However isolationist British intentions may have been, they were thwarted by the metamorphosis of the Anglo-French colonial agreement. The fact that it was immediately dubbed the second *entente cordiale* intimated that it might develop a wider dimension. As early as 1905 Germany sought to sever the new Anglo-French tie by challenging France in Morocco and by forcing Delcassé's resignation under threat of war. The seriousness of the crisis demanded of Britain something more than diplomatic support. Although no promise of military aid was forthcoming, the next year annual staff talks began and produced contingency plans in the event Britain should intervene in a hypothetical Franco-German conflict. Strategic cooperation took another step forward after the second Moroccan crisis in 1911. A naval understanding allowed France to concentrate its fleet in the Mediterranean while Britain transferred more ships to the North Sea and the English Channel. In effect, this left the Royal Navy to protect France's northern coast against a German amphibious attack.

The military talks and naval dispositions constituted the essence of a conventional alliance, and not unreasonably the French began to hope for a formal Anglo-French pact. But mindful of Britain's isolationist principles, they did not insist on an 'alliance or any obligation to take action'. Paris had to rest content with an exchange of private letters dated 22–3 November 1912 between Grey and Paul Cambon, the French ambassador in London, which pledged prompt discussion between the two governments in future international crises when 'what measures they would be prepared to take in common' would be decided. In addition, this vague undertaking was hedged by the preamble that the ongoing 'consultations' by military and naval experts were 'not to be regarded as an engagement that commits either Government to action'.[16] Taxed later in the House of Commons on rumours of a British commitment to France, the government replied through Prime Minister Asquith: 'If war arises between European Powers there are no unpublished agreements which will restrict or hamper the freedom of the Government or of Parliament to decide whether or not Great Britain should participate in a war.' This public denial was later repeated by Grey and maintained right up to the outbreak of war in 1914. Various explanations have been advanced for the economy with the truth exhibited by Grey and Asquith, but there can be no doubt that some of their disingenuousness with both the French and Parliament arose from an accountability they felt to the dogma of splendid isolation.[17]

The *entente cordiale* blossomed in proportion to the decay of Anglo-German friendship. At the opening of the twentieth century Britain and Germany were adjudged to be natural associates by reason of racial and cultural ideology. Joseph Chamberlain talked of the Germans 'bred of our race' who 'speak our language'; William II was wont to refer to the 'two great Protestant powers' in the van of civilization. But these traits availed little against the spirit of Social Darwinist competitiveness that came to prevail in both countries. 'You may roughly divide the nations of all the world as the living and the dying,' remarked Lord Salisbury in 1898, 'the weak states are becoming weaker and the strong states are becoming stronger.'[18] To many on both sides of the Channel Germany appeared the living, and Britain the dying nation. Germany had overtaken Britain in many crucial economic respects, producing by 1914 twice as much steel, for example. What registered more in the public consciousness, though, was the building of a German high-seas fleet too big for the Royal Navy to destroy without suffering such loss as would impair its overall naval supremacy. The German 'risk navy' struck at the heart of British power and prestige.

Within less than a generation the popular British mood swung around to view Germany as a mortal enemy. This was reflected in the vogue for adventure tales featuring a German invasion: *The Riddle of the Sands* (1903) by Erskine Childers; William Le Queux's *Invasion of 1910*, serialized in 1906 in the jingoist *Daily Mail*; Saki's *When William Came* (1913). On a different plane, a host of pressure groups sprang up to argue that to compete with Germany it was necessary to follow the German model – introduce conscription and other schemes to toughen the 'national fibre', halt 'deindustrialization' and promote 'national efficiency'. Encouraged by 'public chauvinism' aimed at Germany, British policy moved steadily in an anti-German (and pro-French) direction, a classic instance of the enhanced role of the new popular and journalistic nationalism.[19] In any case, there was plenty of antagonism towards Germany in high places to begin with. Grey himself, coming as he did from a liberal imperialist background, always harboured suspicion about Germany's ambitions. Within the Foreign Office worked a coterie of senior Germanophobe diplomats whose influence grew with time. Their most extreme statement was a famed memorandum of 1 January 1907 composed by Eyre Crowe, the office's senior clerk – over twenty closely printed censorious pages on 'the generally restless, explosive and disconcerting activity of Germany' since 1871.[20] In short, an important segment of official opinion shared the general public's perception of Germany.

Initially, the *entente cordiale* had been in no sense anti-German; not so the Anglo-Russian entente that was formed in 1907. Admittedly, the substance of the agreement concerned imperial problems on the Indian frontier, but a common distrust of German *Weltpolitik* drove negotiations from the start. Multiple motives were required to bring about an Anglo-Russian *rapprochement* perhaps more remarkable than that between France and Russia. Of all the powers, Britain had opposed Russia most persistently throughout the nineteenth century, and the ideological gulf between British parliamentarianism and tsarist autocracy was at least as broad as that which once divided republican France and monarchical Russia. Hence, the first Anglo-Russian talks were assisted by the Russian revolution of 1905, which constrained the tsar to tolerate an elected parliament or duma. Unfortunately, before the Anglo-Russian accord was concluded this duma was dissolved. The instinctive response of Sir Henry Campbell-Bannerman, the British prime minister, was 'la douma est morte, vive la douma.' Despite this *contretemps*, the negotiations suffered only a slight hiatus; like the French, even a British Liberal cabinet felt the need to line up Russia against Germany strongly enough to ignore the return of reaction within Russia. Predictably, the Anglo-Russian entente provoked an outcry from British radicals. But their criticism was diffuse and not unanimous. After all, many had welcomed the entente with liberal-democratic France, and the Anglo-Russian entente was the diplomatic complement to that with France.[21]

Although Britain signed no military pact with either France or Russia, 1907 witnessed the completion of the division of Europe's great powers into two armed camps. The bipolar balance between Triple Entente and Triple Alliance furthered the blurring of traditional ideological boundaries. Russia's partnership with the Western liberal democracies was the most obvious ideological anomaly. On the other side of the fence, Italy's presence in the Triple Alliance was something of an aberration, for the body politic of united Italy had much more in common with western liberalism than with the more authoritarian systems of Berlin and Vienna. Yet the Italians remained at least nominally members of the Triple Alliance, while making it clear that they could not be counted on in a war against France or Britain.[22] The Anglo-German antagonism was another breach of an established ideological pattern for a loose affinity between the two so-called Anglo-Saxon peoples dated back to 1756. In all these instances ideology appeared to have yielded to the higher claim of national self-interest. But this was not old-fashioned *raison d'état*. In an age of democracy national interest cloaked itself in the new ideologies spawned by Social Darwinism. Pursuit of a state's self-interest was now driven by the immense ideological force of popular nationalism. Such was the recipe for the disaster of 1914.

IDEOLOGY AND THE THIRD BALKAN WAR

The diplomatic scene immediately preceding the First World War used to be popularly known as the 'international anarchy', by which was meant that international relations, always intrinsically anarchic, had simply become more unpredictable than customary.[23] It was a fair enough judgement. Social Darwinism and populist nationalism were eroding the patrician cosmopolitanism that had underpinned the 'solidarism' of the great powers, and the Concert of Europe functioned only intermittently amid the confrontation between Triple Alliance and Triple Entente. On the other hand, to concentrate on the schematic frailties of the states system is sometimes to overlook the war's actual roots in that hardy perennial, the Eastern Question. It can be argued that the First World War began as a 'third Balkan war'.[24] In the series of crises that plagued Southeastern Europe before 1914 the new nationalism and its ideological offshoots were prominent in aggravating the geopolitical issues.

The Eastern Question had stayed in the background during the 1890s mainly because Russian imperialism was temporarily directed to the Far East. But with the defeat administered by Japan in 1904–5 Russia's gaze swung back westward to the Balkans and its Slavic peoples. Meanwhile, in the Balkans themselves, Serbia had ceased to be an Austrian client state as the result of a palace revolution in Belgrade engineered by Slav nationalist elements. Thus, the foreign policy of two key players in Danubian politics took on new overtones of pan-Slavism. At the same time the Austro-Hungarians kept their face adamantly set against trialism or power-sharing with their Slav minorities whose restiveness mounted accordingly. The stage was being set for a Habsburg–Slav showdown from which the Russians would find it hard to stay apart.

Austro-Russian conflict was not foreordained, however. For example, in the autumn of 1908 Alexander Isvolsky, the Russian foreign minister, reached a secret agreement with his Austrian counterpart, Count Aehrenthal. In return for Austro-Hungarian support of a Russian proposal to revise the Straits regime, Russia would raise no objection to Austria-Hungary's annexation of Bosnia-Herzegovina, the Turkish provinces administered by Vienna since the Congress of Berlin in 1878. But whereas Isvolsky anticipated implementing these arrangements in an indeterminate future, Aehrenthal took advantage of the domestic turmoil in the Ottoman empire to proclaim annexation at once, leaving the Russians empty-handed. The ensuing Bosnian crisis fanned pan-Slavism in the Balkans to a frenzy.

The most violent reaction came from the Serbs, who had earmarked Bosnia-Herzegovina for their own as a step on the way to a Greater Serbia, by which they envisaged a confederation of all southern Slavs. Since so many of the latter lived within the Habsburg borders, a Greater Serbia was a direct threat to Austro-Hungarian integrity, and it was to forestall Serbia playing the role of 'Piedmont of the southern Slavs' that Aehrenthal snatched Bosnia-Herzegovina from under Belgrade's nose. In Serbia's capital the rebuff was met by the founding of nationalist organizations. The most notable was the part cultural, part paramilitary *Narodna Odbrana* (National Defence) which, within a few years, boasted over 200 branches and launched a newspaper ominously called *Piedmont*. In 1911 the *Crna Ruka* (Black Hand), a terrorist group, came into existence and proceeded to infiltrate the *Narodna Odbrana*. The links between these pan-Slav societies and Serbian authorities were complex and have never been totally unravelled.[25]

The Serbs on their own could do nothing; they looked to their Slavic big brother in St Petersburg. But the Russian position was desperately weak. Militarily drained after defeat in the Far East and haunted by the spectre of the revolution which that defeat had triggered, Russia also found its French ally reluctant to become involved in a Balkan dispute. In contrast, Austria-Hungary received the promise of armed support from Berlin which was fearful lest an international setback trigger the collapse of the Habsburg empire, now Germany's only reliable ally among the powers. In these circumstances, St Petersburg had little choice but to tolerate Aehrenthal's duplicity and suffer diplomatic humiliation. 'Shame! Shame! It would be better to die,' exclaimed General Kireyev, a prominent pan-Slav who resigned his post.[26] After the Bosnian crisis Russia renounced any hope of reaching accommodation with Austria-Hungary in the Balkans, and trusted instead to deterrence.

The events of 1908–9 inevitably stimulated pan-Slavism within Russia, but it would be quite wrong to see Russian foreign policy on the eve of the First World War as determined by a simple ethnic ideology. The government in St Petersburg was much less in thrall to a Slavic lobby than was the Serbian administration, and Isvolsky and his successor, Sergei Sazonov, came under frequent nationalist fire for failing to conform to a rigid pan-Slav line. It was more a question of unconscious assumptions about Slavdom's uniqueness and mission among Russian officials. 'Most of Russia's ruling élite did not share Kireyev's extreme Panslav sympathies but, as the Austrian ambassador in St Petersburg commented in 1912 with slightly exaggerated gloom, there was "a certain degree of Slavic solidarity in all of them".'[27] Arguably, the major impact of Russian pan-Slavism on international affairs was not that St Petersburg's diplomacy was locked into a Slavic tunnel vision, but that Austria-Hungary, and Germany too, believed it to be so.

For sure, pan-Slav sentiments were openly expressed, often in high places. The household of the tsar's uncle, the Grand Duke Nicholas, and his Montenegrin wife was a hotbed of Slav fanaticism. Russia's leading newspaper, *Novoye Vremya*, which the tsar was known to read, frequently couched its opinions in pan-Slav terminology. The most effectual pan-Slav figure proved to be N.V. Hartwig, a former *Novoye Vremya* journalist appointed minister to Belgrade in the wake of the Bosnian crisis. In this capacity Hartwig went his own way, scarcely bothering 'to conceal the fact that he considered M. Sazonov's policy despicable and misguided'. His 'incurable Austrophobia' and 'enthusiastic identification of Russia's interests with the Serb national cause and the semi-imaginary "Slav idea"' was a gift from heaven to the Serbs whose foreign policy, it was generally recognized, came to be made only with Hartwig's closest guidance.[28]

In 1912 St Petersburg brokered a Serb–Bulgar alliance as a preliminary to a larger agreement that would embrace Turkey, but with Hartwig's blessing Serbia torpedoed the scheme.[29] Instead, Serbia and Bulgaria united in a Balkan league, and then enlisted Greece and Montenegro in an attack on the Ottoman empire to drive the Turks out of Europe. Turkey, still racked by internal dissension and also under Italian assault in Libya, was quickly beaten in this First Balkan War (1912). Although retaining a toehold in Europe, they surrendered considerable territory to the Balkan League. It was only a matter of time before these Balkan upheavals impinged on Habsburg–Slav relations. The victorious Serbs laid claim to an outlet to the Adriatic Sea, which was promptly opposed by Austria-Hungary. A full-scale international crisis was averted by the restraint of both Russia and Germany, neither power being militarily ready for war. This permitted Britain, uneasy at the Balkan League's original designs against the Ottoman empire, to step in and host an international conference. In 1913, for the last time, the Concert of Europe saved the peace. In particular, an international fiat denied Serbia access to the sea by creating an autonomous Albania.

But Serbian ambitions were not so easily repressed. Hartwig's encouragement did not flag, and his government's award of the Order of the White Eagle could be taken as official endorsement of his pan-Slav stance.[30] Squabbling within the Balkan League over the Turkish spoils played into Serb hands. No sooner had the London Conference concluded than Bulgaria attacked its recent allies. From this Second Balkan War Serbia once more emerged victorious, its reward great tracts of Macedonia that doubled the country's size. This progression towards a Greater Serbia, coupled with the subversive propaganda directed by *Narodna Odbrana* at southern Slavs within the Habsburg empire, constituted a rising tide of pan-Slavism that threatened to engulf Austria-Hungary. 'Diplomacy no longer appeared adequate', and Vienna was disposed to think of preventive war, to destroy Serbia before its activity destroyed the Habsburg empire.[31]

The Dual Monarchy's chance to strike at Serbia came with the murder of the Habsburg crown prince at Sarajevo on 28 June 1914, an incident appropriately replete with connotations of Slavic self-consciousness. Not only was Franz Ferdinand's purpose in the Bosnian capital to review Austrian troops in the heartland of the south Slavs, but he was doing so on St Vitus day, the Balkan Slavs' national holiday commemorating the anniversary of the fourteenth-century battle of Kosovo against the Turks. A deliberate provocation to Slav nationalism, one might think; a fair parallel would have been for the Prince of Wales to attend a British military parade in Dublin on St Patrick's day. The assassination was executed by members of the pan-Slav Black Hand with the assistance of Serb officials, although the Belgrade government's participation in, or even knowledge of, the plot remains problematical. But the Serbian connection served Vienna's purpose. The Austro-Hungarian ultimatum, by demanding intervention in Serbian internal affairs, was crafted to be rejected and to pave the way for war. But the hope for a localized third Balkan war was on this occasion dashed by great power partisan involvement.

Unlike the crises of 1908–9 and 1912–13, that in 1914 put Serbia's own integrity at risk, and Russia was therefore more receptive to an appeal to the tsar's 'generous Slav heart'.[32] Nevertheless, the Russians, while giving Belgrade a green light to reject the most offensive sections of the ultimatum, also urged the Serbs to make as conciliatory a reply as possible – a clear sign St Petersburg was not carried away by pan-Slav euphoria. Then, in the midst of the July crisis Hartwig died of a heart attack, oddly enough on a visit to the Austro-Hungarian legation, which of course gave rise to wild rumours of foul play. Without Hartwig to countermand St Petersburg's advice, the Serbs' answer to Vienna was surprisingly mild, albeit a negative one.

If pan-Slavism supplied a pervasive ideological background to Russian decision-making, pan-Germanism played a similar role in Berlin, though to a lesser degree. William II was prone to windy declamations on the historic struggle between Teuton and Slav, but in handing the notorious blank cheque to Austria-Hungary on 5 July 1914 he was moved by power-political considerations and horror at a regicidal act rather than any ethnic ideology.[33] For a stronger ideological factor in Berlin's conduct during the July crisis one must return to the internal mainsprings of German foreign policy, as developed by the Fischer school of thought. According to this, the sense of desperation among Germany's elites reached a peak with the SPD's success in the *Reichstag* elections of 1912. Heinrich Class, head of the Pan-German League, reflected his organization's preoccupation with the spectre of revolution within the *Reich*: 'The entrepreneurs who . . . have become the pillars of our national economy see themselves exposed to the arbitrary power of the working-class which are spurred on by socialism.' The entire power structure in Germany fixed on war as 'an antidote to revolution', and no distinction could be drawn between a war and peace party.[34] *Weltpolitik* having been curbed by the Triple Entente, however, the German right, of necessity looked to war in Europe, or at least a grand diplomatic triumph won by threatening war, as in the Bosnian crisis. To which the German military added their opinion that, if war was to come, it was better sooner than later; Russian and French military preparations would be more advanced by 1915 or 1916, the Triple Entente stronger and the Triple Alliance weaker.[35] All this conservative and pessimistic rationale for war in July 1914 certainly helps to explain German rashness during the Sarajevo crisis – the almost cavalier way in which the blank cheque was given, the persistent urging of Austria-Hungary to invade Serbia at once and, most contentiously, the two-faced treatment of Sir Edward Grey's *démarche* to defuse the crisis as he had the Balkan crisis of 1912–13.[36]

But in one respect the situation imposed caution on Germany. That was to avoid appearing the aggressor. Rather, in the words of the enigmatic Chancellor Bethmann-Hollweg, 'it is imperative that the responsibility for any extension of the conflict to Powers not directly concerned should under all circumstances fall on Russia alone.' The ploy was geared to encourage British neutrality in a forthcoming conflict and, more important, to trade on the German socialists' pathological dislike of Russia. In the event, Russia obliged; on 31 July, three days after Austria-Hungary had declared war on Serbia, a hesitant Tsar Nicholas gave the order for total mobilization. Faced with an ostensibly belligerent Russia, the SPD adopted a patriotic attitude which met the chancellor's wish that 'there will be no question of a general or partial strike, or of sabotage'.[37]

As for British neutrality, German military dispositions already in place nullified Bethmann's hope. To cope with the two-front war augured since the Franco-Russian alliance, the general staff had adopted the plan named after their quondam chief, General Schlieffen, which predicated a sudden knockout blow to France before conducting a more drawn-out campaign against Russia. Sensible enough strategy, one might think, although the codicil added in 1905 to march on Paris through Belgium and Luxemburg was less so. For one thing, it allowed the French, well aware of the Schlieffen plan, to assume a reactive posture throughout the July crisis; in a gesture aimed at winning British sympathy, they deployed their main body of troops ten kilometres short of the national frontiers.[38] And if there was one thing likely to bring the British out of their official isolation, it was an invasion of Belgium – as the French themselves had discovered in 1793.

In fact, the invasion of Belgium rescued the British government from the embarrassment of its moral obligation to France incurred by the military and naval arrangements, even though the cabinet lost two members who resigned on learning of the secret Anglo-French strategic planning. Radical critics of British foreign policy, for their part, were lulled by a reconciliation of sorts between themselves and the foreign secretary over the two previous years. The radicals interpreted a relaxation of Anglo-German tension and even the abortive attempt to reach a naval-building holiday in 1912 as Grey's conversion to their own internationalist principles, whereas in reality, 'it was not the Foreign Secretary who adopted their case but the radicals who accepted his'.[39] Most radicals in July 1914 were conditioned to swallow passively the official line that intervention was

forced on Britain by the violation of Belgium. In sum, left-wing internationalists in both Germany and Britain were domesticated.

Statesmen were swept along in 1914 by the speed at which the Sarajevo
crisis unfolded – less than two weeks passed from the delivery of the
Viennese ultimatum on 23 July to the British declaration of war on
4 August.[40] One reason for this was the 'short war illusion', the almost
universal conviction of military and civilians alike that the next war
would follow the pattern of Prussia's swift victories in 1866 and 1870, if
only because modern warfare was too expensive to sustain for long.[41]
The lesson drawn was that the side that got its blow in first would prevail
– hence the importance attached to mobilization and to Schlieffen's plan.
Additionally, under the short war illusion it seemed plausible that one
could still wage war without imperilling the social order or rending the
fabric of Western civilization by a lengthy conflict. In this way a short
war appeared compatible with continued progress. The sort of maelstrom
unleashed in 1914 was inconceivable to a generation thoroughly indoc-
trinated in the idea of ineluctable progress. So statesmen complacently
subjected diplomacy to militarist fiat, and the public indulged in 'a widespread fascination with war' in expectation that a historical law of linear
progress would save them from the worst.[42]

The presence of ideological factors in the prelude to the First World
War is undeniable – ethnic sentiments, especially Russian and Balkan
pan-Slavism; social imperialism operative most clearly in the case of
Germany; British isolationism; the idea of progress. But in the final analysis, the war was fought not for ideological reasons but to repair the
balance of power. Germany protested the Triple Entente's encirclement
and wanted to break the stranglehold. The Entente powers held that a
united, industrialized and militaristic Germany had already disturbed the
European equilibrium. Indeed, the bipolar balance between Triple Entente
and Triple Alliance proved ephemeral, a transitional stage in the construction of an old-style coalition against hegemonical Germany. The First
World War ended with Germany and a few weak allies (not even Triple
Alliance partner Italy, which declared its neutrality in 1914) ranged against
a combination of two dozen states – a scenario reminiscent of the wars
against Napoleonic France. However, this traditional strategic contest
was disguised between 1914 and 1918. All the combatants, to rally their
citizen armies and civil populations, coated their war aims with an ideological gloss, and the longer the war lasted, the more ideological it became.

TOTAL WAR AND PROPAGANDA

The spontaneous outburst of patriotism that almost everywhere and at all
social levels greeted war in 1914 astonished most observers. Socialists
were understandably dismayed but took refuge in the slogan 'better to be

wrong with the working class than right against them'. The SPD did not dare vote against war credits in the *Reichstag* lest they 'rouse a storm of indignation among men at the front and the people at home'.[43] Their socialist colleagues in Vienna felt and behaved in exactly the same way. At the opposite end of the spectrum Freud confessed that his 'whole libido' went out to the Habsburgs, while Class of the Pan-German League rejoiced 'how people who did not know one another at all were profoundly moved as they shook hands, as if making a silent vow to stand together until the end'.[44] The delighted William II declared a *Burgfrieden* or civil peace, and boasted he no longer recognized parties, only Germans. Similarly, in France President Raymond Poincaré, a Lorrainer who acquired the nickname of Poincaré-la-guerre, issued a call for a *union sacrée*. The response, shaped by remembrance of 1870, was a mix of resigned and enthusiastic acceptance of war. Crucially, the trade unions abjured strike action and, in return, the government forbore to arrest the suspected subversives listed on the infamous police *Carnet B*. A number of French leftists recalled the revolutionary patriotism of 1793 when nation, state and citizenship were first synchronized. In the van was Gustave Hervé, whose notoriety rested on his earlier derision of the national flag as fit only to be planted on a dunghill; now he exclaimed, 'National defence before everything! They have assassinated Jaurès, we shall not assassinate France!'[45]

The nationalist efflorescence was no less in the least militarist of the powers. A young bank clerk returning from the country on the bank holiday evening of 3 August found the British capital 'in a state of hysteria':

> A vast procession jammed the road from side to side, everyone waving flags and singing patriotic songs . . . We were swept along . . . to Buckingham Palace, where the whole road in front of the palace was chock-a-block with shouting demonstrators. Police were powerless to control the flood as people climbed the railings; sentries were clapped on the back or even chaired. 'The King! The King!' they yelled and chorused, and then broke into the national Anthem. After this pandemonium had lasted for a considerable time the king and queen appeared on the balcony waving to the crowd. Only then did the multitude disperse.

The next day the recruiting office at Great Scotland Yard was a 'seething mass'. In the words of a poet, 'Never such innocence, never before or since'.[46] By the end of September over three-quarters of a million men volunteered for military service, and in the first sixteen months of war some two and a half million; conscription was avoided until 1916. Such statistics were the fruit of a popular nationalism that had germinated in democracy's garden for half a century.

Only in Russia, in the absence of any real semblance of democracy, was the national rallying abridged. Enthusiasm for war extended no further than the educated classes, the patriotic street demonstrations were partly organized by the police, while the vast peasantry were bewildered and unmoved – all ominous signs for the Russian war effort.[47]

But patriotism was not enough. As the short war proved illusory, the belligerents were forced to mobilize their resources for a war of attrition. This required the allotment of all productive forces to the war effort and the compliance, voluntary or otherwise, of the civilian masses. The nineteenth-century liberal values of *laisser faire* and the rights of man were replaced by 'state socialism' and integral nationalism; the war of 1914–18 was the first total or 'hyperbolic' war.[48] Morale needed to be sustained not just in the armed forces but among entire populations harnessed to the war machine. This was attempted negatively by censorship, both official and self-administered by the press, which minimized losses, exaggerated military advances, and held out the hope of victory around the next corner.[49] But it was impossible to disguise completely the horrendous and futile slaughter that occurred on every battlefront. Therefore, in all countries official committees, departments and even full ministries of information adopted the more positive tactic of contriving lofty purposes, beyond simple patriotism, for which the war was being fought. As the bloodletting continued and war weariness grew, reaching its apex in 1917, ideological justifications for all the suffering became more shrill and extreme; 'propaganda and ideology usurped the place of genuine feeling'.[50]

It is important here to recognize that wartime ideologies were not the same thing as war aims, although sometimes they overlapped. In the case of Germany, early wartime victories prompted Berlin to draft plans for a postwar Europe. German war aims were, in fact, summed up as early as 9 September 1914 in a memorandum that bore Bethmann-Hollweg's name. By this France was to be 'so weakened as to make her revival as a great power impossible for all time', while Russia was to be 'thrust back as far as possible from Germany's eastern frontier and her domination over the non-Russian vassal peoples broken'.[51] The net result would be a gigantic Central European zone subject to German political and economic direction, a prospect articulated publicly in Friedrich Naumann's enormously popular *Mitteleuropa* (1915). All Germany's elites, civilian and military, and indeed much of German society to the right of the social democrats, nursed annexationist war aims, and Berlin's official position did not move far from Bethmann's memorandum of September 1914 throughout the war. The fortunes of war caused Germany's annexationist gaze to be fixed particularly on the east; the trench stalemate on the western front was offset by the collapse of the Russian war effort in 1917 and subsequent Treaty of Brest-Litovsk (March 1918), which transferred the bulk of European Russia to the Central Powers. This temporary realization of German aims in the east gratified the historic Teutonic sense of racial superiority over the Slavs which was a staple of pan-German ideology. Fritz Fischer, among others, has remarked how closely German war aims matched the programme of the Pan-German League, and also how the pan-German 'ideas of 1914' became the ideology of the next *Reich*.[52]

The war aims of the entente powers, however, bore little relation to the ideological messages purveyed. In the eyes of the administrations in London and Paris the war's purpose was initially to address the political origins of the conflict – Belgian independence, Alsace-Lorraine, the German battle fleet. But imperial calculations soon entered, and Japan was first off the mark. Using the Anglo-Japanese alliance as a specious pretext, Tokyo entered the war on 23 August 1914 and set about filching German colonial assets in China and the Pacific. In the west, Britain and France, in order to hold isolated and embattled Russia in the war, promised the tsar Constantinople and the Straits, thus defying the shades of Palmerston and Disraeli. For their own equivalent compensation London and Paris looked elsewhere in the Ottoman empire and to Germany's African colonies. Further territorial rewards at the expense of Germany, Austria-Hungary and Turkey were offered to neutrals to enter the war.[53] These diplomatic deals were kept secret; cynical power-brokering, if revealed, was more likely to depress than augment popular endurance of the war's destructiveness. Instead, more inspirational reasons were required, and in the contest of ideological rationalization the western powers, the British above all, came out ahead.

From the start, their propaganda organs tried to delineate the war as a collision between liberal democracy on the one hand and Prussian military authoritarianism on the other. This simplistic picture was, of course, marred by the presence of autocratic Russia in the entente camp. But the ruthless breach of Belgian integrity rekindled memories of Bismarck's dictatorial blood-and-iron methods, and the British seized the opportunity to compile a lurid report of atrocities committed in Belgium (nearly all of which proved after the war to be grossly exaggerated or totally fabricated). In any event, some ideological distinction between Germany and the Western democracies was evident from the start, and it was accentuated in 1916 when Generals Hindenburg and Ludendorff took charge of their country's entire war effort, on the home as well as the fighting front, thus transforming Germany into a veritable military dictatorship. The Germans themselves ineptly provided much fodder for the entente jibes of 'Hun' and 'Boche'. But probably the most potent British propaganda tactic was to proffer a vision of some brave new world that would dawn at war's end. The slogan 'houses fit for heroes to live in' encapsulated the dream at home. Its international equivalent was the phrase coined by the novelist

H.G. Wells, 'the war that will end war'. This promise was all the more effective for responding to the immediate cause of the present miseries.

British and entente propaganda, then, translated wartime objectives into universalist terms – permanent peace and democracy – which the Germans found hard to answer. Only grudgingly in 1917, in response to SPD pressure, did the German emperor promise a degree of political liberalization and social reform. The Prussian military tradition inhibited any preaching of a world without war, and the ideological message that the war was being fought to save German *Kultur* from Slav barbarism, French frivolity and British materialism was not much advance on a conventional nationalist appeal. This constricted range of German propaganda mattered because the public relations battle of 1914–18 was not just to sustain the morale of populations at war, but also to win over neutrals.

Italy provided a good case in point. Italy was not consulted by its Triple Alliance partners in the July crisis and its neutrality was not unexpected. Although 'the least of the great powers', Italy was courted because its war potential was considerably overestimated. The bare truth is that Italy entered the war on the entente side for purely mundane reasons. By the Treaty of London of 26 April 1915 Britain and France bid higher in a territorial auction than Vienna was prepared to offer in the region of *Italia irredenta*. Moreover, these diplomatic machinations proceeded against a backdrop of opinion voiced mainly by lawyers, journalists and intellectuals who tended to take at face value the Anglo-French claim to represent the cause of democratic freedom. The leading liberal paper, *Corriere della Sera*, 'preached war for British-style liberalism against the violators of Belgium and oppressor of Small Peoples', and other left-of-centre interventionists extolled France as the 'Home of Revolution and the People, and enemy of militarism and authoritarian empires'. Among those recruited by the entente was Mussolini who, having broken with most of his fellow Italian socialists, accepted French money in order to advocate a revolutionary war.[54] In the impassioned public and parliamentary debate of 'radiant May', during which the Italians resolved to ratify the Treaty of London, the interventionists did not shrink from advertising the war's ideological aspect, if only to obscure the government's unguarded admission of its 'sacred egoism' in choosing the entente over the Central Powers.

But the real neutral prize was the United States, which the British hoped to win over by dint of a common language and social contacts. The British propaganda campaign in the USA was guided by Sir Gilbert Parker, Canadian by birth and a popular novelist; other writers who lent their pens and reputations included such Anglo-American literary lions as Henry James and Edith Wharton. Furthermore, it was no coincidence that Lord Bryce, one of the most respected pre-war British ambassadors to Washington, was appointed head of the Belgian atrocities committee;

his report was aimed directly at the USA. But on the whole, British propaganda in the United States indulged less in strident messages to the populace than in low-key approaches to pillars of society and decision-makers.[55] Britain's expectations were raised by the fact that, at this stage of American history, most of the political power structure still came from British stock; many had relatives fighting with the British forces. President Wilson's mother was English-born and his personal diplomatic advisor, Colonel House, was decidedly pro-British.

Wilson himself, though, perhaps better than any other incumbent of the White House, embodied the spirit of American 'liberal exceptionalism'.[56] This sense of unique destiny flavoured his call in 1914 to the American people to be 'impartial in thought as well as in action', in order to fulfil the 'proper performance of our duty as . . . the one people holding itself ready to play a part of impartial mediator and speak the counsels of peace and accommodation'. Again, after the sinking of the *Lusitania* in May 1915 shocked the US conscience, the president explained to an audience of newly naturalized US citizens that 'Americans must have a consciousness different from the consciousness of every other nation . . . The example of America must be a special example' that made it 'too proud to fight'.[57]

It has been noticed earlier that from the birth of the republic exceptionalism pulled in different directions. On the one hand, it dictated isolation from Old World quarrels; Wilson's neutralist injunction was an obedient response, and it helped him to win re-election in 1916. On the other hand, there was the compulsion to bring America's moral superiority to bear on world affairs, which contained the germ of paternalistic imperialism. Significantly, Wilson had approved the Spanish–American War and US annexations as a 'moral obligation', and a sense of 'service to humanity' lay behind his administration's interference in Mexico, Haiti and the Dominican Republic.[58] The Latin American record suggested an interventionist reading of exceptionalism. In the First World War Wilson may have honestly sought a balance between international isolation and involvement, but it was the latter that not surprisingly prevailed.[59]

Nuances rather than major differences of opinion divided the president from his isolationist secretary of state, William Jennings Bryan. Nevertheless, the latter's resignation in June 1915 was a sign of things to come. Wilson's first interventionist efforts took the form of trying to persuade the warring states to accept his arbitration. Colonel House's mission to Europe in 1916 aimed at extracting a statement of war aims from both sides. However, the cost of total war constrained the belligerents to demand total, or at least substantive, victory, and the incompatibility of stated war aims was stark. By default, Wilson was driven to enunciate his own version of a desirable settlement, namely a compromise or 'peace without victory'. To sell such an idea in Europe's capitals a bribe was added. The president held out the promise that the USA would 'join the other civilized nations of the world in guaranteeing the permanence of peace'. Again, the exceptionalist note was struck:

> It is inconceivable that the people of the United States should play no part in that great enterprise. To take part in such service will be the opportunity for which they have sought to prepare themselves . . . ever since the days when they set up a new nation in the high and honourable hope that it might in all that it was and did show mankind the way to liberty. They cannot in honour withhold the service to which they are now about to be challenged. They do not wish to withhold it.[60]

But US advice and promises from a distance were to no avail. In the last resort, Wilson was only able to promote the American ideal worldwide through US intervention in the war itself.

The reasons for US entry into the war in April 1917 have been hotly debated.[61] Germany's resumption of unrestricted submarine warfare was the immediate cause. The defence of neutral trading rights had been for over a century a staple of US foreign policy, and recently American delegates to the Hague Conferences had pleaded for the validity of international law. Yet Washington's principled stand was compromised by its reaction to the British blockade's infringement of international law, against which the US never offered more than verbal protests. America thus joined the thieves to fight against the murderers. Furthermore, material factors behind the US declaration of war were not hard to find. Wall Street loans to the entente governments were mostly expended on war *matériel* produced in the USA, thus averting an economic recession that loomed in 1914. (Britain's blockade, of course, inhibited the Central Powers from such purchases.) Loan-servicing and the continued flow of war orders comprised a vested American interest in an entente victory. In short, the profit motive and ideological purpose mingled uneasily in 1917.

In presenting his war resolution to Congress on 2 April, President Wilson understandably stressed the idealistic grounds for abandoning neutrality. Like Monroe's speech announcing his doctrine in 1823, broad principles took up only a fraction of Wilson's address, but it was these that attracted attention. The United States was to fight 'for the rights of nations great and small and the privilege of men everywhere to choose their way of life and of obedience. The world must be made safe for democracy.' He repeated his pledge of US participation in a postwar international system

> to vindicate the principles of peace and justice . . . as against the selfish and autocratic power and to set up amongst the really free and self-governed peoples of the world such a concert of purpose and of action as will henceforth ensure the observation of those principles.[62]

The president received healthy congressional approval (in the Senate by 82 to 6, in the House of Representatives by 373 to 50), and a Committee of Public Information was struck to convince the American people of their just cause. It followed the propaganda agencies in Europe in teaching hatred of the foreigner, which sometimes included 'hyphenated-Americans', while couching war aims in terms of high-minded precepts.

Wilson's designation of the conflict as a war to end war and save democracy reiterated entente propaganda almost exactly, although his facile linking of individual freedom and national self-determination found no echo in London and Paris, which had hitherto steered clear of the tricky question of self-determination. But whereas necessity obliged the entente states to mouth the slogans of peace, liberty and justice, the United States – or at least its president – was sincerely committed to their universal application. Hence, US cooperation with its European partners was restricted, much to the frustration of the American representative on the Supreme War Council. The USA was an associated not an allied power, unbound by secret treaties, its ideological virginity intact.

The year 1917 changed the face of the war, for America's entry was complemented by Russia's exit. The March revolution in Petrograd (St Petersburg renamed for patriotic reasons), which saw the tsar abdicate in favour of a species of representative government, was welcomed by the Western powers. It gave substance to the entente's claim to be a democratic coalition. Moreover, Russia's provisional government undertook to stay in the war. This decision, however, proved its undoing by playing into the hands of the Bolsheviks. The Germans scored a spectacular success by affording Lenin and other anti-war Russian revolutionaries transit home from their Swiss exile, and probably money too.[63] Once in Petrograd Lenin told a Bolshevik caucus that 'the basic question is our attitude towards the war'. For Lenin it was an imperialist outgrowth of the highest stage of capitalism and opened the door to revolution. Not many Russians were interested in Leninist theory, but the Bolshevik anti-war stand met the popular mood. The provisional government's refusal to extricate Russia from the war was largely responsible for the November revolution during which Lenin took advantage of the revolutionary chaos to mount a Bolshevik *coup d'état*. He moved immediately to realize his ideological conception. On 8 November the Congress of Soviets issued a Decree on Peace that called for 'the immediate opening of negotiations for a just and democratic peace'.[64] Receiving no worthwhile response from the other belligerent governments, the new Bolshevik regime published and repudiated the secret agreements that Russia had signed with the entente powers earlier in the war. This evidence of an imperialist war served to justify the Bolsheviks' pursuit of a separate peace with the Central Powers. Germany drove a terrible bargain, but Lenin accepted the Treaty of Brest-Litovsk in the firm expectation that it would not survive the future world revolution. Lenin resisted calls to gamble on the instant export of Bolshevism, but he had no doubts about the inevitability of revolution in the long run.[65]

The words and deeds of the Russian Bolsheviks brought back to life the socialist hope of proletarian internationalism, which had been so damaged by the upsurge of working-class patriotism in 1914. Since then several attempts to revivify the Second Socialist International had failed. But now many on the Left who had initially backed the war effort began to have second thoughts as the carnage in the trenches continued unabated and voices of protest mounted, if not in international concert, then in individual nations. Germany was an exemplar. There, a breakaway movement of 'independent' socialists or Spartacists was formed in April 1917. At its core were those orthodox Marxists such as Rosa Luxemburg and Karl Liebknecht who had never accepted the war in the first place, but it also recruited members among the disillusioned 'majority' wing of the SPD. Under pressure from the Independent Socialists, the SPD combined with the centre parties on 19 July to push through the *Reichstag* a resolution in favour of a peace without annexations.[66] It did not deflect the imperial German government one whit, as Brest-Litovsk proved. But the gathering strength of the far left was significant, for the Independent Socialists took their cue from Lenin and, by 1918, aspired to duplicate in Germany what he had accomplished in Russia. That meant peace abroad but civil or revolutionary war at home.

Both Lenin and Wilson preached peace among the nations, although they arrived at a common position by dissimilar routes and their visions of a postwar order differed markedly. It was Lenin's foray into the peace-making arena that induced the American president to refine and reiterate his own high-minded objectives. Wilson's celebrated Fourteen Points were drafted by the Inquiry, a task force charged with enunciating US war aims. The Inquiry was staffed by liberal intellectuals temperamentally disposed to Wilsonian international morality and ideally suited to concoct a direct riposte to the Bolshevik Decree on Peace. The Fourteen Points, unveiled before Congress on 8 January 1918, dealt for the most part with the specific international problems of the 1870–1918 period. But the underlying principles were consistent with Wilson's previous statements – national determination (or at least 'autonomous development') to provide the moral basis of a European territorial settlement, neutral rights at sea, general disarmament. The fourteenth point postulated more emphatically than hitherto a league of nations, with American participation, to uphold the postwar settlement and the peace. In addition, it was necessary to mitigate the odium cast on the entente powers by the revelation of the secret treaties, which was attempted in the very first of the Fourteen Points: 'Open covenants of peace, openly arrived at, after which there shall be no private international understandings of any kind, but diplomacy shall proceed always frankly and in the public view.'[67] Thus, democratic diplomacy was appended to the other elements of democratic ideology that the US prescribed for a war-torn world.

Wilson's natural constituency was the moderate left. As a Progressive in domestic politics, he instinctively looked for foreign allies among reformers, and found them especially among those British radicals on the flank of the Liberal party who had sniped at Grey's entente policy from 1906 to 1912. Predictably, the war roused these radicals to fresh attacks on an international system that had produced Armageddon. Their umbrella organization, the Union of Democratic Control (UDC), was founded in November 1914, won support from well beyond radical ranks and by the end of the war boasted a membership of 650,000. The programme of the UDC anticipated many of Wilson's pronouncements – on open diplomacy for instance – and the term 'league of nations' was invented in Britain. In fact, there was considerable intellectual interchange between the American president and British radicals, a 'community of opinion and . . . conscious harmony'.[68] But when, in April 1917, Wilson became another war leader, some radicals showed signs of withdrawing their trust; the Russian revolution in its libertarian phase was an alternative avatar. But after the Bolshevik coup most radicals were forced to recognize the American president as the most practical embodiment of their international hopes. They acclaimed the Fourteen Points *faute de mieux*.

Since the United States entered the war Wilson had been committed to achieving his new international order, not without victory but through victory. This involved converting or coercing the entente governments and whosoever ruled in Berlin to accept the principles inherent in the Fourteen Points. The entente powers, incapable of winning the war without US help, were malleable. But the German situation was more intricate. Wilson's protestation that 'we have no quarrel with the German people' identified the emperor and his militarist regime as the real enemy, and the promise of a just peace in the Fourteen Points was clearly intended for a Germany that had democratized itself. Above all, Wilson aimed to persuade Germany's moderate Majority Socialists that, rather than following the Independent Socialists into the Bolshevik camp, they should stand ready to take over the reins of government in Berlin.[69]

In the concluding months of the war, then, the Fourteen Points became the focus of a quadrille among the American president himself, the imperial German government, the SPD, and the administrations in London and Paris. In October, with Austria-Hungary, Bulgaria and Turkey all about to capitulate, the German high command knew that the war of attrition was lost and recommended that Washington be approached for an armistice and peace on the basis of the Fourteen Points. Wilson was to be Germany's shield against entente vengeance.

The US president seized the chance to exert pressure on both sides. A scarcely veiled American threat to reach a unilateral agreement with Germany brought London and Paris to heel. They agreed in principle to negotiate within the framework of the Fourteen Points, although Britain imposed a reservation regarding freedom of the seas and France one regarding war reparations.[70] As for Germany, Wilson was determined to exact an ideological price. In his reply to Berlin's *démarche* he refused to

> deal with any but the veritable representatives of the German people who have been assured of a genuine constitutional standing as the real rulers of Germany. If it must deal with the military masters and the monarchical autocrats of Germany now, or if it is likely to have to deal with them later in regard to the international obligations of the German Empire, it must demand, not peace negotiations, but surrender.[71]

The Germans had no choice but to comply. On 9 November 1918 William II was prevailed upon to abdicate, to be replaced by a republican government of Majority Socialists that was granted an armistice on the 11th.

This was an opportunistic, even artificial revolution. The appearance of soviets or worker councils in German factories and military units, as well as a fleet mutiny, was evidence of grass-roots unrest. But the revolution succeeded so painlessly and swiftly in a matter of forty-eight hours because the old imperial order declined to oppose it. It was not only the emperor who abdicated but also the generals and conservative politicos; they backed down in order to regroup. What is more, they launched an immediate counter-attack by circulating the legend that the German army had not been defeated but stabbed in the back by a socialist conspiracy. Conceived out of deference to a foreign ideology, Germany's new-born democracy was fragile from the start. As a device to secure a non-punitive peace settlement, its survival depended heavily on Wilson's ability to fulfil this promise.[72]

The war, which some in 1914 had calculated would avert social change, ended with much of Europe ablaze with revolution. It may have started as a war for the balance of power, but its concluding revolutionary tumult revealed the accretion of broader, ideological complexities. The ideological tactic of subverting the enemy state was practised more frequently as the war continued, to an extent unseen since the French revolutionary wars. Russia was twice a target. First, driven by the exigencies of war, Berlin defied the principle of monarchical solidarity by transporting Lenin and his comrades to the Finland Station. Then, with the Bolshevik seizure of power, the western liberal states found themselves faced with a new ideological challenge. Even while Wilson's propaganda was undermining the right-wing imperial regime in Germany, the entente and associated powers turned their attention to the adversary on the left.

Well before the armistice of 11 November 1918, British, French, American and Japanese troops arrived in Russia ostensibly to prevent war supplies sent by the west from falling into German hands. But the major contacts made were with White anti-Bolshevik forces fighting the Red Army, and the foreign contingents immediately ran the risk of being sucked into the Russian civil war. Naturally, Lenin depicted them as imperialist agents of the counter-revolution, and indeed for many in the West, such as Winston Churchill, the intention was 'to strangle bolshevism at birth'.[73] Ideological hostility between the Soviets and the capitalist states was as inevitable as historians will allow; the powers' intervention in Russia, ineffectual though it was in the end, confirmed and intensified it.

Appealing across the battle lines to disaffected national minorities was a time-honoured device. In the First World War it was a double-edged sword because both sides were vulnerable. In 1916 the desperate Germans proclaimed an independent Poland carved out of Russia's Polish provinces, intrigued in Ireland to set off the Easter uprising, and introduced measures in occupied Belgium to promote Flemish separatism. Elsewhere, Britain encouraged Arab nationalism against the Ottoman empire while courting world Jewry with the Balfour Declaration's promise of a national home in the Near East. In return, the Turks tried to rouse the Muslim world against the Western colonialists. Most exposed to this kind of subversion, however, was the Habsburg empire whose multinational character had sparked the war in the first place. Out of respect for the balance of power, Britain and France did not include in their initial war aims the dismemberment of Austria-Hungary. But the US entry into war brought it into view. Wilsonian emphasis on national self-determination gave the cause ideological bite, and US influence on entente war aims was apparent in the Versailles Declaration of 3 June 1918. Issued by the Supreme War Council, it expressed 'warm sympathy' for the Czechs, Slovaks and Yugoslavs (south Slavs) in 'their struggle for liberty and the realization of their national aspirations', and went even further towards the Poles by guaranteeing them 'a united and independent' state.[74] Polish, Czechoslovak and Yugoslav exile committees, the nuclei of future national governments, gained status in western capitals. Battlefield defeat was in the process of shattering the Habsburg empire in any case, but the currency that the entente and associated powers gave to national determination made doubly sure of its collapse. In the final week of October 1918 the empire disintegrated; on 1 November the Austro-Hungarian tie was dissolved; ten days later the last Habsburg emperor abdicated.

With the disappearance of all three empires of East Central Europe, the ideological shape of international relations was drastically altered. But the role of ideology was not reduced. On the contrary, the First World War increased the general proclivity to view things from an ideological perspective. Wilson and Lenin had made the war into a crusade. Neither liberal democracy nor radical socialism was exactly a new creed, but suddenly both basked in the limelight of international politics. Just as important, war propaganda had from the start peddled ideological images – a combination of simple stereotypes of the enemy and elevated, magnanimous goals. 'A war between Christ and the Devil', Britain's poet laureate called the struggle.[75] Again, nationalist sentiment was nothing new and hardly ideological save in the sense of a cast of mind. But the war's paramount lesson was that ideological thinking, even without an intellectual rationale, was sufficient and necessary to mobilize an entire nation.[76] In this broad context, the war of 1914–18 was the first *total* war of doctrine, for which reason if no other, it probably deserves to retain its original title of the Great War. It has been said that the Great War provided an analogue for the next generation;[77] this was particularly so in demonstrating the uses of ideology in an age of mass politics. In effect, it prepared the way for the totalitarian ideologies and new levels of fanaticism.

7

ENTER TOTAL IDEOLOGIES

LENIN, WILSON AND REACTION

To the war-weary millions Lenin and Wilson appeared as alternative mes-
siahs, and indeed since 1917 each had been projecting himself as a saviour
from outside Europe. Each held out the twin lures of social and economic
justice at home and peace abroad. In one case the promised land was to be
attained according to Lenin's radical world view; in the other, according to
Wilson's reformist principles.

Lenin's recipe for eternal peace was the familiar Marxist one of the
international brotherhood of the working class, although he operated on
two presuppositions neither of which owed much to Marx and Engels
themselves. First, the latter had not envisaged capitalism as a cause of
quarrel among the nations, but rather as a bond among the bourgeois
ruling class and governments everywhere. Second and in consequence,
they had largely ignored the possibility of international conflict as a platform for revolution. However, as we have seen, the new imperialism
before 1914 persuaded much of the socialist community that the wellspring
of the international anarchy was monopoly capitalism. At the same time,
the Second International showed increasing awareness of war's potential
to create revolutionary conditions. Lenin took special note how defeat at
the hands of Japan set off the Russian revolution of 1905 which, in fact,
turned out to be a dress rehearsal for 1917. But it was the First World
War that provided Lenin with a paradigm for his own interpretation of
history's continuum. According to this, the capitalist system bred nationalist rivalries which led through imperialism to war, as allegedly happened in
1914. Modern war, especially defeat in total war, so disrupted bourgeois
society as to clear the way for a workers' revolution. What the Bolsheviks
wrought in Russia was destined to be repeated over and over. Thus, the
Marxian prophecy of universal proletarian revolution would be fulfilled
by exploiting the strife among nations which Lenin asserted to be endemic
to capitalism. The linkage between world politics and world revolution
was a cardinal feature of the new Marxist–Leninist ideology.[1]

Marxist writings implied that capitalism everywhere would disappear in one fell revolutionary swoop, and some of the early conduct of the Soviet regime reflected its conviction that the millennium was at hand. If the economic foundations of modern society were fated to be swept away, then the nation state in its allegedly class-based form would, along with the rest of the capitalist superstructure, automatically disappear too. One could therefore dispense with the apparatus of conventional diplomacy, including foreign ministries themselves. Thus Trotsky's avowed intent on assuming the democratically styled post of people's commissar of foreign affairs was to 'issue a few revolutionary proclamations to the people and close up shop', and in this vein the famous Decree on Peace was addressed in particular to 'the class-conscious workers' of Britain, France and Germany.[2]

It was to Germany above all that the Trotskyites looked for the extension of their revolution. The German working class was large and its organizations formidable, potentially an ideal revolutionary weapon; the Bolsheviks in 1918 clung to the Marxist dogma that revolutionary prospects were brightest where the proletariat was strongest, their own success in backward Russia notwithstanding. Furthermore, Germany appeared to be passing through the same cycle of war, defeat and revolution that Russia had already experienced. The German imperial abdication and constitutional revolution of November 1918 was the rough equivalent of the March 1917 changes in Russia. Why should the revolutionary tide not continue to flow and produce a second, more radical upheaval in Germany, as it had in Russia? It was the burning question of the postwar hour, for conservatives and the extreme left alike. Indeed, in January 1919 Germany's Spartacists took to the streets of Berlin in order to carry forward the November revolution, only to be suppressed with extreme viciousness by a combination of regular army (*Reichswehr*) and paramilitary (*Freikorps*) forces acting with the approval of the Majority Socialists in the provisional government. The failure of the Spartacist uprising turned out to be a death blow to imminent world revolution, although this was not immediately apparent. Radical groups remained active elsewhere, in Bavaria and Hungary for example. And on 2 March 1919 the First Congress of the Comintern or Communist International assembled in Moscow, which the Soviets had made the new Russian capital.

The Russian Bolsheviks having by now adopted the name of the Communist Party, the Comintern was to be an association of like-minded socialists worldwide. Its establishment was Lenin's ideological response to the continued presence of foreign troops on Russian soil. If the victors of the First World War could meddle in Russia's civil war (and refuse to admit the Soviets to the postwar peace conference), then Moscow would give history a push by promoting subversion in the capitalist nations. Lenin did offer to muzzle Bolshevik propaganda outside Russia as part of a deal to end foreign intervention in Russia. But his sincerity was not put to the test. All efforts, mostly American-inspired, to open a dialogue with Moscow foundered on the anti-Bolshevik objections of the European allies, especially the French who had lost most when the Soviets reneged on tsarist debts.[3] Therefore, the invitation to the first Comintern meeting, which was accepted by more than thirty socialist delegations, was couched in unequivocal revolutionary terms: 'The present epoch is the epoch of the disintegration and collapse of the entire capitalist world system . . . The task of the proletariat now is to seize State power immediately.'[4]

Only a fraction of the world socialist community was invited to join the Comintern. Ignored were those who represented the tradition of pre-1914 reformist Marxism, the wartime 'social patriots' and, naturally, the German Majority Socialists because of their role in suppressing the Spartacist revolt. In fact, news that such 'renegades' and 'Judases' were planning to revive the Second International hastened the calling of the first Comintern congress.[5] The Comintern's exclusivity was emphatically confirmed at its second congress in July and August 1920. On this occasion the Comintern received its real organization based on 'democratic centralism' and shaped by Lenin's Twenty-one Conditions for membership, the second of which read:

> Every organization which wishes to join the Communist International must, in an orderly and planned fashion, remove reformists and centrists from all responsible positions in the workers' movement . . . and replace them by tried communists, even if, at the beginning, 'experienced' opportunists have to be replaced by rank and file workers.[6]

The institution of the Comintern thus brought to a head the split between revolutionary communism and evolutionary socialism, or social democracy, the prevailing leftist doctrine outside Russia. In this way, Russian communism became insulated from extraneous and differentiated socialist influences, and Marxism–Leninism developed within an exclusively Russian context. From the beginning, it was questionable whether communist ideology would surmount or be subservient to Russia's national interests. The Comintern, for instance, was nominally independent of the government in Moscow but, in reality, operated as an arm of Soviet foreign policy. A balance had to be struck between the requirements of the Russian state and the promotion of revolution abroad. At least one expert asserts that Lenin's overbearing behaviour at the Comintern's second congress proved his priority was already Soviet power, not global revolution.[7]

Because the Spartacist debacle suggested a lack of revolutionary fervour on the part of the European proletariat, subversive opportunities elsewhere deserved to be explored. Hence, the first Comintern congress issued a call to 'the colonial slaves of Africa and Asia. The hour of proletarian dictatorship in Europe will also be the hour of your own liberation.'[8] The appeal to colonial nationalism was in line with the Leninist theory expounded in his *Imperialism*; empire-building was a mark of the crisis of mature or 'rotten-ripe' capitalism, and it behoved Soviet Russia to encourage all anti-imperialist forces to hasten the demise of capitalism. The moment also appeared propitious because the First World War had had a radicalizing effect outside as well as within Europe. Stirrings of colonial discontent were widespread but those in the British Empire, the cradle of capitalist imperialism in Leninist eyes, were particularly significant. The massacre of 500 unarmed Indians at Amritsar in April 1919 gave tremendous impetus to Mahatma Gandhi's *satyagraha* (non-violent passive resistance) campaign for Indian independence. But in singling out British India for particular attention, Lenin departed from strict class ideology, for the alliance he sought was not with the illiterate masses, but the disaffected middle-class nationalists. The simplistic equation of nationalism and red revolution did not go undisputed; a most vociferous early critic was M.N. Roy, himself an Indian nationalist and later a member of the Comintern's executive committee.[9]

Nevertheless, in tandem with the first Comintern meetings, representatives of all the 'Oppressed Peoples of the East' were brought together in conference. The assemblage at Baku in September 1920 was a particularly histrionic affair at which more than one contradiction surfaced. Predictably, communists and bourgeois nationalists clashed. Even more explosive was the presence of Turkish opponents of Western imperialism who had to be separated from the Armenians struggling to escape Turkey's yoke.[10] But such quarrels were of little immediate concern; the Soviets were more interested in preparing the ground for later ideological penetration of the Third World (see Chapter 9).

In the short term, the Russian communist regime was more preoccupied with its own security in a world of hostile capitalist powers. In the spring of 1920 fighting broke out on the undefined Soviet–Polish border. It was, in a sense, an extension of foreign intervention in Russia's ongoing civil war; the Poles, with special encouragement from France, aimed not only to push their own frontier as far east as possible, but also to carve an independent Ukraine out of western Russia. After initial reverses Soviet forces unexpectedly began to advance and by August reached Warsaw. There was an upsurge of joy in the Comintern at the sudden prospect of spreading the communist revolution on the bayonets of the Red Army. But just as suddenly the mirage faded; Soviet forces were repulsed and thrown into disorderly retreat. The Treaty of Riga (1921), which concluded the war, consigned large tracts of Byelorussia and the Ukraine to Poland, a lesser Brest-Litovsk. Thereupon, Soviet Russia axiomatically became an aggrieved and revisionist power. Just as important, the battle of Warsaw deflated Comintern optimism and accelerated the *pro tem* shift away from the policy of exporting revolution westward.

The retreat from an ideological foreign policy and recourse to more customary diplomatic methods was closely linked to the departure from Marxist–Leninist orthodoxy on the home front. Although civil war petered out in 1921, Russia was left with a terrible legacy of economic ruin and famine. To cope with the overwhelming crisis Lenin abandoned his 'war communism', a crash programme to eradicate capitalism, in favour of his New Economic Policy (NEP). The NEP licensed a certain amount of private ownership and a free market in trade, small business and farming. Were a form of capitalism to become the road to recovery, cooperation with the West was vital; specifically, the Soviets needed western capital investment and technological assistance. Out of this exigency was born the doctrine of peaceful coexistence (*sosushchestvovanie*), or cohabitation (*sozhitel'stvo*) as Lenin preferred.[11] In this new phase of Soviet foreign policy revolutionary ideology did not disappear but, to propitiate the west, it ceased to be front and centre. 'In the life of European Communism the romantic and adventurist period came to an end.'[12]

Peaceful coexistence instantly threw up some ideological peculiarities. The major part of foreign relief of the great Russian famine in 1921–2 came from the United States where red-baiting was in full spate. But the relief effort did not lead on to further US–Soviet economic ties. A more natural Russian partner was Germany, both by reason of geography and a joint animus against the victors of the First World War. The year 1921 saw the launch of several mixed Russo-German industrial and agricultural enterprises and, significantly, the groundwork was laid for cooperation in military training.[13] In the latter negotiations the Soviets found themselves working with the reactionary *Reichswehr* general staff which, in the Spartacist revolt, had shown its determination to use brute force within Germany to eliminate communists and their sympathizers.

A broader *rapprochement* with the West seemed to open up with an invitation to attend an international economic conference in Genoa, Lloyd George's last fling to salvage postwar European rehabilitation. But Moscow suspected, not without cause, that others in the West planned the economic exploitation of Russia in neocolonial fashion. Consequently, while virtually nothing was accomplished in the Genoa Conference itself, the Soviet representatives, who were staying in nearby Rapallo, entertained their German confrères there on 16 April 1922 and signed a bilateral pact. The terms of the Rapallo treaty were innocuous enough; a financial and commercial accord was accompanied by the resumption of full diplomatic and consular representation. Symbolically, however, it was much more; Rapallo splintered the united capitalist front against Soviet Russia.[14]

If in one sense Rapallo was a Soviet ideological victory, it had been won by Moscow's new pragmatic diplomacy. What drew Moscow and Berlin together was from first to last their condition as defeated states, and the tactic of allying with the enemy of one's own enemy was pure *Realpolitik*. In turn, the Western powers responded to Rapallo in time-honoured fashion. At Locarno, in circumstances described below, they tried to separate Germany from Russia. And to counter the economic march stolen by Germany in the Soviet Union they developed a sudden enthusiasm for commercial accords with Moscow which, in turn, led to *de jure* diplomatic recognition. Led in 1924 by supposedly bitter ideological antagonists of communism, imperialist Britain and Fascist Italy, a parade of states accorded recognition. The USA was last to do so, withholding recognition until 1933.

The ideological edge in the Soviet–Western relationship may have been much diminished, but in the Kremlin world revolution had been only set aside, not forgotten. The Comintern continued to churn out proletarian rhetoric, and its personnel to move easily to and from the Commissariat for Foreign Affairs (*Narkomindel*). In view of the latter's evolution, this was bound to create tension. Under Georgy Chicherin, who took over the commissariat from Trotsky after Brest-Litovsk, professional agitators rapidly gave way to members of Russia's radical intelligentsia, many of them with cosmopolitan experience from time spent in exile from tsarism. Chicherin, whose own background included aristocratic connections and a spell in the pre-1917 foreign ministry, and his colleagues of upper middle-class origin were perfectly suited to conduct conventional diplomacy in the era of peaceful coexistence. 'As the interests of the Soviet state came to predominate over those of proletarian imperialism, the techniques and style of the Narkomindel's diplomats became less and less distinguishable from those of their bourgeois colleagues'.[15] To such bureaucrats Comintern activities were an embarrassment. Even the Soviet newspaper, *Pravda*, carried a cartoon of Chicherin clutching his head in despair behind the back of the Comintern president, Gregory Zinoviev, while the latter indulges in an anti-capitalist rant.

Pravda was prophetic, for shortly afterwards occurred the affair of the Zinoviev letter. Western intelligence agencies more or less regularly intercepted Comintern instructions to national communist parties. Those of 15 September 1924 to a British communist leader, possibly forged but probably authentic, were unduly provocative in that they concerned the infiltration of army and navy units. British authorities saw fit to leak the text to the press and promptly created a red scare reminiscent of 1919. In actual fact, this Zinoviev letter appears to have sprung from a brief flurry of Comintern 'adventurism' made possible by a lack of central direction in Moscow during the power struggle that followed Lenin's death. In no way did it betoken a swing away from peaceful coexistence, and its main effect was to ensure defeat in the pending British election of the first Labour government, which was in the process of extending diplomatic recognition to the USSR. Subversion and revolution were of less immediate use to Soviet foreign policy than to western anti-communists eager to scare the middle classes into voting for conservative parties.[16]

Out of peaceful coexistence grew the doctrine of 'socialism in one country'. Ever since 1918 Lenin had cautioned against a premature and risky launch of class war on an international scale. Now it was his purpose to use the breathing space provided by peaceful coexistence to build the Soviet Union with capitalist help into a fortress invulnerable to capitalist assault. Within secure frontiers the communist experiment, after NEP had done its work, would be resumed and completed. Hence 'socialism in one country', a phrase bandied about well before Stalin elevated it into dogma.[17] The very words connoted delay in the revolution elsewhere. On the other hand, 'socialism in one country' bore its own ideological and revolutionary subtext. Since the eighteenth century US isolationists had preached the dictum that their country should stand alone as a beacon of enlightenment, an exemplar to all other nations. In much the same way, the promise that a socialist paradise was under construction in one corner of the universe was an invitation for revolutionaries everywhere to look to the USSR for inspiration and imitation. As Italy's leading socialist newspaper put it after the Bolshevik revolution, 'The Soviet republic is our country today. The proletariat finally has a homeland.'[18] In sum, Soviet foreign policy was never really without ideological reverberations.

Lenin's efforts to create a new world order out of the opportunity presented by the First World War paralleled those of US President Wilson. But where the Bolshevik leader's postwar revolutionary message was addressed to the masses who were bidden to confront their governments, his rival sought to implement popular Wilsonianism by persuasion, first of the other world leaders and then of the US political elite. His labours began at the postwar peace conference that opened in Paris on 18 January 1919, and it must be stressed that at Paris Wilson was from the outset handicapped by the mere existence of the coincident Marxist–Leninist phenomenon.

In spite of Soviet Russia's exclusion from the Paris deliberations, it was present in spirit like 'Banquo's ghost sitting at every Council table'. In brief, the conference met amid apprehension that a 'red tide of Bolshevism' was about to overwhelm Europe. As one participant commented, 'Paris cannot be understood without Moscow . . . Russia played a more vital part at Paris than Prussia. For the Prussian idea had been utterly defeated, while the Russian idea was still rising in power.'[19] Many conservatives did indeed trade on the great fear of Bolshevism to discard the wartime promises of social and economic justice. But in addition, it has been argued that the use of the Bolshevik bogey to resist any and all change applied equally to international relations, and especially to the Wilsonian peace with justice which was supposed to usher in a new era in 1919:

> The forces of order appear to have taken advantage of the intoxication of victory either to preserve or advance their class interests and status positions under an ideological cover which was a syncretism of jingoist nationalism, baleful anti-Wilsonianism, and rabid anti-Bolshevism. Whoever was not a superpatriot was denounced as a fellow traveler of the Bolsheviks and stood accused not only of disloyalty but of advocating a sellout peace.[20]

There is more than a whiff of exaggerated conspiracy theory in this view, as well as the danger of discounting the magnitude of the German problem which was more immediate and closer to hand. Yet, undeniably, the Paris Conference was haunted by the spectre of Bolshevism which created a climate of opinion inimical to reform of any kind. It is difficult to evaluate exactly the impact on Wilson's ambitious project for a 'new diplomacy', but it was assuredly detrimental.

Unlike Lenin, who proposed to tear down the existing system before rebuilding, Wilson aimed to repair it. The American president had no quarrel with capitalism *per se*, and his domestic policy followed the US Progressive line of simply curbing its worst abuses. Similarly, on the international stage he proffered no alternative to the nation states system, but rather a means of controlling its internecine competition. Wilson's Progressivism derived from his nineteenth-century liberal background, and his policies were a liberal's response to the problems posed by mass politics and total war. This was apparent in the three cardinal features of his prospective new international order – open diplomacy, self-determination and the concept of collective security.

The cult of democratic diplomacy rested on the postulate that the public, once properly apprised of an international issue, would demand a pacific solution. 'Just a little exposure will settle most questions,' Wilson remarked on arriving in Paris.[21] His belief that the masses everywhere shared his own passion for international conciliation was strengthened by the enthusiastic crowds he attracted as he toured France, Britain and Italy before the peace conference opened. Such faith in the basic rationality and peaceable inclinations of humankind was a trait that nineteenth-century liberals had inherited from the Enlightenment, and it blithely overlooked the explosion of popular nationalism and kindred ideologies in the half-century before 1914.

Nor was Wilson's emphasis on national self-determination anything new; self-determination had been on the march since the French revolutionary wars. Like the romantic nationalism of the nineteenth century the Wilsonian crusade embraced both individual liberty and the freedom of national groups. In effect, Wilson was trying to reclaim nationalism from the *Realpolitik* conservatives and return it to the liberal fold. And, again like the nineteenth-century liberal nationalists, he did not see self-determination as an end in itself but as a means to a higher goal; the removal of nationalist grievances was a prerequisite step towards inter-nationalism. Hence, a world body to formalize the achievement of international harmony was central to Wilson's grand design.

A league of nations providing 'collective enforcement' and 'pooled security' (hence collective security) for all members had the air of a genu-inely innovative proposal, not least because it was presented as an alternative to the mechanism of the balance of power. The Wilsonians regarded the balance as discredited partly because it had been used at the Congress of Vienna in 1815 to thwart just national aspirations, partly because it was supposed to have caused the Great War. This latter criticism was directed at the 1914 balance, bipolar and 'adversarial'; it disregarded the classical or 'associative' type of balance that had been more common over the centuries.[22] Nevertheless, the balance was to yield to collective security – a notion that was intended to mean a greater degree of inter-national *dirigisme* than, say, the old Concert of Europe. In other words, it held out the promise of restricting for the first time the sovereign independence of the nation state. Prior to the peace conference, however, Wilson refused to be drawn on details of his putative league of nations, and it remained unclear how revolutionary an experiment he actually intended.

Details of the new diplomacy took second place to the 'great wind of moral force' which the American president felt to be 'moving throughout the world'.[23] The assumption was that the Great War had taught a salutary lesson, and now civilization was set to resume its onward march. In this fashion, the liberal idea of progress survived the war in the Wilsonian constituency. Wilson himself certainly approached the postwar negotiations in Paris with the sense that he rode an advancing tide of history, and that his ideas had destiny on their side. It contributed to what his critics called his 'messiah complex'.[24]

Predictably, Wilson won some battles at Paris but lost others. Open diplomacy proved a non-starter. The public adulation of the US president on his arrival in Europe was misleading; it signified no diminution in the spirit of popular nationalism. A British khaki election was held in the closing weeks of 1918 and, although Prime Minster Lloyd George shunned rhetorical extremes, his followers won strong approbation with the slogan that Germany should pay for the war 'until the pips squeaked'. In France public opinion was, if anything, more xenophobic in support of Clemenceau; this tigerish war leader felt little need to consult the Chamber of Deputies and relied more on the backing of an improvised 'French National Congress' composed mainly of superpatriots and veterans.

Later, in mid-conference, in order to rebut Italy's claim to Fiume, Wilson tried to appeal to the Italian people over the head of their government; this proved a sorry error of judgement for it incited a fierce nationalist backlash.[25]

The persistence of a fervid populist nationalism meant that no diplomatic compromise could be negotiated in the public gaze. The peace conference itself reflected this reality. No material business was conducted in the occasional plenary sessions. Decision-making took place, first, in a council of ten consisting of the heads of governments and foreign ministers of the USA, Britain, France, Italy and Japan, and later, with European issues paramount, in a council of four of Wilson, Lloyd George, Clemenceau and Orlando. A further reduction occurred when the last named, the Italian premier, stalked out. And when Wilson fell ill at the height of a giant influenza epidemic, some meetings were held in the intimacy of his hotel bedroom. This was traditional conference diplomacy in which bargains were struck privately and communiqués couched in bland generalizations, much to the chagrin of the horde of journalists lured to Paris by the prospect of public negotiation and daily scoops. In the end, not much was left of the original dream of open diplomacy save for certain facets of the pristine League of Nations, namely, open discussion in its Assembly and a requirement that member states register, and thereby publish, their international engagements with the League secretariat.

National self-determination fared somewhat better at Paris but hardly lived up to the universal panacea the Wilsonians predicted. A prime site for its application was the Danube valley where the dissolution of the Habsburg empire made self-determination unavoidable. Notable among the successors to the Habsburg inheritance were the brand-new federal states of Czechoslovakia and the south Slavs (Yugoslavia), while out of the additional collapse of the Romanov and Hohenzollern empires emerged an independent Poland for the first time in a century and a quarter. All this resulted in the reduction by almost half of those peoples in Eastern and Central Europe under alien rule in 1914. Yet populations were so mixed throughout Eastern Europe that it was impossible to do more than correct the most glaring anomalies, and the 1919 settlement still left some thirty million people living as national minorities. Moreover, the ethnic feeling of these 'peasant nationalities' was tribal and savagely intolerant of neighbours. Irredentism was rife among states such as Hungary and Bulgaria that had lost territory, and even among the victorious Poles, who coveted Czechoslovak Teschen. In short, nationalist ideology at its most malevolent was set to flourish in Eastern Europe *sine die*. The hopelessness of the task that faced the postwar peacemakers drove one British statesman to comment, 'We should put the whole area in charge of a genius. We have no genius's [*sic*] available.'[26]

The main business of the Paris conference was, of course, a settlement with Germany, and here too the principle of national self-determination was at stake. The notorious war guilt clause of the Versailles treaty blamed the First World War on German 'aggression' in 1914. But beyond this specific charge, it could be argued that Germany's responsibility went deeper in that its very unification had upset the European balance. If this was the real cause of the war, why not dismember the troublesome hegemonic state which, in 1919, was less than a half-century old? However, this was never on the peace conference agenda. The most that France felt able to urge for its own security was the creation of a separate Rhineland state, and even this was thwarted by Wilson's use of the national determination argument. In lieu, Wilson offered the French demilitarization of the Rhineland and an Anglo-American guarantee of the frontier with Germany. Yet if the Paris conference's acquiescence in Bismarck's work was a triumph for self-determination, it also represented a setback for a different Wilsonian ideal, for a united Germany was, in the *Realpolitik* calculation of the European victors, a buffer against Bolshevik Russia. In other words, the balance-of-power factor, which the Wilsonians hoped to banish, was alive and well in Paris.

In Germany, on the other hand, attention was fixed not on the preservation of German unification, but on perceived offences against German nationality in the border regions. In truth, several decisions taken at Paris were conspicuously at odds with national determination. With the disappearance of the Habsburg empire, the question was raised whether those Germans left outside Bismarck's *Kleindeutschland* should now 'come home'. The answer was in the negative. Although the Austrian rump state was exclusively Teutonic in ethnicity, both the Treaty of Versailles with Germany and the Treaty of St Germain with Austria specifically forbade *Anschluss*, despite a strong popular current in postwar republican Austria for joining the new democratic Germany. In former Habsburg Bohemia, the heavily German Sudetenland was placed within Czechoslovakia in order to give that state a defensible northern boundary and possession of the Skoda industrial complex. However, the major German nationalist grievance concerned the Polish Corridor which, created explicitly to give another new state economic access to the sea, cut the Prussian heartland of the old Germany in two. The cession of territory to Poland rankled most because it constituted a retraction of Germany's own 1914 frontiers. So too, of course, was the return to France of the mixed provinces of Alsace-Lorraine, but Western Europe by this time took second place. Germany's annexationist ambitions towards the end of the First World War had focused nationalist eyes on the east, and in the interwar period German revisionism continued to look first and foremost to Central and Eastern Europe. It was no coincidence that the next war in 1939 arose out of successive crises in Austria,

Czechoslovakia and Poland, precisely where the Paris peace conference rejected German nationality claims.

For Wilson, as for Lenin, the criterion of his new order resided in Germany. An immediate Marxist–Leninist cosmic revolution would start in Germany or not at all; likewise, the fate of Wilsonian liberal democracy at large hinged on the success or failure of the German venture in constitutional government currently being drafted in Weimar. In turn, the Weimar regime's initial standing with its own people was contingent on the realization of the peace with justice heralded in the Fourteen Points and promised Germany in the armistice. Objectively speaking, the Germans might have been treated much more harshly in the 1919 settlement. So long as a united Germany continued in being, so did the 'German problem'; that country's dominance of the European continent remained in the offing.[27]

Unfortunately, Versailles was a matter of perception, and the Germans widely held the treaty to be punitive and unfair. It was not just a question of the departures from national self-determination, the war guilt clause justifying reparations, limitation of the German army, loss of colonies, etc., but also of the imagery with which the treaty came to be shrouded. For a start, there was the victors' refusal to negotiate face to face with the German delegation in Paris, a sop to Germanophobe opinion back home. In reality, there were extensive written negotiations with the Germans but these were not publicized; the impression left was that terms were presented as a *fait accompli*. Nor was the ceremonial manner of the treaty's signing conducive to heal the wounds of war; it took place on 28 June 1919, the fifth anniversary of the shot fired at Sarajevo, in Versailles' Hall of Mirrors in retaliation for Germany's provocative announcement there of the Bismarckian *Reich* in 1871. The predictable outcome was a German nationalist hue and cry against the *Diktat* or 'slave-treaty'. Democratic Weimar thus started out burdened with an unacceptable settlement on which all Germany's postwar problems could be and were blamed. From an international perspective, the Treaty of Versailles, far from providing an *entrée* to a fresh and peaceable world, erected a formidable barrier.

The many compromises that Wilson tolerated at Paris are susceptible to two explanations. Either they were wrenched from him by force of circumstance and, as many at the time assumed, the superior diplomatic skill of Lloyd George and Clemenceau. Or else he was not the utter idealist that some of his followers imagined, in which case he was less committed to absolute self-determination and more disposed towards balance-of-power politics than is often supposed.[28] But whether Wilsonian concessions were wrung or calculated, they were made to serve his diplomatic priority – the establishment of a league of nations. At the outset of the Paris conference Wilson demanded that this item be placed at the head of the agenda, and his retreat on other points of principle was the price paid for the *sine qua non* of his international programme. After all, once in place the league's machinery would, as Wilson assured his wife, 'correct mistakes which are inevitable in the treaty we are trying to make at this time'.[29]

It was Wilson who insisted on the title of covenant, with its overtone of a solemn religious vow, for the constitution of the League of Nations. The actual text emerged principally from Anglo-American exchanges during January 1919, and at each stage of the negotiating procedure genuine collective security surrendered more and more to individual states' freedom of action.[30] In the Covenant national sovereignty was safeguarded in two crucial ways. First, decisions of the League's executive council required a unanimous vote on substantive matters, parties to a dispute excepted. Second, member states were under no legal obligation to abide by a League council resolution; the Covenant permitted the Council merely to 'advise' (article 10) or 'recommend' (article 16) a course of action. As Lord Robert Cecil, one of the League's chief architects, privately acknowledged, his brief at Paris was to help 'devise some really effective means of preserving the peace of the world consistently with the least possible interference with national sovereignty'. There was 'no attempt to rely on anything like a superstate'.[31]

Subject to the pleasure of its members, the League could respond to international aggression by imposing on the guilty party three kinds of sanctions – moral, economic and military. The French seized on the last category and suggested a permanent military force be put at the League's disposal, but the USA and the British rejected the proposal in favour of the member states' voluntary secondment of armed forces on an *ad hoc* basis. Whereupon the French to all intents turned their back on the League and went in search of security by the tried-and-true methods of bilateral alliances and the balance of power. Truth to tell, the framers of the Covenant placed their trust in moral sanctions, meaning world opinion, or at worst economic measures; they regarded military sanctions as a remote hypothesis. 'Armed force is in the background of this program,' explained Wilson to a plenary session of the peace conference, 'but it *is* in the background.' The League was 'intended as a constitution of peace, not as a league of war'.[32]

A 'great experiment' Cecil called the League of Nations ensconced in the Palais des Nations in Geneva, though there was perhaps less novelty involved than his title implied.[33] Particularly redolent of past diplomatic practice was the concentration of the decision-making power in the hands of the victorious allied and associated powers, which constituted the permanent members and a permanent majority of the League Council. Indeed, whatever the internationalist intent, the Council came out resembling the condominium of great powers that had tried to direct international affairs in the post-Napoleonic era, the old Concert of Europe made global. This amounted to a great disappointment for those reformers who dreamed of a clean break with the tainted multi-state system and its replacement by some sort of world government. On the other hand, the Covenant in its finished form may not have departed too far from the American president's own expectations. It bears repeating that he was not the foe of national sovereignty that many wanted him to be and, in any case, he was conscious of the need to get the work of the peace conference accepted in the USA. Thus, the League Covenant was purposely included in all the peace treaties on the presumption that the US Senate would not dare refuse ratification of the whole package. Indeed, during a quick trip home in February and March 1919, Wilson discovered a mounting unease at the international obligations he was asking his country to assume. In part, this derived from partisan politics, for Wilson had unwisely excluded prominent Republicans from his Paris delegation. On returning to Paris, he pushed belatedly for amendments to the Covenant which might mollify the domestic opposition; his most notable success was the insertion of a clause that recognized the validity of regional understandings and made specific reference to the Monroe Doctrine.

The fight for the treaties and League of Nations was joined in earnest after Wilson's final return from Paris in the summer of 1919. From a distance it appears a straightforward contest between those at the two ideological poles of US foreign policy – isolationists and interventionists. In fact, the situation was more complex because it is far from certain that Wilson, in campaigning for the League, meant to cut himself totally adrift from the tradition of American isolationism. The Wilsonian conception of a league of nations owed much to the liberal or Progressive ambience in which the president worked.[34] In domestic policy he relied on the notion of 'social control', a collective recognition of what was needed to produce both reform and civil harmony (much the same objective as that of the original French *idéologues*). The extension of the Progressive philosophy of social control from the arena of domestic reform to that of world politics was the precise recommendation of a group of American sociologists, most notably C.H. Cooley, whose printed academic paper, *Social Control in International Relations* (1917), reached a wide audience, including Wilson, who kept up his contacts with the world of scholarship. According to this fashionable current of thought, the League of Nations was cut out to perform as the instrument of international social control. If it succeeded, the USA would then be at liberty to resume its traditional aloofness, and the old fear of 'entangling alliances' would be set at rest. In the context of social control theory, then, the American president appears 'at once interventionist and isolationist', his objective a synthesis of 'control, universalism and unilateralism'.[35]

But whatever Wilson's ulterior purpose, his actual conduct of the League of Nations campaign managed to polarize the forces of American isolationism and interventionism as never before. He was always stubborn in his beliefs, and a physical collapse while on a gruelling cross-country speaking tour in September appeared to increase his obduracy. A stroke after his return to Washington left the president crippled and heavily dependent on his second wife, who encouraged him to stick to the letter of the League Covenant drafted in Paris. His refusal to accept any but minuscule modifications stood in sharp contrast to the concessions of principle he had made in the rest of the peace treaties. It was clear, moreover, that the European allies would not balk at watering down the Covenant. But the League's pivotal role in his new diplomacy precluded that he yield on this issue. His intransigence undercut the efforts of his party political lieutenants to meet the League's critics halfway, and drove waverers into the camp of the 'irreconcilables'. This played into the hands of Henry Cabot Lodge, the powerful Republican chairman of the Senate foreign relations committee. Lodge himself was a pragmatic opponent of Wilsonianism rather than a doctrinaire isolationist, but the president's attitude enabled him to forge a formidable, if variegated, coalition against the League.[36] Although almost certainly a majority of American public and congressional opinion favoured a league of nations in one form or other, the Treaty of Versailles with the essentially unamended Covenant failed twice, in November 1919 and March 1920, to gain the two-thirds Senate majority necessary for ratification.

The subsequent presidential election was something of a referendum on the League. With Wilson too ill to run for re-election, the Democrats held out the prospect that the USA might join the League 'with reservations', and a committee of thirty-one prominent Republican internationalists contended that their candidate had the same goal in mind. But once elected, Republican President Harding wasted no time in declaring US membership in the League as 'dead as slavery'.[37]

To all appearances, events in Paris and Washington had shattered the Wilsonian hope of liberal internationalism. The old diplomacy remained in place as foreign ministries were largely unchanged in personnel and ethos. In Britain the UDC and other critics kept up a running attack on the aristocratic foreign office, although the principal effect was to loosen restraints on Lloyd George's penchant for personal diplomacy. The French and German foreign ministries continued to work with minimum public review.[38] The European balance of power was back in full operation as the Treaty of Rapallo indicated. The French, meanwhile, had resumed their ancient policy of cultivating allies to the east of Germany; Poland took the place of tsarist Russia.[39] To crown it all, the League of Nations was what its name stated: a partnership of sovereign nation states. Coupled with a shortfall in delivery of the pledges of social and economic justice, it all led a host of Europe's 'disillusioned intelligentsia' to accuse Wilson of a great betrayal. From a short-term perspective, it is true that 'the great promises of 1917–18 turned out to have been a pipe dream'.[40]

Yet, just as Marxism–Leninism retreated to fight another day, so Wilsonianism lived on beyond 1919. Its resilience was demonstrated within a few years by efforts at Geneva to 'put teeth' in the League of Nations Covenant. The first of these was prompted by Cecil, British representative in Geneva, who often acted beyond his official remit in the interests of a League of Nations Union lobby. A draft treaty of mutual assistance, drawn up in 1923, proposed to tighten member states' obligations under article 10 with an eye to facilitating military sanctions. The French and their allies were interested, but the project foundered on a contradiction in the minds of many liberal internationalists. Being antimilitarist, they could not abide the thought of war to keep the general peace; they wanted collective security without the price. Prototypical was Ramsay MacDonald, Labour prime minister from January 1924, who dismissed the draft treaty as an 'old-fashioned military compact' whose 'first result would be the increase of the British army'. But having scuppered the draft treaty, MacDonald felt constrained to find a substitute, especially when French elections brought a left-of-centre coalition, the *Cartel des gauches*, into power. MacDonald traded on the ideological similarity of the London and Paris administrations to persuade the *Cartel* leader, Edouard Herriot, to evacuate the Ruhr valley, which the French had occupied for eighteen months to force payment of German reparations; Britain owed something in return. Together, the two premiers of the democratic left contrived the Geneva Protocol, a package of arbitration, disarmament and security, to be supervised by the League of Nations and to give France its longed-for security. Whether MacDonald was as sincerely committed to the Geneva Protocol as his oratory in introducing the measure suggested must be doubted; he began to back off as soon as the French emphasized the military implications of the 'enforcement of arbitration'.[41] But in any event, Labour fell from office before 1924 was out, and its Conservative successor terminated all essays in belated Wilsonianism forthwith.

But once again, lingering guilt over the demise of a pact was assuaged by the invention of a new one. Britain's Conservative foreign secretary, Austen Chamberlain, seized on a German overture and the result was the Locarno accords of October 1925. In retrospect, one can see the flaws of Locarno all too clearly: a guarantee by four powers of the West European frontiers fixed six years earlier fell far short of universal collective security and also cast doubt on the validity of the rest of the territorial peace settlement. Nevertheless, Locarno at the time was greeted with euphoria because it was no *Diktat* and laid to rest the most exigent threat to peace, the Franco-German quarrel. Germany's foreign minister, Gustav Stresemann, saw in Locarno 'the basis of great developments in the future. Statesmen and nations therein proclaim their purpose to prepare the way for the yearnings of humanity after peace and understanding.'[42] The architects of Locarno, Chamberlain, Stresemann and their French counterpart, Aristide Briand, won the Nobel Peace Prize.

For the short period known as the Locarno era (1925–9) the Wilsonian faithful took heart; the dream of international conciliation might be coming true after all. Robert Graves, composing his war memoir, chose a title that summed up the feeling that the real end of the First World War had been reached, *Goodbye to All That* (1929). Even the United States had emerged sufficiently from isolation to superintend an interim reparations settlement – the Dawes plan in 1924 – and went on to provide investments and short-term loans, especially to Germany, which contributed heavily to the European economic recovery which underlay the international goodwill. Moreover, though *détente* had been engineered outside the League of Nations, the Wilsonian cynosure enjoyed a reflected glory. By agreement at Locarno Germany entered the League and, after some haggling among the minor states, secured a permanent Council seat. With Locarno affording Europe at least temporary security, it was possible to entertain another of Wilson's ideals – general disarmament. The League of Nations was charged with preparing the ground rules for an international disarmament conference, a long and tortuous process as it transpired. Elsewhere the League succeeded in imposing its collective will on minor states squabbling over frontier delimitation. Inflating the organization's bubble reputation still further, the world's leading foreign ministers during the Locarno era put in regular attendance at Geneva.

It all proved an illusion as in the 1930s the Great Depression and international discord, each fuelling the other, engulfed the world.[43] None the less, Wilsonianism persisted, above all in the 'myth of collective security'.[44] As we shall see later in this chapter, a residual longing for something better than old-style power politics inhibited at least the English-speaking world in responding to the dictators. Furthermore, the American exceptionalist mission of bringing the world a new and peaceable order resurfaced in the guise of 'universalism' at the end of the Second World War (see Chapter 8). It should be added here that Wilson's call for democracy and national self-determination probably played as large a part in stirring up colonial unrest as Lenin's more studied propaganda. But again, the international consequences were not clearly apparent until after 1945 (see Chapter 9).

The contest between Wilsonianism and Leninism after the First World War was one between old and new fashions in ideology. Wilson was a nineteenth-century figure, his creed a slightly updated liberalism. Liberalism lacked structural rigour; it was more an implicit set of attitudes. Classical liberalism eschewed dogma; it sought to persuade rather than assert. Its truths were relative; thus national self-determination was ancillary to universal well-being, what Mazzini called humanity and Wilson meant by internationalism. In most respects, Wilsonian liberalism was a partial ideology. By contrast, Marxism–Leninism was the very model of a total ideology, an intellectual, exclusive and messianic *Weltanschauung*. Lenin's brutal decimation of enemies and inconvenient associates alike after November 1917 and, on the international stage, his propensity to browbeat the Comintern bore the unmistakable stamp of the ruthless dogmatist. Yet it was Lenin who, albeit for strategic reasons, reined in an ideological, that is to say subversive, foreign policy. Even more significant, he established a tradition of equating the advance of world communism with the health of the Russian state. The heed accorded *raison d'état* cushioned Soviet diplomacy from the full impact of the regime's total ideology. This remained broadly true under Stalin as well, just one dimension of the larger argument whether the later totalitarian state was built on Leninist precedents.[45] Ideology would continue to cast a long shadow over Soviet foreign policy; on the other hand, it never came close to constituting the sole and categorical imperative.

In the meantime, total ideology was arriving from another quarter. While Wilson and Lenin competed for souls on the left, right-wing factions rode a backlash against both Wilsonian reform and Leninist revolution. In addition, these groupings of old conservatives and a new radical right had no compunction about exploiting the latent nationalist zealotry which the First World War had failed to chasten. Out of this volatile compound burst fascism and Nazism, and it was these movements that elevated ideology to be the pole star of international affairs.

FASCISM AND NAZISM

Fascism was a direct consequence of the First World War. The fascists themselves, as distinct from their conservative allies, were overwhelmingly members of the 'front generation' of 1914–18 – returned soldiery who found it hard to adjust to civilian life – as well as their younger brothers cheated of the great adventure of war. Such were the blackshirted followers of Mussolini, who became Italian premier in 1922. Their very name resonated with the spirit of battle – *fasci di combattimento* (action groups).

In the beginning, Italian Fascism was so anxious to oppose Marxism in every form that it set its face against any and all ideologies. In the words of a seminal work on fascism,

> By invoking the superiority of action, Italian fascism spared itself the constant evolution of a doctrine. Fascism has therefore at times been described as 'unideological' in nature . . . a typical antithesis to the

constant efforts of Marxism to establish a relationship with a great and tangible intellectual tradition.[46]

And yet, the cult of action for its own sake bespoke a generic ideological outlook. The generational revolt that was Fascism brought to peacetime politics the symbols of the battlefield and the intransigence towards opponents fed by wartime propaganda. The 'will, firm and decisive' of which Mussolini boasted clearly indicated opinions held viscerally and dogmatically.[47] Furthermore, it was in foreign policy that passion and bias could be expected because Fascism absorbed the Italian Nationalist party and appropriated its entire ideology.

Fascism rode to power on two waves of sentiment: anti-Bolshevism and nationalist discontent. The latter was expressed in the nationalists' description of their country as a 'proletarian nation'. According to this slogan Italy lacked both adequate raw materials and a compensatory empire for great-power status.[48] To this was added the notion of the 'mutilated victory' whereby the Paris Peace Conference was accused of reneging on promises made to Italy in the Treaty of London and subsequent arrangements. The literary *condottiere* Gabriele D'Annunzio made Fiume the emblem of nationalist vexation when, at the head of a private army, he seized and held the town for fifteen months in defiance of the international community. Fiume was not covered by the wartime agreements because no one had foreseen the collapse of the Habsburg empire or the creation of Yugoslavia. In truth, Italy was more than amply requited at Paris for rebuffs in the Adriatic and elsewhere. On the northeast Alpine frontier – the locus of the nation's primary war aims – the new borders were tailored expressly to suit Italian strategic requirements; 200,000 Germans in the South Tyrol and half a million Slavs in the Trentino and Istria were put under none-too-tender Italian rule. Apropos the mutilated-victory syndrome, one Italian critic dubbed his nation, after Molière, a 'malade imaginaire'.[49]

D'Annunzio's Fiume episode impressed upon Mussolini the value of playing the nationalist card. It was by doing so that Fascism gained unusual popularity in Italy's frontier regions. In foreign policy Mussolini's goal was parity with Britain and France, which was to be won by national self-assertion summed up in his aphorism 'niente per niente' (nothing for nothing).[50] At first, though, he was occupied mainly with the establishment of his own position at home as *duce* of a one-party state; a serious campaign to satisfy Italian nationalist ideology awaited the 1930s.

The question was whether the Fascists would add beliefs of their own to traditional nationalism. And in fact, with time the Fascist distaste for ideology *per se* abated remarkably. Mussolini was the first of the interwar dictators to boast that his regime was a totalitarian one, which seemingly necessitated a sustaining doctrine. The *Enciclopedia italiana* of 1932 contained a Mussolinian definition of 'the Fascist political doctrine – different from all others either of the past or the present day'. It extolled the virtues of the absolutist state and went on to suggest that Fascist ideas had worldwide relevancy: 'If every age has its own characteristic doctrine, there are a thousand signs that point to Fascism as the characteristic doctrine of our time'.[51] Taking this literally, a group of young Italian intellectuals launched plans for a fascist international. But a meeting at Montreux in 1934 disclosed a great gulf between two sets of participants: the Italians proposed achieving national integration by a corporative socio-economic polity while others, especially the Romanians, favoured an appeal to race. Pretensions to an ecumenical ideology could not survive the rift, and universal fascism offered no counterbalance to the Comintern.[52]

Fascist ideology, however, offered an advantage in one particular question. Italy's hold on the German-speaking South Tyrol made the preservation of an independent Austria as a buffer state against German revisionism imperative. Concern for their northern neighbour led to the Italian Fascists' patronage of like-minded Austrian groups such as the paramilitary *Heimwehr* and the Fatherland Front, a clerico-corporative coalition headed by Engelbert Dollfuss. After Dollfuss became chancellor in 1932 Mussolini traded on the loose fascist empathy between Rome and Vienna in order to treat Austria as a client state. This was his tactic to ward off *Anschluss*, for, with the accession of Hitler to power in January 1933, German nationalism was deemed to be on the march. The mere presence of a National Socialist regime in Berlin was enough to incite Austria's own Nazis and their contacts in southern Germany to a frenzy of plots, and in July 1934 a Viennese *Putsch* resulted in the murder of Dollfuss. It was Mussolini's disagreeable duty to communicate this news to Frau Dollfuss, whom he was entertaining. He then promptly announced the dispatch to the Brenner frontier of 'land and air forces . . . large enough to deal with any eventuality', a move which helped to save Austria's integrity *pro tem*.[53]

Mussolini's Austrian policy in 1934 illustrated further the lesson of the abortive fascist international, namely, that there was no automatic ideological affinity between fascism and National Socialism. The clerico-corporative fascism of Dollfuss and his successor, Kurt Schuschnigg, the *Duce* found congenial, but not Hitlerian racism, even though the *Führer* acknowledged a debt to his Italian precursor as a radical right-winger. Mussolini often scoffed at Hitler's obsessive antisemitism, 'a joke that will be over in a few years'.[54] Ideological differences were coincident with, though probably secondary to, *raison d'état*. The revival of German power heralded by Hitler rang alarm bells nowhere more loudly than south of the Alps. When, in March 1935, Hitler broke the Versailles treaty by announcing mass German rearmament, Mussolini responded by hosting a meeting of British and French premiers and foreign ministers at Stresa. This Stresa front produced nothing beyond verbal resolutions, but it kept alive the unity of the the First World War victors.

It was at this point that Italy embarked on its African imperial adventure, which was destined to reverse totally the train of both Fascist foreign policy and ideology. Behind the assault on Ethiopia lay a dual motivation. First, the *Duce* was driven forward by the dynamism of his own regime. Fascism never reached its 'second wave', the promised transformation of Italian social patterns, succumbing instead to compromises with Italy's elites. The Great Depression exposed the hollowness of the corporative state. Now that the time had come, in Mussolini's words, for 'reaching out to the people', the only ideological *raison d'être* he had to fall back on was militant nationalism. Therefore, 1930s Italy was deluged with slogans at once minatory and somehow ridiculous: 'Better one day as a lion than a hundred years as a sheep'; 'War is to man what motherhood is to woman'; 'Whoever has iron has bread'.[55] The object of this warlike rhetoric was a third Roman empire to succeed that of the caesars and the popes, another conceit Mussolini borrowed from Italy's pre-1914 nationalists. The cult of *romanità* registered with Italy's middle class whose education was heavily classical, and the neoclassical reconstruction of Rome included large marble maps of ancient Roman conquests that hinted at the scope of the regime's imperial ambitions.[56] The initial trophy was to be Ethiopia, which liberal Italy had tried but failed to conquer forty years earlier.

Second, Mussolini calculated that he could secure his prize swiftly, in good time to resume his watch on the Brenner before German rearmament got into gear. This expectation was not misplaced. Britain and France, the other colonial players in East Africa, gave ample indication – before, during and after the Stresa Conference – that they were ready to countenance Italy's acquisition of Ethiopia in return for its support in Europe.[57] Thus, the Anglo-French encouragement of the League of Nations to come to Ethiopia's rescue had a distinct air of artifice. The League became involved largely because of the sudden revelation that the British public was still attached to the doctrine of collective security. With the National government approaching the end of its term in 1935, the League of Nations Union (LNU), by far the most effective Wilsonian lobby in the interwar years, organized a ballot to gauge support for the League. Of ten million respondents to this misnamed peace ballot, over 90 per cent proved in favour of their country's membership in the League and of the use of economic sanctions against an aggressor. But to the question, 'Do you consider that, if a nation insists on attacking another, the other nations should combine to compel it to stop by, if necessary, military measures?', affirmative answers dropped off sharply. The old dilemma whether to fight to preserve the peace still haunted liberal internationalism. The British government interpreted the peace ballot as recommendation of 'all sanctions short of war'.[58]

From the start, military sanctions were ruled out, and the French told Mussolini so. Economic sanctions, for that matter, were applied less than wholeheartedly; oil was not embargoed nor was the Suez canal closed to Italian shipping. Then, with the British election out of the way, the Hoare–Laval plan of December 1935 offered Mussolini two-thirds of Ethiopia if he would call off his armies. Leaked to the French press, the plan was officially disavowed in London, and one will never know whether the *Duce* would have accepted it. But revelation of the Hoare–Laval intrigue undermined the sanctions experiment fatally. The episode finally exploded the myth that collective security was operative. It therefore marked a turning point, not just in the Ethiopian crisis, but in the whole history of the League of Nations.[59]

Fascist Italy now used aerial bombardment and poison gas to subjugate Ethiopia by mid-1936. Mussolini had won his gamble on a quick victory, but there was no return to the Stresa front. In fact, he had sold out to Hitler soon after the Hoare–Laval plan collapsed. In January 1936 Mussolini informed the German ambassador that 'if Austria, as a formally quite independent State, were . . . in practice to become a German satellite, he would have no objection.' This statement so astonished the ambassador that he asked for it to be repeated. Berlin too was sceptical at first. None the less, the result, six months on, was an Austro-German accord by which Austria affirmed itself a Germanic state and agreed to align its foreign policy with that of Germany. Although this made *Anschluss* only a matter of time, Mussolini 'expressed lively satisfaction over the event which . . . would finally remove the last and only mortgage on German–Italian relations'.[60]

How to explain this apparent desertion of a vital national interest? The fact that Hitler had consistently and openly recognized Italian possession of the South Tyrol as the price to be paid for Rome's friendship presumably carried some weight with Mussolini in 1936.[61] However, the Hitlerian promise had cut no ice as recently as a year earlier at Stresa. On balance, it would seem more profitable to consider the psyche of the *Duce*. Mussolini had always adhered to the doctrine that 'strife is the origin of all things'.[62] By the mid-1930s he was in the grip of a simplistic Social Darwinism that categorized states as either rising or declining. Germany under Hitler plainly fell into the former category, while in Rome considerable propaganda energy was put into depicting Fascist Italy as virile and youthful. It has been argued that Mussolini always harboured the totalitarian dream of creating a new sort of Italian (*uomo fascistus*): hard, ruthless and bellicose.[63] On the opposite side of the ledger, the *Duce* drew on a bizarre array of sources (some Fascist propaganda took P.G. Wodehouse seriously) to build up a picture of the effete 'demo-plutocracies'. There, drunkenness, sexual perversion and material-ism were allegedly rife. Mussolini relished demographic figures – the low French birth rate, a surplus of spinsters in Britain, populations too old to fight.[64] To a certain extent, his contempt arose from the Ethiopian affair. He was particularly scornful of London's deference to LNU-swayed public opinion, and of Anglo-French vacillation between sanctions and appeasement.

None of this made for an ideology in any intellectual sense; just as Mussolinian totalitarianism was an empty boast, the ideology of the Fascist regime remained a 'cultural blank'.[65] On the other hand, excessive Social Darwinism induced in the *Duce* a fatalism characteristic of the ideo-logue. Shortly after inviting Hitler to make Austria a satellite, he assured a Nazi press correspondent that 'between Germany and Italy there is a common fate . . . Germany and Italy are congruent cases. One day we shall meet whether we want to or not. But we want to! Because we must!'[66] The word 'destiny' was frequently on his lips. On 1 November 1936, Mussolini announced a special relationship between Rome and Berlin and named it an axis – initially no more than a statement of vague ideological empathy. He also took the occasion to gloat over the League of Nations' failures in disarmament and collective security, 'the debris from the great shipwreck of Wilsonian ideology'.[67] The *Duce* knew what he was against, although his own ideology remained inchoate. But the ideological temperament was evident in the vision of a 'new man', the Social Darwinian banalities and the credulous trust in a tide of history.

In joining Hitler, however, Mussolini found himself sucked into an ideo-logical world of an entirely different complexion. The *Führer* too cherished a Social Darwinian *Weltanschauung*, but in his case it formed part of a teleological and 'self-consistent system'. Whereas the Fascist *Duce* at first steered clear of ideology, Hitler in *Mein Kampf* (1925) boasted of being a 'programmatic thinker'.[68] Whereas all Social Darwinians viewed the nation state as a biological organism, Hitler found in biological racism alone the motivating force in history past, present and future.

Like many ideologues, Hitler sought scientific evidence for his beliefs; hence his affirmation of the pseudo-scientific concept of an Aryan race. In reality, Aryanism was a convenient counterpoint to Jewry, which sym-bolized all that Hitler hated about the modern world; his ideal was a racially homogeneous, pre-modern *Volksgemeinschaft* (folk community). Thus he denounced the Jews as cosmopolitans and liberals, humanitarians and intellectuals, and at one and the same time as 'parasitic' capitalists and the authors of Bolshevism. Of these charges the last was the most sig-nificant, for the Soviet Union was the hinge where Hitler's racist ideology joined his foreign policy.

In 'the relation of Germany to Russia', Hitler wrote in *Mein Kampf*, 'we are dealing with the most decisive concern of all German foreign affairs'.

To the old German *Drang nach Osten* he added his ideological mission to vanquish Jewish Bolshevism:

> For centuries Russia drew nourishment from [the] Germanic nucleus in its upper leading strata. Today it can be regarded as almost totally exterminated and extinguished. It has been replaced by the Jew. Impossible as it is for the Russian by himself to shake off the yoke of the Jew by his own resources, it is equally impossible for the Jew to maintain the mighty empire forever. He himself is no element of organization, but a ferment of decomposition. The Persian empire in the east is ripe for collapse. And the end of Jewish rule in Russia will be the end of Russia as a state. We have been chosen by Fate as the witnesses of a catastrophe which will be the mightiest confirmation of the soundness of the folkish [*völkisch*] theory.[69]

This was the stuff of Austrian romantic fantasy now able to call on the resources of the Prussian state.

It is useful to remember that Hitler was an Austrian, and in *Mein Kampf* described how he arrived at his racist convictions in Vienna before 1914. One does not have to accept all his anecdotal account to recognize the Habsburg experience behind Hitlerian ideology. Hitler's loathing of the mélange of races that was Austria-Hungary echoed and amplified the views of such pre-First World War Austrian politicians as Georg Schönerer and Karl Lueger. Austria's Germanic identity was held to be threatened by Jewish prominence in Viennese cultural and business life, and by 'Slavization' encouraged by Russian patronage of pan-Slavism.[70] Hitler's animus against Habsburg multiracialism goes a long way towards explaining the venom against Czechoslovakia, a microcosm of the old Austro-Hungarian state, that he exhibited in the diplomatic crises of 1938–9.

But race coupled with anti-Bolshevism was not the only ideological imperative to justify Teutonic expansion eastward. Hitler was a devotee of the fashionable cult of geopolitics. This school of thought originated in Germany in the work of Friedrich Ratzel, notably his *Politische Geographie* (1897). Inspired by the German wars of unification, Ratzel employed Darwinian biology to advance the concept of *Lebensraum*, every nation's drive for its natural living space. In the interwar years geopolitical study was centred in Munich, home also, of course, to National Socialism, where a former army officer, Karl Haushofer, headed an *Institut für Geopolitik*. Haushofer himself, though, looked beyond Germany to England for one of his central tenets. In a famous scholarly paper delivered in 1904, Halford Mackinder had challenged Admiral Mahan's emphasis on sea power in history by postulating a 'geographical pivot' as the determinant of world politics. This was 'that vast area of Euro-Asia which is inaccessible to ships, but in antiquity lay open to the horse-riding nomads, and is to-day about to be covered with a network of rail-ways'. In this perspective, Russia, heir to the Mongol empire, became the 'pivot state'. After the First World War Mackinder revised his theory, adding Eastern Europe to Russia to constitute the 'heartland', and he coined the maxim:

> Who rules East Europe commands the Heartland:
> Who rules the Heartland commands the World-Island:
> Who rules the World-Island commands the World.[71]

Haushofer took up the notion of Russia and Eastern Europe as the natural seat of power. But while Mackinder became a Wilsonian inter-nationalist, Haushofer remained in Ratzel's Social Darwinian tradition and was not backward in asserting Germany's claim to *Lebensraum* in the east.[72] And indeed a majority of the German academic community engaged in research into the eastern lands and peoples also either explicitly or implicitly endorsed the *Drang nach Osten*.[73]

But it was Haushofer's geopolitics that provided particular sustenance for Hitler's ideological foreign policy, even if Haushofer's influence was exerted indirectly through Hitler's deputy, Rudolf Hess, who had been his student at the University of Munich. As an old-fashioned conservative, Haushofer was never an intimate in the upper echelons of the Nazi party (NSDAP). He later claimed that the Nazis misused his ideas, and it is true that he advocated the acquisition of *Lebensraum* by peaceful redistri-bution of territory, not by conquest. Moreover, although subscribing to the concept of the *Volk*, he was no thoroughgoing racist and commended Japan's imperial growth as a model. 'Nevertheless, Haushofer's ideas (and to a lesser extent Ratzel's) were open to the interpretation which Hitler put on them.'[74] Certainly, the *Führer* drew freely on geopolitical theory and terminology – the need for economic self-sufficiency (autarky) as a basis of national strength, frontier fluctuations according to a Social Darwinist law, the discourse of *Lebensraum*, and the division of the world into ethnic or pan categories. In the final analysis, however, it was the deterministic certitudes of geopolitics, above all the heartland formula for world power, that made its doctrines perfect ideological fodder. They pro-vided a social scientific framework for what Hitler in *Mein Kampf* termed his soil policy:

> The right to possess soil can become a duty if without extension of its soil a great nation seems doomed to destruction . . . If we speak of soil in Europe today, we can primarily have in mind only Russia and her vassal border states.[75]

For Hitler *der Primat der Aussenpolitik* (primacy of foreign affairs) was an article of faith, and a sequel to *Mein Kampf* composed in 1928, albeit not published until after his death, was devoted exclusively to international politics.[76] In both *Mein Kampf* and Hitler's second book, Social Darwinism, anti-Marxism, antisemitism and geopolitics all pointed to the fulfilment of Nazi ideology at Russia's expense. The German assault on the Soviet Union in 1941 was the apogee of Hitler's career, and significantly coincided with the high-water mark of his racial policy, the Holocaust. It is the manifest concordance between the early writings and later politico-military actions that lies behind the dominant interpretation of the Nazi phenomenon, namely the 'intentionalist' thesis. This rests on two contentions. First, that all important policy decisions in Germany between 1933 and 1945 were Hitler's and his alone – hardly an aberrant opinion of a totalitarian regime where the leadership principle (*Führerprinzip*) was avowed at least as much as *ducismo* in Fascist Italy. Second, that Hitler was one of the greatest literalists in history whose intentions were laid out almost from the start. This is not to say that Nazi foreign policy followed a blueprint limned in *Mein Kampf*, but rather that it must always be analysed in the light of Hitler's inflexible *Weltanschauung*.[77]

The intentionalist argument has not gone unchallenged. Some contend that Nazi economic policy and the need to conquer markets to the east drove Hitler to war. Others dwell on the dynamism of Hitler's own propaganda that carried both leader and followers further than intended, in which context *Lebensraum* appears simply an 'ideological metaphor'. (In parenthesis, it is interesting to note that the same sort of 'functionalist' interpretation has been advanced for the Holocaust.) However, as the history of terrorism illustrates, propaganda and deed overlap in the extremist's mind,[78] and Hitler was an extremist if nothing else. Alternately, there is the view of Hitler as no more than a consummate opportunist. He was indeed most successful in seizing on events but, in Alan Bullock's lapidary phrase, 'Hitler's opportunism was doubly effective because it was allied with unusual consistency of purpose.'[79] Efforts to bridge various schools of thought have resulted in the construction of 'polycratic' models of foreign policy-making and of distinctions between a 'programmatic' ideology and a looser 'goal-setting' one. But in the final analysis, the historian, even if taking on board some functionalist refinements, cannot escape the intrinsic validity of an intentionalist reading of Nazi policy.[80]

In its comprehensiveness, exclusivity and fanaticism Hitler's *Weltanschauung* met the definition of a total ideology symptomatic of a totalitarian regime. But while the Third Reich has invariably been cited as an archetypal totalitarian society, the degree to which Germans in the mass subscribed to all the Hitlerian doctrines is problematical. On the one hand, those who regard Nazism as the culmination of the special path or *Sonderweg* taken by German history imply that Hitler tapped strains deep in the Teutonic mentality. In this connection, a prominent German civil servant compared him to a reflector that intercepts light rays and transmits them onward in an intensified form.[81] On the other hand, the wilder flights of *Lebensraum* fancy were, so far as we can tell, confined to the Nazi party faithful. Elsewhere in the German population 'admiration for Hitler rested less on bizarre and arcane precepts of Nazi ideology than on social and political values'.[82] Yet Hitler retained the respect and active cooperation of most Germans, his wartime blunders notwithstanding, up to 1945. This has to be attributed to the impact of an unfolding *Stufenplan* (plan by stages) on the growth of a Hitlerian charisma.

Hitler expected his grand design to proceed in phases, the first of which would see Germany freed from the restraints imposed by the treaties of Versailles and Locarno. This he accomplished in three years. Withdrawal from the League of Nations' disarmament conference was followed by exit from the League itself, and then in March 1935 by the announcement of full-scale German rearmament. A year later, taking advantage of the disarray among the victors of 1918 caused by the Ethiopian affair, Hitler moved troops into the demilitarized German Rhineland. Thereby one guarantee of French security was removed, while at the same time Poland's willingness to listen to Hitler's blandishments undercut France's East European alliance system. By 1936 the continental outcome of the First World War was well on the way to being reversed. This was what in the 1920s all German governments had dreamed of but hardly dared hope for. However, 'what for Stresemann . . . had served as the final goal was for Hitler only the jumping-off point'.[83]

The second stage of Hitler's *Stufenplan* was the creation of a Germanic *Mitteleuropa* coupled with the drive east for *Lebensraum*. Even here, the *Führer* was not far ahead of many Germans. The Pan-German League had kept alive the memory of the eastern annexations of 1917–18, and in fact had joined Hitler in 1929 in a nationalist coalition that hounded Stresemann to his death. The percolation of pan-German expansionist ideas throughout German society was perhaps indicated by the success of Hans Grimm's novel, *Volk ohne Raum* (1926), which sold 315,000 copies by 1935.[84] *Mein Kampf* may have sold more but we may be sure it was read less. On the whole, though, it remains undeniable that Hitler's foreign policy ambitions outstripped those of the old conservative elites and of the bulk of the German people. By the late 1930s, however, circumstances so combined that he was able to carry most Germans with him by means of a charismatic authority.

Max Weber in his studies of charisma maintained that it is in times of 'extraordinary needs' that people turn to 'an individual personality . . . endowed with supernatural, superhuman, or at least specifically exceptional powers or qualities'. This bearer of charisma 'proves' his calling by performing 'heroic deeds'. The Great Depression and the series of international crises in the 1930s supplied the appropriately unstable environment for the emergence of charismatic leadership; Germany's recovery from the depression, for which Hitler fairly or unfairly took credit, as well as his foreign policy triumphs represented the requisite notable deeds. Between the charismatic leader and his disciples exists 'an emotional form of communal relationship', an intensely personal bond that, in the case of Nazism, was forged by oaths of personal allegiance to the *Führer*. 'It is recognition on the part of those subject to authority', wrote Weber, 'which is decisive for the validity of charisma.'[85] The Germans in their stubborn loyalty to Hitler amid disaster bore witness to his charismatic hold over them. And since personal charisma and ideology issued from the same source, in this case the *Führer*, the former reinforced the latter. Hitler himself acknowledged the linkage when he wrote of 'that great magnetic attraction which alone the masses always follow under the compelling impact of towering great ideas, the persuasive force of absolute belief in them, coupled with a fanatical courage to fight for them'. Hitler succeeded in blending his 'natural charisma with his providential charisma'.[86] Or as the *alte Kämpfer*, the old Nazi fighters, would say: 'Adolf Hitler is our ideology.'

To what extravagant lengths the *Führer* intended by means of his charisma to lead the German, or Aryan, people is a matter of debate. Did Hitler have in mind absolute world dominion, which geopolitical dogma taught was assured by control of the East European and Russian heartland? Was there, then, a third stage of the *Stufenplan* beyond *Lebensraum*? The answer must remain speculative; Hitlerian writings and oratory offer no infallible guide and, in practice, Russia was never overcome to allow passage to a global strategy. Yet there are broad hints aplenty of a cosmic phantasmagoria. Specifically, if Hitler indeed nursed schemes for world hegemony, they would assuredly bring him into conflict with the English-speaking powers. Hence, some clue to the terminus of his *Stufenplan* can be gleaned from Hitler's attitude to the British empire and the United States.

In both *Mein Kampf* and his second book he chided the Wilhelmine regime for having alienated Britain. An alleged racial kinship between the two peoples tempted Hitler to urge an Anglo-German understanding, but his real purpose was power-political. A friendly Britain would offset a hostile France, and the stalemate between the Western powers would leave Germany a free hand to achieve hegemony in the east. In a wider perspective, British toleration of Germany's command of the Eurasian heartland was to be balanced by German recognition, for the time being at least, of Britain's overseas empire.[87] On 18 June 1935 occurred an event which suggested that this Hitlerian strategy might be realized. An Anglo-German naval agreement that projected a German fleet of up to 35 per cent of British tonnage was significant because it came hard on the heels of the Stresa Conference's condemnation of German rearmament. If the spirit of Stresa could be so cavalierly violated, how much further might not London go to strike a bargain with Nazi Germany?[88] But expectations were not met. The British, convinced 'the bomber will always get through', wanted an air pact to complement the naval agreement, and this Hitler would not countenance. In turn, London offered 'economic appeasement' which, in large measure, was an attempt to divert Hitler's gaze from continental Europe and, not surprisingly, proved ineffective[89]. On the broader European stage, after the Ethiopian affair and Mussolini's announcement of a Rome–Berlin axis, Hitler found it difficult to stay on good terms with Fascist Italy and Britain simultaneously. Moreover, following the Rhineland reoccupation in March 1936, London and Paris set in motion plans for military and naval coordination. By late 1937 Hitler saw fit to lump Britain and France together as 'hate-inspired antagonists'.[90]

Nazi policy towards Britain continued to exhibit ambivalence. On the one hand, gratification was in order for Britain's recognition and even encouragement of German national self-determinist claims in Central Europe. On the other, Ribbentrop, who was made foreign minister in February 1938, returned from the London embassy a rabid Anglophobe, having failed to deliver the anticipated entente. Hitler's own thinking increasingly matched that of his new foreign minister.[91] It was probably represented by Berlin's mounting emphasis on planning for war at sea. As a senior naval officer pointed out, 'If Germany is to gain a secure position as a world power, as the *Führer* wishes, then . . . it will require secure naval routes and communications and guaranteed access to the high seas.'[92] Accordingly, the naval high command in September 1938 drew up a draft study of naval war strategy against Britain. The following January a so-called Plan Z allocated resources to the navy ahead of the other services. Nevertheless, the pace of naval building was measured; the Z Plan was not to be fulfilled until 1944. In other words, Hitler appeared to envisage a global collision with Britain but not for several years.[93]

Beyond the British empire stood the USA. In *Mein Kampf* Hitler remarked how difficult it would be 'to attack the gigantic American colossus of states', which none the less did not deter him from imagining an ultimate confrontation.[94] In the short run, to 'show the United States a bold front', the *Auslandsorganisation*, the NSDAP foreign office, came in useful. As the name implied, its principal function was to disseminate Nazi ideology among German-speaking communities abroad. It was particularly active in the Latin American countries, where it operated in defiance of the Monroe Doctrine, but to the advantage of British intelligence eager to alert the USA to a Nazi threat. Within the USA it found a potential Trojan Horse in the German–American *Bund*. Although founded only in 1936, the *Bund* was successful enough to attract the attention of the congressional committee set up under Martin Dies to investigate subversion.[95] For a more forceful if distant challenge to the United

States, Hitler counted on eventual American usurpation of the British empire bringing Britain to his side. He clung to this prospect in spite of deteriorating Anglo-German relations, even after the outbreak of the Second World War. He was by then reduced to imitating the tactic of Bismarckian and Wilhelmine Germany, that of bullying Britain into an alliance:

> I believe that the end of this war will mark the beginning of a dur-
> able friendship with England. But first we must give her the k.o. . . .
> If America lends her help to England, it is only with the secret thought
> of bringing the moment nearer when she will reap her inheritance. I shall
> no longer be there to see it, but I rejoice on behalf of the German
> people at the idea that one day we will see England and Germany
> marching together against America.[96]

That Hitler had the USA in his sights is perhaps finally borne out by Germany's entirely gratuitous declaration of war on America in December 1941. By this point Hitler, mindful of his self-proclaimed destiny and his own mortality, was telescoping the *Stufenplan* severely.

Any description of Hitler's schemes for world dominion must sound utopian at best, lunatic at worst. The permutations, convolutions and lacunae are mind-boggling; the place of the growing Japanese empire in Hitler's schema, for instance, is not easy to fathom. Yet nothing is out of character of the true ideological believer who was convinced 'he both understood and could control the course of centuries'. More than one observer compared the *Führer* to a Dostoevskyan character, a man possessed.[97] Ironically, Hitler's global vision had deeper roots in conventional German policy than had the lesser target, in a spatial sense, of *Lebensraum*. To enter the lists against the British empire and the United States recalled the pre-1914 *Weltpolitik* cultivation of economic imperialism, while *Lebensraum* derived from a more radical conservative tradition of racism and annexationism. But, as one author asserts, Hitler's skill lay in reconciling *Lebensraum* and *Weltpolitik* in a 'composite' or 'integrated' Nazi ideology. He accomplished this by 'a schedule of imperialist expansion' in which *Lebensraum* laid the groundwork for later *Weltpolitik*.[98] It is worth recalling that in the 1930s Hitler was unmoved by British offers to open the colonial question. The time was not ripe for such *Weltpolitik* issues; *Lebensraum* had first to be won and settled.

Hitler's imperialist ideology, not to mention his Social Darwinian proclivities, made war virtually inevitable. His calculation was that, in the early phases of the aggrandizement of the Third Reich, he could prevail over inferior foes by blitzkrieg without interference from the major powers. But he knew that sooner or later he would have to fight a general war. He began to make this plain in a number of remarks over the winter of 1937, especially at a much-discussed meeting on 5 November of civilian and military chiefs that was minuted by his military adjutant, Colonel Hossbach. The Hossbach memorandum figured prominently in the postwar Nuremberg trials of the major Nazis on the count of conspiracy to commit aggression. It may prove less than the Nuremberg prosecution charged, but it still revealed that 'Hitler spoke more openly on 5 November of his intention to use force in the pursuit of his objectives than ever before'.[99] He set out three cases in which general and offensive war might be entertained: two rested on the contingency of French incapacity by reason of civil strife or hostilities with another country; failing this eventuality, war was predicated between 1943 and 1945. By this juncture, he explained to his listeners, Germany would enjoy an advantage in war preparations over its potential foes. Therefore, 'it was his unalterable resolve to solve Germany's problem of space at the latest by 1943–45'.[100] These years were crucial to Hitler's long-range scheme. They conform to what we have seen of his naval plans and ultimate showdown with Britain. It is perhaps of further significance that German rearmament and the autarkic planning of the economy did not peak until 1944,[101] from all of which follows that the war with Britain and France that broke out in 1939 arrived earlier than Hitler expected. Nevertheless, that war must remain Hitler's war because its fundamental cause was his ideological foreign policy programme. Its timing, however, was determined as much by his adversaries as by the *Führer* himself.

POPULAR FRONTS AND APPEASEMENT

The balance of power in the interwar years was a triangular one. It has been suggested that the entire story of international relations in this period was nothing more or less than a competition between Britain and France on the one hand and Russia on the other to win the allegiance of Germany, a struggle to create a grouping of two against one.[102] This struggle, of course, had its ideological overtones. As we have seen, in the aftermath of the First World War, Weimar Germany was the battlefield of Wilsonianism and Leninism. Then, with Hitler's accession to power in 1933 and the Rome–Berlin Axis of 1936, the ideological divisions in Europe came to correspond to the power-political triptych: the Anglo-French bloc represented liberal democracy, Hitler and Mussolini the authoritarian doctrines of Nazism and fascism, and Soviet Russia the Marxist–Leninist tradition. In the ongoing triangular contest *Realpolitik* and ideology now overlapped at almost every point. This can be explored in two contexts. First, Soviet diplomacy during the so-called popular front era canvassed an understanding with the West against the Axis states. Second, Western appeasement after a fashion aligned London and Paris with Germany against Russia.

The Soviet Union could hardly be expected to ignore the arrival in power of two stridently anti-communist regimes in Rome and Berlin. Although Italo-Soviet relations continued to be surprisingly cordial,[103] the emergence of Nazi Germany brought to a head a raging ideological battle which marked the early years of Stalin's dictatorship. It was at his insistence that the Sixth Comintern Congress in 1928 had given top billing to 'fascism', under which rubric were subsumed all right-wing forces. Capitalism was declared to be in crisis and fascism its last, desperate offensive. The forecast was for 'a fresh era of imperialist wars among the imperialist States themselves; wars of the imperialist States against the USSR; wars of national liberation against imperialism; wars of imperialist intervention and gigantic class battles'. Lest opportunist elements usurp the forthcoming revolution, as allegedly they had in Germany in 1919, communist parties everywhere were instructed to purge themselves of all bourgeois influences. In practice, this meant breaking links with nationalist movements in the colonial world, and in the industrialized countries with the social democrats who were now dubbed, in a phrase that had been bandied about for some time in Comintern circles, 'social fascists'.[104] One stunning effect of this tactic was to prevent a united front of German communists and socialists, which greatly facilitated Hitler's rise to power.

Having helped to create a monster, Stalin after 1933 registered palpable alarm. Russo-German military and economic collaboration, which dated from the Treaty of Rapallo, faded away as Moscow clearly took Hitler's public statements about eastern *Lebensraum* at face value. Moreover, at the same moment that Nazism materialized as a real international threat, the Chinese situation was becoming a cause of perturbation. There, the nationalist movement, the Kuomintang under Chiang Kai-shek, appeared more inclined to harry Chinese communists than resist a Japanese invasion. The transformation of Manchuria into the Japanese protectorate of Manchukuo in 1932 created a threat from Japan on Russia's Far Eastern border. Faced with the possibility of war on two fronts, the Kremlin set out to cultivate friends in the capitalist world. The enterprise was conducted on two levels – that of diplomatic *haute politique* and that of mass politics.

Beginning in 1932 the USSR signed a series of non-aggression pacts – with the Baltic states, Poland, France and even Fascist Italy. In 1935 the agreement with France was augmented by a treaty of mutual assistance, although in the absence of joint military planning it never went beyond a toothless paper pledge. The Soviet Union created an even greater stir when, in 1934, it accepted an invitation to join the League of Nations and occupy the permanent Council seat vacated by Hitler's Germany. In this forum the shift in Russian foreign policy was epitomized in the person of Maxim Litvinov, commissar for foreign affairs. Of Jewish parentage and with an English wife, he conveyed the impression of a broad-minded cosmopolite rather than a hard-line communist. Assessing his contribution to Moscow's new conciliatory image, an American diplomat reported that Litvinov's 'courage, effrontery, articulate and irrepressible energy have been invaluable at a time when Soviet representatives are usually regarded as nuisances'.[105] At Geneva Litvinov threw himself into the lagging Wilsonian causes of general disarmament and collective security. But despite his personal popularity, ingrained Western distrust of all Soviet manoeuvres caused his dramatic proposal for across-the-board disarmament to be dismissed out of hand, and the League's disarmament conference collapsed amid a welter of Franco-German recriminations. As for the League's credibility as a shield against aggression, this suffered badly from its failure to do no more than remonstrate against Japan's activities in Manchuria. Then, in the Ethiopian affair, while the Soviets stayed loyal to a sanctions policy, London and Paris hatched the Hoare–Laval plan which gave the *coup de grâce* to collective security.

The dearth of positive results on the diplomatic front lent urgency to the Soviets' campaign to win popular support through the Comintern. This entailed a total ideological volte-face. The discipline for which the Comintern was notorious, constrained national communist parties to abide by the ban on cooperation with social democrats imposed by the sixth congress. But many nursed doubts, which increased when events in Germany demonstrated the folly of the party line. On request, the Comintern began to permit deviations on an *ad hoc* basis. The most famous occurred in France, after a fascist march on the National Assembly on 6 February 1934 ended in riot and bloodshed. On 29 July French communists and socialists signed a non-aggression pact, and the French Communist Party called for a 'rassemblement populaire' to include radicals as well as social democrats.[106] It was another year, however, before a formal Comintern congress, the first since 1928, openly endorsed the idea of a popular anti-fascist front:

> The Seventh Congress of the Comintern welcomes the aspiration of the social-democratic workers to establish a united front with the communists, regarding this as a sign that their class consciousness is growing, and that a beginning has been made towards overcoming the split in the ranks of the working class in the interests of a successful struggle against fascism, against the bourgeoisie. In the face of the towering menace of fascism . . . it is the main and immediate task of the international labour movement to establish the united fighting front of the working class.[107]

From such language, as well as from Litvinov's behaviour at the League of Nations, one might deduce that the Soviets were issuing an invitation for an offensive against fascism and Nazism. But it is a question of how much was for show. We can be certain Stalin did not fully share Litvinov's Western orientation, and in all probability his objectives were limited and defensive. Bilateral accords and the encouragement of collective security seem to have been geared simply to ensuring that Russia was not alone when and if attacked by Germany or Japan. In the same vein, the popular front was more likely intended as a precaution than a crusade. 'It was not to provide Western countries with the resolution and the material means to fight Hitler. It was to make sure that they would not fall prey to fascism themselves.'[108] But whatever the Kremlin's immediate purpose, it succeeded in raising ideological consciousness in world politics. The result was seen before long in the internationalization of the Spanish Civil War.

Since its inauguration in 1931 the second Spanish republic had been plagued by violent clashes between Right and Left. As the result of a general election in February 1936 a broad *Frente Popular* took office, an event that galvanized a junta of conservative nationalists into action. On 19 July General Franco announced armed rebellion against the government and republic alike. Immediately Fascist Italy and Nazi Germany came to his aid with *matériel*, and Italian and German military personnel soon followed. Each of these interventionist states had its own agenda. Mussolini was eager to supplant French influence in the western basin of the Mediterranean and perhaps annex the Balearic Islands. Hitler was interested in gaining access to the mineral resources and naval stations of Spain and Spanish Morocco. The *Führer* also quickly appreciated the Spanish Civil War's utility in diverting the Western powers' gaze from his own ambitions in Eastern Europe; to prolong this distraction, German assistance to Franco was sufficient to avert his defeat but not enough to clinch victory before the spring of 1939. Yet Mussolini and Hitler shared one overriding motive: anti-communism. Both expressed overt alarm lest Spain fall to communism by popular front tactics and other nations follow suit. Of the two, Mussolini seemed the more genuinely convinced that the Spanish conflict was one episode in a universal struggle. But both dictators harboured a real ideological antipathy towards popular frontism, which helps to account for the speed of Italian and German intervention.[109]

The loyalist republicans, however, believed they had a counter at hand. In May French elections had brought to power a popular front administration headed by the socialist Léon Blum. It was in the natural order of things that one popular front government should help to save another from outside interference. Indeed, Blum's impulse on the outbreak of war in Spain was to send the Loyalists military supplies. But in the course of two weeks and three fraught cabinet sessions, the Blum ministry opted for non-intervention. It is now generally accepted that 'the decisive, proximate, factor . . . was the domestic French political situation'. In mid-1936 France was convulsed by labour unrest, and right-wing groups were openly threatening to carry Spain's civil war across the Pyrenees. Blum's reluctant resolve for inaction was strengthened by British advice, which ranged from the moderate 'be cautious' to the British ambassador's expostulation that the Spanish government was a 'screen for anarchists'.[110] The French found a way out of their dilemma by proposing a multilateral non-intervention agreement and committee; the British at once seconded the idea. This scheme put both sides in the Spanish conflict on the same footing and, however inadvertently, gave status to Franco's rebels. More important, it denied the republican regime in Madrid the right to purchase arms abroad, which as the legitimate, recognized government of Spain it had every right to do according to international law and custom. In any event, the non-intervention agreement, although signed by all the powers, was blatantly flouted by Italy, Germany and the third interventionist state, the Soviet Union.

The West's non-intervention left the Loyalists dependent on the USSR for outside help. As the patron of popular frontism, the Soviet Union could hardly refuse to assist the embattled regime in Madrid. Yet Stalin proceeded circumspectly. He evinced no real affection for the *Frente Popular*, and his strategy was to prop up the republic at minimal cost in the hope that the democracies would eventually come to its aid. Soviet supplies to the Spanish Loyalists were in any case limited by problems of both logistics and Russia's economic condition. Manpower came from two sources. The Soviets sponsored international brigades of volunteers from everywhere save Russia. From Moscow they dispatched, instead, foreign communists who had taken refuge from fascist and Nazi persecution in the Russian capital; they were to serve the republicans as 'technical advisers'. Disputes between these multinational communists and their Spanish hosts began immediately over both military and political matters. Ironically, one cause of dissension was the Soviet insistence that the *Frente Popular* moderate its socialist economic policies in order to propitiate London and Paris.[111] Without alternative outside help and riven by internal factionalism, the Loyalists gradually surrendered to the dictates of their so-called advisers. In taking over the Spanish popular front, Moscow and its agents displayed the same ruthlessness that had characterized the Bolshevik–communist movement since 1917. The experience horrified many who had enlisted in the international brigades, and on their return they set about exposing what they regarded as communist duplicity. George Orwell, to cite only the most famous example, experienced great difficulty in persuading left-wing publishers to accept his account, but eventually his *Homage to Catalonia* (1938) came to be recognized as a classic of the genre.[112]

But until disillusion set in, the Spanish Civil War engaged the conscience of the European intellectual left like no other interwar cause. Here was a classic case of intellectuals' fascination with ideology, for what appeared to be at stake in Spain was the triumph of one or other of the two total ideologies of the twentieth century: communism and fascism–Nazism. This was at best an oversimplification; the Spanish communist and fascist parties were only minor units in their respective coalitions. But the angle of vision was everything, and foreign intervention produced the outward spectacle of ideological polarization. In a titanic struggle of 'isms', half measures and compromise customarily invite scorn, and so in the fraught atmosphere of the 1930s the Anglo-French non-interventionist policy was criticized as especially craven. In contrast, one power stood out, prepared to resist fascism in Spain and by extension the world – the Soviet Union. The anti-fascist credentials the Soviets had earned in Spain made for a per-suasive argument among Western intellectuals. Faced with an ostensible stark choice between communism and fascism, they chose the former in their thousands, becoming either communist party members or else fellow travellers. In the words of a sardonic contemporary, 'Stalin became their antidote to Hitler; Marxist hate should abolish Nazi hate, and Marxist falsifications correct Nazi ones.'[113]

Ideological polarization carried over from Spain on to the international stage. Against popular frontism was posited an anti-Comintern pact signed during the Spanish war by the three expansionist powers, Germany, Japan and Italy. The pact's text was short on content but long on dire warnings of the communist menace to civilization. If nothing else, it illu-strated the growing international habit of rallying around an ideological issue. All this placed the Western democracies in a quandary, caught in the dichotomy between communism and fascism–Nazism. Anxious to check the aggression of the Anti-Comintern Pact powers, they were loath to do so in association with the USSR. This stemmed, of course, from twenty years of ideological wrangling, and more storm signals flew with the Soviets' brutal appropriation of the anti-fascist cause in Spain. The spread of communist influence among Western intellectuals and workers was of further concern. Ideological discord, then, continued to hold the West and Moscow apart. But in the prevalent triangular balance of power London and Paris could not afford unalloyed hostility towards the Axis powers. The alternative to keeping company with communists was to fall back on the policy, which antedated the Spanish crisis, of appeasing the dictators.

Britain and France practised appeasement for various pragmatic reasons. The financial orthodoxy of a balanced national budget in a depression, coupled with the need to relieve social distress at home, inhibited rearma-ment; the French defensive posture behind the Maginot line and the disper-sal of Britain's energies on imperial obligations foreclosed strategic options; the new independence and isolationism of the British dominions and the unreliability of some of France's East European allies argued further for appeasement. Nevertheless, there were also more principled motives at work. These were to be observed in British rather than French policy, for they were derivative of Woodrow Wilson's influence in the English-speaking world.[114]

Arguably, the fundamental emotion behind appeasement was revulsion against the carnage of 1914–18. The memory of the trenches haunted public figures and public alike. It is noteworthy that Neville Chamberlain, prime ministerial appeasement activist from 1937 to 1940, had earlier conveyed his message of the wastage of war in a privately printed memoir of his cousin Norman Chamberlain, killed in France. Among the general public, it is significant that in 1939, unlike 1914, no crowds flooded into the streets rejoicing.[115] Wilson's meteoric popularity at the end of the First World War was due to his articulation of anti-war feeling and his crusade for international reconciliation. The appeasers translated the latter into conciliation at almost any cost. In the Wilsonian scenario peace was to be preserved by adhering to international justice which, as we have seen, more often than not resolved itself in practice into the application of the principle of national self-determination. Here again, English-speaking appeasers followed in the American president's footsteps. Guilt at the injustice of the Versailles treaty had first arisen over France's attempt to wrest heavy reparations from Germany. But a decade later, the morality of Versailles at large was called into question as publicists and historians undermined the thesis of Germany's sole responsibility for the war.[116] And because Hitler's early international revisionism concerned Germanic peoples, he was able to seize the high moral ground of self-determination and win a sympathetic ear; the remark ascribed to a London taxi driver summed up the British attitude: 'I suppose Jerry can do what he likes in his own back garden.'

There was rich ideological paradox in all this. After the First World War international conciliation was a watchword of the democratic Left; twenty years later its precepts were being put into practice by conservative governments. The Left had apparently converted the Right, although oddly at the very moment when the bogey of Fascism was pushing many on the left to relinquish their pacifist or pacificistic stance. The British Labour Party, for example, edged towards acceptance of rearmament.[117] The Left's inhibition against using force to keep international order had bedevilled collective security for a generation; now it was belatedly being overcome – after collective security was defunct.

The Western democracies' embrace of Wilsonian ideology was manifest in their acquiescence in the Rhineland remilitarization of March 1936 and the *Anschluss* two years later. The same trust in conciliation and national-determinist morality marked the apogee of appeasement – the surrender of the Czech Sudetenland to Hitler at the Munich Conference of 29–30 September 1938. Although France was bound to Czechoslovakia by a pact of mutual assistance signed in 1924, all the running in this crisis was made by the British; this was due partly to France's strategic reliance on Britain after the Rhineland reoccupation, partly to the French government's desire to hide its own appeasement mentality behind that of Britain.[118] Thus it was Chamberlain, meeting Hitler at Berchtesgaden on 15 September, who readily conceded the principle of the transfer of the Sudetenland to the Third Reich. On the 22nd in Bad Godesberg Hitler presented Chamberlain with an ultimatum for the territorial transfer by 1 October without the cloak of a plebiscite, and for the satisfaction of Polish and Hungarian claims on Czechoslovakia. After several days of contemplating war, the British prime minister's face was saved by Hitler's assent to an international conference at Munich where, in fact, the substance of the Bad Godesberg demands was granted.

In return for redressing the injustice of three million Sudeten Germans subject to alien rule, Chamberlain won Hitler's signature to an agreement 'that the method of consultation shall be the method adopted to deal with any other questions that may concern our two countries'.[119] This new *détente* to secure 'peace in our time', like Chamberlain's whole policy in the Munich crisis, presumed a mutual sense of international goodwill and morality. In the deliberately provocative words of one historian, Munich 'was a triumph for all that was best and most enlightened in British life; a triumph for those who had preached equal justice between peoples . . . Chamberlain brought first the French, and then the Czechs, to follow the moral line.' The other side of the coin was illuminated by a contemporaneous historian who, deploring the emphasis on Wilsonian moralism, pointed to 'the glaring and dangerous defect of nearly all thinking, both academic and popular, about international politics in English-speaking countries from 1919 to 1939 – the almost total neglect of the factor of power'.[120]

If appeasement stood in the liberal democratic tradition of Cobden and Bright, Gladstone and Wilson, it also marched to a harsher, twentieth-century ideological drummer: anti-communism. Because of the polarization of French domestic politics, the sentiment was more intense in Paris than in London. In Britain conservatives spoke in terms of 'better Hitler than Stalin', in France, 'better Hitler than Blum'. The French nationalist right was torn between its historic Germanophobia and philofascism; a portion of the French right-wing press condemned Munich while the rest applauded it. On the official level, Premier Daladier was terrified lest war unleash a Bolshevik revolution after which 'Cossacks will rule Europe', while Foreign Minister Bonnet clung to the belief that 'Stalin's aim is still to bring about world revolution'.[121] Similar alarmist premonitions could be heard in London too. A debate among British diplomats on whether fascism or communism posed the greater danger found a number of participants plumping for the latter. Chamberlain himself was deeply distrustful of Stalin whose strategy, he suspected, was 'to see the "capitalist" powers tear each other apart'.[122]

Anti-communism sprang still further to the fore of international affairs as a result of events in the spring of 1939. The entry of Nazi troops into Prague in March could in no way be rationalized by national self-determination. Next on Hitler's agenda, plainly, was the Polish Corridor where, ironically, population figures favoured German and Polish self-determinist claims about equally. None the less, on 31 March Britain issued a unilateral guarantee of Polish integrity. Similar promises followed to other states deemed threatened by the Axis powers. Possibly the Chamberlain cabinet was at this point ready to fight to prevent Eastern Europe falling to Hitler. But gestures of appeasement continued to be made during the summer, and the more likely explanation of the guarantees is that they were intended to deter by threat of war.[123] To make any deterrent credible to Hitler, however, it was necessary to threaten the *Führer* with a major war on two fronts, which meant bringing Russia into play.

Following this logic, the Soviets now approached Britain with a suggestion to transform the ineffectual Franco-Soviet pact of 1935 into a tripartite military alliance. Chamberlain immediately erected roadblocks. Besides his ingrained ideological bias, he set a very low value on the Red Army whose officer corps had been decimated in Stalin's purges; in this estimate he accepted the opinion of the Foreign Office and ignored that of his chiefs of staff.[124] To be fair to Chamberlain, an accord with Russia was feasible only in so far as the Poles were prepared to cooperate with Moscow, and this they adamantly refused to do. Nevertheless, pressure for a 'grand alliance' encompassing the Soviet Union built up in British opinion. The most powerful voice of this lobby was that of Churchill, who conveniently dropped both his anti-communist fulminations and the occasional compliments he was wont to pay Mussolini and Hitler. The Labour Party, although steering clear of a popular front, called loudly for negotiations with the USSR, and even Chamberlain's foreign secretary, Lord Halifax, urged the same thing in cabinet. By the end of May the weight of this opinion forced Chamberlain to accept in principle an overture to Moscow.[125] But it was not until mid-August that an Anglo-French military delegation, travelling slowly by sea and devoid of plenipotentiary powers of negotiation, reached the Russian capital. Whatever the intent, this show of reluctance contrasted sharply with Chamberlain's three urgent visits by air to meet Hitler the previous September.

Once talks began, a fundamental disagreement came into the open. If the Russians were to fight Germany, they wanted their troops in Poland and Romania even before hostilities; they also sought a green light to establish bases in the Baltic states guarding the approaches to Leningrad. Neither the small states nor the Western powers would accede to these demands. The Soviet response was swift; on 23 August a Nazi–Soviet non-aggression pact was announced. This had been in the cards for some time, probably since the West had refused aid to the Spanish Loyalists, and certainly since Munich. 'My poor fellow, what have you done?' said a *Narkomindel* official to the French ambassador in October 1938. 'For us, I see no other consequence but a fourth partition of Poland.'[126] The replacement of Litvinov by the antisemitic and anti-Western Molotov in May 1939 was a clear signal of Moscow's drift. The Nazi–Soviet Pact, by a secret protocol for the division of Poland, gave Stalin the geographical space for defence that the democracies refused him. It also afforded him temporal breathing space before Hitler's drive for *Lebensraum* carried him into Russia, and thus freed the Soviets from the immediate peril of a two-front war against both Germany and Japan.

Ideologically, of course, the pact seemed a monstrosity. David Low captured the universal reaction in his famous cartoon, 'Rendezvous', wherein Hitler and Stalin greet each other over the corpse of Poland: 'The scum of the earth, I believe?' says the former; 'The bloody assassin of the workers, I presume?' replies the latter. Both Germans and Russians were candid about the travesty they were making of their erstwhile propaganda, and Ribbentrop joked with Stalin about the Soviets joining the Anti-Comintern Pact.[127]

On the other hand, there is an ideological rationale to be discovered on both sides. The Kremlin still held firm to its 1920s definition of fascism–Nazism as the product of monopoly capitalism, while contending that the appeasement of the 1930s was a capitalist conspiracy to use Nazi Germany as a strike force against communist Russia.[128] The non-aggression pact turned the tables on the capitalist world; it set up a likely war between two sets of capitalist powers – the dictatorships and the democracies – a stratagem 'well within a Leninist analysis of the European situation'. *Glasnost* has brought forth hints that in 1939 Stalin indeed calculated on a repetition of the collapse of tsarism on a larger scale. If so, the Nazi–Soviet Pact was for the Kremlin less of a defensive manoeuvre than an ideological offensive.[129] As for Hitler, he had merely deferred his assault on Jewish Bolshevism. Subsequent events would bear out the truth of what, in mid-August, he told the League of Nations commissioner for Danzig, who was expected to transmit his thoughts to the West:

> Everything I am doing is directed against Russia. If the West is too obtuse to grasp this, then I shall be forced to come to terms with the Russians and turn against the West first. After that I will direct my entire strength against the USSR.[130]

In neither Moscow nor Berlin, then, did the opportunistic non-aggression pact deflect the signatories from their long-term ideological ambitions.

By any *Realpolitik* calculation the Nazi–Soviet Pact ought to have prevented the outbreak of a general war, for there was now no way in which the Western states could save Poland. On the eve of the pact a euphoric Hitler had advanced the date of the projected invasion of the Polish Corridor from 1 September to 26 August. On the 25th, however, two unwelcome pieces of news reached Berlin. First, the belated conclusion of a formal Anglo-Polish treaty suggested that Britain was going to fight for Poland after all. Second, Rome sent a 42-page memorandum of *matériel* that Germany would have to supply before Italy could contemplate war. Hitler put back the attack on the Corridor to 1 September in the hope that the Western powers might lose their nerve and desert Poland. But he was determined on war against Poland and would brook no talk of another Munich. Moreover, he was prepared to risk a wider war with the West for the sake of a smaller one with Poland. If this involved departing from a measured, ideological *Stufenplan*, the *Führer* justified an immediate confrontation with the democracies by reference to Germany's current armaments advantage and by musings on his own mortality and shortage of time to fulfil his destiny.[131] In any event, whatever sort of war developed, local or general, Nazi Germany was left to take it on alone.

Although leaving Hitler in the lurch, Mussolini had fallen heavily under his spell, and the Italian Fascist state took on some of the trappings of the Third Reich. Most startling was the unpopular imitation of Nazi race laws inflicted on Italy in 1938. On the diplomatic front, two years earlier the *Duce* had entrusted the foreign ministry to his son-in-law, Count Ciano, with the express purpose of imbuing Italy's foreign policy with an ideologically correct or Fascist tone. This resulted administratively in the centralization of Italian diplomacy in the hands of Ciano and his friends, and politically in the translation of the Rome–Berlin Axis into an offensive and defensive alliance, the Pact of Steel of 22 May 1939. On this document's signing, Ribbentrop gave a verbal promise to avoid general war until 1943 at the soonest; on the 31st the Italians took the precaution of putting this proviso in a written memorandum.[132] Thus, Mussolini had an excuse for neutrality on the outbreak of war on 3 September. But Italian unpreparedness rankled. It contradicted his warrior image of Fascist Italy, and neutrality was an embarrassing repetition of his liberal predecessors' position in 1914. Therefore he termed Italy's stance twenty-five years later 'non-belligerency', a phrase chosen in fact to convey his resolve to enter the war at the first propitious moment. So he informed Hitler.[133] To this extent, the ideological bond of the Axis remained valid.

Ideology commanded a much higher profile in the diplomatic origins of the Second World War than it had before 1914, a testimony to the twentieth century's increasing predilection for framing political matters in doctrinal terms. First and foremost, there was the looming presence of the two total ideologies, Marxism–Leninism and fascism–Nazism, which in turn bred the countervailing ideological mentalities of anti-communism and popular frontism. Of the traditional right- and left-wing ideologies, nineteenth-century conservatism had become compromised with, and in some cases subsumed by, the radical rightist movements. Nineteenth-century liberalism survived, particularly in its internationalist and pacificistic aspects, thanks to the Wilsonian impulse. Furthermore, in the inter-war years all these 'isms', old and new, were engaged in an urgent and common pursuit – accommodation of the one omnipresent and thriving ideology, that is to say, nationalism. Marxism–Leninism looked to nationalism to induce a capitalist civil war and downfall; fascism–Nazism aspired to extend nationalism in imperialist directions; liberalism hoped to tame and integrate nationalism into a universal states system.

Yet, when all is said and done, the cause of quarrel in 1939 was not fundamentally ideological. The liberal democracies did not fight Hitler *ab initio* in order to destroy National Socialism, and certainly not to stop his anti-semitism; Western inaction when the Nazis turned to genocide in 1942–5 would tragically prove the latter point. Rather, they resorted to war to forestall German hegemony. The basic cause of the Second World War was the same as that of the first; both conflicts began over the vexatious question of Germany's proper place in the balance of power. What was different in 1939 was that German national self-assertion was now yoked to Hitler's peculiar and obsessive *Weltanschauung*, already evident in his 'deviant diplomacy'.[134] This factor alone guaranteed that the coming struggle would turn into a second and greater total war of ideologies.

8

A SECOND GLOBAL CONFLICT
Test of total ideologies

EUROPEAN WAR, 1939–41

Like the First World War, the second began as a European civil war.
Within this initial European context, it soon shed further light on the ideological patterns in both Soviet and Nazi foreign policy.

Once Poland was overwhelmed by attack from both west and east,
Berlin and Moscow on 28 September 1939 signed another pact recognizing
each other's conquests and redefining their respective spheres of interest in
Eastern Europe. This allowed the USSR to begin the process of returning
the three Baltic states of Estonia, Latvia and Lithuania to the Russian
orbit, which was plainly a precautionary measure directed against
Germany as well. For the same reason, Moscow demanded bases in southern Finland, whereupon the Finns' refusal brought on a Soviet invasion on
30 November. The West responded to this Winter War with outrage and
the token gesture of Soviet expulsion from the moribund League of
Nations. In addition, communist ranks outside the USSR were thrown
into turmoil. Those who had fought in Spain found the Nazi–Soviet agreements hard to stomach, and Russia's aggression against its small neighbours was all too reminiscent of tsarist imperialism. Many fellow
travellers and members of communist front organizations deserted the
cause.[1] The Comintern struggled to hold the line. Soviet expansion was
justified as a defensive measure to protect 'fortress socialism', and the
absorption of eastern Poland was presented as the recovery of Byelo-
russian and Ukrainian lands lost in 1921 (most of which admittedly the
Paris Peace Conference had recognized as Russian territory). Parentheti-
cally, it was a means, so the claim went, of saving some Polish Jews from
the Nazis. But the main Comintern argument was the ideological one
that the war of 1939 was the 'second imperialist war'; it was being fought
between capitalist states as the result of 'the insurmountable contradictions
of the capitalist system'. The French and British communist parties were
instructed to oppose their countries' war effort and, after some initial hesi-
tation and individual protests, did so.[2] They thus emulated their German

colleagues who, ten years earlier, had also found their resistance to Hitler paralysed by Moscow's orders.

Meanwhile, in the west the winter of 1939 was taken up by the *drôle de guerre* or phoney war. This passivity testified that war with the democracies at that time was not what Hitler had intended, and the contrast with the military and political commotion in Eastern Europe indicated where his priorities lay. The same conclusion can be drawn from his conduct after the Nazi blitzkrieg swept through Western Europe in May 1940. Following the fall of France, Hitler gave instructions to plan an invasion of the British Isles under the code name of Operation Sealion. His commitment to the venture, however, seemed strangely suspect: 'I have decided to prepare a landing operation against England and, if necessary, to carry it out.' Probably he expected a British overture to sue for peace, which never came, and Operation Sealion always depended on the Germans' control of the air space over the English Channel, which they never secured. Even so, in July, well before the aerial Battle of Britain had been fought, he issued further orders to his generals to prepare for an attack on Russia. In other words, while his victories in Western Europe were piling up, the *Führer* never lost sight of his paramount ideological purpose of *Lebensraum* at the opposite end of Europe. 'The compass needle of nazi policy swung erratically in the summer and autumn of 1940, but it came to rest pointing east.'[3]

By mid-1940 continental Europe was well on the way to Nazification. Even countries that kept a formal independence felt constrained to adjust their foreign policy and adopt the accoutrements of a Nazi or fascist regime in order to curry favour with Berlin. Hungary and Romania, for example, had little choice but to follow the German lead. But the most significant case was that of France, a third of which remained nominally independent after the armistice in June. It is a moot point to what extent France's 'strange defeat' in 1940 can be attributed to a widespread collapse of morale stemming from disillusion with the regime for which the *poilu* was asked to fight and die.[4] None the less, it is remarkable how emphatically the politicians of the Third Republic, once ensconced in their new capital, Vichy, turned their back on the democratic past. Without pressure from Germany, they erected an authoritarian system with fascistic overtones. Marshal Pétain, given unlimited power as president of Vichy France, voluntarily agreed to collaborate with the Nazi war effort. Collaborationism, a new word imparted to political discourse by this decision, is made somewhat explicable by the fact that Western Europeans, unlike the Poles, were not immediately exposed to the brutal impact of Hitler's racist policies. Failure to appreciate Hitler's true ideological calling enabled some patriotic Frenchmen, like Pétain, to imagine that a defeated France's interests were best served by carving out a respectable niche in Hitler's 'new order'.[5]

A similar if more even-handed choice was available to Britain: acquiescence in Germany's European conquests in order to attend to extra-European affairs. Although the British cabinet considered the option, it was dismissed. It would have meant renouncing the war's original purpose – preservation of a balance of power in Europe. But this was not the sole consideration, for perception of the conflict as a clash between two fundamentally incompatible world views was gaining ground. On this score, appeasement was a posthumous 'unifying force'. That the utmost in international conciliation had been tried and failed left the impression that Hitler was beyond the pale of normal political discourse, and Chamberlain had struck this note in announcing war.[6] Then, on 10 May 1940, the war's transformation into a crusade took a large step forward in Britain with the replacement of Chamberlain by Churchill. The latter, since his advocacy of a 'grand alliance' against Nazi Germany, had become the symbol of unbending hostility to Nazism itself, underscored by his deliberate mispronunciation of the word. The new prime minister at once applied his histrionic skills to raising spirits, not just by his oft-quoted patriotic oratory, but also by his depiction of the war as a cosmic ideological competition: 'We have become the sole champions now in arms to defend the world cause. We shall do our best to be worthy of this high honour.' The duel between Hitler and Churchill was that between 'a visionary of a new, heroic, pagan and scientific world' and 'the defender of a traditional and now antiquated world; a defender of Western Civilization'.[7] The argument can be made that Churchill, the arch nationalist and imperialist, by spurning a global deal with Hitler, engaged his nation in so exhausting a struggle as to induce the demise of the British empire and of Britain as a major power.[8] Yet the fact that the British took on so hazardous a challenge (and the consequences were not hard to envisage in 1940) amounts to an admission that more than power politics was held to be at stake.

In the meantime, the question for Hitler was how, in default of a cross-Channel invasion, to contrive the defeat of Britain and the dominions fighting on alone. One answer was to round up as many diplomatic allies as possible. Already Mussolini, true to his promise, had jumped into the fray on 10 June 1940 with a Social Darwinian flourish: 'An hour signalled by destiny is sounding . . . This is a struggle between peoples fruitful and young against those sterile and dying.'[9] But from the Nazi viewpoint the Italian entry proved a great disappointment. Mussolini intended to fight a 'parallel war', distinct from Hitler's. Accordingly, on 28 October, without giving the *Führer* prior notice, he launched an attack on Greece. The outcome was catastrophic; the Italians were soon in retreat and had to be rescued by their Axis partner. The same thing happened during the ensuing winter in the North African theatre. The parallel war, undertaken as a gesture of independence, in less than a year 'became a subsidiary part of the larger German war . . . and Italy a German satellite'.[10] But if Italy's help in bringing Britain to its knees was negligible, that of Franco's Spain was non-existent. Franco had, in truth, offered to join the war at the height of the Nazi victories in June 1940. However, four months later, his demands for French North African territory in addition to Gibraltar alarmed Hitler eager to keep Vichy France on his side. At a much-discussed meeting at Hendaye Franco and the *Führer* failed to strike a bargain, and the moment when Spain might have intervened in the Second World War passed for ever.[11]

Hitler's foremost diplomatic success came on 27 September 1940 with the conversion of the Anti-Comintern Pact into a defensive alliance, the Tripartite Pact. But in the negotiations leading up to the signing Tokyo made it perfectly plain that it had its own fish to fry.[12] As will be recounted shortly, Japan and the US were locked in a deadly Asiatic rivalry, and therefore the Tripartite Pact was as much anti-American as anti-British. What it did was to create a potential alignment of three militaristic, authoritarian states – Germany, Italy and Japan – against the English-speaking liberal democracies; ideological lines in the sand were being drawn ever more clearly.

The war in the interim lapsed into stalemate that seemed set fair to continue in the near future: Germany ruled the Continent but was incapable of invading the British Isles; Britain dominated outside Europe but was powerless to assault the Continent. Economic warfare, whether by British blockade or Nazi submarine, was a slow process. And in any case, a war of attrition had little appeal to Hitler's impatient mind. In this deadlocked situation his thoughts turned back to his pristine ideological mission to vanquish the Soviet Union.[13]

The Nazi–Soviet Pact began to sour in the middle of 1940. The German conquests in the west prompted Stalin to seek compensatory territorial gains in Eastern Europe which, in turn, rankled in Berlin. In an attempt to patch up differences Molotov visited the German capital in November. The Germans hinted that the USSR might adhere to the Tripartite Pact but backtracked when Stalin showed interest. All Berlin wanted was an economic agreement to continue receiving supplies from Russia but it offered no concessions in Eastern Europe in return. The talks for a new political deal, then, ended frostily and without resolution. On 18 December Hitler signed the directive for an attack on the Soviet Union, Operation Barbarossa, and henceforth it was a matter not of whether, but when the blow would be struck.[14]

Operation Barbarossa was launched in the small hours of 22 June 1941, and Hitler's explanations at the time make interesting reading. In public it was billed as a preventive strike, but no evidence of an imminent Soviet offensive has ever been adduced. To his entourage Hitler presented Russia as a latent threat, and it is true that the Soviet Union was in a position to do harm. Nazi Germany depended for raw material supplies on the USSR, which also since 1940 had controlled vital supply lines in the Balkans and Baltic area. Furthermore, in return for raw material the Soviets were receiving German armaments which one day might be turned against their manufacturer. These apprehensions surfaced two days before Barbarossa when Hitler delivered himself of the maxim, 'What one does not have, but needs, one must conquer.'[15] Put another way, Stalin could not be left free to enter the war at his own convenience. On the other hand, Stalin showed no sign of interrupting Russo-German trade and, in fact, sanctioned a new commercial accord as late as April 1941. In any event, it has been trenchantly observed that there existed a glaring contradiction between all this fearful Hitlerian prognostication and his opinion expressed in *Mein Kampf* and elsewhere that the Russians and their so-called Judaeo-Bolshevik leaders were totally incapable of state building and management. In the summer of 1941 he was still expounding the latter view with unfeigned earnestness.[16]

The biggest puzzle about Operation Barbarossa, though, concerns its timing. Why would Hitler open a second front in the east while the British empire was still in the field? The German high command, on being asked to plan the invasion of Russia, had posed this question and received the reply:

Russia [is] the factor on which England is mainly betting . . . Russia never need say more to England than that she does not want Germany to be great, then the English hope like a drowning man that things will be entirely different . . . Should Russia, however, be smashed, then England's last hope is extinguished.[17]

This was precisely the same strategic argument that had driven Napoleon I, thwarted by the Continental System's failure to subdue Britain, to his invasion of Russia in 1812. It is scarcely surprising that not all Hitler's listeners were convinced by his logic, and in May 1941 Rudolf Hess parachuted into Scotland in the vain hope of patching up an Anglo-German peace before the Russian adventure began. Hess always denied knowledge of the forthcoming attack on the USSR, but this is hard to credit and, if true, would make the timing of his escapade an extraordinary coincidence. Most likely Hess, although acting on his own, represented many in the upper echelons of the Third Reich who had qualms about Hitler's Napoleonic hubris.[18] All of which leads one irresistibly to ask how meaningful Hitler's linkage of Barbarossa to the defeat of Britain really was. Was his exposition perhaps rationalization for a decision taken on instinctual grounds? And indeed one is forced to conclude that the attack on Russia in 1941 was at least as much an emotional response to ideological fixations as it was rational calculation.[19]

Hitler had been moving steadily towards an invasion of Russia for almost a year. Buoyed by easy conquests in the west, he looked forward to another blitzkrieg victory over a weak and despised foe. He seemed increasingly prone to a characteristic affliction of ideologues, that of supposing that an ineluctable fate will somehow provide the wherewithal of success. How else to account for the German shortage of military transport, clothing and footwear suitable for a Russian winter? In a famous bout of self-revelation, Hitler once declared, 'I go the way that Providence dictates with the assurance of a sleepwalker.'[20] That remark, made originally apropos his course in the Rhineland crisis of 1936, might equally well have applied to Operation Barbarossa. Ideological thinking tends to simplify and categorize, and it irritated Hitler to conceive of the Soviets as anything other than a sworn enemy. It is worth remembering too that in Hitler's grand *Stufenplan* the destruction of the Soviet Union was supposed to come before the global conflict with the Anglo-Saxon powers. In sum, the Nazi–Soviet *détente* was a detour to be travelled as quickly as possible. His satisfaction at returning to the ideological highway shines through in a message to his Fascist comrade-in-arms, Mussolini, on the eve of 22 June 1941:

I again feel spiritually free. The partnership with the Soviet Union, in spite of the complete sincerity of the efforts to bring about a final conciliation, was nevertheless very irksome to me, for . . . it seemed to me to be a break with my whole origin, my concepts, and my former obligations. I am happy now to be relieved of these mental agonies.[21]

The ideological motif sprang into glaring prominence when it came to planning the administration of the conquered territories in the east, on which the *Führer* lavished more care than he did on the logistics of victory. Among the Nazi elite who shared Hitler's racial and geopolitical sentiments there was a scramble for part of the action. Himmler and Goering engaged in their habitual competition in bureaucratic empire building, and a number of overlapping offices were created. In a sinister move, the ideological vanguard of the Nazi movement, the *Schutz-Staffeln* (SS), was given authority to operate in the occupied lands independently of military commanders. At first, the job of coordinating all Nazi efforts in the east was surprisingly entrusted to Alfred Rosenberg. Few in Berlin had any respect for this windy and self-appointed philosopher of the NSDAP, but his alleged expertise in Nazi ideology earned him a place in its implementation. Orders to all agencies, civil and military, called in so many words for the extermination of Russia's communist leadership and Jewish intelligentsia, while an economic programme for the pillaging of the Soviet Union amounted to starvation of the Slavic populace. The fanaticism of a total ideology designated Jews and Slavs as biological *Untermenschen* (subhumans), a word that from 1941 became a cliché in Nazi mouths.[22]

This genocidal policy went into immediate effect as the *Wehrmacht* swept to the gates of Moscow and Leningrad before the onset of winter. The speed of the German advance was due overwhelmingly to a woeful lack of Soviet precautionary measures. Although the Soviets were rearming furiously, they had made no provision for defence in depth.[23] Communications between Moscow and the front were immediately cut, and a large part of the Russian air force was caught and destroyed on the ground. Yet there was ample notice of a German attack long before 22 June 1941, which raises the troublesome question of why and how Stalin could have been so remiss. One clue might be found in the provenance of much information received in Moscow. British and American warnings in April were presumably distrusted as ideologically tainted; Moscow feared the Hess flight to be the prelude to an Anglo-German peace and anti-Soviet agreement. The same alarm that the West was planting 'provocations' may have balked Richard Sorge, the famous Soviet spy in Tokyo, who predicted the date of Barbarossa to within forty-eight hours.[24]

Stalin's gnomic characterization of these forewarnings as 'clumsy fabrications' has prompted interpretations that run the gamut of extremes. In one view, the key to Stalin's behaviour was a 'self-confidence', born of his many 'fantastic gambles' won over the years, that 'he might still fool Hitler'. So in 1941 he set too much store by a Russo-Japanese neutrality treaty signed on 13 April, and by Hitler's coincidental diversion into a Balkan campaign against Yugoslavia. At the opposite pole, Stalin was supposedly 'semi-paralyzed' at the demonstration of German military might in 1940. He remained fearful of putting the USSR on a war footing lest it incite Hitler (as Russian mobilization had provoked Germany in 1914), a prey to 'wishful thinking' and the 'anguished hope that Hitler . . . would hold off and thereby give him another year in which to get ready for war'.[25] From the ideological angle, it is just possible that the Russian leader was blinded by the outbreak of war in 1939 among the bourgeois powers as forecast by Lenin. But while he might well have anticipated capitalist civil war and self-destruction in 1939, it is hard to credit that he still clung to such a fond belief two years later in the light of Nazi Germany's rude health. As we have already seen, a Stalinist addendum to Marxism–Leninism taught that National Socialism's historical function was to assail the Soviet socialist fortress on behalf of the capitalist world *in extremis*. The fact is that his ideology should have made Stalin more, not less, alert to the Nazi danger in 1941. In sum, Stalin's miscalculations and neglect remain a riddle, inexplicable in ideological or any other terms.[26]

Operation Barbarossa, of course, had wide international ramifications. Contingents from all over Europe flocked to join in the assault on the Soviet Union. Undoubtedly, some were racist but the main attraction was that here, at long last, was the counter-revolutionary crusade promised since 1917. Non-German forces came from the Nazi-occupied countries and from neutrals such as Hungary, Romania, Finland and Vichy France; even Franco's Spain sent a 'blue division' east. Mussolini insisted on contributing troops, much to the annoyance of Hitler who wanted the Italians to concentrate their strength in the Mediterranean. More significant, however, Japan abided by its recent neutrality pact with the Soviets and declined to attack Russia in the rear, despite Hitler's urging.

The Soviets drew added comfort from another quarter. On the very day of the Nazi invasion Churchill gave a public and unconditional pledge of help to the USSR. Stalin did not respond at once, understandably wary of the veteran anti-communist who, as recently as 1940, had advocated aiding the Finns in their Winter War against the Soviet Union. 'If Hitler invaded Hell he would at least make a favourable reference to the Devil!', remarked Churchill on 21 June 1941, implying that he still regarded the Soviets as diabolical.[27] But now he resurrected his grand-alliance theme of 1938–9; the common cause against Hitler demanded an Anglo-Russian alliance which was duly concluded. Western communists, ever obedient to Moscow, immediately ceased their clamour against an imperialist war and endorsed all forms of anti-Nazi struggle.[28] And so cooperation between the West and the Soviets against fascism, first bruited at the League of Nations and in the Spanish Civil War, only to be thwarted by both parties' appeasement of Hitler, was finally realized. None the less, the ideological configuration of the Second World War was not yet complete; this awaited the war's wholesale globalization. In bringing this about, the year 1941 was very like 1917 in the First World War. Within six months of the Russo-German passage of arms, the USA and Japan were involved in hostilities, imposing further ideological dimensions on the conflict.

AMERICA'S MISSIONARY ROLE AND JAPANESE 'NATIONAL POLITY', 1941

After the spectacular entry of the United States as a major player on the world stage in 1917–19 came a slow but sure isolationist reaction and retreat. It was not that the US was cut off from international affairs, if only because the overseas scope of American business was growing by leaps and bounds – a process hastened enormously by the crippling effect of the First World War on America's competitors. Moreover, this economic activity frequently had political reverberations. In one instance, business interests paved the way to US patronage of a German reparations agreement; in another, to Washington's indulgence of the Italian Fascist regime exemplified by the American ambassador who later ghost-wrote a Mussolinian autobiography.[29] Indeed, in the 1920s the United States practised selective intervention. Hence, Secretary of State Kellogg lent his name to the Pact of Paris (also known as the Kellogg–Briand Pact of

1928) which ostensibly outlawed war. Of course, before the Senate ratified the pact, the isolationists added sufficient riders to make it worthless. A few years later, Washington worked closely with the League of Nations in the abortive attempt to halt Japan's incursion into Manchuria. Isolationism in these circumstances could be no more than uneven.[30]

But in the 1930s the American will for disengagement gathered startling momentum. It stemmed in the first place from disillusion with the outcome of the First World War which became coupled with scepticism about US intervention. Europeans appeared to feel little gratitude for American services rendered. The Continent's recurrent nationalist bickering and drift to authoritarianism mocked the US crusading war aims of international conciliation and democracy. The American acclaim that greeted Erich Maria Remarque's anti-war novel, *All Quiet on the Western Front*, translated into English in 1929 and filmed in 1939, bore witness to the popular judgement of the First World War's futility. On a more mundane level, the European victors incurred transatlantic odium in the matter of the war debts they owed the USA. Having in the 1920s obtained generous repayment settlements, by 1933 all but one nation had seized on the Great Depression unilaterally to cancel all payments. The following year, the historical debate over the US declaration of war in 1917 came to a head in a senatorial investigation. Needless to say, no firm conclusion emerged as to what, if any, sinister economic forces pulled strings for intervention. But on the principle of no smoke without fire, the impression was left that somehow the USA had been mendaciously inveigled into war.

Isolationist sentiment, which in the previous decade had mostly advocated a benign non-involvement, now demanded positive steps to avoid foreign entanglements. Presidents Washington and Jefferson were frequently invoked in doctrinaire fashion. This 'isolationist tornado' brought in its train a spate of neutrality legislation (1935–8) prohibiting those economic ties with belligerents that had allegedly dragged the USA into the First World War. One newspaper wittily dubbed the 1937 law 'An Act to preserve the United States from Intervention in the War of 1917–18'. US isolationism reached its zenith in 1938 with a proposal introduced into the House of Representatives, albeit never accepted, to hold a national referendum before any declaration of war.[31]

In the executive branch of government the isolationist impulse was decidedly weaker than in the legislature. President Franklin Roosevelt and his secretary of state, Cordell Hull, were by temperament internationalists, and they urged that congressional legislation should distinguish between the aggressor and the victim in an international crisis. But the effort was in vain, and the White House was resigned to swimming with the isolationist tide in order to retain support for its domestic programme. Roosevelt's first presidential term was notable in international affairs for the continuation of restrictive trade practices and the application of the

neutrality act to the Italo-Ethiopian dispute. But in his re-election campaign of 1936, the president saw fit to draw attention to the mounting
ideological polarization between liberal democracy and authoritarianism
of both the right and the left. This was a useful electoral ploy. He was
able to cast his New Deal policies as the liberal-democratic solution to
the Great Depression while, at the same time, appealing to those who
believed US duty ceased with presenting a model for imitation: 'Here in
America . . . we are fighting to save a great and precious form of government for ourselves and for the world.'[32] Abroad, however, Roosevelt was
powerless to do more than offer such passive nostrums as quarantining
aggressors.

At the same time, international upheavals lent urgency to the question
of America's world role. Membership in the League of Nations had postulated US overseas obligations in the abstract at some future date; the
aggressiveness of Japan, Germany and Italy made the issue real and
immediate. The Ethiopian affair, the Spanish Civil War, the Munich
Conference all left an imprint on American opinion. Further disquiet was
caused by renewed Japanese incursions on the Chinese mainland; by the
late 1930s Washington's gaze wavered between Europe and Asia. But the
memory of 1917–18 meant that it was over policy towards Europe that
American interventionists and isolationists quarrelled. It is appropriate
therefore to deal with the US response to the European crisis before turning to the Asian scenario.

Since 1937 Roosevelt had been begging Congress to allow some relaxation of the arms embargo in the neutrality laws. The outbreak of war in
Europe in 1939 added a spur to his plea. In October the president won a
repeal of the arms embargo, with the proviso that belligerents should pay
in cash and carry *matériel* bought in the USA in their own ships. To
mollify isolationist feeling specific war zones were designated from which
American merchantmen were banned. But it was the fall of France in the
summer of 1940 that concentrated US minds powerfully on the European
scene. The Atlantic ocean now seemed less a moat than a channel for
invasion, and fear of National Socialist penetration of the American hemisphere, while somewhat fanciful, was keenly felt. Polls showed that a solid
majority of Americans favoured supplying Britain with all material aid.
Significantly, a number of Progressive isolationists from the First World
War took the same position, as did Wendell Wilkie, the Republican chal-
lenger in the 1940 election. On the other hand, the electorate overwhelmingly opposed a US declaration of war, and Roosevelt explicitly
promised 'your boys are not going to be sent into any foreign wars'.[33]
Matching policy to public opinion meant that the Roosevelt administration paid lip service to the neutrality laws while bending them beyond
recognition.

In September 1940 fifty mothballed US destroyers were transferred by presidential fiat to Britain in return for the American lease of British bases in the western Atlantic and the Caribbean. But the greater part of US help came to be provided under the Lend–Lease Act of 11 March 1941, for which Roosevelt found more than enough votes in both House and Senate. By the loan or lease of *matériel* to be returned or replaced at war's end, it was calculated that the ghost of the war debts from the previous world war might be laid to rest. After the Nazi invasion of Russia lend–lease was extended eventually to the Soviet Union, although the lion's share went to the British empire. Of course, lend–lease by itself was little use without the means of delivery which, in view of the strain imposed on the British and Canadian navies by Nazi U-boat packs, was far from assured. To implement lend–lease, then, the USA moved inexorably into sharing in the protection of Atlantic convoys. In September and October several US–German clashes at sea resulted in torpedoes and depth charges being launched and lives lost. If on the US part this was still an 'undeclared war', it had still progressed into a shooting war.[34]

Washington spelled out its commitment to the defeat of the Axis states on 14 August 1941 at Argentia Bay, Newfoundland. There, Roosevelt met Churchill, and together they drew up the Atlantic Charter. This was nothing less than a statement of ideological war aims to which the neutral United States bound itself, a circumstance so odd as to drive one historian to quote the poetic couplet,

At least such subtle Covenants shall be made,
Till peace it self is War in Masquerade.[35]

In drafting the Charter American influence was uppermost, for it was essentially a reformulation of Woodrow Wilson's vision. The 'common principles . . . for a better future for the world' included national self-determination and democracy; freedom of the seas and, Britain's system of imperial preference notwithstanding, free trade and equal access to the world's raw materials; disarmament and 'a wider and permanent system of general security' – a hint of another league of nations.[36]

The Atlantic Charter had less immediate impact on American public opinion than Roosevelt hoped, but in retrospect it may be seen to mark the final round in the long-running debate over how best to express United States exceptionalism. Wilson had sought to export American virtue only to run afoul of his country's isolationist mentality. Roosevelt a generation later took up the fight to universalize US liberal ideology: 'If war does come', he remarked in 1940, 'we will make it a New Deal war.'[37] The Atlantic Charter, together with the US role in the battle of the Atlantic, pointed irresistibly to another bout of interventionism, and this time there was to be no turning back. After 1941 the isolationists were forced to take a back seat, as the 'great cycle theory' took over.

This cited the interwar years as a cautionary tale of what America's lapse from internationalism after the First World War had entailed; economic protectionism and the Great Depression, isolationism, and the Second World War itself, were all joined in one seamless tragedy. To Roosevelt and most of Washington's foreign policy elite a repetition was unthinkable, and in 1941 they succeeded in setting US diplomacy irreversibly on a missionary path.[38]

Over the summer the president came to the decision that, to save the world, his nation could no longer stay out of the war; but he was still fearful of the America Firsters and was 'waiting to be pushed'. At Argentia, in a foretaste of imperial presidencies to come, he mentioned that he was looking for an 'incident' in the Atlantic to justify a declaration of war on the Axis without recourse to a lengthy congressional debate.[39] In Roosevelt's eyes the war in Europe took precedence over the brewing storm in Asia. Accordingly, since the beginning of 1941 Anglo-American military planning had proceeded on the assumption that, once at war, the USA would deploy its military strength to achieve victory in Europe before turning to tackle the problem of Japanese aggression. In part, the European priority arose from geopolitical considerations and the fear that Hitler was about to develop a decisive secret weapon. But also, Roosevelt and most of his advisers, coming from an 'American East Coast elite', exhibited a commensurate 'ideological view of the world'.[40] Anglophile and steeped in Old World culture as they were, their instinct was Eurocentric and attuned to regard Nazism's assault on western liberal values as the prime challenge. Against this it could be claimed that America's material stake was greater in Asia than in Europe, and the collision between US and Japanese interests and ideals certainly predated the rise of European fascism.[41] It was perhaps apposite, then, that Roosevelt's anticipated 'incident' should occur first in the Pacific.

Japan's emergence as a major power dated from that country's astonishingly swift modernization following the Meiji restoration of 1868. For economic progress the Japanese adopted and adapted Western models, but to instill civic dedication to national greatness they had deliberate recourse to ancient precepts. Emphasis was placed on duty, honour, loyalty, filial piety and obedience, especially to the emperor, who was made the focus of the entire belief system. The constitution of 1889 described him as 'sacred and inviolable', not perhaps a god himself but partaking of divine attributes. Japanese myth had it that emperors were directly descended from the sun goddess Amaterasu, one of many deities in the animistic Shinto religion. 'State Shinto', in fact, enjoyed the stature of 'a national religion' and 'a moral and patriotic cult'.[42] Another retrieval from the past, and most germane to Japan's position in the world, was the military ethos of *bushido*; this code of the old samurai warriors was incorporated into the new Japan's armed forces remodelled on Western lines. The entire complex of revived traditions was subsumed under the rubric of *kokutai*, a word simply translated as 'national polity' but also pregnant with the idea of a unique state character or essence. In the Meiji period *kokutai* served as immunization against the cultural Westernization that accompanied industrialization. *Kokutai* was perhaps most successfully implanted in modern Japanese society by an imperial rescript on education in 1890. An all-encompassing and collectivist social and political code, it flourished as a national ideology up to 1945.[43]

The beginnings of Japanese national assertiveness coincided with the age of new imperialism. Japan's drive for empire was in many respects imitative of the European fashion (see Chapter 5). The same ingredients were present – strategic and economic interests, an atavistic military aristocracy, a sense of superiority towards other peoples.[44] Japanese imperialism enjoyed some early successes. A short war against the crumbling Chinese empire gained economic privileges there. Emphatic victories over Russia in 1904–5 paved the way for conquest of Korea in 1910. But further penetration of the Chinese mainland, on which Japanese expansionism had set its sights, was blocked by Europe's colonial powers. The distraction of European war in 1914, therefore, was Japan's opportunity to demand, and obtain, further concessions in China. But as Europe retreated in the Far East, the United States advanced. America's own informal imperialism, executed through the open door policy, obliged Washington to become China's protector. The confrontation of two imperialisms was postponed from one world war to the next, but found its outlet at Pearl Harbor.

During the years of so-called Taisho democracy (1912–26) it appeared that Japan might evolve into a modern, even liberal, state on Western lines. At home a species of parliamentarianism functioned; abroad Japan adhered to the 'Washington system' named after several agreements for Asian–Pacific stability and naval disarmament concluded at the Washington Conference of 1921–2.[45] But whether the Japanese would rest content within these bounds was doubtful. Criticism of the Washington system fixed on the Tokyo government's apparent submission to Western pressure, a resentment fuelled by British blocking of a racial equality clause in the League of Nations Covenant and America's discriminatory immigration laws. Overall, Japanese opinion of Western political culture, parliamentarianism and the Washington system was always ambivalent.

As in Europe, so in Japan it was the Great Depression that tipped the scales against domestic liberalism and international cooperation. Economic and social dislocation provided the backdrop to an upsurge of radical forces and, again as in Europe, it was the radical right in Japan that carried the day. The latter's impetus sprang from younger intellectuals and army officers who had been educated in the spirit of *kokutai* in the early twentieth century. They rejected alien Western doctrines and practices, their hates ranging from liberalism and communism to base-ball, and they condemned their elders for inadequate promotion of traditional Japanese verities. Some looked for inspiration to Kita Ikki, guru of National Socialism in Japan. Their forums were small, grass-roots nationalistic associations such as the Cherry Blossom Society, a title that equated the short life of the cherry blossom with samurai readi-ness to die gloriously. In reality, the militant nationalists were infatuated with death and violence and, between 1931 and 1936, they made political assassination into a habit. The climax was reached on 26 February 1936, when a thousand troops led by junior officers occupied government build-ings in downtown Tokyo for three days, killed two ministers and came close to murdering the prime minister. The insurrection was suppressed only when the military high command, at the urging of the emperor, turned its back on the rebels. The ringleaders were executed, as was the fascist Kita Ikki. But only on the surface was the 'February incident' a set-back for the radical right, because after 1936 the ideology of the nation-alistic societies became to all intents official policy. The truth was that much of the Japanese elite shared the aims of what the press called 'sincere young officers being driven to action by their sense of patriotism'.[46]

The outward sign of the changing order was the post-1936 pre-dominance of the armed forces over Japanese civilian authorities. Since the seizure of Manchuria several years earlier the army had determined policy towards China; now the military imposed their values in all walks of life. An army memorandum demanded 'the establishment of a strong political structure at home' to support overseas expansion.[47] Against a background of political and economic uncertainty and the outbreak of full-scale war with China in 1937 Japan acquired the trappings of totali-tarianism. Ideological conformity was addressed by the ministry of educa-tion's publication of *Kokutai no Hongi* (Principles of National Polity), which sold over two million copies. Its purpose was to clarify and reassert the dogma of Japan's uniqueness:

Filial piety in our country has its true characteristics in its perfect con-formity with our national polity by heightening still further the relation-ship between morality and nature. Our country is a great family nation, and the Imperial Household is the head family of the subjects and the nucleus of national life . . . Filial piety is a characteristic of oriental morals; and it is in convergence with loyalty that we find a character-istic of our national morals, and this is a factor without parallel in the world.

Some occidental influences, notably individualism, were to be shunned; others (fascism was mentioned as an example) needed 'sublimating' to suit the 'Imperial Way'.[48] To drill home the lesson a bureau of thought control was set up, and state Shinto became more than ever a vehicle of official propaganda. The kernel of *Kokutai no Hongi* was the 'emperor system', but the actual emperor, Hirohito (1926–89), was something of a cipher. His views, which were usually of a moderating nature, were frequently overridden by his militant advisers, although they still did everything in his name.[49]

The Japanese regime that emerged after 1936 invites comparison with the contemporary Hitlerian and Mussolinian systems. Japanese scholars are more inclined than their Western counterparts to perceive a Japanese fascism.[50] Some parallels stand out. Japan's reverence for a past society recalled the Nazi *Volksgemeinschaft*, joined in both cases to a readiness to use modern technology to resurrect the golden age. The plaint of being a 'have not' nation, which Japan frequently voiced, was the same as Fascist Italy's self-definition as a 'proletarian nation'. Common to all three regimes were ties between government and capitalist interests, the pursuit of autarky and a vision of the world in geopolitical blocs. The Japanese fascist party itself was minuscule, and no mass fascist movement ever developed. On the other hand, in 1940 Japan became effectively a one-party state under Premier Konoe who was by then, in one historian's view, the 'nominal leader of fascist forces'[51] – which is not to say that Konoe or his successor, General Tojo, ever achieved *Führer* or *duce* status. It has been suggested that there was really no need for a fascist party in Japan since its functions were already performed by a 'sacerdotal corps' of Shinto priests. And since *kokutai* corresponded to long-cherished Japanese beliefs, the inculcation of a 'political religion' went much deeper and wider in Japan than in either Nazi Germany or Fascist Italy.[52] In any event, an ideological mentality lay behind an ultra-nationalist foreign policy in each case.

Japan's repudiation of Western values in the 1930s was mirrored in its pattern of diplomacy.[53] When in 1933 the League of Nations condemned the Japanese establishment of the puppet state of Manchukuo, Japan withdrew from the organization, and soon after refused to countenance any further limitation on its naval building – an emphatic rejection of the Washington system. Japan's signature on the Anti-Comintern Pact in 1936 was motivated primarily by concern for the Russo-Manchurian frontier, but Tokyo was also happy to be aligned with the European enemies of liberalism and Marxism–Leninism. The Nazi–Soviet Pact upset this ideological calculation, and it fell to Foreign Minister Matsuoka to repair the situation. A rabid anti-Westerner and hero of the Japanese walkout from the League of Nations, he was the chief negotiator of the Tripartite Pact (1940) with the Axis states, and then in April 1941 signed a neutrality agreement with the Soviet Union. His ideological objective at this point was a front of authoritarian states against the democracies. But once more a Hitlerian action, this time in the form of Operation Barbarossa, nullified Japan's international expectations.

The symbol of noxious Western ways as well as the most formidable obstacle to Japanese expansion remained the United States. The American reaction to perceived aggression in Asia was markedly different from the posture assumed *vis-à-vis* Europe. Until 1939–40 US policy towards the Axis can only be described as appeasement, but against Japan, relatively unhindered by isolationist protest, 'it had more activist implications'.[54] For a start, the Roosevelt administration took advantage of the lack of a formal declaration of war in the Sino-Japanese conflict of 1937 to avoid invoking the neutrality laws. In due course, this opened the door for credits and supplies to the embattled Kuomintang.

A quantum deterioration in US–Japanese relations began in September 1940 when Tokyo activated its 'southern strategy'. This involved avoiding military engagement with Russia on the Manchurian border, where the Japanese had suffered heavy losses in the previous year, in order to concentrate on pushing southward into French Indochina. Even after the Nazi invasion of the Soviet Union in 1941 and Hitler's urging notwithstanding, Tokyo declined to become embroiled with Russia. By this juncture the southern strategy had, with the connivance of Vichy France, won Japan a foothold in southern Indochina and was threatening the British in Burma as well as the Dutch East Indies. All of which antagonized a bloc of ABCD states – America, Britain, China and the Dutch. Of the four ABCD countries only the USA was in a position to hinder Japan. The brutal fact was that the USA supplied Japan with 90 per cent of its petrol, 80 per cent of its oil, 74 per cent of its scrap iron and 60 per cent of its machine tools.[55] The deeper Japanese armies penetrated into China and Southeast Asia, the more extensive became Washington's embargo of these goods. The vicious circle was completed as America's economic warfare added urgency to Japan's advances on the Asian mainland in search of substitute resources. A turning point was reached on 26 July 1941 with the freezing of Japanese assets in the United States. Unless the USA rescinded these measures, Tokyo resolved to strike directly at its tormentor.

Japan acted on the calculation that its situation would only deteriorate with time. The records of the imperial conferences held in Tokyo between July and December 1941 exude a sense of desperation. Pessimism was expressed about the outcome of a protracted war and reliance placed in a quick knockout blow. It was generally agreed that war was inevitable because national honour allowed no evasion of Japan's imperial destiny. In other words, the ideology of *kokutai*, which was invoked in word and spirit throughout the imperial conferences, imposed a duty to be fulfilled regardless of cost.[56] As so often, with ideological imperatives went a sense of self-righteousness. Pronouncements regarding the New East

Asian Order of 1938 and later a Greater East Asia Co-Prosperity Sphere often made reference to 'international justice' and to *kodo* (literally the moral way in which Japanese emperors rule). Upon entering the Second World War, Japan would pose as the moral opponent of colonialism: 'It is necessary to foster the increased power of the empire, to cause East Asia to return to its original form of independence and co-prosperity by shaking off the yoke of Europe and America'.[57] To crown everything, a war blessed by Shinto and ordered in the name of a semi-divine emperor could be and was designated a 'holy war'. In sum, there may have been an element of *Realpolitik* in the Japanese attack on the USA but, equally, a large measure of ideological conviction was present, making for a wishful underestimation of the enemy.

Linkage of the European and Asian wars was completed following Japan's destruction of America's Pacific fleet at Pearl Harbor on 7 December 1941. Four days later the Axis powers declared war on the United States. This Hitlerian step, with Mussolini following tamely in his wake, was not entirely unexpected; Japanese imperial conferences had presumed as much.[58] In Berlin war with the USA was judged to be imminent anyway, so Roosevelt's policy in the Atlantic indicated. Moreover, fear of America's economic potential was balanced by the hope, still alive at the end of 1941, that the Russian campaign might soon draw to a successful close.[59] But as with the rationalization of Operation Barbarossa, one wonders what *idées fixes* lay behind the strategic reasoning. After all, Japan had not run to Germany's assistance by attacking the USSR, so the *Führer* hardly owed Tokyo a favour. It has often been remarked that Hitler's view of the USA was shallow, shaped perhaps by the cowboy stories he enjoyed as a youth and the Hollywood films he watched in his private cinema. Most pertinently, to what extent did the 'primacy of race' in his mind blind him? His vituperative speech of 11 December excoriated Roosevelt as a tool of Jewish Wall Street, and in the new year he told his cronies, 'I don't see much future for the Americans. In my view, it's a decayed country . . . they have their racial problem.'[60] It is difficult to believe that his racist ideology played no role in Hitler's decision.

Whatever Hitler's deeper motivation, the timing of his declaration of war on the USA was an unmitigated political blunder. Roosevelt's commitment to Britain to give priority to the European over the Asian theatre of war appeared, on the morrow of Pearl Harbor, extremely rash. To respond to an attack in the Pacific by a stepped-up involvement in Europe would open the president to the charge of using the Asian conflict as a 'back door' to war against the Axis.[61] Here was an opportunity to embarrass Roosevelt and raise the flagging spirits of the America Firsters. But Hitler's rush to arms cut the ground from beneath their feet. His haste to take on the United States must be attributed to a doctrinaire belief in a tide of history, which convinced the *Führer* at the apex of his career that his star was in the ascendant. 'I can only be grateful to providence that it has entrusted me with the leadership in this historic struggle,' he said in his war message. 'A historical revision on a unique scale has been imposed on us by the creator.'[62]

For once Hitler's hyperbole was not misplaced. With the entry of Japan and the United States, the conflict was now a genuine world war in which the two sets of antagonists stood and fought for mutually exclusive *Weltanschauungen*. The Grand Alliance of the USA, Britain and the USSR brought into one camp the three salient ideologies of the nineteenth century; these were personified in the 'big three' war leaders: the liberal-democratic Roosevelt, the traditional conservative Churchill and the ostensibly socialist Stalin. It bears restating that nineteenth-century liberalism, conservatism and socialism (at least in its reformist guise) were in a way embryonic ideologies in that they lacked a quintessential dogmatic rigour. Certainly, the Anglo-Americans pursued a liberal-democratic ideology but it consisted of rather inchoate Western values; Stalin for his part, as we shall see, subordinated Marxism–Leninism after 1941 to the demands of an old-fashioned nationalism. On the other side, Nazi Germany, Fascist Italy and Imperial Japan rejected the main tenets of modern Western thought, save for a warped Darwinism that found expression in ultra-nationalism and febrile imperialism. Decision-making responded to their different forms of Darwinian ideology, and their foreign and military policies were submitted to the dictates of an ideological destiny. It was not that they all subscribed to a tightly knit theoretical construct; Mussolini and Japan's militarists were deficient in this regard. But their thoughts and actions were circumscribed by a blinkered and categorical perspective of the world. In this sense the leaders in Berlin, Rome and Tokyo were of the same ideological species.

Thus, the Second World War after 1941 was not merely a clash of particular political philosophies, fascism–Nazism against anti-fascism. It was also a contest between two styles in ideological thought – the loosely formulated ideological doctrines of an earlier age against the mindset of absolute conviction prevalent in the twentieth century.

TOTALITARIAN IDEOLOGIES REBUFFED

The zealotry endemic to ideologies came to the fore in the war policies of Japan and Germany, on the battlefield and in the occupation of conquered territories. In brief, Japanese and German conduct represented the ultimate in the subjugation of both self and others to a larger ideological cause. Moreover, this denial of individual human worth was not confined to national elites, but was encountered throughout the fighting forces and civilian bureaucracy.

In the Japanese case, absolute credence in the 'national polity' assured a sufficiency of volunteers as *tokkọtai* (kamikaze) pilots or human torpedoes. As for non-Japanese denizens of the co-prosperity sphere, they were expected to bow to Nippon's 'destiny to become the light of Greater East Asia'.[63] This meant ruthless economic exploitation and brutal suppression of any dissent; pan-Asianism and equal partnership against Western colonialism proved a mirage. Collaborators with the Japanese – Wang Ching-wei in China, Ba Maw in Burma, Subhas Chandra Bose in India – were pushed to the fringes of their countries' nationalist struggles. In other words, Tokyo's own imperialist ideology thwarted any chance of rallying Asian anti-colonial sentiment to its side.[64]

In the same way, ideological blinkers prevented Nazi Germany from exploiting analogous advantages in its war against the USSR. The Leninist and Stalinist denial of autonomy to the non-Russian peoples of the Soviet empire left simmering nationalist and separatist anger to be exploited. A number of Ukrainian villages at first greeted German troops as liberators, and Rosenberg, the coordinator of Nazi occupation policies, envisaged working closely with a range of discontented nationalists. Alternately, there existed the opportunity to explore, and take advantage of, unrest provoked among Russians and non-Russians alike by the Stalinist purges and tyranny. However, Hitler turned his back on all such possibilities. His racist dogma rendered any Slavic state, even a puppet one, anathema to him. All Slavs, being biologically worthless, were to be dragooned into the service of an Aryan *Herrenrasse* (master race) planted in the conquered regions. 'This space in Russia must always be dominated by Germans,' insisted the *Führer*; the method was 'to germanize this country by the immigration of Germans' and in a favourite Hitlerian metaphor 'to look upon the natives as Redskins'.[65] The viciousness with which this programme was put into effect guaranteed a nationalist backlash *against* the Nazi invader. In a pragmatic way, the hard-pressed occupation authorities did employ as camp guards and general labourers some half a million collaborators drawn mostly from the Soviet minorities. On the other hand, no attempt was made to mobilize Soviet dissidents into an armed force until late 1944 when fifty thousand of them were put under the command of the captured General Vlasov. But even with defeat looming, Hitler remained lukewarm, and this Russian 'liberation army' never saw serious action.[66]

The central place that the Soviet Union occupied in Nazi ideology contributed to the savagery of four years of war and conquest on the eastern front. Moreover, it was not only the SS and party fanatics who were responsible for the innumerable atrocities. By a process of 'ideological internalization' the *Wehrmacht* succumbed to Nazi racial doctrines, and the participation of both the professional officer corps and the rank and file in the liquidation of 'subhuman' Slavs and Jews has been amply documented.[67] Indeed, the *Vernichtungskrieg* (war of extermination) in the east was inextricably mixed with the climax of Nazi racial policy which evolved as more Jews fell under Nazi rule. In 1941 the conquest of vast tracts of Russia with a large Jewish population radicalized the Nazi outlook. It made increasingly difficult the prior policy of ghettoizing Europe's Jews in the so-called General Government of southern Poland, and the failure to overcome British sea power ruled out the alternative of shipping them to Madagascar. Hitler had already resolved on the genocidal 'final solution of the Jewish question' before the German armies were checked before Moscow in November, and the infamous Wannsee Conference in January 1942 merely concerned the logistics of the solution. The actual Holocaust, then, grew out of the nature of Operation Barbarossa itself. The no man's land between Europe and Asia had always been Hitler's target. There, Jewry was populous and Bolshevism flourished, and the two remained inseparable in his ideological fantasy.[68]

If Nazi ideology was given tangible shape in the Russo-German war, Stalin on the contrary rallied the Soviet peoples by shunning Marxism–Leninism. The name given the struggle speaks volumes: the Great Patriotic (or Fatherland) War was fought with the symbols of old Russian and Slav nationalism.[69] The Soviet media took to eulogizing national heroes of the feudal past, and the German capture of Tolstoy's country house provided an opportunity to recall his classic account of Russian resistance to the Napoleonic invader in *War and Peace*. The atheistic Kremlin lifted restrictions on the Russian Orthodox church and invited this bastion of the tsarist state to bless its war effort. Stalin addressed public audiences as 'brothers and sisters' instead of 'comrades', and he opened a competition for a new Russian national anthem to be played instead of the revolutionary *Internationale*. On the international stage, a parallel departure from orthodox Soviet ideology was the dissolution of the Comintern in May 1943. Again, this was a gesture to nationalism, 'a license issued to foreign communists to become nationalists' in the anti-fascist resistance. Yet Moscow intended no relaxation of control; it was rather that national communist parties were now tame enough not to need Comintern supervision.[70] Additionally, of course, the end of the Comintern improved Stalin's relations with his Western allies, which had recently been badly bruised by the revelation of the Soviet massacre of Polish officers in the Katyn forest.

Here, one touches on perhaps the most pregnant issue of Second World War diplomacy – the difficulty of holding together the incompatible elements of the Grand Alliance. The defeat of Nazi Germany was assured, if not immediately apparent, when in the winter of 1942 Hitler, still arrogantly confident of his own destiny, refused to allow his sixth army to retreat from Stalingrad. During 1943 the tank engagement at Kursk, the rout of the Afrika Korps, the subsequent Anglo-American landing in Sicily and overthrow of Mussolini, all left the Allies confident of victory sooner or later. Axiomatically, as the dread of fascism–Nazism receded, the old distrust between capitalist West and communist East, between liberal democracy and dictatorship in the name of the proletariat, returned.

Contention arose over three matters above all. Two were of immediate concern and interlinked: the Anglo-American launch of a second front in Western Europe to relieve the burden on the Red Army, and the potential for a separate peace with Hitler by one side or the other. Rashly, Churchill and Roosevelt had promised Stalin a second front in 1942, and were then forced by strategic considerations to go back on their word. The Russian leader was incensed, probably because he feared that lengthy German occupation of Russian lands was sure to foment anti-Soviet dissidence. But the Soviet media ascribed the delay to a plot, reminding their audience that Western appeasement in the 1930s had been a device to turn Hitler against the USSR. Indeed, there were still some Western voices in mid war to be heard advocating that the two totalitarian regimes be left to bleed each other to death.[71]

Soviet distress at the tardy second front occupied the minds of Churchill and Roosevelt when they met in January 1943 at Casablanca. Their public resolution there to accept nothing short of German unconditional surrender suggested, and was in part motivated by, an awareness of the ideological gulf that separated the West from the regime in Berlin, which rendered any compromise impossible.[72] The statement was thus intended to convince Stalin that an Anglo-American separate peace with Nazi Germany was inconceivable. The same message was conveyed by the dismissive Western attitude to Germany's conservative anti-Nazi opponents who hoped that, on getting rid of Hitler, they could then negotiate a moderate peace settlement.[73] Unconditional surrender dashed this hope; there was to be no repeat of the 1918 scenario when the Germans fabricated a stab-in-the-back legend. But in the final analysis, the Casablanca Conference was as much concerned with the USSR as with Germany; it was the West's refutation of Soviet charges of duplicity.

Stalin himself was not guiltless of double-dealing. In 1943 and 1944, presumably reacting more to the Western powers' tardy second front than their unconditional surrender protestation, he made tentative overtures for a peace with Nazi Germany on the basis of the 1941 frontiers. These were clandestine and unofficial contacts. How serious they were is unclear as Hitler, deaf to the pleas of his Italian and Japanese allies for a separate peace, intervened twice to break off exploratory talks in Stockholm. He preferred to believe the Grand Alliance would fall apart of its own accord. In any event, the absolute destruction of the Soviet regime was his life's work, and in so far as he entertained a separate peace at all, it would more likely be with the West than the Judaeo-Bolsheviks.[74]

The third and most consequential cause of dispute within the Grand Alliance involved planning for the postwar world. On being drawn into the Second World War, Russia had guardedly adhered to the Atlantic Charter, including its espousal of national self-determination. But within months the Soviets asked the British for a guarantee of their 1941 borders, which implied approval of the seizure of areas in the Balkans, Poland and the Baltic states. The request was refused largely at Washington's behest, whereupon Stalin muted his territorial demands, temporarily of course, in the hope of inducing the West to launch its second front without delay.[75] Nevertheless, from the earliest stages of the Grand Alliance, a Wilsonian–Rooseveltian liberal world order based on international justice was set to clash with old-fashioned power politics marked by spheres of influence.[76] The postwar plans that the big three Allies concocted were an uneasy compromise of the two international modes of international relations.

During the Second World War both Churchill and Stalin gave precedence to *Realpolitik* over past ideologies and future idealism. In 1943, for example, Churchill switched British support among Yugoslavia's partisans from the royalist Mihailovic to the communist Tito. For his part, Stalin's preoccupation with the USSR's western frontiers was in keeping with his embrace of Russian nationalism in the Great Patriotic War. The two leaders were on the same wavelength as regards spheres of influence; Churchill thought to safeguard the British empire, Stalin to construct an East European buffer zone of satellite states. Meeting in Moscow in October 1944 they reached an informal Balkans understanding that effectively traded Western predominance in Greece against Russian in Romania and Bulgaria, while giving each an equal say in Hungary and Yugoslavia.[77]

A more sensitive issue, however, concerned Poland, partly because the war started there, partly because an anti-communist Polish government-in-exile operated in London and enjoyed the backing of a Polish lobby in the USA. Stalin's intent to bring Poland within the Soviet orbit was patently clear.[78] The Russians made no effort in August 1944 to aid the anti-Nazi Warsaw uprising which was directed by known anti-communists. The resultant annihilation of the Polish underground opened the door to a committee of Polish communists gathered on Kremlin orders at Lublin. With the advance of the Red Army the Western powers were forced to accommodate Stalin's wishes. At the Yalta and Potsdam conferences in 1945 a Declaration on Liberated Europe paid lip service to the principle of free and democratic elections throughout Eastern Europe, including Poland. But ominously the Lublin Poles were recognized as the nucleus of the provisional government in Warsaw. The same conferences endorsed a shift of the Polish frontiers westward, at Germany's expense, while in the east the Soviet gains of 1939 that three years earlier the Anglo-Americans had refused to recognize were now ratified. The imposition of Stalinist dominion over Eastern Europe was accompanied by the division of occupied Germany into Allied zones of occupation, thus completing the severance of Europe into Western and Soviet halves.

In Washington there were those prepared realistically to recognize Russian predominance in Eastern Europe and to accept the concept of spheres of influence.[79] President Roosevelt himself was not immune to thinking in regional terms – witness his enthusiasm for the policy of pan-Americanism. Yet fundamentally 'he never abandoned his commitment to avoid creating a confrontational world', and it is significant that he was not a party to the informal Churchill–Stalin spheres-of-influence deal. Roosevelt's clear preference was for universalist solutions.[80] Because the Great Depression was believed to have occasioned the nationalist excesses of the 1930s, the Bretton Woods Conference of 1944 aimed at establishing a stable international monetary system. On the political front, the comparable international decision was that to build a united nations organization. The United States was the moving spirit behind the idea that reached fruition in San Francisco in April 1945. Like its predecessor, the United Nations gave national sovereignty due respect; all the powers, the USA included, agreed in principle that each permanent member of the Security Council should be allowed to wield a veto. None the less, the UN was at the heart of Roosevelt's universalist hope of engaging the Soviet Union in an international security system. He told Congress in the spring of 1945 that he looked forward to

> the end of the system of unilateral action, the exclusive alliances, the spheres of influence, the balances of power, and all the other expedients that have been tried for centuries – and have always failed. We propose to substitute for all these, a universal organization in which all peace-loving nations will finally have a chance to join.[81]

Although Roosevelt affected to be more 'realistic' and 'pragmatic' than Woodrow Wilson, echoes of Wilsonian internationalism were never far away.[82]

The post-1945 Cold War between the USA and the USSR, then, started from the dichotomy in Grand Alliance tactics. While Moscow played by the rules of balance of power and spheres of influence, Washington at first put its faith in resurgent collective security. A classic dialogue of the deaf ensued.[83] Inevitably, this intellectual misunderstanding was reflected ideologically. In Eastern Europe local communists pretended that the workers' embrace of Marxism–Leninism, and not the Red Army, accounted for their nations' incorporation into the Soviet empire. But in the West Stalin's instruction to the Italian and French communist parties to support post-liberation bourgeois cabinets, in reality conceding the Mediterranean and Western Europe to the Anglo-Americans, betokened a retreat from world revolution. Stalin might be engaged in extending

Soviet power on the ground, but in the ideological realm it was rather the United States that, at the close of the Second World War, aspired to make its principles ecumenical. Roosevelt was 'a true twentieth-century American liberal' in that he 'possessed a calm, quiet conviction that Americanism (a better word than liberalism) was so very sensible, logical and practical, that societies would adopt those values and systems if only given the chance'.[84] Such values were embodied in the prospectus of the UN, which was thus to serve as the medium for fulfilment of the American dream.

One further ideological ingredient of postwar expectations deserves mention. This is the 'resistance ideology' of the anti-Nazi underground in Western Europe, which was directed not just against German occupation but against the socio-economic system blamed for the rise of Hitler. Resistance was 'one step toward a higher goal – the renovation of the nation's society, economy and political structure', or, as the masthead of a French underground paper put it, 'From resistance to revolution'. Furthermore, the resistance was largely the inspiration behind the dream of a united democratic Europe, an explicit riposte to Hitler's hegemonic new order. All of which signified a general anticipatory mood similar to that of 1918. There was the same conviction that with peace would dawn a new era of social and economic justice and of international conciliation. But euphoria had to be restrained lest history repeat itself. Indeed, the post-First World War bogey of anti-communism reappeared. Since communists, with Moscow's approval, had assumed a high profile in the French and Italian resistance movements, the Anglo-Americans showed themselves eager to employ De Gaulle in France and Christian Democracy in Italy to resist, or at least control, the 'wind of revolutionary change' at liberation.[85]

Most of the ideological passion of the Second World War was traceable to Hitler, either in his support or, as the European resistance illustrated, in opposition. And the *Führer* decreed that ideology should predominate to the end. Nazi Germany's total mobilization came late in the day, when the looting of Europe no longer sufficed for the war effort. Even in 1944–5, though, this was an ideological rather than physical mobilization, 'disproportionate hopes being placed on will, fanaticism and propaganda as a means of winning the war'. Rosenberg's 'ideological ceremonies' retained top priority while the slaughter of the Jews went on relentlessly at the cost of resources wasted. Some around Hitler were prepared for compromise solutions and dreamed of a last-minute peace overture to the Western powers. But the *Führer* was adamantly locked into the 'all-or-nothing approach [he] had adopted since Barbarossa'.[86]

In fact, it has been argued that the real ideological frenzy of Nazism was only disclosed in the last mad days of the Third Reich when the *Führer* and his staff retreated to the bunker beneath the Berlin *Reichskanzlei*.[87]

There, they consulted horoscopes which foretold a great eleventh-hour victory in April 1945. Hence, news of Roosevelt's death on the 12th was greeted ecstatically, and a parallel drawn with the collapse of the alliance against Frederick the Great on the death of the tsarina in 1762. 'We felt the Angel of History rustle through the room,' wrote one Nazi in his diary.[88] Ideological faith in providence denied the possibility of defeat even as the Red Army was poised to begin its final assault on the German capital. On the other hand, Hitler's *Weltanschauung* provided a stratagem in the event that the unthinkable should happen. Twenty years earlier he had written, 'Germany will be a world power or there will be no Germany.'[89] With the fanatic's absolutist vision still prevailing in the spring of 1945, he ordered the razing of Germany's industrial infra-structure in the face of the Allied advance. With Hitler, ideology came before Germany's future. His political testament dated 2 April enjoined the Germans to persist in the struggle against 'our enemies . . . Jews, Russian Bolshevists', and concluded:

> And so in this cruel world into which two great wars have plunged us again, it is obvious that the only white peoples who have any chance of survival and prosperity are those who . . . have shown themselves capable of eradicating from their system the deadly poison of Jewry.[90]

He seemed oblivious to the irony that his own pursuit of this ideology had brought the Satan of his demonology in the form of the Red Army into the heart of Europe.

Remarkably, the bulk of the German populace stayed loyal to their *Führer*. Although the managerial class were persuaded to ignore Hitler's destructive order, the German war machine continued to function until Hitler's suicide on 30 April and the subsequent armistice of 9 May. In part, this must be attributed to the guile of the Nazi propaganda minister, Josef Goebbels. In the last year of the war he seized somewhat belatedly on the Allied policy of unconditional surrender, which he coupled with a US State Department paper proposing the pastoralization of postwar Germany, to preach that there was no choice but to go down fighting. The fate of Hitler's regime was thus confounded with that of Germany itself, which detracts somewhat from the common impression that the German people 'held solidly to their [Nazi] faith and their madness to the very end'.[91] Their tenacity in 1944–5 was arguably as much a nationalist statement as an endorsement of Hitler's world view. Nevertheless, the Allies, assuming the Germans had imbibed a full draught of Nazi ideo-logical fantasies, determined on a programme of denazification. The first lesson in this educative process took the form of the trial of major war criminals.

After the nuclear attacks on Hiroshima and Nagasaki brought the war to an end on 14 August 1945, Allied international tribunals were set up in Nuremberg and Tokyo.[92] Their task was, in a manner of speaking, to enunciate the principles for which both the European and the Far Eastern wars had been fought. Automatically, they illustrated some of the ideological intricacies bequeathed by those conflicts. For one thing, the war crimes trials responded to the state of relations between the liberal-democratic West and communist Russia; keeping the spotlight on their mutual German and Japanese enemies, which had brought them together in the first place, might help to heal the growing breach. However, the proceedings at Nuremberg and Tokyo were supposed to be more concerned with political principle. On this count, morality and conscience were declared to be paramount; neither *raison d'état* nor *respondeat superior* (execution of orders from above) were recognized as defence against the charges of crimes against the peace and against humanity. This perspective ignored over a century of growing pressure on the individual citizen to obey the state at all costs and brushed aside the spell cast by nationalist and other ideologies. Being contrary to modern nation-state philosophy, this doctrine has for the most part lain dormant.

The most abiding memory of the trials of war criminals is, of course, the evidence brought forward of atrocities against both civilians and prisoners of war. Initially, this was done to destroy popular German and Japanese respect for the Nazi and Imperial regimes, although for its intended audience the message was vitiated by the Allies' own commission of acts capable of being called war crimes. The horror tales from Nuremberg and Tokyo made a greater impression elsewhere. In Western eyes particularly, they suggested that the millions of casualties might not be too high a price to pay for the extirpation of regimes so alien to humane values. The Second World War did a great deal to refute the message of 1914–18 regarding the futility of armed conflict, which had constituted the *Ursprung* of so much interwar appeasement. The Second World War refurbished the image of a just, or at least justifiable, war – that is, one fought to eradicate a way of life deemed irrefutably wicked. In this way, the war crimes trials helped to habituate the world to an international relations system riven by combat between irreconcilable ideologies. They created an international ambience in which the ideological fire of a smouldering cold war was easily ignited.

This is simply to say that the Second World War may have seen the defeat of specific ideological tendencies in Berlin, Rome and Tokyo, but that it hardly reduced the general inclination to couch foreign policy in some sort of doctrinal terminology. War propaganda on all sides had the same result as in 1914–18. Furthermore, it soon transpired that Europe's thirty years' war from 1914 to 1945 had exported ideological thinking and parlance to the Third World.

9

IDEOLOGY AND GLOBAL POLITICS

THE COLD WAR

From 1945 until 1989 international relations revolved around the resumed quarrel between the Stalinist version of Marxism–Leninism and the forces of capitalist liberal democracy. Scarcely an international episode in this period escaped the imprint of the East–West altercation. Since international politics as the result of two world wars had ceased to be Euro-centric, the ideologies of the conflict, to which the American journalist Walter Lippmann attached the phrase 'Cold War', were transported around the globe.

The extension of ideology to a universal diplomatic terrain was furthered by the invention of the atomic bomb. The failure of the USA and USSR to agree on an international atomic energy control system left the West in sole possession of nuclear weaponry until 1949 when the Soviets exploded their first nuclear device and then, some years later, acquired a missile-delivery capability. The frightening power of nuclear weapons imposed a bar on their use, a 'self-deterrence' that operated even when the West enjoyed a monopoly.[1] Furthermore, once both super-powers came to possess the ultimate weapon, parity was less important than mutually assured destruction (the sardonic acronym MAD seemed appropriate), some degree of which was guaranteed and constituted an even greater inhibition. On several occasions the USA threatened to drop the bomb, but there was always a strong element of bluff involved. One historian has facetiously suggested that the atomic weapon deserves the Nobel Peace Prize.[2] Fearful of an armed clash with each other, then, Washington and Moscow were compelled to turn to twin surrogates. First, they had recourse to proxy wars in the Third World fought, initially at least, by clients of the superpowers guided by American or Russian 'advisers'. These were contests for the political allegiance of Asians, Africans and Latin Americans, and involved promotion of the capitalist and communist ways of life in an either/or ideological fashion. The second alternative to a nuclear Armageddon was to conduct the Cold

207

War with words, using ideological slogans as a substitute for bombs and missiles – by psychological warfare within a 'balance of ideologies'.[3] Much of the propaganda so generated can be dismissed as rhetorical froth. None the less, the constant depiction of an apocalyptic struggle between pure and impure ideologies could not fail to create certain expectations and apprehensions, a belief system or 'operational code' that found expression in diplomatic behaviour.[4]

Ideology's power to distort policy was never better exemplified than in the fate of the American objective of 'containing' communism. If an exact date is sought for the start of a containment policy, it must be 22 February 1946 when the minister-counsellor at the US embassy in Moscow, George Kennan, dispatched his 'long telegram' to the State Department. This sixteen-page missive purported to explicate Russia's hostility to the West, becoming daily more manifest in the postwar era; its immediate inspiration was the election campaign for the Supreme Soviet during which Stalin had spoken at length about the incompatibility of capitalism and communism. The tenor of Kennan's message duly dwelled on the ideological factor. While disparaging Marxism as 'the fig leaf of [Soviet] moral and intellectual respectability', he also warned that 'no one should underrate [the] importance of dogma in Soviet affairs'. As to foreign policy, 'the party line is not based on any objective analysis of [the] situation beyond Russia's borders . . . it arises mainly from basic inner-Russian necessities which existed before [the] recent war and exist today.' Specifically, Moscow needed to paint the outside world as 'evil, hostile and menacing' in order to sustain the communist dictatorship within the Soviet Union. Where once Germany and Japan had been Russia's 'implacable enemies', it was now the turn of the USA and the UK 'to fill this gap'. Although discounting the danger of outright Soviet aggression, Kennan predicted remorseless pressure:

> We have a political force committed fanatically to the belief that with [the] US there can be no permanent *modus vivendi*, that it is desirable and necessary that the internal harmony of our society be disrupted, our traditional way of life be destroyed, the international authority of our state be broken, if Soviet power is to be secure.

In the long term, the internal stresses in the Soviet system could be expected to bring it down. But meanwhile, the Soviets being 'impervious to [the] logic of reason', normal diplomatic bargaining was impossible; only the 'logic of force' would suffice. Less than a year after Roosevelt's death nothing more contrary to his universalist vision could be imagined.[5]

There existed, in Kennan's own words, a 'subjective state of readiness on the part of Washington officialdom' to accept his homily.[6] Rooseveltian optimism had given way to President Truman's mounting exasperation at perceived Soviet provocations on a dozen fronts – a Russian spy

ring uncovered in Canada, Soviet troops encamped in Iran, stalled negotiations for a German peace treaty and, above all, the violation of the
Allied Declaration on Liberated Europe in Eastern Europe. We now
know that the US president gave prior approval to Churchill's famous
speech in March 1946 at Fulton, Missouri, that blamed the Soviets for
lowering an iron curtain down the middle of Europe. Moscow's behaviour
seemed to go far beyond any tacit understanding about respective East–
West zones of influence. Lessons of the recent past came into play. The
image of a totalitarian state ideologically driven to boundless expansion
called Nazi Germany to mind. The fashionable concept of totalitarianism
encouraged the notion of 'red fascism', equating Stalin with Hitler.
As Truman remarked, 'There isn't any difference in totalitarian states.
I don't care what you call them, Nazi, Communist or Fascist.'[7] This
parallel, in turn, drew attention to the failure of appeasement to cope
with Hitler; thus the 'Munich syndrome' ruled out concessions to the new
totalitarianism.

Kennan articulated this temper perfectly and propitiously. His long telegram was circulated in Washington's corridors of power and its gist leaked
to the press. Early in 1947 Kennan was appointed head of a new office
within the Department of State known as the Policy Planning Staff.
Because of his official position he signed an anonymous X to an article
published in October 1947 rehearsing the themes of the long telegram.
This article also became required Washington reading and was excerpted
in the popular journals *Life* and *Reader's Digest*. It gave wide currency to
the strategy of containment, which indeed had already been put into
effect, to wit, 'United States policy toward the Soviet Union must be that
of a long-term patient but firm and vigilant containment of Russia's
expansionist tendencies.'[8] 'George Kennan came as close to authoring
the diplomatic doctrine of his era as any diplomat in our history'; Henry
Kissinger's verdict is telling.[9]

'Policy began to catch up with ideology' on 12 March 1947 when the so-
called Truman Doctrine was enunciated before Congress. The immediate
issue at stake was US funding to replace faltering British support of
Greek monarchists assailed by local communists reliant on neighbouring
communist states, and of Turkey under Soviet pressure to cede a base in
the Straits. But the president chose to phrase his request in broad ideological terms, an 'all-out speech' in the words of a White House aide.
Communism was not mentioned but the code word 'totalitarianism' was,
and Congress was told humankind was faced with 'alternative ways of
life'. Most startling was a blanket pledge: 'It must be the policy of the
United States to support free peoples who are resisting attempted subjugation by armed minorities or outside pressures.' Here, containment shaded
into anti-communist worldwide commitment.[10] The alarmed Kennan protested at the failure to distinguish between vital and lesser US interests,

and at the tendency to focus exclusively on the messianic ideology of the Soviet Union. In light of the texts of the long telegram and X article it was perhaps disingenuous to claim his recommendations were distorted; containment always held the seeds of an anti-communist crusade.[11]

The globalism of the Truman Doctrine, however, remained latent so long as the US confrontation with communism centred on Europe, as it did to the end of the 1940s.[12] The Truman administration followed up its stand on Greece and Turkey by proposing to rehabilitate the Continent's war-ravaged economies. The offer was extended to all European countries and the Soviet Union too. But the USSR, after first giving the scheme a guarded welcome, refused the overture and also compelled its satellites to stay aloof. Thus, the Marshall Plan, named after the US secretary of state, became a means of restoring the capitalist, or at least Keynesian, mixed economies of Western Europe. The communist–capitalist economic divide went to the root of East–West ideological differences. In fact, one United States motive from the start of the Marshall Plan was to preserve the free markets of Europe from socialist experimentation and their accessibility to American exports.[13] In return, the Soviet Union set out to sabotage the Marshall Plan. The French and Italian communist parties, no longer partners in postwar coalitions, received orders to stir up trade union and proletarian unrest. In another gesture to world revolution Moscow revived the Third International in the shape of a truncated and short-lived Cominform. In Eastern Europe a new round of purges ensured ideological purity, and in February 1948 the Kremlin orchestrated a coup in Prague that put the Czechoslovak government into the hands of obedient communists.

Europe's postwar economic recovery depended, after both the First and Second World Wars, on the condition of Germany. The main thrust of the Marshall Plan therefore was to create prosperity in West Germany, which required the industrial development of the American, British and French zones of occupation and their economic integration into Western Europe. Predictably, Moscow interpreted this move as a Western plot to resurrect German militarism for use against Russia. A Soviet counter-offensive in June 1948 took the form of a blockade of West Berlin. For several months the risk of a third world war existed before Moscow drew back. This prospect of moving from Cold War to shooting war persuaded Washington the following year to organize the military complement to the Marshall Plan – the North Atlantic Treaty Organization (NATO).

This rapid sequence of critical episodes, coupled with President Truman's alarmist language, comprised a necessary prologue to a global strategy. In 1949 China's communists emerged victorious from the long civil war in that country. The Truman Doctrine notwithstanding, the United States had declined to intervene militarily, partly out of preoccupation with Europe, partly out of disenchantment with its protegé, Chiang

Kai-shek. The following year another sputtering civil war exploded as the communist troops of North Korea crossed into the southern half of the Korean peninsula. The American resolution to oppose this move in a lesser Asian theatre sprang straight from the ideological world view reigning in Washington by June 1950. This may be traced in reports emanating from the Joint Chiefs of Staff and from an advisory body minted in 1947, the National Security Council (NSC). Especially significant was its report dated 14 April 1950 (NSC-68) because in apocalyptic tones it provided the theoretical platform for action in Korea: 'The issues that face us are momentous, involving the fulfilment or destruction not only of this Republic but of civilization itself.' Here and in similar documents the USSR was routinely depicted at the heart of an organized worldwide communist conspiracy.[14] Cracks in the monolith, such as the revolt of Tito's Yugoslavia against Stalin in 1948, were noted and more were pleasurably anticipated. But they were not allowed to detract from the short-term strategy of rearmament and the frustration of communism everywhere. In this scenario East Asia's communists, Chinese as well as North Korean, were puppets of the Kremlin. The outbreak of the Korean War on 25 June 1950 crystallized America's growing conviction of a world ideologically polarized.[15]

Although Stalin apparently gave a green light for North Korea's incursion, his boycott of the UN Security Council in protest at Chiang Kai-shek's continued occupancy of a seat played into the hands of the Western powers. In the absence of a Soviet veto they were able to undertake military operations against North Korea under the banner of the United Nations. The internationalist cause of impartial collective security was hardly advanced thereby. Moreover, while fifteen nations fought alongside American forces in Korea, the police action was conducted and financed overwhelmingly by the United States of America. The objective of the exercise was also American; the UN 'endorsed the principle of containment' hatched in Washington.[16]

Whether containment was implemented multilaterally or unilaterally, there was a virtual American consensus on the policy itself. Three polls taken between January 1950 and June 1951 asked the question, 'How important do you think it is for the United States to try to stop the spread of communism in the world?' Some 80 per cent responded 'very important'; those answering 'fairly important' boosted the affirmative total to 90 per cent, and less than 5 per cent thought the task 'not important'.[17] The heir of Rooseveltian universalism, Henry Wallace, having been dismissed from Truman's cabinet for advocating conciliation with the USSR, ran dismally on a third-party ticket in the 1948 presidential election. He was deserted by America's liberals who, after their love affair with the USSR during the war, turned out to be the fiercest cold warriors. The Americans for Democratic Action, founded amid the Cold

War atmosphere of 1947, formally endorsed the hard-line anti-Soviet stand of Truman and his second-term secretary of state, Dean Acheson. As for the Republican party, the majority were persuaded by Senator Vandenberg, isolationist turned interventionist, to subscribe to a broad bipartisan foreign policy.[18]

But after Vandenberg's death and from mid-1950 up to the election of 1952, a noisy opposition came to be voiced by a group of mostly Republican ultra-conservatives sometimes described as 'new isolationists'.[19] Their critique began with an issue of domestic politics – budget deficits incurred to finance rearmament and containment. The inference was that the USA should defend only what it could afford, and the Republican right repeated the demand of the America Firsters ten years earlier that Asia take precedence over Europe. A further sign of isolationist nostalgia was the call for a more unilateralist foreign policy, and less reliance on allies. In any case, the methods employed by Democratic administrations were alleged to be proven failures because they had not checked communism's advance. Much was made of the 'sell-out' of Eastern Europe at Yalta (decisions taken on Russian soil being automatically suspect) and of the 'loss' of China. Moreover, to the charge of incompetence was added that of treason suggested by Senator Joseph McCarthy's hunt for communists in the State Department, a classic example of 'the paranoid style in American politics'.[20] The McCarthyite obsession with communists at home clearly betokened an inward-looking and Fortress America mentality. Yet there existed a decided incongruity between this residual isolationism and McCarthy's conspiracy theory of an international communist network busily undermining the United States. If the latter were real, it permitted no withdrawal from the global struggle, in Korea or elsewhere. On the contrary, containment might be too defensive an attitude to take. Significantly, the Republican platform in 1952, written for tactical reasons with the far right in mind, reached just such a conclusion.

It was in deference to the Republican right that the new Eisenhower administration raised the decibel count in the verbal Cold War. Secretary of State Dulles spoke of 'liberating' Eastern Europe and 'rolling back' communism, and even hinted at a preventive war. More chillingly, he popularized the phrase 'massive retaliation', which implied that the USA could achieve its goals by nuclear weapons without the expense of conventional armaments. 'Brinksmanship' gave the impression of a vigorous anti-communist campaign.[21] But behind the screen of words Eisenhower's policy differed little from Truman's containment. A greater emphasis on psychological warfare and propaganda perhaps, but otherwise anti-communist resolve was still tempered by caution lest military confrontation result in an atomic war. Neither in 1953, when anti-communist riots convulsed East Germany, nor in 1956, when Hungary briefly threw off the Russian yoke, did the West attempt to invade the Soviet sphere of influence. Similarly, in Korea a stalemate was accepted by an armistice (1953). The none-too-savoury regime of Syngman Rhee survived in South Korea which, nevertheless, was declared saved for the so-called free world; but contrariwise, communism was not rolled back in either North Korea or China.

Meanwhile, also in Asia there was germinating the imbroglio that was to expose beyond doubt the spell that anti-communist ideology was casting over US foreign policy. In 1954 the French, who had been fighting to keep a foothold in Indochina, were overwhelmed by the Vietminh, the anti-colonialist coalition led by Ho Chi Minh. Washington's appraisal of the situation was bedevilled by the McCarthyite climate; it was sufficient to know that Ho was a communist and backed by China to locate his movement within the worldwide communist conspiracy. Of the Department of State's Far Eastern experts, some hesitated to advance a more subtle analysis out of fear, while those who did were disregarded. Yet the Eisenhower administration, its bark ever greater than its bite, shied away from saving France on the battlefield. On the other hand, it was at this moment that the president and Secretary Dulles began to preach the 'domino theory': the Southeast Asian states were a row of dominoes that would topple one by one if the first, Vietnam, fell to communism. US sponsorship of the Southeast Asia Treaty Organization (1954), the equivalent of NATO, was one symptom of domino fever.[22] On the ground in Southeast Asia, however, the immediate crisis was averted by a conference in Geneva that provided for Vietnamese independence but, pending internationally supervised elections within two years, divided the country into two – a communist North Vietnam and a non-communist South Vietnam.

The head of the new government in the south, Ngo Dinh Diem, had been living in the USA, and he received prompt American diplomatic and economic support. All-Vietnam elections were never held because Ho Chi Minh was regarded as a near certain winner. This evasion, combined with the nepotism and brutality of the Diem regime, brought into play the Vietcong, an indigenous South Vietnamese guerilla army that, not surprisingly, accepted the patronage of communist North Vietnam and China. By the end of the 1950s Vietcong growth posed the threat, supposedly exorcised in 1954, of a Vietnam unified under communism. This was the poisoned chalice Eisenhower passed to his successor.[23]

John F. Kennedy entered office in 1961 promising a policy of 'flexible response'. This was intended both as a military alternative to massive retaliation and a reply to stepped-up Soviet encouragement of 'wars of national liberation' in the Third World. But flexible response did nothing to relieve the rigour with which Washington interpreted containment. On the contrary, the siren call of the domino theorists became more insistent. 'If you don't pay attention to the periphery,' warned Dean Rusk,

Kennedy's secretary of state, 'the periphery changes. And the first thing you know the periphery is the center . . . What happens in one place cannot help but affect what happens in another.'[24] By this logic US vital interests were at stake wherever and whenever a communist movement reared its head. Hence the Kennedy administration committed 15,000 US personnel to Vietnam in a counter-insurgency capacity. This proved insufficient, and Lyndon Johnson, after Kennedy's assassination and his own re-election in 1964, proceeded to bomb North Vietnam and dispatch American troops as a combat ground force. Ultimately, almost half a million United States soldiers were serving in Vietnam.

No declaration of war was made. Instead, following a murky naval engagement in the Tonkin gulf, a congressional resolution gave the president *carte blanche* in Southeast Asia; it passed the House by 146–0 and the Senate by 88–2. If this was an imperial presidency, its foreign policy was not imposed on an unwilling nation. Public opinion polls revealed at least two-to-one support for the US course in Vietnam, and after each escalation of the war President Johnson's approval rating rose. The White House did not lose the trust of most Americans until 1968 when the communist Tet offensive, albeit not a Vietcong victory, exposed the ineffectiveness of US military technology in jungle warfare.[25]

For over twenty years both the US people and its government had been locked in a mindset that was the basic reason for the Vietnam cataclysm. The incubus of international communism so weighed on the country that no challenge could go unanswered.[26] In Asian affairs the spectre of communist China was ever present and Vietnam, like Korea, was a surrogate for outright war against China. McCarthy's demagogic use of the fall of China to communism was never far from Lyndon Johnson's mind: 'I am not going to be the President who saw Southeast Asia go the way China went,' and in typical language he described the McCarthyite furore of the 1950s as 'chickenshit compared with what might happen if we lost Vietnam'. Fear of a populist right-wing anti-communism goes a long way towards explaining 'the imperative not to lose' in any round of the Cold War.[27] The original premise behind the containment policy was that Soviet diplomacy was shaped by its domestic ideological needs. It might be argued that, in an ironic twist, US foreign policy became similarly inner-directed; the dragon of anti-communist ideology at home required feeding with an aggressive anti-communist containment abroad.

Elsewhere in the Western world Vietnam furthered a growing sense of unease about America's leadership. In the case of Western Europe this derived in large measure from a transatlantic divergence of interpretation as to the nature of the Cold War. There, in the immediate postwar era, the locus of ideological opposition to communism was to be found in the Vatican under the governance of the rigid Pope Pius XII. With the emergence and electoral success of centre-right Catholic parties, the stage appeared set for an international polarization between Roman Catholicism and communism. However, the Catholic parties, outside Italy at least, proved themselves to be independent of the Holy See, and papal fulminations against godless communism fell on more receptive ears in the USA and east of the Iron Curtain. In due course, the accession in 1958 of the flexible Pope John XXIII and the pronouncements of the Second Vatican Council (1962–5) attenuated the earlier visceral Catholic antipathy to communism.[28] The truth was that Western Europe on the whole, while not unmoved by the Soviet threat, perceived it less in ideological than geopolitical and historical terms, as another episode of the age-old balance-of-power struggle in which Russia was prepared to take advantage of Europe's postwar disarray.[29] Thus, an exaggerated calculation of Soviet conventional military strength led to grateful acceptance of US protection, even by Britain's Labour government, whose foreign policy rested in the hands of Ernest Bevin, a fierce cold warrior. Whether Bevin's stance was an ideological reaction to his trade-union experiences with communists or a pragmatic attempt to prop up the special Anglo-American relationship for economic reasons remains an open question.[30] In any event, America's membership in NATO provided Europe's shield against the USSR. Still, to some Europeans this was no simple anti-communist emanation. As NATO attached more and more importance to West Germany, French President De Gaulle took to complaining of it as an Anglo-Saxon condominium based on Washington, London and Bonn[31] – coincidentally the grouping propounded by some cultural and quasi-racist ideologues at the opening of the twentieth century.

But the deeper cause of NATO disharmony was that, quite simply, Western Europe did not share America's paranoid apprehension of communist ideology; significantly, there was no European equivalent of McCarthyism. This distinction has been well captured in fiction. Arthur Koestler's *Age of Longing* (1951) is a parable set in Paris of the postwar lack of an ideological faith among Western Europeans (save for the committed Marxists): the desperate will to believe of a pair of lovers, one a Soviet diplomat and the other a lapsed Catholic daughter of an American colonel, is set against the scepticism of an archetypal French intellectual who symbolically carries a facial scar from the Spanish Civil War. Europe had suffered enough from ideologies is the message. In the same way, a weary distrust of the communist and the anti-communist cause alike pervades John Le Carré's spy novels set on the European front line of the Cold War. This mood, translated into political terms, saw America's allies offer only token support for, and sometimes covert objection to, the United States' ideological rationale for the Vietnam War. Not one of America's NATO allies shared in the fighting.[32]

Admirers of the United States in 1945 were appalled at how the anti-communist fixation altered within twenty years the whole complexion of

American foreign policy. At the end of the Second World War the US vaunted its tradition as the champion of the oppressed against old-fashioned colonialism. It was the defender of liberal pluralist values, never slow to extol the virtue of 'preserving and protecting a world of diversity'.[33] But withstanding Marxist–Leninist totalitarian conformity was one thing, persuading the world to accept the American values of economic and political liberalism was another. The temptation for the USA to use its superpower weight to impose its own model on others proved irresistible. Washington fell into the trap outlined in the conclusion of Kennan's long telegram: 'The greatest danger that can befall us in coping with this problem of Soviet communism is that we shall allow ourselves to become like those with whom we are coping.' A kind of liberal intolerance and self-assurance prompted US interventions, open and clandestine, around the globe. This was imperialism American-style. Again, a literary work provides a vivid representation. Graham Greene's *Quiet American* (1955) 'had pronounced and aggravating views on what the United States was doing for the world' and, despite his decency and best intentions, wrought havoc around him in Indochina. Lesser and more didactic writers invented the image of the 'ugly American'.[34]

A further defect of America's missionary endeavour was that too often the pursuit of liberal-democratic idealism yielded to short-term anti-communist strategy. In brief, the United States associated itself with the forces of the *status quo* and privilege merely because they were anti-communist; Rhee and Diem personified this predisposition. For the same reason Washington changed its attitude towards colonialism. Once, the campaign for black civil rights inside the USA had drawn sustenance from the felt need to appeal to Third World peoples. But this gave way to collaboration with the relics of European empires. Africa provided a benchmark. In 1970 Washington adopted a 'tar-baby option' that assigned priority to good relations with South Africa and Portugal ahead of those with the emerging black nations. While denouncing apartheid verbally, the USA was conspicuously slow to participate in international sanctions against the stridently anti-communist South African regime.[35] From being the guardian of liberty and individual rights, the US metamorphosed into an imperial power in its own right and the shield of reactionary authoritarian regimes.

Vietnam became the symbol of all America's lapses from grace, 'the culmination not only of the American Cold War in Asia but of an old impulse to impose on the world the patterns of an ideological foreign policy'.[36] As such, it invited a backlash in the form of an anti-Americanism manifest in youthful left-wing disturbances that erupted throughout Western Europe in 1968. Here, anti-Americanism amounted to a counter-ideology to America's own anti-communism. Similar generational protest convulsed the USA itself, as Vietnam overwhelmed the reformist domestic policies of the Kennedy–Johnson presidencies.[37] Out of this internal turbulence emerged a swingeing attack on American policy in the form of a radically revisionist historiography. To find the mainspring of American foreign policy in business interests was not a new argument, but it was the trauma of the Vietnam War that made it fashionable for historians to unmask sinister factors and personalities behind the diplomatic scenery. It might almost be called a therapeutic exercise. The doyen of the revisionists, W.A. Williams, deplored as much in sorrow as in anger the gradual surrender of pristine American ideals to a perceived need for economic expansion.[38] However, many of his followers took a sterner line, execrating what they judged to be the systemic collusion of Wall Street and the State Department.

This 'new left' school set off a re-examination of two centuries of American diplomacy.[39] At the core of their interpretation was the development of the United States as an imperialist power, with much attention paid to the ramifications of 'open door imperialism'. In this *mise en scene*, any anti-colonial rhetoric was a hypocritical device to open up formerly closed markets to American exporters and financiers; the Cold War originated in US machinations to gain economic opportunities in Eastern Europe and Asia; the World Bank and International Monetary Fund established at Bretton Woods, the Marshall Plan, US aid to the Third World were all means to assure America's global economic hegemony. In this massive economic-political design anti-communist sentiment played a part, but a secondary one as a populist screen for the real American ideology – capitalist imperialism. There is no denying the symmetry between US economic interests and anti-communism during the Cold War, but in the last analysis the dynamics of economic determinism lie in the revisionist historian's eye. Monocausal explanations that smack of ideological preconceptions must always be suspect both in history and historical writing alike.[40]

Some of the 'lessons of Vietnam' drawn by the academic community filtered through to the actual conduct of US foreign policy.[41] There was an understandable retreat from open-ended commitment abroad. One departure from international responsibility was already in train. The Bretton Woods monetary system, which rested on the soundness of the US dollar, broke down in 1971, its collapse hastened by the damage the Vietnam War inflicted on the US economy. Politically, Vietnam forced Washington to adopt a damage-limitation strategy, the prerequisite of which was *détente* with the communist powers. The tokens of this *détente* were a strategic arms limitation treaty with the USSR (SALT I) signed in 1972, and in the same year a presidential state visit to red China. In 1973 the USA at last disengaged itself from Vietnam which, two years later, succumbed to the communists. American opinion tolerated these compromises in part because they were executed by President Richard Nixon, who 'had been so staunch an anti-communist over the years that flexibility now took on the aura of statesmanship rather than softness'.[42] In addition, of course, Vietnam had dampened enthusiasm for anti-communist crusading, leaving a climate of opinion more congenial to the limited and 'realist' containment policy advocated for some time by the Kennan–Lippmann school. The beneficiary was Nixon's foreign policy adviser, Henry Kissinger, who ran the National Security Council and in 1973 became secretary of state. Kissinger was enabled to practise his pragmatic, some would say unprincipled, style of diplomacy professedly in imitation of his heroes, Metternich and Bismarck.[43]

In other respects, though, there was no slackening in the prosecution of the Cold War under Nixon and Kissinger or their successors. In Latin America the traditional *dirigiste* role adopted by the United States under the Monroe Doctrine had already combined with the visceral fear of leftist regimes to provoke several interventionist actions – effective in Guatemala (1954) and the Dominican Republic (1965), ineffective in Cuba (1961). In 1970 Chile elected the socialist Salvador Allende as president. The post-Vietnam climate being inimical to armed intervention, Washington responded by unleashing the Central Intelligence Agency (CIA), itself a Cold War creation. The CIA first used the weapons of economic sabotage and black propaganda against Allende, and later became deeply involved in the plot that overthrew and murdered him in 1973. 'We set the limits of diversity,' Kissinger told an NSC review group.[44] This triumph would later encourage President Reagan (1980–8) to use the CIA in a covert war against the Nicaraguan Sandinistas. As for the relaxation in US–Soviet relations, this stalled over the failure to build on SALT I, and the stockpiling of arms continued unabated under four American presidents between 1968 and 1988. A crescendo was reached in 1983 with Reagan's launch of a strategic defence initiative, immediately dubbed Star Wars, which, had it been scientifically practicable, would have upset the delicate stability of mutually assured destruction.

The American tone of ideological moralism *vis-à-vis* the communist world was somewhat muted in the early 1970s by the exigencies of *détente* and by the Nixon–Kissinger style of *Realpolitik*. But it did not disappear altogether. After all, it was Kissinger who negotiated, however cynically, the Helsinki accords (1975) that traded Western recognition of existing East European frontiers against a Soviet acknowledgement of the general principle of human rights. The latter cause, at the heart of liberal-democratic ideology, and Moscow's non-compliance with its promises became a stick with which to beat the Soviets. President Carter (1976–80) took up the international crusade for human rights with the utmost earnestness. According to his credo, 'a nation's domestic and foreign policies should be derived from the same standards of ethics, honesty and morality', from which he concluded that 'there is only one nation in the world which is capable of true leadership among the community of nations and that is the United States of America.'[45]

His successor in the White House subscribed to this traditional American exceptionalism even more strongly:

> The American dream lives – not only in the hearts and minds of our countrymen but . . . of millions of the world's people in both free and oppressed societies who look to us for leadership. As long as that dream lives, as long as we continue to defend it, America has a future, and all mankind has a reason to hope.

The corollary of this lyricism consisted of Reagan's diatribes during his first term in office against the Soviet Union, which 'underlies all the unrest that is going on. If they weren't engaged in this game of dominoes, there wouldn't be any hot spots in the world.' Soviet Russia was categorized a totalitarian state – as opposed to a tolerable 'authoritarian' one such as South Africa. And adjusting his language to suit a fundamentalist Christian audience, Reagan most notoriously denounced the Soviets as 'the focus of evil in the modern world . . . an evil empire'.[46]

Ironically, at the moment that presidential rhetoric was raising bitter echoes of the early Cold War, the Cold War was about to end. Clearly, this was not due to any change in the general line of US policy or principles. It came about because of what was happening on the other side of the Iron Curtain.

The aftermath of the Second World War in Russia saw Stalinism at its worst. It is now fairly well established that Stalin, even more than Hitler, suffered from delusional paranoia. One doctor suggested this diagnosis as early as 1927, and others read something into his relish for *Boris Godunov*, the operatic tale of tsarist intrigue and murder. At all events, in Stalin's final years, his terrified and terroristic reaction to imaginary plots reached patently pathological proportions. Because, according to the testimony of his successor, Nikita Khrushchev, Stalin 'jealously guarded foreign policy . . . as his own special province', his eccentric persona made an imprint on the international scene.[47] The isolation and secrecy of his own existence in the Kremlin was reproduced in the shrinking of Soviet bloc contacts with the West to a bare minimum, and reflected in deep scepticism towards American overtures for UN control of nuclear weaponry which would have put international inspectors on Soviet soil.[48] An echo of Stalin's personal paranoia was audible in accusations of a Western anti-Soviet conspiracy. Here, individual character traits overlapped Marxist–Leninist ideology. US furtherance of the economic recovery of West Germany (and Japan) brought forth the old refrain that capitalism in crisis was conniving with the forces of fascist imperialism.[49] Andrei Zhdanov, the Kremlin's resident ideologue, laid down this line in a landmark speech to the Cominform in 1947; there were two camps in the world – the Western one 'imperialist and anti-democratic', the other dedicated to the 'consolidation of democracy and the eradication of the remnants of fascism'.[50] The invocation of a capitalist–fascist link was communism's ideological reply to the Western taunt of Soviet totalitarian 'red fascism'. Within this ideological context Stalin could still cling to the old Bolshevik hope of a rising of the German proletariat.[51]

Yet it would be totally wrong to pretend that Marxist–Leninist ideology was the final arbiter of Stalinist foreign policy. His conduct in the Great Patriotic War had shown how far *raison d'état* outweighed socialist doctrine when the two were incompatible, and his postwar dominion over Eastern Europe is easily explicable in terms of Russia's historic geopolitical ambitions. Still, Marxist–Leninist theory had definite functions in post-1945 Soviet international relations, specifically to provide 'scholastic ballast' in legitimation of actions taken on a variety of grounds and a 'cohesive moral force' within the communist community.[52] For example, victory in the Second World War was now presented as a 'reminder of the success of the socialist system and its Supreme Leader'.[53] Whereas US policy in the Cold War was taken captive by an anti-communist ideology, the Soviet state remained in firm control of its own ideological doctrine, manipulating it at will. On the other hand, the mere use of ideological discourse by the Soviets was inflammatory enough; it drew the USA into demonizing Soviet intentions, thereby transforming containment into the anti-communist crusade. Furthermore, the ruthlessness with which the Soviets imposed their own system on Eastern Europe did reveal a gulf in political mentality, if not between communism and capitalism, then certainly between autocracy and liberal-democratic pluralism. The two 'alternative ways of life' recited in the Truman Doctrine comprised a not entirely invalid summation of the world situation at the time.[54]

With Stalin's death in 1953 a certain rigidity went out of Soviet foreign policy. It was three more years, however, before Khrushchev felt secure enough to proclaim a new era. This he did by delivering a sweeping denunciation of Stalin to an astonished Twentieth Congress of the Communist Party of the Soviet Union (CPSU). Khrushchev's accusations concentrated on the Stalinist tyranny at home. But more obliquely, he also attacked his predecessor's attitude towards both the hostile West and states within the communist orbit.

As socialism had now been achieved in the Soviet Union, Khrushchev argued, armed confrontation with the Western powers could be ruled out, though fear of nuclear Armageddon and the superior arsenal of the United States was a more probable rationale. At all events, the Leninist stratagem of thirty years earlier, peaceful coexistence, received a new lease on life. But the Kremlin's definition of peaceful coexistence had always been double-edged. Its essence, in the words of one authoritative Soviet publication (1978), lay in both 'co-operation between, and . . . a special form of class struggle between, states with different social systems. The unity of these two aspects consists in the fact that both struggle and co-operation proceed . . . by peaceful means.'[55] Consequently, Soviet policy after 1956 was a curious combination of accommodation and challenge. The Cominform was dissolved, the Stalinist anathema against 'cosmopolitan' western culture was relaxed, and summit conferences of US and Russian leaders became almost commonplace. Against all this was set continued Soviet pressure on Berlin culminating in 1961 in the building of the infamous wall (an 'anti-fascistic protective barrier'), the placing of Soviet missiles on the soil of communist Cuba which in 1962 brought the world to the edge of nuclear war, and in Asia and Africa the intensification of the Leninist tactic of fostering anti-colonial struggles for national liberation.

None the less, these policy contradictions were resolvable within the framework of contemporary Soviet ideology. Moscow never lost faith in the Marxian prediction that socialism was destined to emerge victorious from its conflict with capitalism. Peaceful coexistence was calculated to hasten this outcome by gilding the appeal to the universal proletariat. In the Western world an abatement of the Cold War would lessen the scope for anti-communist propaganda whereby bourgeois governments kept their working classes loyal. On the Soviet side, a reduction in the burden of arms production would allow the socialist states to overtake the capitalist world economically. Khrushchev likened East–West peaceful coexistence to the marriage of a young man (the Soviet Union obviously) with an older woman (the West); however amicable their relationship, she was bound to wilt away. In reality, peaceful coexistence was the 'mirror image of containment theory' in that both anticipated the crumbling of the opposing system from within: 'In the case of containment it was to be democratic change, whereas with peaceful coexistence it was to be progressive change.'[56] On the other hand, Marx and Lenin had advocated giving history a nudge on its predetermined course whenever possible, and Khrushchev's Russia was not averse to doing the same. Hence, the maintenance of global pressure on the West, as long as it did not lead to nuclear incineration – witness his withdrawal of missiles from Cuba.

Although the Cuban debacle led to Khrushchev's fall before the end of 1964, his policy of *détente* mixed with competition began to reap rewards in the next decade. The growth of the Soviet nuclear programme persuaded the post-Vietnam USA to sign SALT I and at least temporarily relax the arms race. In the cosmic ideological combat between communism and liberal democracy also, Moscow was able to count several successes. In Africa national liberation movements in Angola, Mozambique and Ethiopia, all nominally communist, made giant strides towards power. In Europe a similar drift to the left was discernible as right-wing regimes, which Moscow automatically labelled fascist, collapsed in Greece, Portugal and Spain.

In contrast, post-1956 Soviet policy *vis-à-vis* the socialist states floundered badly. Khrushchev's de-Stalinization speech contained veiled criticism of the tight supervision that Moscow exerted over its East European satellites, and his ostentatious rapprochement with the communist rebel, Yugoslavia's Tito, gave promise of a more polycentric system. But the limits of autonomy permitted the satellite communist nations were never clear. In 1956 Russian tanks crushed what the Kremlin regarded as excessive dissidence in Hungary, and a dozen years later the exercise was repeated in Czechoslovakia. Suppression of the 'Prague spring' was retroactively justified by the Brezhnev Doctrine, named after the Soviet leader in 1968 and published in *Pravda* under the heading 'Sovereignty and the international obligations of socialist countries'. It confirmed that foreign socialists' 'freedom to determine their country's path of development' remained secondary to the cause of universal Marxism–Leninism:

> Any decision of theirs must damage neither socialism in one country nor the fundamental interests of other socialist countries nor the world-wide workers movement . . . This means that every Communist party is responsible not only to its own people but also to all socialist countries and to the entire Communist movement.[57]

But doctrinal shibboleths did nothing to relieve the pressures within the Soviet bloc for greater liberalization and nationalist self-expression. Moscow was fighting the same battle as Metternich before 1848, with in due course the same result.

Yet the Kremlin's troubles in Eastern Europe were as nothing compared to those with the second communist power, China. Relations between the Russian and Chinese communist parties had long been ambivalent. For most of the 1920s the Comintern had arranged revolutionary training for young Chinese radicals at Moscow's Sun Yat-sen University for the Toilers of China, and had exercised direct control over the fledgling Chinese Communist party (CCP). But in the next decade the CCP came under the control of Mao Zedong who declined to play the subaltern role that the USSR allotted him. In the Chinese civil strife between the reactionary nationalist Kuomintang (KMT) and the CCP, Stalin declined to take clear sides and, instead, pushed for a common KMT–CCP front against the Japanese. Even after the Second World War, when the CCP was gaining the upper hand over the KMT, Stalin was loath to come off the fence; he did not concede formal recognition of the communist People's Republic of China until the eve of Mao's total victory. But if the CPSU and CCP were at odds over strategy within China, on the international stage in the bipolar postwar era they quickly joined ranks against the Western powers. The major token of this was a Sino-Soviet alliance signed on 14 February 1950, although the drawn-out negotiations hinted at divisive issues beneath the surface. Then the Korean War reinforced the partners' outward solidarity; to the world at large they presented themselves, in the Chinese phrase, 'as close as lips and teeth'.[58]

In spite of his differences with Stalin, Mao never challenged the Soviet leader's status as head of the international communist movement. He showed no such deference to Stalin's successors, especially Khrushchev. In the late 1950s appeared signs of a coming Sino-Soviet rift. Irritation arose over the amount and type of Soviet economic assistance to China, leading to Beijing's accusation that Russia was exploiting its ally. Moscow formally backed Mao's claim to the island of Taiwan, where the defeated KMT had retreated, but refused to countenance military action. Indeed, in 1958 the Chinese bombardment of the offshore islands of Quemoy and Matsu, still held by Chiang Kai-shek's forces, so alarmed Khrushchev that he reneged on an earlier pledge to share the Soviets' nuclear expertise with China. Instead, the USSR went in search of a nuclear test ban agreement with the USA, and in 1960 withdrew all its technical advisers from China.

With two communist nations in disagreement, it was only natural for their quarrelling to be conducted on an ideological plane too. The focus was Khrushchev's famous speech to the CPSU Twentieth Congress in 1956, to which Beijing had initially raised no objection. However, with the general deterioration of Sino-Soviet relations, China in 1959-60 began its campaign of denunciation. Special condemnation was reserved for Khrushchev's arguments that socialism might be achieved without revolution and, more important, that war between the communist and capitalist blocs in a nuclear age was neither unavoidable nor thinkable. Mao, on the contrary, believed the struggle should be stepped up, for he regarded the Soviets' success in space exploration (Sputnik, 1957) as confirmation of socialism's ultimate victory. For several years he had been reminding Moscow of its duty to take a more assertive role in the fight against imperialism. Peaceful coexistence ran directly against the grain of this thinking. Hence, *Red Flag*, the CCP's theoretical journal, did not flinch from the admission that 'imperialist war would impose enormous sacrifices upon the peoples of various countries', because 'on the debris of a dead imperialism, the victorious people would create very swiftly a civilization a thousand times higher than the capitalist system'.[59]

The battle of communist ideology was fought out with great bitterness at two conferences in 1960, one in June in Bucharest, where the Romanian communist party was holding its congress, the other in November at a special meeting in Moscow of eighty-one communist parties. These conferences were conducted behind closed doors and the communiqués spoke of socialist comradeship. But within a year Western European communists began to reveal the conference acrimony, whereupon the USSR and

China saw no further need for dissimulation. In 1962–3 the official media in both countries traded ideological accusations back and forth. China, having opened the offensive, castigated the de-Stalinization programme in Russia: 'In completely negating Stalin . . . Khrushchev in effect negated the dictatorship of the proletariat and the fundamental theories of Marxism–Leninism.' The Soviet Union was charged with revisionism, the most rebarbative word in the communist lexicon. Khrushchev's version of peaceful coexistence was condemned as a distortion of Lenin's 'correct principle', and his retreat in the Cuban missile crisis adduced as evidence of 'capitulationism'. China's real purpose was disclosed when the Beijing *People's Daily* used a pastiche of the phraseology of the *Communist Manifesto* against the Soviet Union:

A spectre is haunting the world – the spectre of genuine Marxist–Leninism, and it threatens you. You have no faith in the people, and the people have no faith in you. You are divorced from the masses. That is why you fear the truth.[60]

Here, the Chinese communists claimed to be the true heirs of Marx and Lenin and, as such, to enunciate official communist ideology.

What rocked the communist world was the extent of the CCP presumption rather than a putative Chinese usurpation of leadership, which was never likely. Khrushchev made much of the mishaps of Mao's Great Leap Forward launched in 1958, an economic plan that implied China would achieve communism before the USSR; the Soviet leader derided it as the equivalent of Soviet primitive 'war communism' after 1917. At the Bucharest and Moscow conferences he succeeded in branding the Chinese as the real deviationists ('left adventurists') and won all the key votes easily. When most of the polemical smoke cleared by the mid-1960s, only Albania had defected from the Soviet bloc.[61] It would be wrong, however, to assume that the Sino-Soviet feud was without consequence. If nothing else, it exploded the notion of communism as a monolithic entity with a single blueprint for world domination. Washington admitted as much in the 1970s by contriving *détente* separately with the USSR and China, and then playing off one against the other – the diplomacy of tripolarity.

Discord among the communist nations vindicated those American containment theorists who had put their faith in the 'wedge' strategy. This meant awaiting patiently, and assisting as far as possible, the development of splits in the enemy camp.[62] But few foresaw the spectacular success of this stratagem within the Soviet bloc by the end of the 1980s. The decade opened with the continued but slow erosion of Moscow's control over the communist outposts. In Eastern Europe old-guard communist leaders breached party orthodoxy with impunity, the Hungarian Kadar in the direction of a free market and the Romanian Ceaucescu with moves towards an independent foreign policy. The Polish non-communist trade union organization, Solidarity, was kept in check but not eradicated, and significantly the Kremlin held back from military intervention. On the other side of the Iron Curtain, the brief phenomenon of Eurocommunism denoted Western communists' anxiety to distance themselves from the Soviet Union. Beyond Europe most of the so-called communist governments and national liberation movements pursued their own agenda, leaving Cuba and Vietnam as Moscow's only reliable 'access points' to the Third World. In sum, the international position of the USSR had undergone a 180-degree turn since 1945: 'In the course of half a century, "Moscow Centre" had exchanged minimal military power and maximum political and ideological status (in the Leninist world) for maximum military power and near-pedestrian status.'[63]

In reality, the Soviet status of military superpower proved to be none too secure either, for the overcentralized and corrupt Soviet economic system ran into increasing difficulties. To the cost of aid expected by Cuba, Vietnam and other clients were added, in 1979, the charges of war in Afghanistan, where Moscow blunderingly imitated America's Vietnamese folly. The last straw, however, was President Reagan's Star Wars programme which opened up the prospect of an unbearable financial escalation of the arms race. Matters were coming to a head in 1985 when Mikhail Gorbachev was elevated to supreme power in the Kremlin.

Reagan's anti-communist hyperbole had put a halt to the earlier East–West *détente*. Hard-liners and the disillusioned in Moscow concluded that 'détente was a tactical expedient for the US [because] the ruling circles did not regard it as a long-term policy', and that Soviet efforts had been wasted.[64] But Gorbachev reasoned conversely that Khrushchev's peaceful coexistence had not gone far enough. Russia's parlous economic condition dictated that the Cold War was no longer sustainable; therefore a new *rapprochement* must be sought, and this time unreservedly. This entailed dropping the element of communist–capitalist competition in Khrushchev's formula. This was at one and the same time the 'diplomacy of decline' and 'new thinking'.[65]

Gorbachev's approach, coupled with Reagan's surprising willingness in his second term to modify his harsh anti-communist rhetoric, resurrected US–Soviet negotiations about armaments, some of which were held at summit level. These went far beyond earlier limitation proposals and aimed at a serious reduction of nuclear stockpiles. But the real international revolution occurred when Gorbachev, visiting Eastern Europe in 1988, made it plain that the Brezhnev Doctrine no longer applied. In a statement issued jointly with the Yugoslav leadership he agreed that they should 'have no pretensions of imposing their concepts of social development on anyone . . . [and] prohibit any threat or use of force and interference in the internal affairs of other states under any pretext whatever'. In Poland he told his hosts that 'equality, independence and joint tackling of problems are becoming the immutable norms of our relations . . . coming to rest totally on the foundation of voluntary, committed partnership and comradeship'. To his critics in the CPSU, Gorbachev cleverly replied in the language of dialectical materialism that 'resisting freedom of choice means placing yourself in opposition to the objective course of history'.[66] To the world at large one of his spokespersons, well versed in American popular culture, summarized the new Soviet view of interstate relations by quoting Frank Sinatra's song, 'I did it my way'.[67] By exchanging the Brezhnev Doctrine for the Sinatra Doctrine, Gorbachev drained the last dregs of socialist ideology from Soviet foreign policy.

The effect on Eastern Europe was electric. Denuded of protection by the Red Army, one communist regime after the other fell during 1989 in a demonstration of the domino theory in action. Astonishingly, this international revolution was accomplished with a minimum of violence.[68] The highlight of an *annus mirabilis* was the destruction of the Berlin Wall in November. The East German communist regime evaporated, and in 1990 the Germans experienced a second unification. The speed of change was overwhelming. As late as the mid-1980s the West German government, despairing of reunification, had authorized construction of an expensive new building to house their parliament or *Bundestag* in Bonn; it was completed in 1992 by which time the official policy was to move the German capital back to Berlin.

In the meantime, it was the turn of the Soviets themselves to suffer upheaval. *Perestroika*, Gorbachev's attempt to jerk the Soviet economy out of its lethargy set off turbulence throughout the nation and confusion at the heart of the communist regime. *Glasnost*, his cult of openness encouraged the non-Russian minorities to take advantage of the commotion to declare their independence. With the implosion of the Soviet Union, Gorbachev was deprived of his CPSU power base.[69] The result, in 1992, was the eclipse of the individual responsible before all others for ending the Cold War. It was an open question how far the dismantling of the Russian empire would proceed. But one thing was sure: were Moscow to reassert its control over the 'near abroad', the Russian euphemism for the Ukraine, Georgia and the rest of the former tsarist and Bolshevik lands, it would be a triumph of Russian nationalism, not of some supranational ideology.

The lesson to be drawn from these shattering events is very simple. Marx and Lenin believed that the masses were at heart internationalist, not nationalist. Hence, Soviet ideology had for seventy years (save for the interlude of the Great Patriotic War) asserted the primacy of universal Marxist–Leninist faith over national feeling. For forty-five years the same doctrine had been imposed on Eastern Europe. The failure in both places was comprehensive. Narrow nationalist dogmas reappeared, arguably stronger than ever for having been pushed underground. And *mutatis mutandis*, we shall find in the next section that, among the ideologies absorbed by the Third World, nationalism has assumed pre-eminence too – in places again at the expense of Marxism–Leninism.

THE THIRD WORLD: DECOLONIZATION AND AFTER

The beginning of the end of formal colonial empires dates from the Second World War in which both sides wittingly and unwittingly promoted decolonization. Of the Tripartite Pact powers Germany and Italy called on Indian and Arab nationalists to destabilize the British empire. It was the Japanese, however, who made the greatest impact in the Third World. Not that Tokyo's overt anti-colonial propaganda left much of a mark in light of its own abominable treatment of subject peoples. But 'what did remain behind . . . among its colonial peoples [was] an appreciation, indeed an outraged envy, of Japanese organization, diligence and competitiveness.'[70] Specifically, Japan's rout of the European colonial powers in Southeast Asia in 1942 destroyed any lingering myth of white imperial invulnerability, and throughout the Third World whetted an appetite for emulation. Conversely, the Third World took note that the West's sole use of the atomic bomb was against the non-white Japanese. It acted as a reminder of the ideological component of race at the core of all Western empires.

As for the victors of the Second World War, their announced war aims served to encourage independence movements in the colonial world. Declarations such as the Atlantic Charter and that of Liberated Europe reasserted the doctrine of national self-determination as a maxim of international order. The Americans, harking back to the tradition of 1776, predicated the application of self-determination to the colonial area.[71] Their Western allies for the most part, hoping to keep or recover their overseas empires after the war, would have preferred to confine the principle to Europe. But needless to say, the indigenous nationalists in the colonies seized on Allied propaganda about the rights of man and self-government and were not slow to cite the West's libertarian texts against their imperial masters.[72]

As the war wound down, however, the American anti-imperialist commitment began to wilt. President Roosevelt, formerly a frank advocate of breaking up empires, was persuaded by Churchill to accept continued colonial rule under UN trusteeship, a resurrection of the League of Nations mandate system. Of course, to America's new left historians all their nation's verbal endorsement of decolonization was so much subterfuge to disguise the replacement of formal European empire by informal US economic imperialism or neocolonialism. A test case of US motives and policy was to be found in the vital region of Indochina where the Japanese, apprehending an Allied invasion, dismantled the French administration in March 1945.[73] This, coupled with Japan's defeat soon after, opened up the prospect of indigenous independence which the Vietminh tried to grasp. But the United States, as we have seen, supported morally and economically the restoration of French colonial government, and ultimately replaced France in the battle against Vietnamese nationalist forces. In Indochina an independence movement that was left of centre and professed a kind of Marxism fell foul of Washington's Cold War mentality. The tendency was set for US anti-colonialism throughout the Third World to succumb to the anti-communist ideology.

A signal exception to this pattern concerned the British empire where the communist bogey, save in Malaya, was absent. Thus, American anti-imperialist sentiment found its outlet after 1945 in criticism of what was still the largest stereotypical colonial empire. Grumbling was heard in Congress that a US postwar loan to Britain subsidized 'too much Socialism at home and too much damned imperialism abroad'. The political implications of this mood became manifest in 1956 when Britain orchestrated a three-power invasion of Egypt after that country's nationalization of the Suez canal. US diplomatic pressure brought about an ignominious retreat from the venture that President Eisenhower characterized as the 'worst kind of Victorian colonialism'.[74] The situation was not without irony, for it was the British who forced the pace of decolonization. The grant of independence to the Indian subcontinent in 1947 acted as a precedent not only for further liquidation of the British empire, but also for the French, Dutch and Belgians to follow suit.

Although the post-1945 drive for national independence in the Third World owed much to the recent war, its origins can be traced back much further. After all, Roosevelt's anti-imperialist posture was Wilsonianism *redivivus*, and decolonization was something of a delayed response to Wilson's earlier crusade. A similar time-lag would seem to have applied to the reception accorded Lenin's revolutionary appeal to the oppressed peoples of the colonial world. Lumping capitalists and imperialists together to make a single enemy was not only good Leninist doctrine, it also suited Stalin's post-1945 vision of a bipolar world. But in the Stalinist era the USSR was too preoccupied with European affairs, and probably too aware of the nuclear imbalance, to pursue a forward policy in the Third World. It was left to Khrushchev, once the balance of terror (or MAD) had been established, to begin the Soviets' subvention of national liberation movements in earnest. In the 1960s and 1970s a score of Third World independence movements styled themselves Marxist–Leninist. But this should not be taken as evidence of a triumphal ideological diplomacy. The Kremlin continued to equate the health of world communism with the strength of the Soviet Union, and therefore 'the promotion of revolution elsewhere [was] seldom the primary consideration for the makers of Soviet foreign policy'.[75]

Furthermore, the place of Marxism–Leninism in the Third World was enhanced, if also complicated, by the emergence of the People's Republic of China in 1949. Here was a living demonstration that communism could rid an undeveloped country of foreign domination. CCP chairman Mao Zedong was confident that the methods that had brought him victory in China's civil war were applicable throughout the Third World. Accordingly, he foresaw a flood of revolutionary movements with a mass base in the rural 'semi-proletariat', but whose ascent to power required the interim tactic of a united front of various anti-imperialist groups (not unlike Europe's popular fronts in the 1930s). Such was the model the new China offered national liberation movements for imitation.

This suggestion of revolution for export, of course, fuelled the emerging ideological dispute between China and the United States, as a result of which Washington's Asian policy was designed to incommode Beijing as much as possible. Hence US insistence that Chiang Kai-shek's regime in Taiwan was the legitimate government of China; not until January 1979 did the USA accord communist China full diplomatic recognition. American actions in Korea and Indochina could not fail to affront Mao on the grounds of both national self-interest and doctrinal anti-imperialism. Finally, red China greeted the US-sponsored recovery of Japan in the same way as the Soviets did US succour to West Germany; both Moscow and Beijing railed at the rehabilitation of a 'fascist' neighbour. In short, power politics and ideology went together to create a Sino-American confrontation. Its *dénouement*, however, could be comfortingly predicted by Marxist–Leninist historical determinism. Thus Mao dismissed US supremacy as 'superficial and transient' and, in a famous phrase, all reactionary imperialists as 'paper tigers'. It is perhaps worth mentioning too that Mao's ideological certitude was bolstered by Chinese tradition, specifically that of the Middle Kingdom's alleged civil superiority over the barbarians without. Communist ideology and pre-revolutionary moralism were the twin engines of Chinese foreign policy for twenty years after 1949.[76]

Revolutionary rhetoric notwithstanding, communist China in the 1950s was, save in the Korean War, a fairly passive member of the international community. This was due in part to the need to consolidate the new regime at home, in part to the Sino-Soviet communist partnership in which Beijing played the junior role. But by the 1960s the Sino-Soviet split, already recounted, released China to take more initiatives in 'the internationalization of class conflict'. The bid to break the Soviets' entail on Marxist–Leninist theory and praxis extended to the national liberation movements in the Third World. Abundant Chinese moral support and considerable economic aid was provided to left-wing nationalists in Asia and Africa. Yet, even in this revolutionary phase of foreign policy, Beijing steered clear of direct military involvement in these 'people's wars'. This offered a sharp contrast with China's use of force on the Indian frontier in 1962 in pursuit of its own national interest. It hardly need be added that the attack on a newly independent nation like India did China's reputation nothing but harm in the Third World milieu. Moreover, Beijing was slow to recognize that a patronizing attitude affronted the sensibilities of Third World nationalists; particularly resented were the Chinese air of moral superiority and disparagement of national liberation regimes as no more than a 'transitional' step on the road to true socialism. Only when and where the Chinese learned to yield on strict adherence to the Maoist revolutionary model – in Tanzania for example – did they win any sort of foothold.[77]

Overall, though, this activity yielded few returns, for the majority of Third World Marxist movements continued to look to Moscow for guidance, which was not at all conducive to healing the Sino-Soviet rift.[78] Indeed, this remained as wide as ever. Skirmishes on the Manchurian border reached frightening proportions in 1969. The Vietnam War caused more alarm in China as Moscow's support of Ho Chi Minh seemed to presage the spread of Soviet influence in Southeast Asia. When therefore the United States, chastened by its own Vietnam experience, held out an olive branch, Beijing eagerly grasped it in 1971–2. This was pure *Realpolitik* statecraft, motivated overwhelmingly by hostility to the Soviet Union. It also signalled the start of China's gradual retreat from an ideological foreign policy.

Marxism–Leninism–Maoism became 'adaptive'. At home the frenzied ideological purification of China begun in 1966 under the rubric of the Cultural Revolution was scaled down. In foreign affairs Beijing developed the 'Theory of the Differentiation of the Three Worlds' which recalled old Chinese legends – *The Romance of the Three Kingdoms* about the 'tripolar interaction of the kingdoms of Shu, Wu and Wei in the third century as well as the ancient parable of the monkey sitting on a hilltop "watching two tigers fight"'. Updated, this concept divided states into the First World of the USA and the USSR, both of which were held to be bent on imperial hegemony, the Second World of intermediate states, and the Third World to which China claimed to belong. In this context China elaborated on a theme hatched at the height of the Sino-Soviet dispute ten years earlier – 'anti-hegemonism'. This called for cooperation between the Second and Third Worlds to counter First World hegemony, a 'front from above' not of classes but of sovereign nations:

> Any country that opposes the two hegemonic powers and gives support for national independence, national liberation and people's revolution, whatever its sociopolitical system and whether or not it has maintained friendly relations with us, can be brought into line with us in a united front.[79]

230

By advocating this kind of united front Beijing combined its familiar revolutionary and anti-imperialist ideology with an acceptance of the existing states system.

China's drift towards conventional diplomacy was accentuated after the death in 1976 of Chairman Mao and Premier Zhou En-lai. Under its new paramount leader, Deng Xiao-ping, China opted unequivocally for the quickest route to economic growth, which meant cooperation with and imitation of the capitalist West. This course was summed up in the wonderfully oxymoronic phrase 'market socialism'. The public portraits of Marx and Lenin began to disappear, sometimes to be replaced by that of Sun Yat-sen, the founder of modern Chinese nationalism. By the 1980s national interest, not communist ideology, was the clear determinant whether in any given question China sided with or against the West. Sino-Soviet relations beginning in 1979 underwent a deliberate process of normalization.[80] This is not to say, however, that strains did not reappear and cause further obfuscation of China's international ideological position. In order simply to oppose the Soviets, Beijing did not hesitate to align itself with some distinctly unprogressive forces – in Afghanistan, for example, where China joined Pakistan's military dictatorship in backing Muslim fundamentalist resistance to the Soviet invasion. When the Soviet Union itself collapsed, China was in no position to pick up the torch of international revolution. In spite of occasional genuflections towards anti-hegemonism and barbs directed at Gorbachev's liberalization programme in Russia, China was now, so to speak, 'socialized' into the international system. The People's Republic of China and the Soviet Union arrived at the same destination; each had tried a foreign policy based on supranational ideology and found it wanting. It is, in fact, a syndrome common to almost all revolutionary states.[81]

Of the so-called Marxist–Leninist regimes that came to dot the Third World map, it must be doubted whether more than a handful had any deep attachment to, and in some cases comprehension of, communist theory. Not surprisingly, Soviet and Chinese influence among the less developed nations must be adjudged 'modest' and 'marginal at best'.[82] There were exceptions: North Korea, Ho Chi Minh's Vietnam, and Fidel Castro's Cuba, which proved its ideological orthodoxy by sending troops to fight imperialism in Angola. But most national liberation movements and post-colonial regimes that adopted the Marxist tag, and especially a 'Soviet reference' and 'Soviet discourse', did so out of pure self-serving calculation. For one thing, the impoverished Third World found Lenin's explanation of imperialism, and by extension the economic neocolonialism that persisted after political independence had been won, a convenient stick with which to beat the rich capitalist nations. In addition, the Leninist–Stalinist dictatorship provided a paradigm and justification for many post-colonial governments that established authoritarian, one-party rule. In other words, a façade of Marxism–Leninism was a response to the bipolar global balance after the Second World War. The more the USA associated with the old colonial powers and itself indulged in neocolonialism, the greater was the temptation for underdeveloped countries to gravitate politically, economically and philosophically to Russia or China.[83]

Cold War polarization dogged the Third World even when it tried deliberately to stand aside from superpower quarrelling. 'It would not be creditable for our dignity and new freedom if we were camp-followers of America or Russia or any other country of Europe,' proclaimed Jawaharlal Nehru, independent India's first prime minister and instigator of a conference of Afro-Asian non-aligned nations at Bandung in 1956. The initial *raison d'être* of non-alignment was deliverance from the 'suicidal and maddening' confrontation of armed blocs of powers. Although no ideologue, Nehru was a political idealist whose vision of peaceful coexistence was the international equivalent of what Gandhi, his mentor, had preached within India. World peace was still in the forefront of the non-aligned movement in 1961 when it expanded (Yugoslavia and Egypt were the most conspicuous additions) and was 'formally baptised' in Belgrade. On the other hand, Nehru's experiment had a specific and regional objective; this was to contain and neutralize the potential power of red China. Defying pressure from the West, he worked hard to include Beijing in the non-aligned cause, to introduce 'the friendly and reasonable face of the new China'.[84] But this linchpin of Nehru's diplomacy was shattered by China's invasion of northeast India in 1962. New Delhi accepted military supplies from the USA, but turned to the Soviet Union for backing in the Kashmir question against Pakistan, which had the support of China. Such tergiversation was not non-alignment but balance-of-power statecraft.[85]

Nor did the non-alignment movement as a whole live up to the moralistic precepts with which Nehru had tried to invest it. From the start, some of its subscribers were unmistakably aligned with either the communist or Western bloc. Furthermore, the non-aligned movement always contained a faction less interested in reducing international tension than in mobilizing the Third World against neocolonialism. President Sukarno of Indonesia was their spiritual father and, with the increase in membership over the years, they came to form a radical majority. This was noticeable within the forum of the (British) Commonwealth and even more so at the United Nations where the non-aligned group dominated the General Assembly. By the end of the 1970s their priorities 'had shifted to the issues of decolonization and international economics – issues on which neutrality toward the blocs proved to be more formal than real'.[86] Since the West represented both old and neo-colonialism, non-alignment assumed an anti-Western complexion. In the final analysis, non-alignment, like much Marxism–Leninism in the Third World, was a thin ideological cover for pursuit of national self-interest. The authentic ideological dynamic of the have-not countries was 'the national idea' which, although ranged against the West, 'was frequently a product of Western impulses'.[87]

In one respect, however, the Third World brought, or more accurately restored, an extra ideological dimension to nationalist strife. This was religion, which, to all intents, had been banished from European interstate relations after 1648. (It goes without saying that Hitler's antisemitic foreign policy was racially, not religiously motivated.) After the Second World War religion announced its reappearance in world politics by deciding the fate of the Indian subcontinent. Communal hatred was both cause and effect of its partition in 1947 into officially secular but predominantly Hindu India and the Islamic Republic of Pakistan. A perennial flashpoint of Indo-Pakistan hostility has been the vale of Kashmir. Although three-quarters of the population are Muslim, most of the area was incorporated into the new India (the Nehru family were Kashmiri Brahmins), and became the direct cause of two Indo-Pakistan wars. In a third bout of hostilities in 1971 the Indian army marched into east Pakistan then racked by civil disobedience, an action that assured the success of Bangladeshi separatism. An uneasy peace ensued, and the rivals engaged in an arms race for which they solicited aid from both sides of the Sino-Soviet divide – India from Russia, Pakistan from China. In the 1980s Indo-Pakistan tension was kept alive by the advance of religious ideology in both countries. Indian coalition governments faced a 'growth of Hindu militancy' and 'explicit and chauvinistic Hinduism' to which they proved susceptible. In Pakistan the regime of General Zia ul-Haq (1977–88) blended 'pannationalist identity and Islamic public morality', just one example of the rebirth of Islam as a global force.[88]

In fact, an upsurge of theologically based political activity was increasingly evident throughout the swathe of countries stretching from the Himalayas in the east to the Western tip of the North African littoral. At the geographical centre of this area and the focus of religious-ideological ferment lies what was once called the Near East, now the Middle East. And predictably, since 1945 international peace has been most seriously threatened where the politics of two religions collide – in Palestine, the cockpit of Zionist–Islamic bad blood.

In the forging of both a Jewish and Arab national identity, religion was never far way. Zionism and Arab nationalism emerged as forces to be reckoned with at roughly the same time, the late nineteenth century, and they unfolded *pari passu* in a symbiotic relationship.[89] The Jewish campaign for a homeland arose out of a double alarm – at increasing assimilation into Gentile society and outbursts of European *fin-de-siècle* antisemitism. In comparison, the religious element was less overt in early Arab nationalism, if only because its aim was to a great extent escape from the rule of the Muslim Ottoman empire. In any event, the fulfilment of national ambitions lay, not in the hands of Jews and Arabs themselves,

233

but of the great powers. The exigencies of the First World War extorted from Britain one promise of a Jewish national home in Palestine (the Balfour Declaration of November 1917), and another of independent Arab kingdoms in the Middle East. Appropriately, the British, within the framework of a League of Nations mandate, took on the burden of regulating Jewish settlement in Palestine and trying to mollify the indigenous Arab population. This delicate balancing act, always precarious, was wrecked by the Holocaust. The press of Jewish refugees from Europe, coupled with the guilt of the Western allies in 1945 at their failure to check Hitler's genocide sooner, brought matters to a head. Pressure built for not merely a Jewish national home but a sovereign nation state. On 29 November 1947 a UN resolution proposed the partition of Palestine into separate Jewish and Arab states.

As the plan met with blanket rejection in the Arab world, the new state of Israel was born, and its borders delineated in 1948, on the battlefield. This was just the first of a series of short, sharp Arab–Israeli wars that became a regular feature of the Middle Eastern scene (1956, 1967, 1973). Of these, the Six Day War of 1967, resulting in Israel's occupation of the entire west bank of the Jordan river, was to have the greatest regional impact. It would be quite wrong to pretend that these were intrinsically religious wars; Israel's very existence was a political *casus belli*.[90] But the factor of Zionism versus Islam lent the conflicts an extra bite and, significantly, the element of religious ideology on both sides came more to the fore with the passage of time.

Zionism, for its part, combined religious millenarianism and socialist idealism, the end of the Diaspora crossed with a fictional *Altneuland* (1902), Theodor Herzl's sketch of a secular utopia. In Israel at first the latter tendency was uppermost and expressed itself through the predominant Labour party. After the Six Day War, however, the tenor of Israeli public life underwent a noticeable change, epitomized in the founding in 1974 of the movement known as Gush Emunim (Community of Believers). Whereas pristine Zionism had anticipated a Jewish nation state on conventional lines, Gush Emunim envisioned a distinctive Israel with a uniquely religious rationale. This was the Zionism of redemption:

> The settlement of Eretz [Land of] Israel through the ingathering of her sons, the greening of her deserts, and the establishment of Jewish independence within it are merely stages in this process of Redemption. The purpose of this process is not the normalization of the people of Israel – to be a nation like all other nations – but to be a holy people, the people of a living God.[91]

In the short term, the militant religious groups assembled under the umbrella of Gush Emunim demanded Jewish settlement in and annexation of the territories on the Jordan's west bank. Their influence was felt in the elections of 1977 which constituted a victory for the right-wing Likud party. The subsequent government led by Menachim Begin was deterred by international opinion from annexing the occupied territories, yet pushed ahead with Jewish settlement there. It must be admitted, of course, that the rise of Israeli religious nationalism was a direct riposte to unrelenting Arab rhetoric about expelling the Jews from the Middle East. In this way, 'Israel developed its imperial personality to correspond with the Arab stereotype of it'.[92]

The Arab nationalist resistance to the creation of Israel at first drew inspiration, as did Zionism, from secular sources. One such was Kemal Atatürk's nationalist revolution which, in the aftermath of the First World War, had thwarted the total dismemberment of Turkey planned by the victorious Western allies. The essence of Atatürk's reform pro-gramme consisted of the modernization and secularization of Turkish society. The heir to this secular nationalist tradition in the Middle East was Gamal Abdul Nasser who, as a result of a military coup in Egypt that in 1952 toppled the monarchy, emerged two years later as that country's all-powerful president. Nasser had a taste for ideological formu-lation. His *Philosophy of Revolution* (1954) was a primer in both Arab socialism and Egyptian nationalism; on the second count he saw Egypt at the confluence of three orbits – Arab, African and Islamic. Some Western alarmists compared Nasser's book to Hitler's *Mein Kampf*.[93]

In practice, Nasser's appeal was primarily to pan-Arabism, which he sought to foster by exploiting Cold War tensions. In Arab eyes, Israel was a Trojan horse of Western imperialism in the Middle East. Even more sinister, with the end of Britain's Palestine mandate, successive US administrations responded to the powerful Jewish lobby in Washington by becoming the patron of the infant Zionist state to the profit of both the Israeli economy and military strength. In these circumstances, there was a certain inevitability about an Arab turn to the Soviet bloc for counterbalance. Nasser's partiality towards the Soviets owed a little to his socialist philosophy, but more to his calculation of material assistance. One of his pet projects was to dam the upper Nile at Aswan, and when after years of vacillation the Anglo-Americans refused financing, Egypt turned to the USSR. In the wake of the Aswan dam crisis and still in search of revenue, Nasser put a socialist precept into practice by nation-alizing the Suez Canal. The consequent Anglo-French-Israeli invasion of Egypt proved unavailing, not because of any Egyptian action backed by the Soviets but because of US displeasure. Nevertheless, Nasser's defiance was crowned with success and won him enormous kudos among the Arab peoples. He used his popularity to take a step towards pan-Arab unity; in 1958 he persuaded Syria to join Egypt in a unitary United Arab Republic. But the association was tempestuous and lasted only three years, after which Nasser's steady slide from grace began. The nadir was reached in 1967 with Egypt's humiliation in the Six Day War, the 'Water-loo of pan-Arabism'.[94]

The failure of Nasserism, and for that matter the more sophisticated Ba'ath socialism of Syria, to rally the Arab world for more than a brief span left something of an ideological vacuum. It has been filled by the force of rejuvenated Islam wherein 'man can fight for religion just as well, if not better, than he can fight for the modern state'.[95] The agenda of Arab nationalism and pan-Islam overlap, of course, and their relation-ship has been a love-hate one. Nationalists like Nasser did not hesitate to appeal to Islamic sentiment, and sometimes they carried Islamic theorists with them. But more often mainstream Islamic theologians have denounced the hijacking of their holy cause for a secular purpose. Typical was Sayyid Qutb, executed by Nasser in 1966, who argued that Arab nationalism 'had exhausted its role in universal history'. Rather,

> the sole collective identity Islam offers is that of the Faith, where Arabs, Byzantines, Persians, and other nations and colors are equal under God's banner . . . The homeland [watan] a Muslim should cherish and defend is not a mere piece of land; the collective identity he is known by is not a regime . . . Neither is the banner he should glory and die for that of a nation [qawm].[96]

Thus, pan-Islam lays claim to a broader constituency than any Arabic ideology; in the Middle East alone it addresses its message also to Turks and Iranians.

The Islamic resurgence may be regarded as an extreme form of anti-colonialism. Whereas Third World secular nationalists use Western weapons and slogans against the West, pan-Islamic ideology rejects Western materialism utterly. The west is the dar al-harb, literally the domain where Islam is not and where the duty of the true believer is to fight against evil. In the Middle East pan-Islam has taken direct aim at surrogate Western regimes, those secular oligarchies that compromise with Western values and have neither relieved the region's mass poverty nor prevented the expansion of the West's client state, Israel. It is no acci-dent that Islamic fundamentalism has found a receptive audience among the poverty-stricken and lower middle-class Palestinian Arabs who, dis-placed by the Israeli victories of 1948 and 1967, launched an uprising or intifada (literally, 'shaking off' the foreign yoke) in December 1987.

On the wider international stage radical Islam espouses doctrines that, in theory at least, offer an outlet for anti-Western feeling. One such concept is that of jihad or holy war, the declaration of which potentially obligates all Muslims to come to the aid of their embattled brethren, thereby transforming any conflict into a global struggle between belief systems. It thus presupposes concerted action by all Islamic states. This, it must be said, has not been readily forthcoming. In addition to the historic Shia–Sunni theological divide, pan-Islam, like pan-Africanism and pan-Asianism, has been torn by internecine nationalist squabbles; both factors were at work in the bitter frontier war between Iraq and Iran (1980–8). Another weapon in the arsenal of pan-Islam is the *fatwa*, a religious decree held to be superior to any civil law and binding on Muslims everywhere regardless of their citizenship. Such a jurisdictional claim has been asserted most forcefully by Iran, the most ostentatiously orthodox of all Muslim states since the shah's overthrow in 1979. In the words of Ayatollah Khomeini, spiritual leader of the new revolutionary regime, 'We live only under the banners of Islam, and no one has any influence over us.'[97] Accordingly, Iranian Islamic authorities in 1989 pronounced a death sentence on the allegedly blasphemous British author Salman Rushdie and promised a monetary reward to would-be executioners. Pan-Islam has been called 'religion-cum-politics', as opposed to the reverse; certainly the precedence accorded the religious component marks it off from all other ethnic or pan ideologies.[98]

Islam's transnational pretensions are emblematic of a genuine total ideology. Therefore, it is pertinent to raise the question asked of those other total ideologies, Marxism–Leninism and National Socialism: to what extent does dogma allow a totalitarian regime to abide by the rules of the international game of diplomacy? In the case of pan-Islam one must face the proposition that 'foreign policy is a European concept . . . alien and new in the world of Islam'.[99] Must Islamic international activity, then, be no more than destabilization and terrorism against the West in the name of *jihad* and *fatwa*?

Plausible reasons to modify this doomsday scenario are not lacking. Islamic theological commandments, it is argued, allow a certain flexibility of interpretation.[100] For example, *jihad* may be a less bellicose concept than it seems; the war it preaches can be rendered defensive action or resistance and, even more innocuously, doing good and resisting evil. Pan-Islam's militant universalism can also be called into question by reference to the Koran, which appears to accept divisions within humankind, and by extrapolation sovereign nations. In a historical perspective, the past Islamic empires of Seljuk and Ottoman Turks entered into what were conventional relations of the day with Christian and other kingdoms. Why should modern Islam not prove similarly adaptable? Indeed, in the 1980s there were signs that this might be happening, that the Islamic belief system was becoming 'the vehicle for political and economic demands', merely a 'convenient, readily available ideological instrument' for material ends.[101] Even Khomeini's Iran was not immune from this trend. Tehran bargained the release of Western hostages seized by shadowy Islamic groups in the Middle East against the provision of arms by the USA ('great Satan') for use against Iraq; the intermediary was Israel ('little Satan') with which Iran had sustained a 'pragmatic entente' for forty years.[102] In certain circumstances apparently *raison d'état* was more important than fidelity to pan-Islam.

In the short term, however, the fortunes of pan-Islam would appear to depend on the Arab peoples, for 'Islam has an Arab face and an Arab soul'.[103] Since 1967 a contest for Arab hearts and minds has been waged between the forces of religious ideology and political compromise. The competition was encapsulated in the last years of the Egyptian president, Anwar Sadat. By the Camp David accords of 1978 brokered by US President Carter, he gave Egypt's formal diplomatic recognition of Israel, the first Arab state to do so, in return for the Sinai peninsula lost in the Six Day War. Sadat then affronted pan-Islam further by affording refuge to the deposed shah of Iran. In 1981 Muslim fundamentalists struck back by assassinating Egypt's president. But the Arabs' main preoccupation has remained Palestine. There, a serious attempt to find a political *modus vivendi* was launched in 1993 when the Palestine Liberation Organization (PLO) and Israel recognized each other and agreed on a measure of Palestinian self-rule on the west bank of the Jordan. Each party gambled on outmanoeuvring religious fundamentalism, Islamic and Zionist, and on breaking the ratchet effect Islamic and Zionist ideology have had on each other. The chronic difficulty of the task was revealed in 1995 when Jewish fundamentalists murdered Yitzhak Rabin, Israeli premier and architect of the accords with the PLO – an exact counterpart to the Sadat killing a dozen years earlier. Religious ideology, inflated rather than diminished over fifty years, still stands in the way of the UN's original solution to the Palestinian problem, namely, the creation of an Arab state alongside the Jewish one.

Among Third World countries at large the defining experience has been Western colonialism and the struggle against it. Independence did not spell the end of subservience. For most of the half-century after 1945 the West managed to keep a stranglehold on world trade and finance, perpetuating a sort of imperialism or neocolonialism, and the economic disparity between the advanced countries and most of the Third World remained largely untouched by Western donor aid.[104] Nor should it be overlooked that the rich nations have been until recently predominantly white while the poorer states are still inhabited by black, brown or yellow peoples, a situation guaranteed to enhance race consciousness. With the exception of Zionism (hardly a Third-World phenomenon), all the ideologies just discussed – pan-Islam, pan-Arabism and other anti-Western nationalisms, Marxism–Leninism–Maoism, even non-aligned neutralism – have been expressions of resentment at Western imperialism, stimulated by some degree of racial, anti-white sentiment. It is noticeable too that the newly independent states have been reluctant to embrace the cherished tenets of triumphant white liberals. Whereas the principles of liberal-democratic pluralism overcame fascism–Nazism in 1945 and Soviet communism in

1989, they have hardly flourished in the Third World. There, authoritarian rule, often undisguised despotism, has been more common. In sum, something of an ideological polarization, based both on race and general political philosophy, has come to characterize the relationship between the developed and still developing parts of the globe.

All of which adds up to a geographical shift in the constellation of nation states. The rich, white nations have traditionally been found in the northern hemisphere, the poorer non-white in the southern half of the globe or at least close to the equator. The global ideological axis has been shifting accordingly. For much of the nineteenth century a basic international ideological divide lay along an east–west line, with the Western liberal powers at one pole and the East European conservative states at the other. In the twentieth century the Cold War (1917–89) was *imprimis* another latitudinal confrontation. But the larger a role the Third World plays on the international stage, the more one must expect the world's axis to swing in a general north–south direction. Ideology cannot be exempt from this process.

CONCLUSION
Power and ideas in international relations

The treatment of international relations in this book has been historical, not theoretical. The historical perspective, it is here contended, allows one to appreciate first the emergence of ideology on to the world stage and then its percolation throughout the entire spectrum of interstate relations. In addition, by emphasizing the role of ideology, this approach runs counter to the thrust of much recent theoretical work on international relations.

The so-called 'grand theories' of modern international relations derive from and reflect the realist schools of thought.[1] The leitmotif of these interpretations is the pursuit and accumulation of power for geopolitical ends; ideas are relegated to the sidelines. The realist writers of the Cold War era reacted against the utopianism of fascism–Nazism, Rooseveltian one-worldism and communism (and also for that matter against the ideological excesses of anti-communism) by according priority to each nation state's own pragmatic interests. In turn, what has been termed the 'systems perspective', a species of neorealism, tried to shift the scholarly gaze away from individual states to international interdependence expressed in a bipolar balance of power and a global economy. Nevertheless, the focus was still on the distribution of power.[2] Now, no one will deny that ideas have a force of their own. On the other hand, military and economic power, in the guise of armament and trade statistics, is so much easier to describe and measure. It is hardly surprising that realist theoreticians were, and still are, drawn to calculate power primarily in those materialistic terms. Ideas and ideologies can then be dismissed in the words of the *doyen* of the realist school as 'pretexts and false fronts behind which the element of power, inherent in all politics, can be concealed'.[3]

The clear implication of the realist arguments is that a Hobbesian power-political pursuit of national or bloc interests can be disentangled from the ideological form in which they may be expressed. But this is a simplistic and false dichotomy. Even realist and neorealist writing that claims to isolate those self-interested factors that allegedly determine all foreign policy-making can be deconstructed to reveal a subtext of 'political idealism'. Alternatively, realist propositions may be regarded as

240

an ideology itself, the ideology of a balance-of-power system in fact.[4] As for the actual conduct of international relations, it may be granted that some regimes have used ideology as a cloak for the prosecution of geopolitical advantage; but equally others, wittingly or unwittingly, have made the national interest subservient to ideology. Either way ideology must be recognized as an integral part of world politics. The process whereby this happened has gathered pace over the past two centuries. Fundamentally, it is the ineluctable price exacted of international statecraft in an environment of mass politics, as the preceding chapters have illustrated.

> By means of high philosophical words rulers can better control the ruled, who are ensnared by their literacy, and obtain their support or their passive acquiescence. Thus, by a natural development, it is not philosophers who become kings, but kings who tame philosophy to their use.[5]

Modern ideologies, in other words, retain something of the nature of a false consciousness, although without the Marxist class connotation.

The linkage between ideology and diplomacy began when the doctrine of the rights of man furnished the *fons et origo* of the French revolutionary wars. In the course of the nineteenth century assent to the rights of man and the concomitant march towards popular sovereignty injected ideology still further into foreign policy making. After the liberals' debacle in 1848–9, Europe's conservatives won widespread support by appropriating the ideologies of nationhood, race and empire. The result was an efflorescence of Social Darwinism that spawned the war mood of 1914. The Great War confirmed the nexus that ideology had come to provide between public opinion and foreign policy. In the majority of combatant nations every resource, human and material, was more or less willingly mobilized for the sake of a crusading war aim. The totalitarian rulers of the interwar years were not, of course, concerned to follow popular opinion but to shape it to accord with a Rousseauite general will expressed as an ideological imperative. As such, this demanded an international policy geared at least rhetorically and often in practice to the global triumph of a class or race. The Western democracies responded in kind by emphasizing their own societal values – in the Second World War a pluralistic liberalism that later in the Cold War degenerated into rigid anticommunism. The nuclear stalemate caused the Cold War itself to be fought mostly as an ideological battle for hearts and minds, especially among Third World populations.

Of the ideologies that have agitated international affairs, few deserve the title of total ideology as that concept was described at the start of this study. Probably, one should restrict the number of overt, categorical systems of belief to three. First, Marxism–Leninism shaped the discourse and sometimes the conduct of Soviet diplomacy. Second, Hitler's *Weltanschauung* supplied the motif for Nazi German foreign policy. And last, if one is permitted to waive the secular definition of ideology, the new religious fundamentalism, especially Islamicism, has potential for creating trouble in the international arena that remains incalculable. It will be noted that all three total ideologies are twentieth-century phenomena, which helps account for the century's reputation as 'an age of ideologies'.[6]

However, the impact of ideology on international relations is hardly exhausted by reference to a few total or pure ideologies. Partial, unsophisticated ideology – ideology in the sense of a collective subconscious mentality or belief system – has brought just as much weight to bear, and over a longer time span. Neither the original left nor right in nineteenth-century Europe subscribed to an unbending doctrine. The classical liberals' worship of liberty, both for the individual and the national group, precluded dogma. Liberalism's ideal world was no monolith but a harmony of divergent interests and peoples. None the less, it comprised a 'messianic' vision or animating ideology that inspired the revolutionaries of 1848, Cobden, Bright and Gladstone, and in the twentieth century Wilson and Roosevelt. At the other end of the political spectrum, conservatism began without theory at all; it was simply a rejection of all that the French Revolution stood for. Yet this amorphous conservatism provided the scaffolding on which Metternich rebuilt the Concert of Europe after 1815, and it was a vital ingredient in Bismarck's international system half a century later. Some twentieth-century enemies of the left also followed an ideological path without declaring too coherent a doctrine. By common consent, Italy's Fascists never succeeded in formulating a clear-cut ideology, certainly none comparable to Nazi racial theory. On the other hand, Mussolini's goal of a new Roman empire was pursued with a fixity of purpose and a deadly fatalism worthy of the sternest ideologue. Much the same can be said of the Japanese imperialists who succumbed to the dictates of the diffuse notion of *kokutai*. These generic ideological impulses were succeeded by another, namely formless Western anti-communism in the Cold War. In short, a strict theoretical formula has not proved prerequisite for an ideological foreign policy.

This point is conclusively demonstrated by the phenomenon of nationalism. No real intellectual construct, it has been aptly called 'the last great image of unsophistication'.[7] In spite of its intellectual imprecision, nationalism constitutes another of those sentiments that predispose peoples and their governments to zealotry and hubris. And it supplies a consistent ideological thread running through the entire course of modern and contemporary history.

The birth of nationalist ideology in the French revolutionary wars and its spread to become a populist *mentalité* before the First World War have been described above (Chapters 2 and 5). Its pervasiveness can be observed in the need felt by other ideologies, total and partial, to come to terms with nationalism. Liberalism has been concerned to reconcile national self-determination with its dream of international harmony; this was the liberal objective in 1848 and at the end of both world wars. Initially, conservatives regarded national sentiment as an aspect of dangerous Jacobinism but, by the late nineteenth century, swung around to harnessing it for their own ideological purposes. Not surprisingly, conservatism and nationalism combined to truncate the Wilsonian experiment after the Great War. Lessons in the manipulation of nationalism were not lost on the interwar radical right. Hitler was particularly adept at blending his racist ideology with traditional German nationalism; his drive to the east responded both to the *völkisch* conceit of *Lebensraum* and to pre-Nazi nationalist ambitions encapsulated in the annexationism of the First World War. The ideological cast of mind of Fascist Italy's *duce* and the Japanese warlords injected a new fanaticism into their countries' foreign policy, but in substance their aim was the actualization of standard if extravagant nationalist and imperialist rhetoric. As for the socialists, they might deplore but could not ignore the force of nationalism. It prompted the founding of the Second International in 1889 and its wreckage in 1914. Lenin and his heirs contained nationalism for a while but only by identifying the well-being of world communism with the aggrandizement of the Soviet or Russian nation state. In the same way, the reverse ideology of anti-communism became fused with American patriotism.

The ubiquity of nationalist feeling has been matched by its endurance in the face of twentieth-century efforts to promote a contrary internationalism. These emanated from several quarters. The generic peace movements, galvanized by the world wars and the potential for a nuclear conflict, preached international goodwill as a matter of course. But they have advanced no systemic alternative to the existing international anarchy, and apart from isolated successes, notably in the case of the Vietnam War, have exercised little political impact.[8] More tellingly, Presidents Wilson and Roosevelt carried the liberal universalist tradition forward into the twentieth century and sought to incarnate it through schemes of collective security. Collective security, however, has foundered precisely on the inability of either the League of Nations or the United Nations to confront and dent the national sovereignty of its member states. Essentially these organizations have been 'accessory' to great-power diplomacy: 'Notwithstanding the lip service that the project of setting up a collective security system recurrently enjoys . . . the idea has in fact been almost universally and quite definitively rejected.'[9] Moreover, as an ideology liberal internationalism has never aroused the emotional commitment – save perhaps in the immediate aftermath of each world war – so freely ignited

243

by nationalism. The attraction of this species of internationalism is rational and practical, hardly conducive to ideological fervour.

The same difficulties have attended the most ambitious regional exercise in overcoming national rivalries, namely the European Community (EC), which has grown out of a common market established by the Treaty of Rome (1957) and aspires to become a fully-fledged European union (EU).[10] To be sure, the EC has laid to rest those animosities among the major West European powers that led to the Continent's second Thirty Years War. But its appeal, like that of liberal internationalism, is to pragmatism and material benefit, and the community's bureaucratic nature does not stir ideological blood. Furthermore, while the EC has brought about an increase in international interdependence, it has achieved considerably less international integration. The Treaty of Maastricht (1991) postulates common foreign and defence policies, but so far the EC remains what De Gaulle minimally advocated – a 'Europe des patries'. In other words, the nation state continues to be the 'organizational concept' of the EC, no less than of the League of Nations and the UN. For this reason, it can be argued that such success as the Community has enjoyed has contributed to the 'reassertion' of the nation state, the legitimacy of which was under challenge in 1945.[11]

More important than the preservation of the nation state has been the perpetuation of the *mentalité* of nationalism, the fact that the largest act of empathy of which humans (and not just Europeans) have so far shown themselves capable remains the nation. This is manifest in the form of traditional patriotic feeling (British isolationism, for instance). But it also appears in the twentieth-century upsurge or revival of unfulfilled nationalisms, in the dozens of separatist movements catering to national or local minorities. The consequence is the paradox of, on the one hand, the advance of multinational political and economic associations and, on the other, a proliferation of nationalist and ethnic feelings. Indeed, the 'large-scale continental identities may actually reinvigorate the specific nationalisms of *ethnies* within the demarcated culture area'.[12] The truth is that the loose structure of the new multinational organizations appears to offer more space for separatist self-realization than does the traditional centralized nation state.

Whereas the League, the UN and the EC have all sought to curb nationalist excesses and impose some restrictions on the sovereign state, they have not proposed the absolute eradication of the nation state and national sentiment. However, this was the long-term aim of Marxism–Leninism. In this scenario, class consciousness was destined to override nationalist allegiance, and then the revolutionary elimination of class differences would usher in the brotherhood of man. But communism could not exorcise nationalism either. It was always present in the form of Russian *amor patriae*, which was openly invoked to save the Soviet

244

system in the Great Patriotic War. Elsewhere, when much of the Third World embraced Marxism–Leninism, it did so more often than not as a gambit in the struggle for national liberation. The death of Yugoslavia's Tito in 1980 heralded the return of old Balkan hatreds. Finally, with the collapse of the Soviet communist empire in 1989, the survival of nationalist passion, in spite of tsar and commissar, was unmistakably clear for all to see.[13] Ominously, the forces that re-emerged in the former communist lands have disclosed the so-called 'dark side' of nationalism. Based largely on ethnic identity often with racial overtones, they resemble in their intolerance and violence the earlier pan movements. In brief, this is the sort of nationalism readily transmuted into the most bigoted ideological thinking.[14]

The role and record over two centuries of the ideology of nationalism cannot been gainsaid. 'Nationalist ideology', writes one expert, 'is based on important responses to modernity and, when deployed in symbolic and ceremonial forms, can have a real power of attraction.'[15] That is to say, nationalism has surpassed all other 'isms' in disseminating, not so much an ideology itself as the *spirit* of ideology in international relations. Needless to add, the continued prevalence of nationalist attitudes makes nonsense of the claim heard in the West on the downfall of communism that ideological conflict had been extinguished and the end of history reached.[16]

It is undeniable that the odium incurred by both National Socialism and Marxism–Leninism has driven total ideological concepts (secular if not religious) out of favour. But more significant in the arena of interstate relations is the durability of an ideological *mentalité*, of 'lived' ideologies. The habit of couching foreign policy in terms of values, identities, cosmic fears and aspirations gathered momentum throughout the nineteenth century and drew enormous impetus from this century's two world wars. It led to what one political philosopher aptly called 'the organization of enthusiasm'.[17] In this climate the substance of ideology often takes second place to the sustenance of ideological belief for its own sake. This was a truth that George Orwell recognized in the aftermath of the Second World War and conveyed in his *Nineteen Eighty-Four* (1949). No citizen in the fictional community of Oceania could be sure at any given moment whether the other power blocs, Eurasia and Eastasia, were allies or enemies; reality was irrelevant to the stimulation of 'passionate intensity'. Historical parallels lay close at hand: popular frontism slipped in and out of respectability in the Comintern; Fascist Italy embraced racism more or less out of the blue; Hitler contradicted his anti-Bolshevism in the Nazi–Soviet non-aggression pact and his Aryanism in the Tripartite Pact. Yet there was no slackening in any of these cases of the ideological commitment with which international ambitions were pursued. In the familiar phrase, the medium had become the message.

One study of ideology states as its premise that 'men act as they think'.[18] This is true of this book too so long as 'think' is understood broadly. Intellectuals may claim to create or approve an ideology on the basis of cool ratiocination, but at the popular level ideology is accepted viscerally. False consciousness is more a matter of feeling than of thinking. Thus, any interpretation that views international relations solely as a rational exercise – the realist schools in particular – will automatically undervalue the emotional appeal of ideology. Democracy introduced a Dionysian element into international affairs, and ideology has been its mode of expression.

NOTES

INTRODUCTION

1 J. Larrain, *Concept of Ideology*, London, 1979, p. 13; A. Giddens, 'Four theses on ideology', *Canadian Journal of Political and Social Theory*, 7 (1983): 18; T. Eagleton, *Ideology*, London, 1991, p. 1.

2 Phrases drawn from *Oxford English Dictionary*, *Webster-Merriam's* and *Encyclopédie Larousse*. The reference work with the most comprehensive definition of Ideology is *Geschichtliche Grundbegriffe*, Stuttgart, 1972–92, vol. 2, pp. 131–68.

3 Destutt de Tracy, quoted in E. Kennedy, *Philosophe in an Age of Revolution: Destutt de Tracy and the Origins of Ideology*, Philadelphia, 1978, p. 47.

4 W.J. Stankiewicz, *In Search of a Political Philosophy: Ideologies at the Close of the Twentieth Century*, London, 1993, p. 6.

5 E. Carlton, *War and Ideology*, London, 1990, p. 193; J.L. Talmon, *Origins of Totalitarian Democracy*, London, 1952, pp. 5, 12–13, 21–4. See also O. Chadwick, *Secularization of the European Mind in the Nineteenth Century*, Cambridge, 1975.

6 Napoleon I, quoted in Kennedy, *Philosophe*, p. 215.

7 K. Marx and F. Engels, *The German Ideology*, C.J. Arthur, ed. London, 1974, p. 47.

8 G. Lichtheim, *Concept of Ideology and Other Essays*, New York, 1967, p. 19. See also J. Larrain, *Marxism and Ideology*, Atlantic Highlands, 1983; D. Meyerson, *False Consciousness*, Oxford, 1991; C.L. Pines, *Ideology and False Consciousness*, Albany, 1993.

9 Engels to Mehring, 14 July 1893, in K. Marx and F. Engels, *Selected Correspondence*, Moscow, 1956, p. 459.

10 S.V. and P. Utechin, eds, *What Is To Be Done?*, Oxford, 1963, p. 71.

11 *Ideology and Utopia*, London, 1936.

12 Q. Hoare and G. Nowell Smith, eds, *Selections from the Prison Notebooks*, London, 1971.

13 J. Habermas, *Legitimation Crisis*, London, 1975; L. Althusser, 'Ideology and ideological state apparatuses', in *Lenin and Philosophy*, New York, 1971, pp. 127–86.

14 W. Stark, *Sociology of Knowledge*, London, 1958, p. 48; H.M. Drucker, *Political Uses of Ideology*, London, 1974, p. 140.

15 The compatibility of reason and ideology is argued by M. Seliger, *Ideology and Politics*, London, 1976; G. Therborn, *The Ideology of Power and the Power of Ideology*, London, 1980; G. Walford, *Ideologies and Their Function*, London,

1979. See also the debate in M. Cranston and P. Mair, eds, *Idéologie et politique*, Florence, 1981.

16 Quotations are all from L.S. Feuer, *Ideology and Ideologists*, Oxford, 1975, though the same views can be found in myriad books and articles, e.g. selections in C.I. Waxman, ed., *The End of Ideology Debate*, New York, 1968.

17 *The Hedgehog and the Fox*, London, 1953.

18 Eagleton, *Ideology*, pp. 3, 221–2; M. Billig *et al.*, *Ideological Dilemmas*, London, 1988, pp. 27–34. Similarly, J.B. Thompson, *Ideology and Modern Culture*, Cambridge, 1990, examines ideology's dissemination at the popular level through the 'mediazation of culture'.

19 J. Plamenatz, *Ideology*, London, 1970, pp. 17–23. Plamenatz's contention that total ideologies are the product of literate societies is unassailable, but I would take issue with his restriction of partial ideologies to primitive communities. The historical survey offered in this book shows clearly that non-intellectual, unsophisticated ideological notions are just as common in materially advanced societies.

20 K.R. Minogue, 'On identifying ideology', in Cranston and Mair, eds, *Idéologie et politique*, p. 27.

21 O. Holsti, quoted in R. Little and S. Smith, eds, *Belief Systems and International Relations*, Oxford, 1988, p. 12.

22 J. MacLean, 'Belief systems and ideology in international relations', in Little and Smith, eds, *Belief Systems and International Relations*, pp. 57–82; M. Vovelle, *Ideologies and Mentalities*, Oxford, 1990, pp. 5–17.

23 J.S. Roucek, 'History of the concept of ideology', *Journal of the History of Ideas*, 5 (1944): 479–88.

24 C. Geertz, *Interpretation of Cultures*, New York, 1973, ch. 8; E. Carlton, *Ideology and Social Order*, London, 1977, pp. 24–32.

25 J. Breuilly, *Nationalism and the State*, Manchester, 1993, p. 54; B. Anderson, *Imagined Communities*, London, 1991, p. 5. Nationalism is treated as *mentalité* by M. Howard, 'Ideology and international relations', *Review of International Studies*, 15 (1989): 1–10. M. Knox, 'Continuity and revolution in the making of strategy', in *Making of Strategy*, W. Murray *et al.*, eds, New York, 1994, pp. 628–38, also presents nationalism as a diffuse kind of ideology.

26 E. Shils, *Intellectuals and the Powers*, Chicago, 1974, p. 29.

27 K. Minogue, *Alien Powers: The Pure Theory of Ideology*, London, 1985, p. 128; Carlton, *War and Ideology*, p. 189.

28 Plamenatz, *Ideology*, pp. 75–6.

29 D. Bell, *The End of Ideology*, New York, 1960, p. 370; J. Keane, 'Democracy and the theory of ideology', *Canadian Journal of Political and Social Theory*, 7 (1983): 5.

30 R.R. Palmer, *Age of the Democratic Revolution, 1760–1800*, 2 vols, Princeton, 1959–64; J.J. Rousseau, *Du contrat social*, Amsterdam, 1762.

31 R.V. Burks, 'Concept of ideology for historians', *Journal of the History of Ideas*, 10 (1949): 190.

32 G.L. Mosse, *Nationalization of the Masses*, New York, 1975, p. 2. The title is drawn from Hitler's *Mein Kampf*, New York, 1943, pp. 336–44.

33 See e.g. R. Luxemburg, *The National Question*, H.B. Davis, ed., New York, 1976.

34 D. Kaiser, *Politics and War*, Cambridge, MA, 1990, pp. 271–82; K. Boulding, 'National images and international systems', *Journal of Conflict Resolution*, 3 (1959): 121–2.

35 Bell, *End of Ideology*, p. 373. See also H. Arendt, *Origins of Totalitarianism*, New York, 1958, p. 470.
36 Arendt, *Origins*, p. 468.

1 *RAISON D'ÉTAT* MEETS THE ENLIGHTENMENT

1 The anarchic nature of international society is implicit in F.H. Hinsley, *Power and the Pursuit of Peace*, Cambridge, 1963, and P.M. Kennedy, *Rise and Fall of the Great Powers*, London, 1987. The nations' acceptance of tacit rules and restraint is more to the fore in H. Bull, *The Anarchical Society: A Study of Order in World Politics*, London, 1977, and M. Wight, *Power Politics*, ed. H. Bull and C. Holbraad, London, 1986.
2 H. Nicolson, *Evolution of Diplomatic Method*, London, 1954, pp. 27, 31.
3 J.T. Johnson, *Ideology, Reason, and Limitation of War, 1200–1740*, Princeton, 1975.
4 G. Parker, 'The making of strategy in Habsburg Spain', in *Making of Strategy*, W. Murray *et al.*, eds, New York, 1994, pp. 115–50; G. Parker *et al.*, *The Thirty Years' War*, London, 1984.
5 H.M.A. Keens-Soper and K.W. Schweizer, introduction to F. de Callières, *The Art of Diplomacy*, ed. H.M.A. Keens-Soper and K.W. Schweizer, Leicester, 1983, p. 32.
6 H.M.A. Keens-Soper, 'The French Political Academy, 1712: school for ambassadors', *European Studies Review*, 2 (1972): 329–55.
7 F. Meinecke, *Machiavellism*, London, 1957, p. 338.
8 Quoted in J. Black, *Rise of the European Powers, 1679–1793*, London, 1990, p. 207.
9 Callières, *Art of Diplomacy*, p. 86.
10 M.S. Anderson, *Rise of Modern Diplomacy*, London, 1993, pp. 80–94, 100–2, 119–23.
11 Bull, *Anarchical Society*, pp. 238–9.
12 See e.g. Samuel Pufendorf, quoted in D. McKay and H.M. Scott, *Rise of the Great Powers 1648–1815*, London, 1983, p. 1; Emeric de Vattel, quoted in F.E. Manuel, *Age of Reason*, New York, 1951, p. 113.
13 Heeren, quoted in A. Watson, *Evolution of International Society*, London, 1992, p. 208.
14 Frederick the Great, quoted in G. Blainey, *Causes of War*, London, 1988, p. 108.
15 J. Black, *European Warfare, 1660–1815*, London, 1994, pp. 218–31; C. Duffy, *Military Experience in the Age of Reason*, London, 1977, pp. 7–10.
16 R.L. O'Connell, *Of Arms and Men*, New York, 1989, pp. 148–66.
17 M. Howard, *War in European History*, London, 1976, p. 73.
18 R.N. Rosecranze, *Action and Reaction in World Politics*, Boston, 1963, p. 30.
19 Anderson, *Modern Diplomacy*, pp. 163–4. See also E.V. Gulick, *Europe's Classical Balance of Power*, Ithaca, 1955, pt 1.
20 E. Luard, *The Balance of Power, 1648–1815*, London, 1992, pp. 25–6, 261. For an argument that flexibility was not an unalloyed benefit, see P.W. Schroeder, *Transformation of European Politics, 1763–1848*, Oxford, 1994, ch. 1 *passim*.
21 Hinsley, *Pursuit of Peace*, chs 2–4.
22 F. Gilbert, 'The "new diplomacy" of the eighteenth century', *World Politics*, 4 (1951): 1–38.
23 S. Hoffmann and D.P. Fidler, eds, *Rousseau on International Relations*, Oxford, 1991, p. lxiii.

24 *The Rights of Man*, G. Claeys, ed., Indianapolis, 1992, p. 223.
25 Paine, quoted in J.P. Greene, *The Intellectual Construction of America: Exceptionalism and Identity from 1492 to 1800*, Chapel Hill, 1993, p. 135.
26 F. Gilbert, *To the Farewell Address: Ideas of Early American Foreign Policy*, Princeton, 1961, p. 72.
27 B.I. Kaufman, ed., *Washington's Farewell Address: The View from the 20th Century*, Chicago, 1969.
28 Washington, quoted ibid., pp. 25–6; Winthrop, quoted in P. Miller and T.H. Johnson, *The Puritans*, New York, 1963, vol. 1, p. 199.
29 M.H. Hunt, *Ideology and U.S. Foreign Policy*, New Haven, 1987.
30 Condorcet, quoted in Manuel, *Age of Reason*, pp. 134–5.
31 R.R. Palmer, *Age of the Democratic Revolution*, Princeton, 1959–64, vol. 1, pp. 261–2.
32 Ibid., p. 4.
33 M.S. Anderson, *Europe in the Eighteenth Century*, London, 1987, pp. 414, 417–18.
34 Schroeder, *Transformation of European Politics*, p. 50.

2 THE BIRTH OF IDEOLOGY

1 F.L. Ford, 'The revolutionary-Napoleonic era: how much of a watershed?', *American Historical Review*, 69 (1963): 18–29; F. Fehér, ed., *The French Revolution and the Birth of Modernity*, Berkeley, 1990.
2 *The Ancien Régime and the French Revolution*, H. Brogan, ed., London, 1966, p. 43.
3 Lord Auckland, British ambassador at The Hague, quoted in T.C.W. Blanning, *Origins of the French Revolutionary Wars*, London, 1986, p. 133. This book usefully and directly addresses the question of ideology's part in bringing on war. However, in arguing for a restricted ideological influence, it would seem to overstate its case (see n. 14 below).
4 Leopold II, quoted ibid., pp. 84, 94 n. 88.
5 Declaration of Pillnitz, quoted in J. Godechot, *The Counter-Revolution*, London, 1972, p. 156.
6 Blanning, *Origins*, pp. 80–9.
7 Cloots, quoted in S. Schama, *Citizens*, New York, 1989, p. 474. This work is excellent in capturing the French atmosphere in which events unfolded.
8 Blanning, *Origins*, p. 100.
9 Isnard, quoted ibid., pp. 101, 109; Brissot, quoted ibid., p. 111.
10 Schama, *Citizens*, pp. 581–4; Elie Gandet, quoted ibid., p. 594.
11 Prince Kaunitz, quoted in Blanning, *Origins*, p. 102; Count von der Goltz, quoted ibid., pp. 115–16.
12 Dubois-Dubais and Brissot, quoted ibid., p. 108.
13 G. Blainey, *Causes of War*, London, 1988, p. 114.
14 Blanning, *Origins*, p. 73. Blanning not only coins the Coppelia metaphor, but also cites the thesis of 'recurring optimism' during 'periods of ideological upheaval' (Blainey, *Causes of War*, p. 28). Oddly, however, he ignores the point that illusions in both Vienna and Paris were shaped by ideological prejudices.
15 Robespierre, quoted in Schama, *Citizens*, p. 595.
16 Fraternity decree, quoted ibid., p. 643; W. Doyle, *Oxford History of the French Revolution*, Oxford, 1989, p. 199.
17 D. Armstrong, *Revolution and World Order*, Oxford, 1993, pp. 84–7.

18 Burke, quoted in Blanning, *Origins*, p. 47; Lord Auckland, quoted ibid., p. 133.
19 C. Emsley, *British Society and the French Wars*, London, 1979, pp. 13–18. See also I. Christie, *Stress and Stability in Late Eighteenth-Century Britain*, Oxford, 1984, pp. 158–82, 215–20; L. Colley, 'The apotheosis of George III: loyalty, royalty and the British nation', *Past and Present*, 102 (1984): 94–129.
20 F. O'Gorman, *The Whig Party and the French Revolution*, London, 1967, pp. 104–19.
21 François Noël and Lebrun, quoted in Blanning, *Origins*, p. 153.
22 Danton, quoted in Doyle, *History of the French Revolution*, p. 201.
23 P.W. Schroeder, *Transformation of European Politics, 1763–1848*, Oxford, 1994, pp. 126–7.
24 K.R. Minogue, *Nationalism*, London, 1967, p. 32; C. Brinton, *A Decade of Revolution*, New York, 1934, p. 96.
25 French volunteer, quoted in G. Best, *War and Society in Revolutionary Europe*, London, 1982, p. 79.
26 Convention decree, quoted in Brinton, *Decade of Revolution*, p. 128.
27 J.F. Bosher, *The French Revolution*, London, 1989, pp. 203–7; Brinton, pp. 128–37; Schama, *Citizens*, pp. 755–67.
28 Brinton, *Decade of Revolutions*, pp. 160–1. See also C. Becker, *Heavenly City of the Eighteenth-Century Philosophers*, New Haven, 1932.
29 N. Hampson, 'The French Revolution and the nationalization of honour', in M.R.D. Foot, ed., *War and Society*, London, 1973, p. 209.
30 P.M. Taylor, *Munitions of the Mind*, Wellingborough, 1990, pp. 125–8, refers to the 'monumental propaganda success' of the Committee of Public Safety. On the contrary, A. Forrest, *Soldiers of the French Revolution*, Durham, NC, 1990, pp. 189–97, argues that the 'picture of a politically conscious army . . . must be treated with a certain caution'. For documentary evidence of the troops' state of mind, see J.-P. Bertaud, *The Army of the French Revolution*, Princeton, 1988.
31 Best, *War and Society*, p. 85.
32 Ibid., p. 89.
33 M. Wight, *Power Politics*, London, 1986, pp. 138–41, who here follows Hobbes' division of wars into those of gain, fear and doctrine.
34 B. Jenkins, *Nationalism in France*, London, 1990, p. 21.
35 Jacqueline Chaumié, quoted in Bosher, *French Revolution*, pp. 239–40; G. de Puymège, *Chauvin, le soldat-laboureur*, Paris, 1993.
36 In a famous phrase E. Kedourie, *Nationalism*, 1st edn, London, 1961, p. 9, contends that 'nationalism is a doctrine invented in Europe at the beginning of the nineteenth century'. See also E.J. Hobsbawm, *Nations and Nationalism since 1780: Programme, Myth, Reality*, Cambridge, 1992.
37 A.D. Smith, *Theories of Nationalism*, London, 1983, pp. ix–xi. J. Hutchinson, *Modern Nationalism*, London, 1994, pp. 141–6, echoes this dichotomy in his distinction between political and cultural nationalism.
38 Kedourie, *Nationalism*, p. 76; E. Gellner, *Nations and Nationalism*, Oxford, 1983, pp. 35–8. The former stresses the role of ideas, the latter that of socio-economic forces; but both locate nationalism's genesis in the past two hundred years.
39 A.D. Smith, *Ethnic Origins of Nations*, Oxford, 1986, pp. 7–13, 210–12. See also J.A. Armstrong, *Nations before Nationalism*, Chapel Hill, 1982.
40 Arguably the best brief discussion comprehending various viewpoints but pleading no special theory is P. Alter, *Nationalism*, London, 1994.

41 L. Greenfield, *Nationalism: Five Roads to Modernity*, Cambridge, MA, 1992, pp. 91–133.

42 W. Bagehot, *Physics and Politics*, London, 1887, pp. 20–1; E. Renan, 'What is a Nation?, in A. Zimmern, ed., *Modern Poltical Doctrines*, London, 1939, p. 203.

43 B. Anderson, *Imagined Communities*, London, 1991, pp. 6–7, 36.

44 National Assembly constitution, quoted in Bosher, *French Revolution*, p. 159; Baron Merlin de Thionville, quoted in P. Vansittart, ed., *Voices of the Revolution*, London, 1989, p. 163.

45 N. Hampson, *The French Revolution*, London, 1975, p. 164.

46 *The Prelude*, W.J.B. Owen, ed., Ithaca, 1985, bk XI, ll. 108, 206–9.

47 The best study of this phenomenon is J. Godechot, *La grande nation*, 2 vols, Paris, 1983. Case studies in English include T.C.W. Blanning, *The French Revolution in Germany*, Oxford, 1983; M. Broers, 'Revolution and risorgimento', in H.T. Mason and W. Doyle, eds, *Impact of the French Revolution on European Consciousness*, Gloucester, 1989, pp. 81–90.

48 Schroeder, *Transformation of European Politics*, pp. 166–72.

49 Doyle, *History of the French Revolution*, pp. 218–19. See also J.M. Roberts, *Mythology of the Secret Societies*, London, 1972.

50 Talleyrand, quoted in Blanning, *Origins*, p. 181.

51 P. Geyl, *Napoleon For and Against*, London, 1964; L. Bergeron, *France under Napoleon*, Princeton, 1981.

52 M. Lyons, *Napoleon Bonaparte and the Legacy of the French Revolution*, New York, 1994.

53 G. Bruun, *Europe and the French Imperium*, New York, 1938, p. 61.

54 Frederick William III, quoted in F.M. Kircheisen, *Napoleon*, London, 1931, p. 402.

55 S.J. Woolf, *Napoleon's Integration of Europe*, London, 1991, pp. vii, 32. See also Lyons, *Napoleon Bonaparte*, pp. 230–4.

56 Schroeder, *Transformation of European Politics*, p. 391, seeks a less bland and more opprobrious term than imperialism for Napoleon's international hegemony and chooses to describe it as 'a vast experiment in colonialism within Europe'.

57 N. Hampson, *The First European Revolution*, London, 1969, p. 137.

58 The thesis that Napoleon nursed dreams of a 'universal empire' is developed in A. Thiers, *Histoire du Consulat et de l'Empire*, 20 vols, Paris, 1845–62.

59 Hardenberg, quoted in Bruun, *French Imperium*, p. 174.

60 'October Edict', quoted in J.J. Sheehan, *German History, 1770–1866*, Oxford, 1989, pp. 299–300.

61 Scharnhorst, quoted ibid., p. 309.

62 M. Howard and P. Paret, eds, *On War*, Princeton, 1976, pp. 518, 605.

63 Schroeder, *Transformation of European Politics*, pp. 266–7, 291–4, 322.

64 General Wittgenstein, quoted in D. Seward, *Napoleon and Hitler: A Comparative Biography*, London, 1988, p. 258; Alexander I, quoted in Bruun, *French Imperium*, p. 192. See also G.A. Craig, *Politics of the Prussian Army*, Oxford, 1955, p. 60; Sheehan, *German History*, p. 316.

65 Arndt, quoted in Sheehan, *German History*, p. 387. A good example of later German romanticization of the war of liberation is H. von Treitschke, *Deutsche Geschichte im neunzehnten Jahrhundert*, Leipzig, 1879–94, vol. 1.

66 H.G. Schenk, *Aftermath of the Napoleonic Wars*, London, 1947, ch. 1: 'The ideological background'; M. Forsyth, 'Friedrich von Gentz', *Studies in History and Politics*, 2/2 (1981–2): 127–55.

3 CONSERVATIVES, LIBERALS AND NATIONALIST IDEOLOGY

1 Vicomte de Chateaubriand, quoted in K. Hamilton and R. Langhorne, *The Practice of Diplomacy*, London, 1995, p. 89.
2 R.N. Rosecranze, *Action and Reaction in World Politics*, Boston, 1963, pp. 49–50.
3 J. Droz, *Europe between Revolutions, 1815–48*, New York, 1967, pp. 9–13. Symptomatic of the use of religion to fortify the restoration was the re-establishment in 1814 of the anti-revolutionary Jesuit order.
4 P.W. Schroeder, *Transformation of European Politics, 1763–1848*, Oxford, 1994, p. 582; J.M. Welsh, *Edmund Burke and International Relations*, Basingstoke, 1995, ch. 3.
5 Though, according to Schroeder, *Transformation of European Politics*, pp. 257–62, what St Petersburg and London had in mind was a disguised Russo-British hegemony over Europe.
6 Holy Alliance, quoted in R. Albrecht-Carrié, *The Concert of Europe*, New York, 1968, p. 33.
7 Schroeder, *Transformation of European Politics*, pp. 558–9.
8 Quadruple Alliance, quoted in Albrecht-Carrié, *Concert of Europe*, p. 32.
9 Schroeder, *Transformation of European Politics*, pp. 575–82, considers the post-Napoleonic concert so far an advance on what had prevailed before as to deny that 1815 was, in fact, a restoration.
10 Albrecht-Carrié, *Concert of Europe*, p. 35.
11 S.M. Alsop, *The Congress Dances*, London, 1984. More substantial accounts are C.K. Webster, *The Congress of Vienna*, London, 1919; H. Nicolson, *The Congress of Vienna*, London, 1945.
12 P.W. Schroeder, 'Did the Vienna settlement rest on a balance of power?', *American Historical Review*, 97 (1992): 683–706, contrasts the dog-eat-dog international politics of the eighteenth century with a 'great power cooperative hegemony' after 1815; 'balance of power' is deemed to characterize the former, 'political equilibrium' the latter. Some may think this only a semantic distinction on the grounds that the difference between international relations before and after the French Revolution was more a matter of degree than of kind.
13 E.V. Gulick, *Europe's Classical Balance of Power*, Ithaca, 1955, pp. 227–30.
14 C. von Metternich, *Aus Metternichs nachgelassenen Papieren*, Vienna, 1880–7, vol. 3, pp. 400–20; Metternich, quoted in G. de Bertier de Sauvigny, *Metternich and his Times*, London, 1962, pp. 32, 36–9, 69.
15 Gentz, quoted in P.R. Sweet, *Friedrich von Gentz: Defender of the Old Order*, Madison, 1941, p. 228. On liberal international machinations, see S. Neely, *Lafayette and the Liberal Idea, 1818–24*, Carbondale, 1991, ch. 7, *passim*.
16 H.A. Kissinger, *A World Restored*, Boston, 1957, p. 251.
17 Protocol of Troppau, quoted in F.B. Artz, *Reaction and Revolution, 1814–32*, New York, 1934, pp. 164–5.
18 A. Palmer, *Alexander I*, London, 1974, pp. 333–4, 364–6; P.K. Grimsted, *The Foreign Ministers of Alexander I*, Berkeley, 1969, pp. 149–50, 237–9.
19 Castlereagh's State Paper, quoted in *Cambridge History of British Foreign Policy*, A.W. Ward and G.P. Gooch, eds, Cambridge, 1922–3, vol. 2, p. 627.
20 W. Hinde, *George Canning*, London, 1973, pp. 322–5, 390.
21 *Complete Plays*, London, 1965, p. 171.
22 Monroe, quoted in D. Perkins, *History of the Monroe Doctrine*, Boston, 1955, p. 391.
23 Canning, quoted in H.W.V. Temperley, *Foreign Policy of Canning*, London, 1966, p. 154.

24 Adams, quoted in P.K. Liss, *Atlantic Empires*, Baltimore, 1983, p. 212.

25 A.P. Whitaker, *The United States and the Independence of Latin America*, New York, 1964, pp. 571–82.

26 F.H. Hinsley, *Power and the Pursuit of Peace*, Cambridge, 1963, pp. 213–14.

27 F.R. Bridge, 'Allied diplomacy in peacetime: failure of the congress "system"', in A. Sked, ed., *Europe's Balance of Power, 1815–48*, London, 1979, pp. 34–53.

28 M.S. Miller, 'A "liberal international"? Comparative approaches to the revolutions in Spain, Italy, and Greece in the 1820s', in R.W. Clement, ed., *Greece and the Mediterranean*, Kirksville, 1990, pp. 61–7.

29 B. Lincoln, *Nicholas I*, London, 1978, pp. 105–30.

30 D. Dakin, *The Greek Struggle for Independence*, London, 1973, pp. 107–23.

31 D.H. Pinkney, *The French Revolution of 1830*, Princeton, 1972, pp. 143–4, 293.

32 On the transnational nature of the events of 1830, see C.H. Church, *Europe in 1830*, London, 1983.

33 Pinkney, *French Revolution*, pp. 304–5.

34 M.E. Chamberlain, *'Pax Britannica'? British Foreign Policy, 1789–1914*, London, 1988, pp. 4–8.

35 J. Clarke, *British Diplomacy and Foreign Policy, 1782–1865*, London, 1989, p. 192.

36 Artz, *Reaction and Revolution*, p. 270.

37 Metternich, *Aus nachgelassenen Papieren*, vol. 5, pp. 273–4.

38 Palmerston, quoted in F.R. Bridge and R. Bullen, *The Great Powers and the European States System, 1815–1914*, London, 1980, p. 59; Metternich, quoted in Bertier de Sauvigny, *Metternich*, p. 224; Metternich, *Aus nachgelassenen Papieren*, vol. 5, p. 261.

39 Schroeder, *Transformation of European Politics*, pp. 720–26, 736–56.

40 R. Bullen, *Palmerston, Guizot and the Collapse of the Entente Cordiale*, London, 1974, ch. 2.

41 Ibid., ch. 12; Guizot quoted ibid., p. 336.

42 J.L. Talmon, *Political Messianism: The Romantic Phase*, London, 1960, p. 15; H.G. Schenk, *The Mind of the European Romantics*, London, 1966, p. 4.

43 Victor Hugo, quoted in Artz, *Reaction and Revolution*, p. 196.

44 M. Cranston, 'Romanticism and revolution', *History of European Ideas*, 17 (1993): 24–30.

45 Droz, *Europe between Revolutions*, p. 143. See also H. Kohn, *Idea of Nationalism*, New York, 1945, pp. 329–31.

46 See e.g. D. Beales, *The Risorgimento and the Unification of Italy*, London, 1971 *passim*; F.J. Coppa, *Origins of the Italian Wars of Independence*, London, 1992, p. 1.

47 L.C.B. Seaman, *From Vienna to Versailles*, London, 1955, p. 43.

48 G. de Ruggiero, *History of European Liberalism*, London, 1927, pp. 407–13. Modern attempts to square the liberal-nationalist circle include D. Miller, *On Nationality*, Oxford, 1996; Y. Tamir, *Liberal Nationalism*, Princeton, 1993.

49 D. Mack Smith, *Mazzini*, New Haven, 1994, pp. 11–13, 52–6.

50 *The Duties of Man*, intr. T. Jones, London, 1955, pp. 51–2.

51 Talmon, *Messianism*, p. 29.

52 L.B. Namier, *1848: Revolution of the Intellectuals*, London, 1946.

53 Lamartine's manifesto, quoted in L.C. Jennings, *France and Europe in 1848*, Oxford, 1973, pp. 12–13.

54 G.J. Billy, *Palmerston's Foreign Policy: 1848*, New York, 1993, pp. 45–54, 108–9, 152–3.

55 J. Tulard, 'Le retour des Cendres', in *Les lieux de mémoire*, P. Nora, ed., Paris, 1984–92, vol. 2, pt 3, pp. 81–110. Also on the Bonapartist myth before and since 1848, see R. Gildea, *The Past in French History*, New Haven, 1994, ch. 2.

56 E.-A. de Las Cases, *Mémoriale de Sainte-Hélène*, 8 vols, Paris, 1823.

57 Louis Napoleon, quoted in W.L. Langer, *Political and Social Upheaval, 1832– 52*, New York, 1969, p. 86.

58 Lamartine, quoted in H.A.C. Collingham, *The July Monarchy*, R.S. Alexander, ed., London, 1988, p. 299.

59 J.J. Sheehan, *German History, 1770–1866*, Oxford, 1989, p. 678.

60 Most cogently expressed in A.J.P. Taylor, *The Course of German History*, London, 1945, pp. 77–86. The most balanced study of German liberalism in the mid-nineteenth century is F. Eyck, *The Frankfurt Parliament*, London, 1968.

61 These and similar nationalist remarks uttered in the Frankfurt Assembly are quoted in R. Pascal, 'The Frankfurt parliament of 1848 and the *Drang nach Osten*', *Journal of Modern History*, 18 (1946): 108–22.

62 Gagern, quoted in G. Mann, *History of Germany since 1789*, London, 1968, p. 117.

63 On the events of 1848–9 in Italy, see Coppa, *Origins*, ch. 4.

64 Nicholas I, quoted in Lincoln, *Nicholas I*, p. 313.

65 A.J.P. Taylor, *Struggle for Mastery in Europe, 1848–1918*, Oxford, 1954, pp. 42–3.

66 P. Robertson, *Revolutions of 1848*, Princeton, 1952, pp. 412–19.

67 R.C. Binkley, *Realism and Nationalism, 1852–71*, New York, 1935, p. 123; C. Breunig, *Age of Revolution and Reaction, 1789–1850*, New York, 1977, p. 278. Schroeder, *Transformation of European Politics*, pp. 801–2 casts this new realism as a rejection of post-1815 concert politics and a return to the unfettered power politics of the eighteenth century.

4 IDEOLOGY AND *REALPOLITIK*

1 George Harney, quoted in A.J.P. Taylor, *The Trouble Makers*, London, 1957, p. 59.

2 M.E. Chamberlain, *Lord Aberdeen*, London, 1983, p. 478.

3 P.W. Schroeder, *Austria, Great Britain, and the Crimean War*, Ithaca, 1972, p. 415.

4 On the 'unreason why' of this war, see D.M. Goldfrank, *Origins of the Crimean War*, London, 1994.

5 Chamberlain, *Aberdeen*, p. 502; K.W.B. Middleton, *Britain and Russia*, London, 1947, p. 58.

6 J. Clarke, *British Diplomacy and Foreign Policy, 1782–1865*, London, 1989, p. 251.

7 M.E. Chamberlain, *'Pax Britannica'? British Foreign Policy, 1789–1914*, London, 1988, p. 111. See also E.D. Steele, *Palmerston and Liberalism, 1855– 65*, Cambridge, 1991.

8 J.B. Conacher, *Britain and the Crimea*, London, 1987, pp. 205–6.

9 Cobden, quoted in Taylor, *Trouble Makers*, pp. 53–4; Bright, quoted ibid., p. 63.

10 Cobden, quoted in D. Read, *Cobden and Bright*, London, 1967, p. 147; Taylor, *Trouble Makers*, p. 64.

11 J.M. Hernon, 'British sympathies in the American civil war', *Journal of Southern History*, 33 (1967): 356–67.

12 J. Ridley, *Lord Palmerston*, London, 1970, ch. 38.
13 R.C. Binkley, *Realism and Nationalism, 1852–71*, New York, 1935, pp. 25–32. Cf. modern dictionary definitions: 'politics based on practical and material rather than theoretical and ethical factors' (*Webster-Merriam's*); 'a policy of putting the material greatness of one's own country before other considerations' (*Oxford English Dictionary*).
14 R.N. Rosecranze, *Action and Reaction in World Politics*, Boston, 1963, pp. 112, 126.
15 D. Mack Smith, *Victor Emmanuel, Cavour and the Risorgimento*, London, 1971, pp. 56–76; D. Mack Smith, *Cavour and Garibaldi*, Cambridge, 1985, p. 2.
16 R. Grew, *A Sterner Plan for Italian Unity*, Princeton, 1963.
17 Lord Cowley, quoted in J. Bierman, *Napoleon III and his Carnival Empire*, New York, 1988, p. 150.
18 W. Echard, *Napoleon III and the Concert of Europe*, Baton Rouge, 1983, pp. 4–5, 162–4, 302–4.
19 A.J.P. Taylor, *Struggle for Mastery in Europe, 1848–1918*, Oxford, 1954, pp. 99–101.
20 Mack Smith, *Cavour and Garibaldi*, p. 37. See also A. Blumberg, *A Carefully Planned Accident: The Italian War of 1859*, Selinsgrove, 1990.
21 Baron Thouvenel, quoted in Taylor, *Struggle for Mastery*, p. 119.
22 Mack Smith, *Cavour and Garibaldi*, pp. 381–91.
23 A.W. Salomone, 'The *risorgimento* between ideology and history', *American Historical Review*, 68 (1962): 38–56; R. Grew, 'How success spoiled the risorgimento', *Journal of Modern History*, 31 (1962): 239–53.
24 D. Mack Smith, *Italy*, Ann Arbor, 1969, pp. 69–75.
25 Massimo d'Azeglio, quoted in J.A. Thayer, *Italy and the Great War: Politics and Culture, 1870–1915*, Madison, 1964, p. 38.
26 On Bismarck's fundamental principles, see O. Pflanze, *Bismarck and the Development of Germany*, Princeton, 1990, vol. 1, pp. 32–79.
27 O. von Bismarck, *Die gesammelten Werke*, H. von Petersdorff *et al.*, eds, Berlin, 1923–33, vol. 14, p. 249; vol. 11, p. 46.
28 Taylor, *Struggle for Mastery*, pp. 133–41.
29 J.J. Sheehan, *German History, 1770–1866*, Oxford, 1989, pp. 905–6.
30 Taylor, *Struggle for Mastery*, pp. 155–66.
31 J. Gooch, *Armies in Europe*, London, 1980, pp. 90–1.
32 H. Schulze, *Course of German Nationalism*, Cambridge, 1991, p. 2.
33 National Liberal party constitution, quoted ibid., pp. 145–6.
34 Taylor, *Struggle for Mastery*, ch. 9.
35 *Revue des Deux Mondes*, 70 (15 July 1867): 517.
36 J.M. Thompson, *Louis Napoleon and the Second Empire*, Oxford, 1954, pp. 224–54, 272–86.
37 See e.g. L.C.B. Seaman, *From Vienna to Versailles*, London, 1955, pp. 57–9.
38 Ibid., p. 114.
39 Emile Ollivier, quoted in Thompson, *Louis Napoleon*, p. 300; Binkley, *Realism*, p. 293.
40 Francis Josef, quoted in Taylor, *Struggle for Mastery*, p. 195.
41 For the reasons behind the French defeat, see R. Holmes, *Road to Sedan*, London, 1984.
42 P.M. Kennedy, *Rise of Anglo-German Antagonism, 1860–1914*, London, 1980, pp. 20–7; W.E. Mosse, *The European Powers and the German Question, 1848–71*, Cambridge, 1958, pp. 6–8.
43 This is the theme of Binkley, *Realism*, esp. chs 9–13.

5 IDEOLOGY AND MASS DEMOCRACY

1 A.J.P. Taylor, *Struggle for Mastery in Europe, 1848–1918*, Oxford, 1954, pp. 218–21.
2 S. Hoffmann, 'Paradoxes of the French political community', in *In Search of France*, Cambridge, MA, 1963, pp. 3–21.
3 Bismarck, quoted in W.L. Langer, *European Alliances and Alignments, 1871–90*, New York, 1950, p. 197.
4 J. Stone, 'Bismarck and the containment of France, 1873–7', *Canadian Journal of History*, 29 (1994): 281–304.
5 Langer, *European Alliances*, pp. 44–5. See also J. Stone, 'The war scare of 1875 revisited', *Militärgeschichtliche Mitteilungen*, 53 (1994): 309–26.
6 For an academic account of pan-Slav ideology in the crisis of 1875–8, see D. MacKenzie, *The Serbs and Russian Pan-Slavism*, Ithaca, 1967.
7 O. von Bismarck, *Die gesammelten Werke*, H. von Petersdorff *et al.*, eds, Berlin, 1923–33, vol. 11, pp. 476; vol. 13, p. 212. On Bismarck and European diplomacy in the eastern crisis of 1875–8, see Taylor, *Struggle for Mastery*, ch. 11.
8 J.A. Hobson, *Psychology of Jingoism*, London, 1901, p. 4.
9 C. Holbraad, *The Concert of Europe: A Study in German and British International Theory*, London, 1970, pp. 96–100.
10 Bismarck, quoted in Langer, *European Alliances*, p. 150; Alexander II, quoted ibid., pp. 172.
11 Bismarck, *Gesammelten Werke*, vol. 8, pp. 238–9.
12 Bismarck, quoted in Taylor, *Struggle for Mastery*, p. 263. For Bismarck's attitude to pan-Germanism, see O. Pflanze, *Bismarck and the Development of Germany*, Princeton, 1990, vol. 2, pp. 247–51.
13 Taylor, *Struggle for Mastery*, pp. 263–4.
14 Bismarck, quoted in Langer, *European Alliances*, p. 195.
15 Gladstone, quoted in R.W. Seton-Watson, *Disraeli, Gladstone and the Eastern Question*, London, 1935, pp. 545–8.
16 P.M. Kennedy, *Rise of Anglo-German Antagonism*, London, 1980, ch. 9; Bismarck, quoted ibid. p. 165.
17 Taylor, *Struggle for Mastery*, pp. 304–6.
18 Langer, *European Alliances*, p. 451.
19 Ibid., p. 462.
20 On this vexed question, see ibid., pp. 423–5, and Pflanze, *Bismarck*, vol. 3, pp. 251–2.
21 Taylor, *Struggle for Mastery*, pp. 275–6, 311–14, 319–22.
22 F.R. Bridge and R. Bullen, *The Great Powers and the European States System, 1815–1914*, London, 1980, p. 136. For an excellent survey of historical opinion of Bismarck's accomplishments see Pflanze, *Bismarck*, vol. 1, pp. xvii–xxx.
23 C.J. Hayes, *A Generation of Materialism*, New York, 1941, ch. 2.
24 P.N. Stearns, *European Society in Upheaval*, New York, 1967, p. 113.
25 *Politics*, H. Kohn, ed., New York, 1963, p. 39.
26 P. Alter, *Nationalism*, London, 1994, pp. 26, 28.
27 *On Representative Government*, intr. R.B. McCallum, Oxford, 1946, p. 212.
28 Robert Lowe, 15 July 1875, *Hansard's Parliamentary Debates* (Commons), third series, vol. 188, p. 1549. The phrase has been popularized as 'We must educate our masters.'
29 William II, quoted in E.H. Reisner, *Nationalism and Education since 1789*, New York, 1922, p. 211. See also W.C. Langsam, 'Nationalism and history in Prussian elementary schools under William II', in E.M. Earle, ed., *Nationalism and Internationalism*, New York, 1950, pp. 241–60.

30 Josiah Strong in 1885 and Albert J. Beveridge in 1908, quoted in E.M. Burns, *The American Idea of Mission*, New Brunswick, 1957, pp. 230–1.
31 Hayes, *Generation of Materialism*, pp. 175–6.
32 This thesis is argued by, among many others, M.D. Biddiss, *Age of the Masses*, Harmondsworth, 1977, and A. Green, *Education and State Formation*, London, 1990.
33 C.M. Cipolla, *Literacy and Development in the West*, Harmondsworth, 1969, statistical tables 1, 17–21, 28–30; Hayes, *Generation of Materialism*, pp. 176, 180.
34 Bismarck, quoted in Langer, *European Alliances*, p. 195.
35 O.J. Hale, *Publicity and Diplomacy*, New York, 1940, pp. 16, 27–8.
36 S.B. Fay, *Origins the World War*, New York, 1948, vol. 1, p. 47.
37 B. Bond, *War and Society in Europe, 1870–1970*, London, 1983, p. 63.
38 General André, quoted in D. Porch, 'The French army and the spirit of the offensive, 1900–14', *War and Society Yearbook*, 1 (1975): 119.
39 E. Weber, *Peasants into Frenchmen*, Stanford, 1976, pp. 95–114, 330–8. For a comparative study, see S.C. Watkins, *From Provinces into Nations: Demographic Integration in Western Europe*, Princeton, 1991.
40 J. Van Ginneken, *Crowds, Psychology and Politics, 1871–99*, New York, 1992.
41 Hayes, *Generation of Materialism*, p. 10.
42 G. Himmelfarb, *Darwin and the Darwinian Revolution*, Garden City, 1959, p. 416. It could equally well be argued that evolution would ameliorate competition, and Darwin himself subscribed to this 'peace biology'. But in international relations, as the inefficacy of peace movements would demonstrate, 'biological militarism' was the more conspicuous face of Social Darwinism. On the debate over Darwin's twin legacies, see P. Crook, *Darwinism, War and History*, New York, 1994.
43 Danilevsky, quoted in H. Kohn, *Pan-Slavism: Its History and Ideology*, New York, 1960, pp. 193, 202. See also N.V. Riasanovsky, *Russia and the West in the Teaching of the Slavophiles: A Study of Romantic Ideology*, Cambridge, MA, 1952.
44 R. Chickering, *We Men Who Feel Most German*, Boston, 1984.
45 R. Robinson and J. Gallagher, 'The imperialism of free trade,' *Economic History Review*, 6 (1953): 1–15.
46 See D.K. Fieldhouse, *Economics and Empire*, London, 1973, esp. p. 491, for the distinction between political and economic factors; the book also supplies tables of economic activity in the colonies. For an analysis of schools of thought on imperialism, see B. Semmel, *The Liberal Ideal and the Demons of Empire: Theories of Imperialism from Adam Smith to Lenin*, Baltimore, 1993, who groups them into four categories – classical, sociological, national economist and Marxist.
47 J. Schumpeter, *Imperialism and Social Classes*, New York, 1951, ch. 5.
48 H. Gollwitzer, *Europe in the Age of Imperialism*, London, 1969, p. 13. See also H. Gollwitzer, *Geschichte des weltpolitischen Denkens*, Göttingen, 1972–82, vol. 2, pp. 78–82.
49 Treitschke, quoted in Kennedy, *Anglo-German Antagonism*, p. 169; Bismarck, quoted in Taylor, *Struggle for Mastery*, p. 294. See also Pflanze, *Bismarck*, vol. 3, pp. 119–42.
50 On American business influence, see W. LaFeber, *The New Empire*, Ithaca, 1963, and for an argument that a pervasive profit mentality lay behind US imperialism, W.A. Williams, *The Roots of American Empire*, New York, 1969.

51 F. Merk, *Manifest Destiny and Mission in American History*, New York, 1963, p. 261; M.H. Hunt, *Ideology and U.S. Foreign Policy*, New York, 1987, p. 43.

52 R.A. Rempel, *Unionists Divided*, Newton Abbot, 1972.

53 'Recessional' (1897), *Rudyard Kipling: The Complete Verse*, foreword by M.M. Kaye, London, 1990, p. 266; J.E.C. Welldon, quoted in J.A. Mangan, '"The grit of our forefathers": invented traditions, propaganda and imperialism', in J.M. MacKenzie, ed., *Imperialism and Popular Culture*, Manchester, 1986, p. 120; J.M. MacKenzie, *Propaganda and Empire*, Manchester, 1984, p. 2.

54 W.L. Langer, *Diplomacy of Imperialism*, New York, 1951.

55 R.J. Scally, *Origins of the Lloyd George Coalition: The Politics of Social-Imperialism*, Princeton, 1975; B. Semmel, *Imperialism and Social Reform*, Cambridge, MA, 1960.

56 H.-U. Wehler, *The German Empire*, Oxford, 1985, pp. 24–31, 94–9, 171–6. G. Eley, 'Defining social imperialism: use and abuse of an idea', *Social History*, 1 (1976): 265–90, argues that the notion of an elitist plot obscures the fact of the workers' voluntary acceptance of the *status quo*.

57 P.M. Kennedy, 'German colonial expansion: has the "manipulated Social Imperialism" been ante-dated?', *Past and Present*, 54 (1972): 134–41.

58 H.S. Hughes, *Consciousness and Society: Reorientation of European Social Thought, 1890–1930*, New York, 1958.

59 Ibid., pp. 336–56.

60 Rupert Brooke, quoted in G. Dangerfield, *Strange Death of Liberal England*, London, 1966, p. 352.

61 Z. Steiner, ed., *The Times Survey of Foreign Ministries of the World*, London, 1982.

62 J. Joll, '1914: the unspoken assumptions', in H.W. Koch, ed., *Origins of the First World War*, London, 1972, pp. 307–28.

63 Crook, *War and History*, pp. 9–28.

64 M. Ginsberg, *The Idea of Progress*, London, 1953, p. 2. See also L. Sklair, *The Sociology of Progress*, London, 1970.

65 M. Ceadel, *Thinking about Peace and War*, Oxford, 1987, p. 5; S.E. Cooper, *Patriotic Pacifism*, New York, 1991, pp. v, 141. The word pacificism was first used by A.J.P. Taylor, *The Trouble Makers*, London, 1957, p. 51n.

66 Bloch, quoted in B. Tuchman, *The Proud Tower*, New York, 1966, p. 238. Also on Bloch, see M. Howard, 'Men against fire: the doctrine of the offensive', in *Lessons of History*, Oxford, 1991, pp. 97–101.

67 First Hague Conference resolution, quoted in Tuchman, *Proud Tower*, p. 312.

68 H. Weinroth, 'Norman Angell and *The Great Illusion*: an episode in pre-1914 pacifism', *Historical Journal*, 15 (1974): 574.

69 A.J.A. Morris, *Radicalism against War*, London, 1972. Contrast the high profile achieved by these British pacificists with the marginality of their German counterparts in R. Chickering, *Imperial Germany and a World Without War*, Princeton, 1975.

70 S. Avineri, 'Marxism and nationalism', *Journal of Contemporary History*, 26 (1991): 637–56.

71 V. Kubálková and A.A. Cruickshank, *Marxism–Leninism and Theory of International Relations*, London, 1980, pp. 35–44. See also V. Kubálková and A.A. Cruickshank, *Marxism and International Relations*, Oxford, 1985, ch. 2; R. Szporluk, *Communism and Nationalism*, New York, 1988, ch. 11; and I. Cummins, *Marx, Engels and National Movements*, London, 1980, who concentrates on their attitude to the nationalism of 'backward societies'.

72 K. Marx and F. Engels, *Selected Works*, Moscow, 1969–70, vol. 2, p. 18; cf. p. 190.
73 Second International resolution, Stuttgart Congress, quoted in J. Joll, *The Second International*, London, 1974, p. 208.
74 Bebel, quoted ibid., p. 73, and in R. Hostetter, 'The SPD and the general strike as an anti-war weapon', *The Historian*, 13 (1950): 27; R.C. Williams, 'Russians in Germany, 1900–14', *Journal of Contemporary History*, 1/4 (1966): 121–49.
75 Jaurès, quoted in Joll, *Second International*, p. 114.

6 IDEOLOGY AND THE GREAT WAR

1 G. Barraclough, *Introduction to Contemporary History*, London, 1964, pp. 1–3, 88–118.
2 W.L. Langer, *Diplomacy of Imperialism*, New York, 1951, p. 3; A.J.P. Taylor, *Struggle for Mastery in Europe*, Oxford, 1954, pp. 328–9. For William II's 'new course' speech, see J.A. Nichols, *Germany after Bismarck*, Cambridge, MA, 1958, p. 68.
3 Figures of Germany's economic growth are in H. Holborn, *History of Modern Germany*, New York, 1967, pp. 367–88.
4 On the *Sonderweg*, see G. Iggers, *New Directions in European Historiography*, Middletown, 1980, ch. 3; H. James, *A German Identity*, London, 1990, pp. 88–103. But the *Sonderweg* hypothesis is by no means universally accepted; see e.g. D. Blackbourn and G. Eley, *Peculiarities of German History*, Oxford, 1984.
5 See T. Kohut, *Wilhelm II and the Germans*, New York, 1991, for a psychological portrait of the new emperor.
6 On the connotations of the term *Weltpolitik*, see H. Gollwitzer, *Geschichte des weltpolitischen Denkens*, Göttingen, 1972–82, vol. 2, pp. 23–82, 217–52.
7 This interpretation was pioneered after the First World War by E. Kehr, *Schlachtflottenbau und Partei-politik*, Berlin, 1930, and always thereafter received support in some scholarly quarters, e.g. Taylor, *Struggle for Mastery*, pp. 372–3. But it only gained wide currency with F. Fischer's *Griff nach der Weltmacht*, Düsseldorf, 1961, Eng. trans. *Germany's Aims in the First World War*, London, 1967, chs 1–2. Fischer amplified his views in *War of Illusions*, London, 1973. These and kindred arguments of the *Primat der Innenpolitik* are subsumed in V.R. Berghahn, *Germany and the Approach of War in 1914*, London, 1993, esp. pp. 1–14. For a critique of the Fischer school, see D.E. Kaiser, 'Germany and the origins of the First World War', *Journal of Modern History*, 55 (1983): 442–74, while the essays in G. Schöllgen, ed., *Escape into War? Foreign Policy of Imperial Germany*, Oxford, 1990, demonstrate the tendency of some recent German historians to de-emphasize the internal factors in Wilhelmine diplomacy.
8 Taylor, *Struggle for Mastery*, pp. 318, 325–8; Langer, *Diplomacy*, p. 5.
9 On the ambience in which a Franco-Russian *rapprochement* could develop, see the introduction to G.F. Kennan, *Fateful Alliance*, New York, 1984.
10 Langer, *Diplomacy*, pp. 21–60 *passim*.
11 *The Kaiser's Letters to the Tsar*, N.F. Grant, ed., London, 1920, pp. 23–5.
12 Taylor, *Struggle for Mastery*, pp. 432–4.
13 C. Andrew, 'German world policy and the reshaping of the Dual Alliance', *Journal of Contemporary History*, 1/3 (1966): 137–51.

NOTES

14 Grey to Bertie, British Ambassador to France, 15 Jan. 1906, *British Documents on the Origins of the War, 1898–1914*, G.P. Gooch and H.W.V. Temperley, eds, London, 1926–38 (hereafter *BD*), vol. 3, p. 177.

15 Taylor, *Struggle for Mastery*, p. 400. See also H.W. Koch, 'Anglo-German alliance negotiations: missed opportunity or myth?', *History*, 54 (1969): 378–92; P.M. Kennedy, 'German world policy and alliance negotiations with England', *Journal of Modern History*, 45 (1973): 605–25.

16 For the Grey–Cambon letters, see *BD*, vol. 10/2, pp. 614–15.

17 Asquith reply (drafted by Grey) to questions in House of Commons, 24 March 1913, *BD*, vol. 10/2, p. 689. See also K.M. Wilson, *The Policy of the Entente*, Cambridge, 1985, pp. 40–58.

18 Chamberlain and William II, quoted in Z. Steiner, *Britain and the Origins of the First World War*, London, 1977, p. 17; Salisbury, quoted in J.A.S. Grenville, *Lord Salisbury and Foreign Policy*, London, 1964, pp. 165–6. See also P.M. Kennedy, *Rise of Anglo-German Antagonism*, London, 1980, ch. 19.

19 I.F. Clarke, *Voices Prophesying War*, London, 1963, pp. 142–52; P.M. Kennedy, *The Realities behind Diplomacy*, London, 1981, pp. 57–9. See also A.J.A. Morris, *The Scaremongers*, London, 1984; G.R. Searle, *The Quest for National Efficiency*, Oxford, 1971.

20 Crowe's memo is in *BD*, vol. 3, appendix A. See also K. Robbins, *Sir Edward Grey*, London, 1971, pp. 131–3, 154–9; Z. Steiner, *The Foreign Office and Foreign Policy*, Cambridge, 1969, pp. 83–152.

21 A.J.A. Morris, *Radicalism against War*, London, 1972, pp. 52–70; Campbell-Bannermann quoted ibid., p. 62.

22 R.J.B. Bosworth, *Italy and the Approach of the First World War*, London, 1983, pp. 23, 60–1.

23 The phrase was given currency by G. Lowes Dickinson whose *European Anarchy*, London, 1916, was expanded into *The International Anarchy*, London, 1926.

24 J. Remak, '1914: the third Balkan war', *Journal of Modern History*, 43 (1971): 353–66. See also L. Lafore, *The Long Fuse*, Philadelphia, 1965.

25 See, however, V. Dedijer, *The Road to Sarajevo*, London, 1967, pp. 366–400. For the Habsburg perspective on pan-Slavism, see S.R. Williamson, Jr, *Austria and the Origins of the First World War*, London, 1991, pp. 100–20.

26 Kireyev, quoted in D.C.B. Lieven, *Russia and the Origins of the First World War*, London, 1983, p. 22.

27 Count Thurn, quoted ibid., p. 74. See also D. Geyer, *Russian Imperialism: The Interaction of Domestic and Foreign Policy*, Leamington Spa, 1987, pp. 293–300.

28 Lieven, *Russia*, pp. 41–2.

29 E. Thaden, *Russia and the Balkan Alliance*, University Park, PA, 1965, pp. 53–5, 66–70.

30 A. Rossos, *Russia and the Balkans*, Toronto, 1981, p. 163; Lieven, *Russia*, p. 42.

31 Williamson, *Austria*, p. 155.

32 L. Albertini, *Origins of the War of 1914*, Oxford, 1952–7, vol. 2, p. 350.

33 Ibid., pp. 137–40.

34 Class, quoted in Berghahn, *Germany and the Approach of War*, p. 157; A.J. Mayer, 'Domestic causes of the First World War', in L. Krieger and F. Stern, eds, *The Responsibility of Power*, New York, 1967, p. 293. See also R. Chickering, *We Men Who Feel Most German*, Boston, 1984, pp. 278–83.

35 Fischer, *War of Illusions*, p. 468; Berghahn, *Germany and the Approach of War*, pp. 181–2.

36 All these charges are detailed in Fischer, *Germany's Aims*, ch. 2.

37 Bethmann-Hollweg, quoted ibid., pp. 74, 80–1. See also K.H. Jarausch, *The Enigmatic Chancellor: Bethmann-Hollweg and the Hubris of Imperial Germany*, New Haven, 1973.

38 On the French position in the July crisis, see J. Keiger, *France and the Origins of the First World War*, London, 1983, ch. 7.

39 Steiner, *Britain*, p. 145. See also Morris, *Radicalism*, ch. 10.

40 For an excellent synopsis of the unfolding of the crisis, see J. Joll, *Origins of the First World War*, London, 1992, ch. 1.

41 B. Bond, *War and Society in Europe*, London, 1984, pp. 83–5. See also L.L. Farrar, Jr, *The Short War Illusion*, Santa Barbara, 1973.

42 Bond, *War and Society*, p. 72.

43 Victor Adler and Wilhelm Dittmann, quoted in J. Joll, *The Second International*, London, 1974, pp. 163, 176.

44 Freud, quoted in R.H. Stromberg, 'Intellectuals and the coming of war in 1914', *Journal of European Studies*, 3 (1973): 111; Class, quoted in Chickering, *We Men*, p. 291.

45 Hervé, quoted in J.-J. Becker, *1914: Comment les Français sont entrés dans la guerre*, Paris, 1977, p. 406.

46 E.C. Powell, quoted in W.J. Reader, *'At Duty's Call': A Study in Obsolete Patriotism*, Manchester, 1988, p. 103; Philip Larkin, 'MCMIV', in *Collected Poems*, A. Thwaite, ed., London, 1988, p. 127.

47 H. Rogger, 'Russia in 1914', *Journal of Contemporary History*, 1/3 (1966): 104–9.

48 Georges Sorel, quoted in R. Aron, *Century of Total War*, London, 1954, p. 19.

49 P. Knightley, *The First Casualty*, London, 1975, ch. 5.

50 Aron, *Century of Total War*, p. 25. Cf. M. Knox, 'Continuity and revolution in the making of strategy', in W. Murray *et al.*, eds, *Making of Strategy*, New York, 1994, p. 628: 'Mass warfare [is] almost inevitably ideological warfare.'

51 Bethmann-Hollweg's September memo, quoted in Fischer, *Germany's Aims*, p. 103.

52 Ibid., pp. 106–8; F. Fischer, *From Kaiserreich to Third Reich*, London, 1986, pp. 97–8. See also A. Hillgruber, *Germany and the Two World Wars*, Cambridge, MA, 1981, pp. 41–8.

53 For a survey of entente war aims, see D. Stevenson, *The First World War and International Politics*, Oxford, 1988, pp. 106–31.

54 Bosworth, *Italy*, p. 127. On Anglo-French propaganda in Italy during the period of neutrality, see W.A. Renzi, *In the Shadow of the Sword*, New York, 1988, ch. 8.

55 P. Buitenhuis, *The Great War of Words*, Vancouver, 1987, pp. 17–18, 59–65; M.L. Sanders and P.M. Taylor, *British Propaganda during the First World War*, London, 1982, pp. 143–4, 169–74.

56 N.G. Levin, *Woodrow Wilson and World Politics*, New York, 1968, p. 2. See also T. Smith, *America's Mission*, Princeton, 1994, pp. 84–95.

57 *Papers of Woodrow Wilson*, A.S. Link *et al.*, eds, Princeton, 1966–93, vol. 30, p. 394; vol. 33, p. 149.

58 Ibid., vol. 10, p. 576; vol. 25, p. 629. See also K.A. Clements, *Woodrow Wilson: World Statesman*, Boston, 1987, ch. 8.

59 L. Ambrosius, *Wilsonian Statecraft: Theory and Practice of Liberal Internationalism during World War I*, Wilmington, 1991.

60 Wilson, *Papers*, vol. 40, pp. 534–8.

61 J.A. Combs, *American Diplomatic History: Two Centuries of Changing Interpretations*, Berkeley, 1983, pp. 132–52, 258–63, 378–9.

62 Wilson, *Papers*, vol. 41, p. 523.
63 R. Service, *Lenin*, London, 1985–95, vol. 2, pp. 152–5, 247–51.
64 Lenin, quoted in A.J. Mayer, *Political Origins of the New Diplomacy*, New Haven, 1959, p. 245; Decree on Peace, quoted ibid., p. 262.
65 R.K. Debo, *Revolution and Survival: The Foreign Policy of Soviet Russia, 1917–18*, Toronto, 1979, pp. 19–20, 25, 62–4, 164–8.
66 Mayer, *Political Origins*, ch. 2.
67 Wilson, *Papers*, vol. 45, pp. 534–9.
68 L.W. Martin, *Peace without Victory: Woodrow Wilson and British Liberals*, New Haven, 1958, p. vii. See also M. Swartz, *The Union of Democratic Control*, Oxford, 1971.
69 Wilson, quoted in J.L. Snell, 'Wilsonian rhetoric goes to war', *The Historian*, 14 (1952): 194; Mayer, *Political Origins*, pp. 376–8.
70 R.H. Ferrell, *Woodrow Wilson and World War I*, New York, 1985, pp. 130–2.
71 Wilson, *Papers*, vol. 51, p. 419.
72 K. Schwabe, *Woodrow Wilson, Revolutionary Germany, and Peacemaking: Missionary Diplomacy and the Realities of Power*, Chapel Hill, 1985.
73 Debo, *Revolution and Survival*, pp. 356–7, 378–9. Churchill's *apologia* for intervention is *World Crisis: The Aftermath*, London, 1929, chs 4, 12–13.
74 Versailles Declaration, quoted in Stevenson, *The First World War*, p. 218.
75 Robert Bridges, letter to *The Times*, 2 Sept. 1914, p. 9.
76 Using postmodern literary theory, E. Cobley, *Representing War: Form and Ideology in First World War Narratives*, Toronto, 1994, p. 209, concludes that even the protest literature of the First World War 'did not succeed in escaping ideological complicities' with the war.
77 A. Marwick, *War and Social Change in the Twentieth Century*, London, 1974, pp. 95–6. Other works which explore the Great War's analogical function include E. Leed, *No Man's Land*, New York, 1979; G.L. Mosse, *Fallen Soldiers*, New York, 1990.

7 ENTER TOTAL IDEOLOGIES

1 For the Leninist gloss on Marxist thought in the field of international relations, see A.B. Ulam, *Expansion and Coexistence: Soviet Foreign Policy*, New York, 1974, pp. 12–30; V. Kubálková and A.A. Cruickshank, *Marxism and International Relations*, Oxford, 1985, pp. 76–9.
2 Trotsky, quoted in T.J. Uldricks, *Ideology and Diplomacy: Origins of Soviet Foreign Relations*, Beverly Hills, 1979, p. 17; Decree on Peace, quoted in Ulam, *Expansion*, p. 52.
3 R.K. Debo, *Survival and Consolidation: The Foreign Policy of Soviet Russia, 1918–21*, Montreal, 1992, chs 3–4 *passim*.
4 Invitation to First Congress of the Communist International, *The Communist International*, J. Degras, ed., London, 1956–65 (hereafter *CI*), vol. 1, p. 2.
5 Ulam, *Expansion*, pp. 94, 112–13.
6 Comintern's Twenty-One Conditions, *CI*, vol. 1, p. 169.
7 P. Melograni, *Lenin and the Myth of World Revolution*, Atlantic Highlands, 1989, pp. 121–2.
8 Invitation to First Congress of the Communist International, *CI*, vol. 1, p. 43.
9 B.N. Pandey, *The Break-up of British India*, London, 1969, pp. 105–10; J.P. Haithcox, *Communism and Nationalism in India*, Princeton, 1971, pp. 11–18.

10 Ulam, *Expansion*, pp. 124–5.
11 M. Light, *Soviet Theory of International Relations*, Brighton, 1988, p. 25.
12 Ulam, *Expansion*, p. 121. See also D. Armstrong, *Revolution and World Order*, Oxford, 1993, pp. 126–47.
13 F.L. Carsten, *The Reichswehr and Politics, 1918–33*, Oxford, 1966, pp. 135–47.
14 C. Fink, *The Genoa Conference*, Chapel Hill, 1984; S. White, *Origins of Détente: The Genoa Conference and Soviet–Western Relations*, Cambridge, 1985.
15 Uldricks, *Ideology*, pp. 192–3.
16 C. Andrew, *Secret Service*, London, 1985, pp. 301–13; S. Crowe, 'Zinoviev letter', *Journal of Contemporary History*, 10 (1975): 407–32.
17 On the doctrine of 'socialism in one country', see R.N. Carew Hunt, *Theory and Practice of Communism*, London, 1957, chs 17–18.
18 *Avanti!*, quoted in Melograni, *Lenin*, p. 123.
19 Herbert Hoover, quoted in J.M. Thompson, *Russia, Bolshevism and the Versailles Peace*, Princeton, 1966, p. 2; R.S. Baker, *Woodrow Wilson and World Settlement*, Garden City, 1922, vol. 2, p. 64.
20 A.J. Mayer, *Politics and Diplomacy of Peacemaking*, New York, 1967, p. 14.
21 *Papers of Woodrow Wilson*, A.S. Link, ed., Princeton, 1966–93, vol. 53, p. 462.
22 R. Little, 'Deconstructing the balance of power', *Review of International Studies*, 15 (1989): 87–100.
23 Wilson, *Papers*, vol. 53, p. 462.
24 K.A. Clements, *Woodrow Wilson*, Boston, 1987, p. 204. Interestingly, the classic deterministic statement of human development appeared *after* the First World War: J.B. Bury, *Idea of Progress*, London, 1920.
25 A. Lentin, *Lloyd George, Woodrow Wilson and the Guilt of Germany*, Leicester, 1984, pp. 16–29; D. Stevenson, *French War Aims against Germany*, Oxford, 1992, pp. 149–51; R. Vivarelli, *Il dopoguerra in Italia*, Naples, 1967, pp. 365–84.
26 A.J. Balfour, quoted in A. Sharp, *The Versailles Settlement*, Basingstoke, 1991, p. 158. See also H. Seton-Watson, *Eastern Europe between the Wars*, Cambridge, 1972.
27 A.J.P. Taylor, *Origins of the Second World War*, London, 1961, p. 24.
28 For contemporary statements of how the American president was hoodwinked in Paris, see J.M. Keynes, *Economic Consequences of the Peace*, London, 1919; H. Nicolson, *Peacemaking, 1919*, London, 1933. Biographies which characterize Wilson as an idealist include M. Blum, *Woodrow Wilson and the Politics of Morality*, Boston, 1956; J.W.S. Nordholt, *Woodrow Wilson: A Life for World Peace*, Berkeley, 1991. The realist side of Wilsonian diplomacy figures in E. Buehrig, *Woodrow Wilson and the Balance of Power*, Bloomington, 1955; A.S. Link, *Woodrow Wilson: Revolution, War and Peace*, Arlington Heights, 1979, pp. 99–103; M. Pomerance, 'The United States and self-determination: the Wilsonian conception', *American Journal of International Law*, 70 (1976): 1–27.
29 E.B. Wilson, *My Memoir*, Indianapolis, 1938, p. 239.
30 On these negotiations, see A. Walworth, *Wilson and His Peacemakers*, New York, 1986.
31 Cecil, quoted in G.W. Egerton, *Great Britain and the Creation of the League of Nations*, Chapel Hill, 1978, p. 140, and in Sharp, *Versailles*, p. 62, who provides a text of the Covenant on pp. 64–74.
32 Wilson, *Papers*, vol. 55, p. 175.
33 *The Great Experiment*, London, 1941.

34 This thesis is advanced by T.J. Knock, *To End All Wars*, New York, 1992.
35 L. Ambrosius, *Woodrow Wilson and the American Diplomatic Tradition*, Cambridge, 1987, pp. xii–xiii. On social control, see ch. 1 *passim*.
36 W. Widenor, *Henry Cabot Lodge and the Search for an American Foreign Policy*, Berkeley, 1988.
37 Harding, quoted in S. Adler, *The Isolationist Impulse*, New York, 1957, p. 109.
38 See the appropriate essays in G.A. Craig and F. Gilbert, eds, *The Diplomats 1919–39*, Princeton, 1953, part I: 'The Twenties'.
39 P. Wandycz, *France and Her Eastern Allies*, Minneapolis, 1962.
40 Mayer, *Politics and Diplomacy of Peacemaking*, p. 891.
41 MacDonald, quoted in A. Cassels, 'Repairing the *Entente Cordiale* and the new diplomacy', *Historical Journal*, 23 (1980): 149.
42 G. Stresemann, *His Diaries, Letters, and Papers*, E. Sutton, ed., London, 1935–40, vol. 2, p. 239.
43 S. Marks, *The Illusion of Peace*, London, 1976, chs 4–6. See also J. Jacobson, *Locarno Diplomacy*, Princeton, 1972.
44 G.W. Egerton, 'Collective security as political myth: liberal internationalism and the League of Nations', *International History Review*, 5 (1983): 496–524.
45 S. Cohen, *Rethinking the Soviet Experience*, New York, 1985, ch. 2.
46 E. Nolte, *Three Faces of Fascism*, New York, 1966, p. 29. This is not to deny fascism's intellectual origins in certain late nineteenth-century ideologies, as traced by Z. Sternhell *et al.*, *The Birth of Fascist Ideology*, Princeton, 1994.
47 B. Mussolini, *Opera omnia*, E. and D. Susmel, eds, Florence and Rome, 1951–80, vol. 19, p. 18.
48 E.g. E. Corradini, *Discorsi politici*, Florence, 1923.
49 G. Salvemini, *Prelude to World War II*, London, 1951, pp. 19–28. See also H.J. Burgwyn, *Legend of the Mutilated Victory*, Westport, 1993.
50 Mussolini, *Opera*, vol. 19, p. 19.
51 The article was published in English as 'The political and social doctrine of Fascism', *International Conciliation*, 306 (Jan. 1935): 5–17.
52 M. Ledeen, *Universal Fascism: Theory and Practice of the Fascist International*, New York, 1972.
53 G.-K. Kindermann, *Hitler's Defeat in Austria, 1933–4*, Boulder, 1988, p. 116.
54 Mussolini, quoted in N. Goldmann, *Memories*, London, 1970, p. 160.
55 Mussolini, *Opera*, vol. 25, p. 104; vol. 26, p. 259; vol. 28, p. 60.
56 D. Cofrancesco, 'Appunti per un'analisi del mito romano nell'ideologia fascista', *Storia Contemporanea*, 11 (1980): 383–411; R. Visser, 'Fascist doctrine and the cult of the *romanità*', *Journal of Contemporary History*, 27 (1992): 5–22.
57 On the diplomatic background of the Ethiopian crisis, see E.M. Robertson, *Mussolini as Empire Builder*, London, 1977.
58 D.S. Birn, *The League of Nations Union*, Oxford, 1981, p. 154.
59 G.W. Baer, *Test Case: Italy, Ethiopia, and the League of Nations*, Stanford, 1976.
60 Ulrich von Hassell reports, 7 January and 11 July 1936, *Documents on German Foreign Policy, 1918–45* (hereafter *DGFP*), London, 1949–83, series C, vol. 4, p. 975; series D, vol. 1, p. 283.
61 For Hitler's public view of the South Tyrolean question, see *Mein Kampf*, New York, 1943, pp. 626–9. *Mein Kampf* first appeared in 1925, and soon after Hitler wrote a second or *Secret Book*, New York, 1961, expressly to stress the importance of acknowledging Italian rule in the South Tyrol (see p. 1

and ch. 15). But this second book was not published either in the 1920s or indeed during Hitler's lifetime, maybe to avoid offending Teutonic sentiment.
62 Mussolini, *Opera*, vol. 15, p. 216.
63 M. Knox, 'Conquest, foreign and domestic, in Fascist Italy and Nazi Germany', *Journal of Modern History*, 56 (1984): 1–57.
64 B. Wanrooij, 'The rise and fall of Italian fascism as a generational revolt', *Journal of Contemporary History*, 22 (1987): 401–18; D. Mack Smith, *Mussolini's Roman Empire*, London, 1976, pp. 92–5.
65 A. De Grand, 'Cracks in the façade: the failure of Fascist totalitarianism in Italy', *European History Quarterly*, 21 (1991): 526.
66 SS Hauptsturmführer Strunk, quoted in R.H. Whealey, 'Mussolini's ideological diplomacy', *Journal of Modern History*, 39 (1967): 435.
67 Mussolini, *Opera*, vol. 28, p. 67.
68 E. Jäckel, *Hitler's Weltanschauung*, Middletown, 1972, pp. 13–26.
69 Hitler, *Mein Kampf*, p. 655.
70 Ibid., pp. 15–16, 37–8, 51–65, 91–125. See also A.G. Whiteside, *The Socialism of Fools: Georg Ritter von Schönerer and Austrian Pan-Germanism*, Berkeley, 1975.
71 H.J. Mackinder, 'Geographical pivot of history', *Geographical Journal*, 23 (1904): 421–37; H.J. Mackinder, *Democratic Ideals and Reality*, London, 1919, p. 194.
72 On the intellectual relationship between Ratzel, Mackinder and Haushofer, see G. Parker, *Western Geopolitical Thought in the Twentieth Century*, London, 1985, chs 2–5; W.D. Smith, *Ideological Origins of Nazi Imperialism*, New York, 1986, pp. 146–52, 218–23; G. Stoakes, *Hitler and the Quest for World Dominion: Nazi Ideology and Foreign Policy in the 1920s*, Leamington Spa, 1986, ch. 5.
73 M. Burleigh, *Germany Turns Eastwards*, Cambridge, 1988.
74 Stoakes, *Quest*, p. 161.
75 Hitler, *Mein Kampf*, p. 654.
76 See n. 61.
77 For assertions of the ideological motif in Hitler's foreign policy, see the respective first chapters of G.L. Weinberg, *The Foreign Policy of Hitler's Germany*, 2 vols, Chicago, 1970–80; N. Rich, *Hitler's War Aims*, 2 vols, New York, 1973–4; W. Carr, *Arms, Autarky and Aggression*, London, 1972. Also W. Deist, 'The road to ideological war: Germany, 1918–45', in W. Murray *et al.*, eds, *Making of Strategy*, New York, 1994, pp. 352–92; K. Hildebrand, *Foreign Policy of the Third Reich*, London, 1973.
78 W. Laqueur, *Terrorism*, London, 1977, pp. 49–53.
79 'Hitler and the origins of the Second World War', *Proceedings of the British Academy*, 53 (1967): 286.
80 The functionalist–intentionalist argument was sparked by two essays in particular: T. Mason, 'Intention and explanation: a current controversy about the interpretation of national socialism', and K. Hildebrand, 'Monokratie oder Polykratie', in G. Hirschfeld and L. Kettenacker, eds, *Der Führerstaat: Mythos und Realität*, Stuttgart, 1981, pp. 21–40, 73–97. For overviews of the debate, see I. Kershaw, *The Nazi Dictatorship: Problems and Perspectives of Interpretation*, London, 1993, ch. 6; J. Hiden and J. Farquharson, *Explaining Hitler's Germany*, London, 1989, ch. 5.
81 O. Meissner, *Staatssekretär unter Ebert–Hindenburg–Hitler*, Mannheim, 1950, p. 617.
82 I. Kershaw, *The 'Hitler Myth'*, Oxford, 1987, p. 10.

83 M.M. Lee and W. Michalka, *German Foreign Policy, 1917–33: Continuity or Break?*, Leamington Spa, 1987, p. 156.
84 Stoakes, *Quest*, ch. 2; Smith, *Ideological Origins*, pp. 224–30.
85 *Economy and Society*, New York, 1968, vol. 1, pp. 241–5; vol. 3, pp. 1111–14.
86 Hitler, *Mein Kampf*, p. 377; A. Schweitzer, *Age of Charisma*, Chicago, 1984, pp. 105–6.
87 Hitler, *Mein Kampf*, pp. 139–45, 613–25; Hitler, *Secret Book*, ch. 14.
88 E. Haraszti, *Treaty-Breakers or 'Realpolitiker'? The Anglo-German Naval Agreement*, Boppard, 1974.
89 U. Bialer, *The Shadow of the Bomber*, London, 1980; C. MacDonald, 'Economic appeasement and German moderates', *Past and Present*, 56 (1972): 105–35.
90 Hossbach memo, *DGFP*, series D, vol. 1, p. 32.
91 W. Michalka, *Ribbentrop und die deutsche Weltpolitik*, Munich, 1980, pp. 210–15, 220–2; J. Wright and P. Stafford, 'Hitler, Britain and the Hossbach Memorandum', *Militärgeschichtliche Mitteilungen*, 42 (1987): 77–123.
92 Admiral Carls, quoted in Hildebrand, *Foreign Policy*, p. 76.
93 Ibid., pp. 75, 85; Carr, *Arms*, p. 113. See also A. Hillgruber, 'England's place in Hitler's plans for world domination', *Journal of Contemporary History*, 9/1 (1974): 5–22.
94 Hitler, *Mein Kampf*, p. 638.
95 Hildebrand, *Foreign Policy*, pp. 81–2. See also R.C. Newton, *The 'Nazi Menace' in Argentina*, Stanford, 1992; A. Frye, *Nazi Germany and the American Hemisphere*, New Haven, 1967.
96 *Hitler's Table Talk, 1941–4*, H. Trevor-Roper, ed., London, 1953, pp. 12, 26.
97 Trevor-Roper, 'The mind of Adolf Hitler', ibid., p. xvi; H. Rauschning, *Hitler Speaks*, London, 1939, pp. 253–4; A. François-Poncet, *The Fateful Years*, London, 1949, p. 292.
98 Smith, *Ideological Origins*, pp. 16–20, 250–5.
99 Carr, *Arms*, p. 74.
100 Hossbach memo, *DGFP*, series D, vol. 1, pp. 34–5. The text of the memorandum is also printed in the so-called 'blue series' of Nuremberg documents, *Trial of the Major War Criminals*, Nuremberg, 1947–9, vol. 25, pp. 402–13. An authoritative evaluation of the Hossbach memo is in Weinberg, *Foreign Policy*, vol. 2, pp. 34–42. For criticism of its validity, see Taylor, *Origins*, pp. 131–4; H.W. Koch, 'Hitler and the origins of the Second World War: second thoughts on the status of some of the documents', *Historical Journal*, 11 (1968): 132–5.
101 For differing interpretations of this phenomenon, see A.S. Milward, *The German Economy at War*, London, 1965, and R.J. Overy, *War and Economy in the Third Reich*, Oxford, 1994, ch. 8.
102 L. Kochan, *The Struggle for Germany*, Edinburgh, 1963. See also P.M.H. Bell, *Origins of the Second World War in Europe*, London, 1986, pp. 50–1.
103 S. Slipchenko, 'Veterans speak of the diplomatic service', *International Affairs* [Moscow], (Oct. 1989): 132; C.J. Clarke, *Russia and Italy against Hitler*, Westport, 1991.
104 Theses of Sixth Comintern Congress, *CI*, vol. 2, p. 456. See also L. Ceplair, *Under the Shadow of War: Fascism, Anti-Fascism, and Marxists*, New York, 1987, pp. 47–55.
105 John Wiley, quoted in H.D. Phillips, *Between the Revolution and the West: Political Biography of Maxim Litvinov*, Boulder, 1992, p. 177.
106 J. Jackson, *The Popular Front in France*, Cambridge, 1988, pp. 22–42.

107 Resolution of Seventh Comintern Congress, *CI*, vol. 3, p. 361.
108 Ulam, *Expansion*, p. 229. J. Hochmann, *The Soviet Union and the Failure of Collective Security*, Ithaca, 1984, is emphatic that Stalin's offers of collaboration were spurious; J. Haslam, *The Soviet Union and the Struggle for Collective Security in Europe*, London, 1984, recognizes opposition within the Kremlin to a flexible policy but is more inclined to take the Soviets at their word.
109 J.F. Coverdale, *Italian Intervention in the Spanish Civil War*, Princeton, 1976, pp. 12–13, 78–82; R.H. Whealey, *Hitler and Spain*, Lexington, 1989, pp. 26–36.
110 Jackson, *Popular Front*, p. 208; Anthony Eden quoted ibid., p. 203; Sir George Clerk quoted ibid. p. 205. See also M. Alpert, *New International History of the Spanish Civil War*, Basingstoke, 1994, pp. 13–15, 22–4.
111 Ulam, *Expansion*, pp. 243–5.
112 The most damning indictment of Soviet policy in Spain is B. Bolleten, *The Spanish Civil War*, Chapel Hill, 1991. A more restrained account is H. Thomas, *The Spanish Civil War*, London, 1986.
113 M. Muggeridge, *The Thirties*, London, 1940, pp. 266–7. The Spanish war looms large in the classic memoir of Western intellectual flirtation with communism, R.H.S. Crossman, ed., *The God That Failed*, London, 1949. See also D. Caute, *The Fellow Travellers*, London, 1973, pp. 169–75.
114 The best overview of appeasement is found in the twenty-eight essays which make up W.J. Mommsen and L. Kettenacker, eds, *The Fascist Challenge and the Policy of Appeasement*, London, 1983. P.M. Kennedy, 'Appeasement', in G. Martel, ed., *Origins of the Second World War Reconsidered*, London, 1986, pp. 140–61, is an excellent summary of the factors behind British policy.
115 *Norman Chamberlain* (1923), cited in M. Gilbert, *Roots of Appeasement*, London, 1966, p. 21. The widespread anti-war sentiment in Britain encouraged the growth of outright pacifist movements; see M. Ceadal, *Pacifism in Britain, 1914–45*, Oxford, 1980.
116 See e.g. H.E. Barnes, *Genesis of the World War*, New York, 1926; S.B. Fay, *Origins of the World War*, 2 vols, New York, 1928.
117 J.F. Naylor, *Labour's International Policy*, London, 1969, pp. 189–207; R.P. Shay, *British Rearmament in the Thirties*, Princeton, 1977, pp. 217–19.
118 J.E. Dreifort, 'French role in the least unpleasant solution', in M. Latynski, ed., *Reappraising the Munich Pact*, Baltimore, 1992, pp. 21–46.
119 *Documents on British Foreign Policy, 1919–39*, series 3, London, 1949–55, vol. 2, p. 640.
120 Taylor, *Origins*, p. 189; E.H. Carr, *The Twenty Years' Crisis, 1919–39*, London, 1946, p. vii; the first edition of Carr's book appeared in 1939.
121 Daladier, quoted in A.P. Adamthwaite, *France and the Coming of the Second World War*, London, 1977, p. 108; Bonnet, quoted ibid., p. 109. See also C.A. Micaud, *The French Right and Nazi Germany*, New York, 1943, ch. 9.
122 D. Lammers, 'Fascism, communism, and the Foreign Office, 1937–9', *Journal of Contemporary History*, 6/3 (1971): 66–86; Chamberlain, quoted in J. Charmley, *Chamberlain and the Lost Peace*, London, 1989, p. 185.
123 On this much debated point, see S. Newman, *March 1939: The British Guarantee to Poland*, Oxford, 1976; S. Aster, *1939: The Making of the Second World War*, Aldershot, 1993.
124 R. Manne, 'The British decision for an alliance with Russia', *Journal of Contemporary History*, 9/3 (1974): 3–26; K. Neilson, '"Pursued by a bear": British estimates of Soviet military strength and Anglo-Soviet relations', *Canadian Journal of History*, 28 (1993): 207–21.

125 R.A.C. Parker, *Chamberlain and Appeasement*, London, 1993, pp. 219, 222–31; Charmley, *Chamberlain*, pp. 171–2, 180–5; M. Gilbert, *Churchill*, London, 1991, pp. 614–17; Naylor, *Labour's International Policy*, pp. 293–304; A. Roberts, *The Holy Fox: Biography of Lord Halifax*, London, 1991, pp. 145–8, 156–60.

126 V. Potemkin, quoted in R. Coulondre, *De Staline à Hitler*, Paris, 1950, p. 165.

127 D.C. Watt, *How War Came*, London, 1989, p. 460. On the negotiation of the Nazi–Soviet Pact, see A. Read and D. Fisher, *Deadly Embrace*, London, 1988, chs 19–23.

128 For a standard expression of this Soviet view, see the memoir by Ivan Maisky, Russian ambassador in London in 1939, *Who Helped Hitler?*, London, 1964.

129 Bell, *Origins*, p. 125; R.C. Raack, 'Stalin's plans for World War II', *Journal of Contemporary History*, 26 (1991): 215–27.

130 Carl J. Burckhardt conversation with Hitler, 11 Aug. 1939, quoted in Read and Fisher, *Deadly Embrace*, p. 184. See also H.S. Levine, 'The mediator: Carl J. Burckhardt's efforts to avert a second world war', *Journal of Modern History*, 45 (1973): 439–55.

131 Weinberg, *Foreign Policy*, vol. 2, pp. 653–5, 675–7; G.L. Weinberg, 'Hitler and England, 1933–45: pretense and reality', *German Studies Review*, 8 (1985): 299–309.

132 M. Michaelis, *Mussolini and the Jews: German–Italian Relations and the Jewish Question in Italy*, Oxford, 1978, chs 5–6; F. Gilbert, 'Ciano and his ambassadors', in Craig and Gilbert, *Diplomats*, pp. 512–36; M. Toscano, *Origins of the Pact of Steel*, Baltimore, 1967.

133 M. Knox, *Mussolini Unleashed, 1939–41*, Cambridge, 1984, ch. 2.

134 K. Hamilton and R. Langhorne, *The Practice of Diplomacy*, London, 1995, pp. 181–2.

8 A SECOND GLOBAL CONFLICT

1 D. Caute, *The Fellow Travellers*, London, 1973, pp. 188–91.

2 Communist International Manifesto on 22nd Anniversary of Russian Revolution *The Communist International*, J. Degras, ed., London, 1956–65, vol. 3, pp. 443–4. See also L. Ceplair, *Under the Shadow of War: Fascism, Anti-Fascism, and Marxists*, New York, 1987, pp. 152–3, 179–80.

3 H. Trevor-Roper, ed., *Hitler's War Directives*, London, 1964, pp. 34–8; P.M.H. Bell, *Origins of the Second World War in Europe*, London, 1986, p. 278.

4 For this debate, see A. Adamthwaite, *Grandeur and Misery: France's Bid for Power in Europe, 1914–40*, London, 1995; J.C. Cairns, 'Along the road back to France 1940', *American Historical Review*, 64 (1959): 583–603; D. Porch, 'Arms and alliances; French grand strategy and policy in 1914 and 1940', in P.M. Kennedy, ed., *Grand Strategies in War and Peace*, New Haven 1991, pp. 125–43; E. Weber, *The Hollow Years*, New York, 1994.

5 R. Paxton, *Vichy France*, New York, 1972, pp. 14–38.

6 P. M Taylor, *Munitions of the Mind*, Wellingborough, 1990, pp. 189–90.

7 Churchill, quoted in J. Lukacs, *The Duel: Hitler vs. Churchill, 10 May–31 July 1940*, London, 1990, pp. 146–7; ibid., p. 242.

8 J. Charmley, *Churchill: End of Glory*, London, 1992.

9 B. Mussolini, *Opera omnia*, E. and D. Susmel, eds, Florence and Rome, 1951–80, vol. 29, pp. 43–5.

10 M. Knox, *Mussolini Unleashed*, New York, 1982, p. 272.

11 D. Smyth, *The Diplomacy and Strategy of Survival*, Cambridge, 1986, chs 2, 5; P. Preston, 'France and Hitler: the myth of Hendaye', *Contemporary History*, 1 (1992): 1–16.

12 Hosoya Chihiro, 'The Tripartite Pact', in J.W. Morley, ed., *Deterrent Diplomacy: Japan, Germany and the USSR, 1935–40*, New York, 1976, pp. 179–257.

13 W. Deist, 'The road to ideological war,' in W. Murray *et al.*, eds, *Making of Strategy*, New York, 1994, pp. 388–9.

14 A. Read and D. Fisher, *Deadly Embrace*, London, 1988, ch. 46; G.L. Weinberg, *A World At Arms*, New York, 1994, pp. 199–202; *Hitler's War Directives*, pp. 49–52.

15 Hitler, quoted in N. Rich, *Hitler's War Aims*, New York, 1973–4, vol. 1, p. 208.

16 R. Cecil, *Hitler's Decision to Invade Russia*, London, 1975, pp. 168–9; H. Trevor-Roper, ed., *Hitler's Table Talk*, London, 1953, pp. 3–4.

17 *Documents on German Foreign Policy, 1918–45*, London, 1949–83 (hereafter DGFP), series D, vol. 10, p. 373.

18 P. Padfield, *Hess: Flight for the Führer*, London, 1991. On the interrogation of Hess in 1940, see I. Kirkpatrick, *The Inner Circle*, London, 1959, pp. 170–81. For the unproven conjecture that Hess flew with Hitler's connivance, see J. Costello, *Ten Days to Destiny*, New York, 1993.

19 Bell, *Origins*, pp. 293–4; Cecil, *Hitler's Decision*, p. 167. However, Rich, *Hitler's War Aims*, vol. 1, pp. 162–3, 204–11, appears to accept Hitler's linkage of Russia with the British war effort as plausible motivation.

20 Hitler, quoted in A. Bullock, *Hitler: A Study in Tyranny*, London, 1962, p. 375.

21 *DGFP*, series D, vol. 12, p. 1069.

22 Rich, *Hitler's War Aims*, vol. 1, pp. 211–20; A. Dallin, *German Rule in Russia, 1941–5*, Boulder, 1981, pp. 68–70.

23 Stalin refused to consider exploiting Russia's vast hinterland; see E.F. Ziemke, 'Strategy for class war', in Murray *et al.*, eds, *Making of Strategy*, p. 525.

24 F.H. Hinsley, 'British intelligence and Barbarossa', in J. Erickson and D. Dilks, eds, *The Axis and the Allies*, Edinburgh, 1994, pp. 43–75; G.W. Prange, *Target Tokyo: Story of the Sorge Spy Ring*, New York, 1988, pp. 337–41, 347–8.

25 A.B. Ulam, *Stalin: The Man and His Era*, New York, 1973, pp. 532–5; R.C. Tucker, *Stalin in Power, 1928–41*, New York, 1990, pp. 619–25.

26 D. Volkogonov, 'The German attack, Soviet response, Sunday, 22 June 1941', in Erickson and Dilks, *The Axis*, pp. 76–94, indicates that Stalin's conduct remains unfathomable in Moscow.

27 Churchill, quoted in J. Colville, *The Fringes of Power: Downing Street Diaries*, London, 1985, p. 404. See also G. Gorodetsky, 'An alliance of sorts', in Erickson and Dilks, *The Axis*, pp. 101–22.

28 Caute, *Fellow Travellers*, pp. 197–9.

29 F. Costigliola, 'The United States and the reconstruction of Germany in the 1920s', *Business History Review*, 50 (1976): 477–502; D.F. Schmitz, *The United States and Fascist Italy*, Chapel Hill, 1988, pp. 64–70, 87–100, 108–9. R.W. Child's name appears on the title page of Mussolini's *My Autobiography*, London, 1936.

30 W.I. Cohen, *Empire without Tears: America's Foreign Relations, 1921–33*, New York, 1987.

31 S. Adler, *The Isolationist Impulse*, New York, 1957, pp. 219–42.

32 Roosevelt, quoted in R. Dallek, *Franklin D. Roosevelt and American Foreign Policy*, New York, 1979, p. 137.

33 *Public Papers and Addresses of Franklin D. Roosevelt*, S.I. Rosenman, ed., New York, 1938–50, vol. 9, p. 517. On polls and US popular sentiment, see R.

NOTES

Dallek, *The American Style of Foreign Policy*, New York, 1983, pp. 123–32, and for the debate over the violation of neutrality, J.A. Combs, *American Diplomatic History*, Berkeley, 1983, pp. 199–219, 381–3.

34 W.L. Langer and S.E. Gleason, *The Undeclared War, 1940–1*, New York, 1953.
35 John Dryden, 'Absalom and Achitophel', quoted in D. Reynolds, *Creation of the Anglo-American Alliance*, Chapel Hill, 1982, p. 195.
36 Roosevelt, *Papers*, vol. 10, pp. 314–15.
37 Roosevelt, quoted in E. Janeway, *Struggle for Survival*, New Haven, 1951, p. 71.
38 M. Hunt, *Ideology and U.S. Foreign Policy*, New Haven, 1987, pp. 150–2. The final acceptance by the USA of a global role is the theme of D. Fromkin, *In the Time of the Americans*, New York, 1995.
39 Roosevelt, quoted in Dallek, *Roosevelt*, pp. 265, 285.
40 Hunt, *Ideology*, p. 149.
41 J. Marshall, *To Have and Have Not: Southeast Asian Raw Materials and the Origins of the Pacific War*, Berkeley, 1994.
42 J. Hunter, *Emergence of Modern Japan*, London, 1989, pp. 169, 189.
43 C. Gluck, *Japan's Modern Myths: Ideology in the Late Meiji Period*, Princeton, 1985, esp. pp. 102–56, 279–86.
44 W.G. Beasley, *Japanese Imperialism*, Oxford, 1987, pp. 5–10.
45 A. Iriye, *Origins of the Second World War in Asia and the Pacific*, London, 1987, pp. 2–4.
46 B.-A. Shillony, *Revolt in Japan*, Princeton, 1973, p. 212.
47 Army memorandum, 3 July 1940, quoted in Iriye, *Origins*, pp. 103–4.
48 *Kokutai no Hongi, Sources of the Japanese Tradition*, R. Tsunoda *et al.*, eds, New York, 1958, pp. 785–95.
49 K. Nobura, 'Militarism and the emperor system', *Japan Interpreter*, 8 (1973): 219–27.
50 The prototype of the Japanese approach is Maruyama Masao, *Thought and Behaviour in Modern Japanese Politics*, London, 1963. Western literature in rebuttal includes P. Duus and D.I. Okimoto, 'Fascism and the history of pre-war Japan: failure of a concept', *Journal of Asian Studies*, 39 (1979): 65–76; G.J. Kasza, 'Fascism from below: a comparative perspective on the Japanese right, 1931–36', *Journal of Contemporary History*, 19 (1984): 607–30.
51 I. Nish, *Japanese Foreign Policy, 1869–1942*, London, 1977, p. 219.
52 P. Brooker, *The Faces of Fraternalism: Nazi Germany, Fascist Italy, and Imperial Japan*, Oxford, 1991.
53 Iriye, *Origins*, chs 2–4 *passim*.
54 A. Offner, *American Appeasement: United States Foreign Policy and Germany, 1933–8*, Cambridge, MA, 1969; W. Heinrichs, *Threshold of War: Franklin D. Roosevelt and American Entry into World War II*, New York, 1988, p. 8.
55 M.A. Barnhart, *Japan Prepares for Total War: The Search for Economic Security*, Ithaca, 1987, pp. 144–6.
56 *Japan's Decision for War: Records of the 1941 Policy Conferences*, Nobutaka Ike, ed., Stanford, 1967, pp. 102, 282. On the theme of national honour, see T. Iritani, *Group Psychology of the Japanese in Wartime*, London, 1991, pp. 88, 249.
57 Plan for Greater East Asia Co-Prosperity Sphere, *Sources of Japanese Tradition*, p. 802. See also G.M. Berger, 'Three-dimensional empire: Japanese attitudes and the new order in Asia', *Japan Interpreter*, 12 (1979): 355–82; U. Katsumi, 'Pursuing an illusion: the new order in East Asia', *Japan Interpreter*, 6 (1970): 326–37.
58 Iriye, *Origins*, p. 171.

271

59 Rich, *Hitler's War Aims*, vol. 1, pp. 237–46.
60 *Hitler: Reden und Proklamationen, 1932–45*, M. Domarus, ed., Würzburg, 1962–3, vol. 2, pp. 1802–8; *Hitler's Table Talk*, pp. 82, 188.
61 This criticism was made by, among others, C.C. Tansill, *Back Door to War*, Chicago, 1952.
62 *Hitler: Reden und Proklamationen*, vol. 2, p. 1794.
63 Tokutomi Iichiro, commentary on imperial declaration of war, 1941, *Sources of Japanese Tradition*, p. 800.
64 M.R. Peattie, 'Japanese attitudes to colonialism', in R.H. Myers and M.R. Peattie, eds, *The Japanese Colonial Empire*, Princeton, 1984, pp. 122–6.
65 Hitler, quoted in Rich, *Hitler's War Aims*, vol. 2, pp. 329–30. See also R. Koehl, *RKFDV: German Resettlement and Population Policy*, Cambridge, MA, 1957.
66 Dallin, *German Rule*, chs 26, 28.
67 O. Bartov, *Hitler's Army*, Oxford, 1991, chs 2, 4; G. Hirschfeld, ed., *Policies of Genocide*, London, 1986. The degree to which Germans were infected by Nazi racist ideas is illustrated by the contrast with Fascist Italian attitudes in J. Steinberg, *All or Nothing: The Axis and the Holocaust*, London, 1990.
68 On the link between Operation Barbarossa and the final solution, see C.R. Browning, *The Path to Genocide*, New York, 1993, ch. 1; A.J. Mayer, *Why Did the Heavens Not Darken?*, New York, 1990, chs 8, 9.
69 N. Tumarkin, *The Living and the Dead: Rise and Fall of the Cult of World War II in Russia*, New York, 1994, pp. 61–4.
70 A.B. Ulam, *Expansion and Coexistence: Soviet Foreign Policy*, New York, 1974, p. 346.
71 See e.g. the future President Truman; ibid., pp. 326–7. For the endless east–west bickering over the timing of a second front, see M. Stoler, *Politics of the Second Front*, Westport, 1977.
72 A. Armstrong, *Unconditional Surrender*, New Brunswick, 1961, pp. 15–20, 40–5, 250–3. On the other hand, the Western Allies, for a variety of reasons, declined to emphasize their ideological distance from Nazism by dwelling on news of the Holocaust which was filtering out of eastern Europe in 1942–3; for criticism of this attitude, see W. Laqueur, *The Terrible Secret*, London, 1980; M.N. Penkower, *The Jews Were Expendable*, Urbana, 1983, chs 3, 4.
73 K. von Klemperer, *German Resistance against Hitler: The Search for Allies Abroad*, New York, 1992.
74 H.W. Koch, 'The spectre of a separate peace in the east', *Journal of Contemporary History*, 10 (1975): 531–49; Weinberg, *World At Arms*, pp. 609–11, 719–21.
75 M. Stoler, *Second Front*, pp. 40–51.
76 This distinction was often mirrored in Anglo-American differences during the war; see Weinberg, *World At Arms*, pp. 722–44 *passim*.
77 This agreement quickly scribbled on 'a half-sheet of paper', now lost, is described in W.S. Churchill, *The Second World War*, vol. 6: *Triumph and Tragedy*, London, 1954, p. 198.
78 K. Kersten, *Establishment of Communist Rule in Poland*, Berkeley, 1991, pt 1.
79 E. Mark, 'American policy toward eastern Europe, 1941–6', *Journal of American History*, 68 (1981): 313–36.
80 W.F. Kimball, *The Juggler: Franklin Roosevelt as Wartime Statesman*, Princeton, 1991, p. 104. L.C. Gardner, *Spheres of Influence*, Chicago, 1993, p. 265, argues in a *tour de force* that Roosevelt unconsciously accepted European zones of influence as the only means of averting an East–West confrontation.
81 Roosevelt, *Papers*, vol. 13, p. 138.

82 J.L. Harper, *American Visions of Europe*, New York, 1994, pp. 34–7, 126, 186; T. Smith, *America's Mission*, Princeton, 1994, pp. 329–30.

83 A. Schlesinger, Jr, 'Origins of the Cold War', *Foreign Affairs*, 22 (1967): 25–52.

84 Kimball, *The Juggler*, p. 186.

85 G. Wright, *Ordeal of Total War*, New York, 1968, p. 147; H. Michel, *The Shadow War: Resistance in Europe*, London, 1972, p. 360.

86 E. Hancock, *National Socialist Leadership and Total War*, New York, 1991, pp. 197, 201.

87 H. Trevor-Roper, *The Last Days of Hitler*, London, 1978.

88 Schwerin von Krosigk, quoted ibid., p. 111.

89 *Mein Kampf*, New York, 1943, p. 654.

90 *The Testament of Adolf Hitler: Hitler–Bormann Documents, February–April, 1945*, F. Genoud, ed., London, 1961, pp. 103, 109.

91 H. Heiber, *Goebbels*, New York, 1972, p. 317. See also R.E. Herzstein, *The War That Hitler Won: The Most Infamous Propaganda Campaign in History*, New York, 1978.

92 For the war crimes trials in historical perspective, see B.F. Smith, *Reaching Judgment at Nuremberg*, New York, 1977; R. Piccigallo, *The Japanese on Trial*, Austin, 1979.

9 IDEOLOGY AND GLOBAL POLITICS

1 According to D. Holloway, *Stalin and the Bomb*, New Haven, 1994, pp. 153–61, Stalin in the aftermath of the Second World War did not believe the USA would actually utilize the atomic bomb against the Soviet Union, though he was concerned at Washington's exploitation of its nuclear monopoly to exert diplomatic pressure. This is consistent with, though it does not prove, the argument of G. Alperovitz, *The Decision to Use the Atomic Bomb*, New York, 1995, that America's resort to nuclear weapons to defeat Japan, in preference to an invasion of that country, was precisely a demonstration aimed at cowing the Soviets.

2 A. Schlesinger, Jr., 'Some lessons from the Cold War', in M. Hogan, ed., *End of the Cold War: Its Meaning and Implications*, Cambridge, 1992, p. 54. See also J.L. Gaddis, *The Long Peace: Inquiries into the History of the Cold War*, New York, 1987, ch. 5.

3 R. Pettman, *International Politics*, Melbourne, 1991, pp. 153–5, 164–7.

4 A.L. George, 'The "operational code": a neglected approach to the study of political decision-making', *International Studies Quarterly*, 13 (1969): 190–222.

5 Kennan's 'long telegram', *Containment: Documents on American Foreign Policy, 1945–50*, T.H. Etzold and J.L. Gaddis, eds, New York, 1978, pp. 50–63. D. Yergin, *The Shattered Peace: Origins of the Cold War and the National Security State*, Boston, 1977, chs 1–2, posits the 'Riga axioms', a Kennan-like jaundiced view of the Soviets hatched by American diplomats in their Baltic observation post before the establishment of a Moscow embassy, against Roosevelt's 'Yalta axioms' which envisaged cooperation with Russia.

6 *Memoirs*, Boston, 1967, p. 295.

7 Truman, quoted in L.K. Adler and T.G. Paterson, 'Red fascism: the merger of Nazi Germany and Soviet Russia in the American image of totalitarianism', *American Historical Review*, 75 (1970): 1046.

8 'The sources of Soviet conduct', *Foreign Affairs*, 25 (1947): 575.

9 *White House Years*, Boston, 1979, p. 135.

10 Yergin, *Shattered Peace*, p. 275; George Elsey, quoted ibid., p. 282; Truman, quoted ibid., p. 283. See also H. Jones, *'A New Kind of War': America's Global Strategy and the Truman Doctrine in Greece*, New York, 1989.

11 J.L. Gaddis, *Strategies of Containment*, New York, 1982, p. 26, refers to a 'cottage industry among Cold War scholars, devoted to elucidating "what Kennan really meant to say"'. W.D. Miscamble, *George F. Kennan and the Making of American Foreign Policy*, Princeton, 1992, p. 112, is shrewdest in arguing that the policy of containment was devoid of content until, step by step, 'the Truman administration gave meaning to the notion'. Kennan summarized his intended meaning in his *Memoirs*, pp. 363–7.

12 The centrality of Europe to US postwar global strategy informs J.L. Harper's *American Visions of Europe: Roosevelt, Kennan, and Acheson*, New York, 1994.

13 For a brief excursus on this theme, see W. LaFeber, *America, Russia, and the Cold War*, New York, 1993, pp. 58–63. The standard monograph on the subject is M. Hogan, *The Marshall Plan*, New York, 1987.

14 For a selection of NSC reports, see Etzold and Gaddis, *Containment*, NSC-68, pp. 385–442.

15 M. Jervis, 'Impact of the Korean war upon the Cold War', *Journal of Conflict Resolution*, 24 (1980): 563–92.

16 P. Lowe, *Origins of the Korean War*, London, 1986, p. 70.

17 E.R. Wittkopf, *Faces of Internationalism: Public Opinion and American Foreign Policy*, Durham, NC, 1990, p. 169.

18 Yergin, *Shattered Peace*, ch. 9; S.M. Gillon, *Politics and Vision: The ADA and American Liberalism*, New York, 1987, pp. 26–35, 66–72; D.W. Reinhard, *The Republican Right since 1945*, Lexington, 1983, pp. 29–36.

19 N.A. Graebner, *The New Isolationism*, New York, 1956.

20 R. Hofstadter, *The Paranoid Style in American Politics*, New York, 1965, pp. 6–7.

21 Dulles, quoted in Gaddis, *Strategies of Containment*, pp. 128, 162.

22 P.M. Kattenburg, *The Vietnam Trauma in American Foreign Policy*, New Brunswick, 1980, pp. 39–50. Actually, the domino theory had been propounded in NSC cf. n. 14 124/2 and approved by President Truman two years earlier; see A. Short, *Origins of the Vietnam War*, London, 1989, p. 107. F. Ninkovich, *Modernity and Power: History of the Domino Theory*, Chicago, 1994, locates the theory's intellectual genesis in America's adoption of world-wide axioms in the Wilsonian era.

23 Short, *Origins*, chs 4–5.

24 Rusk, quoted in Gaddis, *Strategies of Containment*, p. 202.

25 L.H. Gelb and R.K. Betts, *The Irony of Vietnam: The System Worked*, Washington, 1979, pp. 129–30, 160–3; Wittkopf, *Internationalism*, pp. 190–3.

26 The distortion wrought in the American policy-making process by obsessive anti-communist ideology is startlingly revealed in the memoir of the US secretary of state for defence during the Vietnam war: R. McNamara, *In Retrospect*, New York, 1995, esp. pp. 19–23.

27 Johnson, quoted in W. LaFeber, *The American Age*, New York, 1994, pp. 606, 611–12; Gelb and Betts, *Vietnam*, pp. 240–5.

28 A.R.E. Rhodes, *The Vatican in the Age of the Cold War*, Norwich, 1992, concentrates on the 1945–50 period. See also O. Chadwick, *The Christian Church and the Cold War*, London, 1992, chs 1–6; H. Stehle, *Eastern Politics of the Vatican*, Athens, OH, 1981, chs 7–9.

29 Ironically, the classic statement of this view was by an American, albeit one working in Europe: L. Halle, *The Cold War as History*, New York, 1967.

30 A. Bullock, *The Life and Times of Ernest Bevin*, London, 1960–83, vol. 3.
31 S. Hoffmann, 'Foreign policy of Charles de Gaulle', in G.A. Craig and F.L. Loewenheim, eds, *The Diplomats, 1939–79*, Princeton, 1994, pp. 235–7. See also C. de Gaulle, *Memoirs of Hope*, London, 1971, pp. 199–206.
32 Kattenburg, *Vietnam Trauma*, pp. 216–18, 253–5.
33 President Kennedy, 1963, quoted in Gaddis, *Strategies of Containment*, p. 201.
34 C. Christie, *The Quiet American and the Ugly American: Western Literary Perspectives*, Canterbury, 1989.
35 LaFeber, *American Age*, pp. 619–21, 662–5, 716–17.
36 M.H. Hunt, *Ideology and U.S. Foreign Policy*, New Haven, 1987, p. 170.
37 P. Hollander, *Anti-Americanism: Critiques at Home and Abroad*, New York, 1992.
38 *The Tragedy of American Diplomacy*, New York, 1962.
39 J.A. Combs, *American Diplomatic History*, Berkeley, 1983, chs 19–21.
40 Extreme new left views can be sampled in the trio of studies of US foreign policy between 1943 and 1980 by G. and J. Kolko: *The Politics of War*, New York, 1968; *The Limits of Power*, New York, 1972; *Confronting the Third World*, New York, 1988. For a critique of the radical revisionists, see J. Siracusa, *New Left Histories and Historians*, New York, 1973.
41 R. Melanson, *Writing History and Making Policy: Cold War, Vietnam, and Revisionism*, Lanham, 1983, pp. 126 35, 174 8, 216–26.
42 Gaddis, *Strategies of Containment*, p. 275.
43 H. Kissinger, *Diplomacy*, New York, 1994, chs 4–5.
44 Kissinger, quoted in R. Morris, *Uncertain Greatness: Henry Kissinger and American Foreign Policy*, New York, 1977, p. 241. See also S. Hersh, *Kissinger: The Price of Power*, New York, 1983, chs 21–2.
45 Carter, quoted in G. Lundestad, *The American 'Empire'*, Oxford, 1990, p. 11.
46 Reagan, quoted ibid., pp. 11–12, and in LaFeber, *American Age*, pp. 704–5.
47 Khrushchev, quoted in W. Taubman, *Stalin's American Policy*, New York, 1982, p. 196. See also A. Bullock, *Hitler and Stalin: Parallel Lives*, London, 1991, pp. 401–4, 1060–5. For a first-hand *exposé* of Stalin's warped personality, see M. Djilas, *Conversations with Stalin*, New York, 1962, and on his total command of Soviet foreign policy, S.M. Miner, 'His master's voice: Viacheslav Mikhailovich Molotov as Stalin's foreign commissar', in Craig and Loewenheim, eds, *Diplomats, 1939–79*, Princeton, 1994, pp. 65–100.
48 Holloway, *Stalin*, pp. 161–6.
49 The thesis of C. Kennedy-Pipe, *Stalin's Cold War*, Manchester, 1995, is that the clue to Soviet foreign policy in Europe after 1953 lies in a paranoid fear of revived German militarism. Preferable to this was the US military presence in its zone of occupation. Of course, West Germany's integration into NATO rang alarm bells anew in Moscow.
50 Zhdanov, quoted in Taubman, *Stalin's American Policy*, p. 176.
51 G. Wettig, 'Stalin and German reunification: archival evidence on Soviet foreign policy in spring 1952', *Historical Journal*, 37 (1994): 411–19, discloses that Stalin's surprising overture for a reunited Germany was aimed at mobilizing the German 'masses' in the communist cause.
52 J.L. Nogee and R.H. Donaldson, *Soviet Foreign Policy since World War II*, New York, 1981, pp. 37–9. In the same vein, see also V. Kubálková and A.A. Cruickshank, *Marxism and International Relations*, Oxford, 1985, pp. 79–86; M. Light, *Soviet Theory of International Relations*, Brighton, 1988, pp. 327–30.

53 N. Tumarkin, *The Living and the Dead: Rise and Fall of the Cult of World War II in Russia*, New York, 1994, p. 101.

54 J.L. Gaddis, 'The Cold War, the long peace, and the future', in M. Hogan, ed., *End of the Cold War*, pp. 23–6.

55 N.M. Nikolsky and A.V. Grishen, *Nauchno-tekhnicheskii progress i mezhdunarodyne otnosheniya*, quoted in S. Shenfield, 'The long and winding road: trajectories to peace and socialism in contemporary Soviet ideology', in S. White, and A. Pravda, eds, *Ideology and Soviet Politics*, London, 1988, p. 206.

56 A.B. Ulam, *Expansion and Coexistence: Soviet Foreign Policy*, New York, 1974, pp. 606–7; Light, *Soviet Theory*, p. 66.

57 Brezhnev Doctrine, quoted in Nogee and Donaldson, *Soviet Foreign Policy*, p. 226.

58 H.W. Nelsen, *Power and Insecurity: Beijing, Moscow, and Washington*, Boulder, 1989, p. viii. See also R.K.I. Quested, *Sino–Soviet Relations*, London, 1983, chs 9–10.

59 *Red Flag*, quoted in A.S. Whiting, 'The Sino-Soviet split', in R. MacFarquhar and J.K. Fairbank, eds, *Cambridge History of China*, vol. 14, Cambridge, 1987, p. 516.

60 *People's Daily*, quoted in W.E. Griffith, *The Sino-Soviet Rift*, Cambridge, MA, 1964, pp. 61, 388–417 *passim*, and in E. Crankshaw, *The New Cold War: Moscow v. Pekin*, New York, 1963, p. 137.

61 Krushchev, quoted in Griffith, *Sino-Soviet Rift*, p. 401. For a full account of the Bucharest and Moscow conferences, see Crankshaw, *New Cold War*, chs 10–12. On Albania, E. Biberaj, *Albania and China: Study of an Unequal Alliance*, Boulder, 1986.

62 On the 'wedge' strategy, see Gaddis, *Long Peace*, pp. 152–94.

63 K. Jowitt, *New World Disorder: The Leninist Extinction*, Berkeley, 1992, pp. 214, 229.

64 Shenfield, 'Long and winding road', in White and Pravda, *Ideology and Soviet Politics*, p. 211.

65 S. White, *Gorbachev and After*, Cambridge, 1992, ch. 6.

66 Gorbachev, quoted in S. Kull, *Burying Lenin: The Revolution in Soviet Ideology and Foreign Policy*, Boulder, 1992, pp. 133–4, and in J.C. Valdez, *Internationalism and the Ideology of Soviet Influence in Eastern Europe*, Cambridge, 1993, p. 114. See also S. Woodby, *Gorbachev and the Decline of Ideology in Soviet Foreign Policy*, Boulder, 1989.

67 Gennadiy Gerasimov, quoted in Valdez, *Internationalism*, p. 124.

68 For a conspectus, see D. Pryce-Jones, *The War That Never Was: Fall of the Soviet Empire, 1985–91*, London, 1995, chs 15–32.

69 Ibid., pp. 366–437.

70 M.R. Peattie, 'Japanese attitudes to colonialism', in R.H. Myers and M.R. Peattie, eds, *The Japanese Colonial Empire*, Princeton, 1984, p. 127.

71 D. Fromkin, *In the Time of the Americans*, New York, 1995, pp. 525–31.

72 F. Ansprenger, *Dissolution of the Colonial Empires*, London, 1989, ch. 7.

73 For contrasting interpretations of American anti-colonialism in Indochina in 1945, see W. LaFeber, 'Roosevelt, Churchill, and Indochina', *American Historical Review*, 80 (1975): 1277–95, and S. Tonnessen, *The Vietnamese Revolution of 1945*, London, 1991.

74 Congressman E. Celler, quoted in R.N. Gardner, *Sterling Dollar Diplomacy*, New York, 1969, p. 237; Eisenhower, quoted in C.J. Bartlett, *'The Special Relationship': Anglo-American Relations since 1945*, London, 1992, p. 86.

75 S.N. MacFarlane, 'Success and failures in Soviet policy toward Marxist revolutions in the Third World', in M.N. Katz, ed., *The USSR and Marxist Revolutions in the Third World*, Cambridge, 1990, p. 9. See also A.Z. Rubinstein, *Moscow's Third World Strategy*, Princeton, 1988, chs 2–4.
76 Mao Zedong, quoted in J. Camilleri, *Chinese Foreign Policy: The Maoist Era and Its Aftermath*, Oxford, 1980, pp. 8, 25; Chih-yu Shih, *China's Just World: The Morality of Chinese Foreign Policy*, Boulder, 1993.
77 For the Tanzanian and other case studies, see J.D. Armstrong, *Revolutionary Diplomacy: Chinese Foreign Policy and the United Front Doctrine*, Berkeley, 1977.
78 Camilleri, *Chinese Foreign Policy*, pp. 105–6.
79 G. Segal, 'China and the Great Power Triangle', *China Quarterly*, 83 (1983): 490; Foreign Minister Huang Hua, quoted in J.R. Walsh, *Change, Continuity and Commitment: China's Adaptive Foreign Policy*, Lanham, 1988, pp. 21.
80 L. Dittmer, *Sino-Soviet Normalization and Its International Implications*, Seattle, 1992, pp. 69–80.
81 See D. Armstrong, *Revolution and World Order*, Oxford, 1993, p. 307: 'The impact of international society on revolutionary states through the socialization process may be judged to have been stronger than the reverse interaction.'
82 A.Z. Rubinstein, ed., *Soviet and Chinese Influence in the Third World*, New York, 1975, p. 221. See also M. Light, ed., *Troubled Friendships: Moscow's Third World Ventures*, London, 1993, ch. 8.
83 Z. Laïdi, 'What use is the Soviet Union?', in Z. Laïdi, ed., *The Third World and the Soviet Union*, London, 1988, pp. 1–23; J. Copans, 'USSR, alibi or instrument for black African states?', ibid., pp. 24–38.
84 Nehru, quoted in B.N. Pandey, *Nehru*, London, 1976, p. 375, and in B.N. Pandey, *South and South-east Asia*, London, 1980, pp. 152, 154.
85 R. Fonseca, 'Nehru and the diplomacy of nonalignment', in G.A. Craig and F.L. Loewenheim, eds, *The Diplomats, 1939–79*, Princeton, 1994, pp. 371–97.
86 W.M. LeoGrande, 'Evolution of the nonaligned movement', *Problems of Communism*, 29 (Jan.–Feb. 1980): 35. See also R.L. Jackson, *The Non-aligned, the UN, and the Superpowers*, New York, 1983, ch. 9.
87 G. Lundestad, *East, West, North, South, 1945–90*, Oslo, 1991, p. 278.
88 V.M. Hewitt, *International Politics of South Asia*, Manchester, 1992, pp. 199, 219; M.K. Pasha, 'Islamization, civil society, and the politics of transition in Pakistan', in D. Allen, ed., *Regional and Political Conflict in South Asia*, Westport, 1992, p. 118. On the unresolved Kashmiri problem, see R.G. Wirsing, *India, Pakistan, and the Kashmir Dispute*, New York, 1994.
89 For an even lengthier historical symbiosis, see S.D. Goitein, *Jews and Arabs: Their Contacts through the Ages*, New York, 1964.
90 R. Ovendale, *Origins of the Arab–Israeli Wars*, London, 1992.
91 Rabbi Yehuda Amital, quoted in A. Rubinstein, *The Zionist Dream Revisited: From Herzl to Gush Emunim*, New York, 1984, pp. 104–5. See also O. Seliktar, *New Zionism and the Foreign Policy System of Israel*, Carbondale, 1986.
92 N. Lucas, *Modern History of Israel*, London, 1974, p. 424.
93 Ovendale, *Origins*, pp. 148–9.
94 F. Ajami, 'End of pan-Arabism,' in *Pan-Arabism and Arab Nationalism*, ed. T. Farah, Boulder, 1987, p. 98.
95 F. Ajami, *The Arab Predicament*, New York, 1992, p. 81.
96 Sayyid Qutb, quoted in E. Sivan, *Radical Islam: Medieval Theology and Modern Politics*, New Haven, 1985, pp. 30–2.

97 Khomeini, quoted in F. Rajaee, *Islamic Values and World View: Khomeyni on Man, the State and International Politics*, Lanham, 1983, p. 73.
98 J.M. Landau, *The Politics of Pan-Islam: Ideology and Organization*, Oxford, 1990, p. 305.
99 B. Lewis, *The Middle East and the West*, New York, 1964, p. 115.
100 J.P. Piscatori, 'Islam and world politics', in J. Baylis and N.J. Rengger, eds, *Dilemmas of World Politics*, Oxford, 1992, pp. 310–33; J. Voll, 'Revivalism and social transformations in Islamic history', *Muslim World*, 76 (1986): 168–76.
101 P.S. Khoury, 'Islamic revivalism and the crisis of the secular state in the Arab world', in I. Ibrahim, ed., *Arab Resources: Transformation of a Society*, Washington, DC, 1983, p. 215.
102 S. Sobhani, *The Pragmatic Entente: Israeli–Iranian Relations*, New York, 1989, ch. 6.
103 B. Tibi, 'Islam and Arab Nationalism', in B.F. Stowasser, ed., *The Islamic Impulse*, Washington, DC, 1987, p. 69.
104 A. Escobar, *Encountering Development*, Princeton, 1995. The enduring gulf between a capitalist 'core' and an undeveloped 'periphery' comprises the essence of A. Wallerstein's noted *Modern World System*, New York, 1974.

CONCLUSION

1 K.J. Holsti, *International Politics*, Englewood Cliffs, 1988, p. 7.
2 M. Hollis and S. Smith, *Explaining and Understanding International Relations*, Oxford, 1990, ch. 2; T.L. Knutsen, *History of International Relations Theory*, Manchester, 1992, ch. 9.
3 H.J. Morgenthau, *Politics among Nations*, New York, 1985, p. 103.
4 M. Griffiths, *Realism, Idealism and International Politics*, London, 1992; J. Rosenberg, *The Empire of Civil Society: A Critique of the Realist Theory of International Relations*, London, 1994, ch. 1.
5 E. Kedourie, *Nationalism*, Oxford, 1993, p. 43.
6 K.D. Bracher, *Age of Ideologies*, London, 1984.
7 K. Boulding, 'National images and international systems', *Journal of Conflict Resolution*, 3 (1959): 131.
8 A. Carter, *The Peace Movements: International Protest and World Politics since 1945*, Harlow, 1992.
9 F.H. Hinsley, *Power and the Pursuit of Peace*, Cambridge, 1963, pp. 335–6; I.L. Claude, *American Approaches to World Affairs*, Lanham, 1986, p. 51.
10 See D.W. Urwin, *The Community of Europe*, Harlow, 1995, for a brief narrative of its development.
11 A.S. Milward, *The European Rescue of the Nation-State*, London, 1992, p. 3.
12 A.D. Smith, *National Identity*, Harmondsworth, 1991, p. 176.
13 On the triumph of nationalism over communism, see J. Lukacs, *End of the Twentieth Century*, New York, 1993; J.L. Talmon, *The Myth of the Nation and the Vision of Revolution*, London, 1980.
14 M. Ignatieff, *Blood and Belonging: Journeys into the New Nationalism*, London, 1993.
15 J. Breuilly, *Nationalism and the State*, Manchester, 1993, p. 72.
16 F. Fukuyama, *End of History and the Last Man*, New York, 1992.
17 E. Halévy, *Era of Tyrannies*, London, 1967, p. 205.
18 E. Carlton, *War and Ideology*, London, 1990, p. vii.

SELECT BIBLIOGRAPHY

HISTORICAL TEXTS AND DOCUMENTARY SOURCES

Albrecht-Carrié, René. *The Concert of Europe*. New York, 1968.
Bismarck, Prince Otto von. *Die gesammelten Werke*, 15 vols, ed. H. von Petersdorff *et al.*, 2nd edn. Berlin, 1923–33.
Burke, Edmund. *Reflections on the Revolution in France*, ed. L.G. Mitchell. Oxford, 1993.
Callières, François de. *The Art of Diplomacy*, ed. H.M.A. Keens-Soper and K.W. Schweizer. Leicester, 1983.
The Communist International, 1919–43, 3 vols., ed. J. Degras. London, 1956–65.
Containment: Documents on American Foreign Policy, 1945–50, ed. T.H. Etzold and J.L. Gaddis. New York, 1978.
Danilevsky, Nikolai. *Russland und Europa*, ed. K. Nötzel. Stuttgart, 1920.
Darwin, Charles. *The Origin of Species by means of Natural Selection or the Preservation of Favoured Races in the Struggle for Life*, ed. C.D. Darlington. London, 1950.
Destutt de Tracy, Comte Antoine. *Eléments d'idéologie*, ed. H. Gouhier. Paris, 1970.
Fichte, Johann Gottlieb. *Addresses to the German Nation*, ed. G.A. Kelly. New York, 1968.
Griffith, William E. *The Sino-Soviet Rift, analysed and documented*. Cambridge, MA, 1964.
Hitler, Adolf. *Mein Kampf*, Eng. trans. R. Manheim. New York, 1943.
—— *Hitler's Secret Book*, intro. T. Taylor. New York, 1961.
—— *Reden und Proklamationen, 1932–45*, 2 vols, ed. M. Domarus. Würzburg, 1962–3.
Hitler's Table Talk, 1941–4, ed. H. Trevor-Roper. London, 1953.
The Kaiser's Letters to the Tsar, 1894–1914, ed. N.F. Grant. London, 1920.
Lenin, V.I. *Imperialism, The Highest Stage of Capitalism*. Moscow, 1947.
Luxemburg, Rosa. *The National Question: Selected Writings*, ed. H.B. Davis. New York, 1976.
Mackinder, Halford J. 'The geographical pivot of history', *Geographical Journal*, vol. 23 (1904), pp. 421–37.
—— *Democratic Ideals and Reality: A Study in the Politics of Reconstruction*. London, 1919.
Marx, Karl and Engels, Friedrich. *The German Ideology*, ed. C.J. Arthur, 2nd edn. London, 1974.
—— *Selected Works*, 3 vols. Moscow, 1969–70.

—— Selected Correspondence. Moscow, 1956.

Mazzini, Giuseppe. The Duties of Man and other Essays, intro. T. Jones. London, 1955.

Metternich-Winneburg, Prince Clemens von. Aus Metternichs nachgelassenen Papieren, 9 vols., ed. Prince R. Metternich-Winneburg. Vienna, 1880–7.

Mussolini, Benito Opera Omnia, 44 vols, ed. E. and D. Susmel. Florence and Rome, 1951–80.

Nasser, Gamal Abdul. Egypt's Liberation: The Philosophy of the Revolution. Washington, 1955.

Paine, Thomas. The Rights of Man, ed. G. Claeys. Indianapolis, 1992.

The Public Papers and Addresses of Franklin D. Roosevelt, 13 vols, comp. Samuel I. Rosenman. New York, 1938–50.

Rousseau on International Relations, ed. S. Hoffmann and D.P. Fidler. Oxford, 1991.

Sources of the Japanese Tradition, ed. R. Tsunoda et al. New York, 1958.

Treitschke, Heinrich von. Politics, ed. H. Kohn. New York, 1963.

Washington's Farewell Address: The View from the 20th Century, ed. B.I. Kaufman. Chicago, 1969.

The Papers of Woodrow Wilson, 69 vols, ed. A.S. Link et al. Princeton, 1966–94.

IDEOLOGY AND IDEOLOGIES

Bracher, Karl Dietrich. The Age of Ideologies: A History of Political Thought in the Twentieth Century. London, 1984.

Brooker, Paul. The Faces of Fraternalism: Nazi Germany, Fascist Italy, and Imperial Japan. Oxford, 1991.

Canadian Journal of Political and Social Theory, vol. 7/1,2 (1983): 'Ideology/Power'.

Carlton, Eric. War and Ideology. London, 1990.

Ceplair, Larry. Under the Shadow of War: Fascism, Anti-Fascism, and Marxists, 1918–39. New York, 1987.

Eagleton, Terry. Ideology: An Introduction. London, 1991.

Geertz, Clifford. The Interpretation of Cultures: Selected Essays. New York, 1973.

Gluck, Carol. Japan's Modern Myths: Ideology in the Late Meiji Period. Princeton, 1985.

Gollwitzer, Heinz. Geschichte des weltpolitischen Denkens, 2 vols. Göttingen, 1972–82.

Howard, Michael. 'Ideology and international relations', Review of International Studies, vol. 15 (1989), pp. 1–10.

Hunt, Michael H. Ideology and U.S. Foreign Policy, New Haven, 1987.

Jäckel, Eberhard. Hitler's Weltanschauung: A Blueprint for Power. Middletown, 1972.

Kennedy, Emmet. A Philosophe in an Age of Revolution: Destutt de Tracy and the Origins of Ideology. Philadelphia, 1978.

Kohn, Hans. Pan-Slavism: Its History and Ideology, 2nd edn. New York, 1960.

Landau, Jacob M. The Politics of Pan-Islam: Ideology and Organization. Oxford, 1990.

Ledeen, Michael A. Universal Fascism: The Theory and Practice of the Fascist International, 1928–36. New York, 1972.

Little, Richard and Smith, Steve, eds. Belief Systems and International Relations. Oxford, 1988.

Meyerson, Denise. False Consciousness. Oxford, 1991.

Mosse, George L. *The Nationalization of the Masses: Political Symbolism and Mass Movements in Germany from the Napoleonic Wars through the Third Reich*. New York, 1975.

Plamenatz, John. *Ideology*. London, 1970.

Rubinstein, Amnon. *The Zionist Dream Revisited: From Herzl to Gush Emunim and Back*. New York, 1984.

Talmon, J.L. *The Origins of Totalitarian Democracy*. London, 1952.

—— *Political Messianism: The Romantic Phase*. London, 1960.

—— *The Myth of the Nation and the Vision of Revolution: The Origins of Ideological Polarisation in the Twentieth Century*. London, 1980.

Vovelle, Michel. *Ideologies and Mentalities*. Oxford, 1990.

NATIONALISM

Alter, Peter. *Nationalism*, 2nd edn. London, 1994.

Anderson, Benedict. *Imagined Communities: Reflections on the Origin and Spread of Nationalism*, rev. edn. London, 1991.

Aveneri, Shlomo. 'Marxism and nationalism', *Journal of Contemporary History*, vol. 26 (1991), pp. 637–56.

Boulding, K.E. 'National images and international systems', *Journal of Conflict Resolution*, vol. 3 (1959), pp. 120–31.

Breuilly, John. *Nationalism and the State*, 2nd edn. Manchester, 1993.

Gellner, Ernest. *Nations and Nationalism*. Oxford, 1983.

Greenfield, Liah. *Nationalism: Five Roads to Modernity*. Cambridge, MA, 1992.

Hobsbawm, Eric J. *Nations and Nationalism since 1780: Programme, Myth, Reality*, 2nd edn. Cambridge, 1992.

Ignatieff, Michael. *Blood and Belonging: Journeys into the New Nationalism*. London, 1993.

Kedourie, Elie. *Nationalism*, 4th edn. Oxford, 1993.

Smith, Anthony D. *Theories of Nationalism*, 2nd edn. London, 1983.

INTERNATIONAL RELATIONS (general and theoretical)

Aron, Raymond. *The Century of Total War*. London, 1954.

Armstrong, David. *Revolution and World Order: The Revolutionary State in International Society*. Oxford, 1993.

Blainey, Geoffrey. *The Causes of War*, 3rd edn. London, 1988.

Bull, Hedley. *The Anarchical Society: A Study of Order in World Politics*. London, 1977.

Carr, E.H. *The Twenty Years' Crisis, 1919–39: An Introduction to the Study of International Relations*, 2nd edn. London, 1946.

Claude, Inis L. *Swords into Plowshares: The Problems and Progress of International Organization*, 4th edn. New York, 1971.

George, Alexander L. 'The "operational code": a neglected approach to the study of political decision-making', *International Studies Quarterly*, vol. 13 (1969), pp. 190–222.

Griffiths, Martin. *Realism, Idealism and International Politics: A Reinterpretation*. London, 1992.

Hamilton, Keith and Langhorne, Richard. *The Practice of Diplomacy: Its Evolution, Theory and Administration*. London, 1995.

Hinsley, F.H. *Power and the Pursuit of Peace: Theory and Practice in the History of Relations between States*. Cambridge, 1963.

Holbraad, Carsten. *The Concert of Europe: A Study in German and British International Theory*. London, 1970.

Kubálková, V. and Cruickshank, A.A. *Marxism and International Relations*. Oxford, 1985.

Light, Margot. *The Soviet Theory of International Relations*, Brighton, 1988.

Murray, Williamson; Knox, MacGregor; Bernstein, Alvin, eds. *The Making of Strategy*. New York, 1994.

Nicolson, Harold. *The Evolution of Diplomatic Method*. London, 1954.

Parker, Geoffrey. *Western Geopolitical Thought in the Twentieth Century*. London, 1985.

Rosecranze, Richard N. *Action and Reaction in World Politics*. Boston, 1963.

Wight, Martin. *Power Politics*, 2nd edn, ed. H. Bull and C. Holbraad. London, 1986.

INTERNATIONAL RELATIONS (to 1815)

Anderson, M.S. *War and Society in Europe of the Old Regime, 1618–1789*. London, 1988.

Blanning, T.C.W. *The Origins of the French Revolutionary Wars*. London, 1986.

Gilbert, Felix. *To the Farewell Address: Ideas of Early American Foreign Policy*. Princeton, 1961.

Godechot, Jacques. *La grande nation: L'expansion révolutionnaire de la France dans le monde de 1789 à 1799*, 2nd edn. Paris, 1983.

—— *The Counter-Revolution: Doctrine and Action, 1789–1804*. London, 1972.

Greene, Jack P. *The Intellectual Construction of America: Exceptionalism and Identity from 1492 to 1800*. Chapel Hill, 1993.

Jenkins, Brian. *Nationalism in France: Class and Nation since 1789*. London, 1990.

Palmer, R.R. *The Age of Democratic Revolution: A Political History of Europe and America, 1760–1800*, 2 vols. Princeton, 1959–64.

Schroeder, Paul W. *The Transformation of European Politics, 1763–1848*. Oxford, 1994.

Sheehan, James J. *German History, 1770–1866*. Oxford, 1989.

Woolf, Stuart J. *Napoleon's Integration of Europe*. London, 1991.

INTERNATIONAL RELATIONS (1815–1914)

Bertier de Sauvigny, Guillaume de. *Metternich and His Times*. London, 1962.

Cooper, Sandi E. *Patriotic Pacifism: Waging War on War in Europe, 1815–1914*. New York, 1991.

Crook, Paul. *Darwinism, War and History: The Debate over the Biology of War from the 'Origin of Species' to the First World War*. New York, 1994.

Geyer, Dietrich. *Russian Imperialism: Interaction of Domestic and Foreign Policy, 1860–1914*. Leamington Spa, 1987.

Joll, James. '1914: The unspoken assumptions', in H.W. Koch, ed., *The Origins of the First World War*, London (1972), pp. 307–28.

Kennedy, Paul M. *The Rise of Anglo-German Antagonism, 1860–1914*. London, 1980.

Merk, Frederick. *Manifest Destiny and Mission in American History*. New York, 1963.

Pflanze, Otto. *Bismarck and the Development of Germany*, 3 vols. Princeton, 1990.
Taylor, A.J.P. *The Struggle for Mastery in Europe, 1848–1918*. Oxford, 1954.
—— *The Trouble Makers: Dissent over Foreign Policy, 1792–1939*. London, 1957.
Wehler, Hans-Ulrich. *The German Empire, 1871–1918*. Oxford, 1985.

INTERNATIONAL RELATIONS (since 1914)

Ajami, Fouad. *The Arab Predicament: Arab Political Thought and Practice since 1967*, updated edn. New York, 1992.
Ambrosius, Lloyd. *Wilsonian Statecraft: Theory and Practice of Liberal Internationalism during World War I*. Wilmington, 1991.
—— *Woodrow Wilson and the American Diplomatic Tradition*. Cambridge, 1987.
Bell, P.M.H. *Origins of the Second World War in Europe*. London, 1986.
Bullock, Alan. 'Hitler and the origins of the Second World War', *Proceedings of the British Academy*, vol. 53 (1967), pp. 259–87.
Cecil, Robert. *Hitler's Decision to Invade Russia, 1941*. London, 1975.
Clements, Kendrick A. *Woodrow Wilson: World Statesman*. Boston, 1987.
Dallek, Robert. *Franklin D. Roosevelt and American Foreign Policy, 1932–45*. New York, 1979.
Egerton, George W. 'Collective security as political myth: liberal internationalism and the League of Nations in politics and history', *International History Review*, vol. 5 (1983), pp. 496–524.
Fischer, Fritz. *Germany's Aims in First World War*. New York, 1967.
—— *From Kaiserreich to Third Reich: Elements of Continuity in German History, 1871–1945*. London, 1986.
Gaddis, John L. *Strategies of Containment: A Critical Appraisal of Postwar American National Security Policy*. New York, 1982.
—— *The Long Peace: Inquiries into the History of the Cold War*. New York, 1987.
Haslam, Jonathan. *The Soviet Union and the Struggle for Collective Security in Europe, 1933–9*. London, 1984.
Hildebrand, Klaus. *The Foreign Policy of the Third Reich*. London, 1973.
Hillgruber, Andreas. *Hitlers Strategie*. Frankfurt–am–Main, 1966.
Hochman, Jiri. *The Soviet Union and the Failure of Collective Security, 1934–8*. Ithaca, 1984.
Iriye, A. *Origins of the Second World War in Asia and the Pacific*, London, 1987.
Jowitt, Ken. *New World Disorder: The Leninist Extinction*. Berkeley, 1992.
Kimball, Warren F. *The Juggler: Franklin Roosevelt as Wartime Statesman*. Princeton, 1991.
Knox, MacGregor. 'Conquest, foreign and domestic, in Fascist Italy and Nazi Germany', *Journal of Modern History*, vol. 56 (1984), pp. 1–57.
Lee, Marshall M. and Michalka, Wolfgang. *German Foreign Policy, 1917–33: Continuity or Break?* Leamington Spa, 1987.
Mayer, Arno J. *Political Origins of the New Diplomacy, 1917–18*. New Haven, 1959.
—— *The Politics and Diplomacy of Peacemaking: Containment and Counter-revolution at Versailles, 1918–19*, New York, 1967.
Melograni, Piero. *Lenin and the Myth of World Revolution: Ideology and Reasons of State, 1917–20*. Atlantic Highlands, 1989.
Nelsen, Harvey W. *Power and Insecurity: Beijing, Moscow, and Washington, 1949–88*. Boulder, 1989.
Ovendale, Ritchie. *The Origins of the Arab–Israeli Wars*, 2nd edn. London, 1992.

Pryce-Jones, David. *The War That Never Was: The Fall of the Soviet Empire, 1985–91*. London, 1995.

Raack, R.C. 'Stalin's plans for World War II', *Journal of Contemporary History*, vol. 26 (1991), pp. 215–26.

Rich, Norman. *Hitler's War Aims: Ideology, the Nazi State, and the Course of Expansion*, 2 vols. New York, 1973–4.

Schwabe, Klaus. *Woodrow Wilson, Revolutionary Germany, and Peacemaking, 1918-19: Missionary Diplomacy and the Realities of Power*. Chapel Hill, 1985.

Shenfield, Stephen. 'The long and winding road: trajectories to peace and socialism in contemporary Soviet ideology', in *Ideology and Soviet Politics*, ed. S. White and A. Pravda, London, 1988, pp. 203–24.

Smith, Tony. *America's Mission: The United States and the Worldwide Struggle for Democracy in the Twentieth Century*. Princeton, 1994.

Smith, Woodruff, D. *The Ideological Origins of Nazi Imperialism*. New York, 1986.

Stevenson, David. *The First World War and International Politics*. Oxford, 1988.

Stoakes, Geoffrey. *Hitler and the Quest for World Dominion: Nazi Ideology and Foreign Policy in the 1920s*. Leamington Spa, 1987.

Ulam, Adam B. *Expansion and Coexistence: History of Soviet Foreign Policy, 1917–73*, 2nd edn. New York, 1974.

Uldricks, Teddy J. *Diplomacy and Ideology: The Origins of Soviet Foreign Relations, 1917–30*. Beverly Hills, 1979.

Weinberg, Gerhard L. *The Foreign Policy of Hitler's Germany*, 2 vols. Chicago, 1970–80.

Yergin, Daniel. *The Shattered Peace: Origins of the Cold War and the National Security State*. Boston, 1977.

INDEX

285

INDEX

Decree on Peace, 1918 (Bolshevik):
133–4, 140
De Gaulle, Charles: 200, 215, 244
Delacroix, Eugène: 'Liberty Leading
the People': 55
Delcassé, Theophile: 117–18
democracy: 7–8, 19, 36, 44, 49, 57–8,
62, 69, 71, 74, 77, 82–4, 93–100,
105–9, 113, 130, 132–3, 135–6, 155,
189, 191, 193, 202, 204, 221, 246;
'democratic centralism' (Leninist):
141; 'democratic international': 33;
demo-plutucracy: 160; see also liberal
democracy, popular sovereignty
Deng Xiao-ping: 231
Denmark: 61, 77–8
Destutt de Tracy, Antoine-Louis-
Claude: Eléments d'idéologie: 1
Diderot, Denis: 14
Diem, Ngo Dinh: 213, 216
Dies, Congressman Martin: 167
diplomacy, Italian and French styles:
9–111, 13; aristocratic (cabinet):
11–14, 41, 82, 93, 107–8, 153; open
(democratic): 16–17, 110, 134–5,
146–8
diplomatic revolution (1756): 10
Directory (French): 31–4, 37
disarmament, general: 109, 134, 154–5,
161, 171, 191; German (interwar):
150, 165; naval: 193, 195; nuclear:
217–18, 223, 225
Disraeli, Benjamin: 82, 88, 90–1, 105,
129
'doctrine, first war of' (French
revolutionary): 29
Dollfuss, Engelbert: 158
Dominican Republic: 131, 218
'domino theory': 213–14, 219, 226
Dostoevsky, Fyodor Mikhailovich: 100,
168
draft treaty of mutual assistance
(1923): 154
Drang nach Osten: 62, 161, 163
Dreikaiserbund: see Three Emperors'
leagues and alliances
Dreyfus affair: 99, 106
Dual Alliance: Austro-German (1879):
89–93, 101; Franco-Russian (1894):
115–17, 119
Dulles, John Foster: 212–13
Dumouriez, Charles-François: 23–4, 26

Eagelton, Terry: 4
East Indies, Dutch: 196; see also
Indonesia
Eastern Question (nineteenth century):
49–50, 53–4, 59, 85–93, 101, 116,
121–4; see also Balkan League and
Wars, Crimean War
education: 7, 96–7, 99, 193–4
Egypt: 32–4, 49, 54, 87, 91, 117, 228,
232, 235–6, 238
Eisenhower, President Dwight D.:
212–13, 228
emigrés: from French Revolution: 18,
20–2, 39; from tsarist Russia: 112
Ems telegram (1870): 81
Enciclopedia italiana (1932 edn): 157
Engels, Friedrich: 2–3, 112, 139
Enlightenment: 1, 13, 15–18, 34, 38,
54–5, 108, 146; enlightened
despotism: 17, 35, 83
Entente Cordiale: first (1840): 54, 58;
second (1904): 117–20
Ethiopia: 221; crisis (1935–6): 159–61,
165, 167, 171, 189–90
ethnicity: 30, 55–6, 61, 126, 148–9,
244–5; see also pan movements
Eugénie, Empress (France): 76, 79
European Community, Union: 244;
antecedents: 35, 204
Eylau, Battle of (1807): 35

false consciousness: see ideology as
false consciousness
fascism, general (fascism–Nazism): 75,
80, 156, 169–76, 178–80, 182, 186,
188, 192, 194–5, 198, 200, 221–2,
229, 238, 240; fascist international:
158; 'red fascism': 209, 220; 'social
fascists': 170
Fascism, Italian: ducismo: 157, 164;
fasci di combattimento: 156; ideology:
156–61, 179, 242; 'second wave': 159;
see also Mussolini, personality and
ideas
Fashoda affair (1898): 117
Fatherland Front: 158
fatwa: 236–7
'February incident', 1936 (Japan): 194
Ferdinand, King (Bulgaria): 91
feudalism: 9, 19, 24, 26, 52, 105, 111,
200
Feuillants: 21

289